CONVERSONS AND SHIFTING IDENTITIES

Conversions and Shifting Identities

RAMDEV PIR AND THE ISMAILIS IN RAJASTHAN

DOMINIQUE-SILA KHAN

MANOHAR

CENTRE DE SCIENCES HUMAINES
2024

First published 1997
Reprinted 2024

ISBN 978-81-7304-181-5

Published by
Ajay Kumar Jain *for*
Manohar Publishers & Distributors
4753/23 Ansari Road, Daryaganj
New Delhi 110 002

Printed and bound in India

Contents

Illustrations

Foreword

I first learnt about Dominique-Sila Khan's original and important research into the forgotten branches of the Ismailis in Rajasthan during a short visit to Paris in May 1993. Dominique had attended a talk I had given at the Sorbonne for a seminar organized by Françoise Mallison. The talk had been about the life and legends of Pir Shams—the celebrated but elusive Ismaili Pir, whose medieval mission of conversion was said to have extended throughout northern India, from Kashmir down to Bengal and Gujarat.

My interest in Shams (whose *gināns* I have known since childhood) had recently been rekindled by a visit to his beautiful mausoleum in Multan, and my talk in Paris had been a fresh attempt to grapple with the rich collection of miracle stories that encrust him to see how far it was possible to recover the Pir's original historical persona. The problem was that outside the traditional *gināns* (the devotional hymns recording the teachings and activities of the Nizari Ismaili Pirs and Sayyids), there was a general absence of reliable historical evidence—just more engaging stories and several confused identities. I was thus both consoled and encouraged to find in the course of our subsequent discussions that Dominique shared my fascination with the elusive Pir. I was still more intrigued to discover that during the previous four or five years she had painstakingly uncovered evidence of a whole new dimension to the early history and development of the Ismaili mission in South Asia, in which Shams himself was said to have played a notable part.

During the next eighteen months, Dominique and I corresponded about the further progress of her research in Rajasthan, and more particularly about the significance of her 'core' investigations into the origins of the Ramdev and other similar traditions, as reflected in the half-hidden beliefs and practices of their Meghval followers. In each letter she would enthusiastically recount the results of her latest field trips to particular shrines, how in this place such and such an interesting legend had surfaced during her interview with a local *pīr* or *mahant* whilst at another *dargāh* she had encountered some new or puzzling architectural feature or motif.

As a result of reading her letters, and after studying her doctoral thesis and several connected articles, I was gradually able to form a clearer picture of the unusual range of her research data and the startlingly bold but convincing nature of her general hypothesis. Essentially, by applying ethnographic and other more traditional techniques to the study of various Hindu 'folk' traditions in Rajasthan (especially those associated with Ramdev, Jambha, Jasnath, Mallinath and Ai Mata), she had reached the conclusion that the untouchable and low caste followers of these cults had originally been converted to Ismailism during the thirteenth and fourteenth centuries by missionaries acting under the direction of the central Ismaili *dawa* in the Multan region. As that central authority had declined from the fifteenth century onwards, such communities had apparently broken away from the parent body and come under the control of various local *pīrs* and *gurus*, whilst at the same time apparently interacting with other religious groups, such as *bhaktas* and Nath Jogis. Although still retaining traces of their former Ismaili affiliation (including the use of self-descriptive term Nizarpanthi, plus a deep reverence for Pir Shams or Samas Rishi), these groups had in modern times come under increasing pressure to either adopt a more conventional Hindu identity, or to assimilate to Sunni/Shia Islam.

My gradual initiation into the disappearing world of the Nizarpanthis took a decisive step forward in January 1995 when Dominique and her husband invited me and my husband to spend a week with them in Rajasthan. This enabled us to join them on several short expeditions to Ramdev/Nizarpanthi shrines in the vicinity of Jaipur, in particular Dudu and Bichun. Near the first of these places, a small town some kilometres from Jaipur, I recall the distant prospect of the white *dargāh* of Khivan set peacefully amidst flat, green meadows. According to the Meghval tradition, Khivan had been a disciple of Pir Shams. After suffering martyrdom with his companion Ransi Tanwar (the grandfather of Ramdev) at the hands of the Delhi Sultan, Khivan's body was said to have been miraculously transformed into milk and laid to rest in Dudu. There was nobody there when we arrived at the *dargāh* of the 'Milk Pir', only the small neat Islamic structure itself, plus a row of white gravestones shaded by a huge tree.

After Dudu we headed down the Jaipur road towards Bichun, the site of another Islamic-style *dargāh,* this time constructed in rocky terrain. As we approached, I was amazed to see a painted inscription over the entrance proclaiming that this was 'the seat of the Samas Rishi's order'. On the verandah we took tea with the *mahant* or priest, a gentleman who spoke freely about the sect's links with the famous Pir from Multan, as well as with the Kabirpanthis. He also told us about the annual gatherings of Meghvals that took place at the *dargāh* at which traditional *bhajans* were sung. As we left, I found I had begun to hum the tune of one of Pir Shams's *ginān*s:

> He brought the whole world into being
> out of clay
> Who in this world is a Hindu
> and who a Musulman?

Dominique-Sila Khan's book incorporates the results of all her previous researches on the lost branches of the Ismailis, and provides a comprehensive overview of her earlier work. As such, it also opens up several new and interesting research prospects, some immediately inviting like the verdant fields that surround the *dargāh* at Dudu, others as demanding as the rocky terrain at Bichun. Like all pioneer studies that embrace a wide range of interpreted details, it will probably inspire some controversy as well as enthusiasm. But as someone who has been involved in related research and who knows the lengthy and painstaking efforts through which it has been thought out and constructed, I have no doubt that her work deserves the most serious scholarly attention. I would further hazard a guess that the general landscape of its major themes, Rajasthan, folk traditions, Ismailism and beyond, has been decidedly altered by these researches and will never be quite the same again.

In so far as my own field is concerned, namely, medieval Ismaili movements in South Asia, the book certainly marks a notable advance. In particular, it presents a range of new data which broadly seem to substantiate the general picture of an expanding Nizari *dawa* as reflected in the early *ginanic* literature, including the *ginān*s attributed to Pir Shams himself. At the same time the book also offers a convincing explanation of how several 'acculturated' Nizarpanthi communities on the margins of that expansion later came to break away, and partly coalesce with more powerful religious groups.

Of special interest in this latter connection is the fascinating correlation to be drawn between the traditional material gathered by Dominique from the Nizarpanthi Meghvals in Rajasthan, and the comparable oral data collected by Sachedina Nanjiani in the late nineteenth century from the Meghvals of Kacch and Gujarat, data which has also been worked over by modern Indian scholars. Thus it now appears that the devotional literature of both groups privileges Ismaili Pirs amongst their founder *gurus* (Pir Shams, Pir Sadruddin, Pir Satgur Nur and indeed Ramdev himself), whilst also sharing certain *ginān*-style texts, and a variety of references to popular Nizari Ismaili themes (e.g. Alamut, Daylam, etc.). It is hoped that these resemblances will be further explored, and, more generally, that the socio-anthropological approaches pioneered in this book will be later extended to the Imamshahi communities in Gujarat. Meanwhile it is clear that Dominique-Sila Khan's work has given a major stimulus to Ismaili studies in South Asia.

London
December 1995

ZAWAHIR MOIR

Acknowledgements

This work is partly based on a Ph.D. thesis submitted to the University of Paris VII in June 1993, with the financial help of the Centre de Sciences Humaines in Delhi. My gratitude goes first to my supervisor, Jean-Luc Chambard, who provided valuable support imparting to me his profound knowledge of field research, and to the French Institute without whose assistance I could not have completed my dissertation. I would also like to express my thanks to the former Director of the Centre de Sciences Humaines Olivier Guillaume, as well as to its successor Director Bruno Dorin for having encouraged and supported this publication.

The present book differs considerably from my thesis, not only because it omits parts of it and includes subjects not tackled there, but also because the basic issues themselves are different, as are the ways in which questions are raised and discussed.

My hypothesis of the Ismaili origin of the Rāmdev movement and other sectarian traditions of Rajasthan was received with much scepticism by French and Indian scholars and even, at times, sharply criticized. At the very beginning of my research, as I was completing my field inquiries with the purpose of writing a thesis, I formulated this hypothesis. I admittedly knew little about Ismailism, guided more by intuition than as the result of a knowledge of this tradition. It was only later that I indulged in Ismaili studies and learned with much relief that my idea had already occurred to other people, for example to the nineteenth-century writer, Nanjiani.

I am particularly grateful to Zawahir Moir whom I first met in Paris in June 1993 on the occasion of her lecture on the hagiography of Pīr Shams: she was the first to openly support my views, and from that time on, never ceased to provide encouragement. Not only did she supply me with a number of invaluable documents and texts which, more than often were not easily accessible, but she generously shared her profound knowledge of the Ismaili tradition and even accompanied me on a few field trips which proved to be particularly fruitful. It is no exaggeration to say that this book which is, in great part, the result of our fascinating exchanges, could not have been conceived without her precious co-operation.

For nearly ten years, my husband Abdul Sattar Khan made himself indispensable as a faithful research assistant, accompanying me to towns, villages and hamlets where we could observe the religious life of communities and talk openly with their leaders, priests, singers and *sādhus.* Having himself taken a deep interest in the subject, although he is not an Ismaili, he spared no effort to support me throughout my difficult quest. I wish to state that his profound knowledge of local Hindu and Muslim traditions has, many a time, filled in for my own shortcomings.

Among my Ismaili friends, my thanks are due to A. Rahmatoullah in Paris, whose sympathy for my views at a time when I felt disheartened by the incredulity of most scholars, helped me to overcome their diffidence. I have learnt much from him. Neither can I forget Iqbal Surani's moral support or the fact that he most generously made available to me his rich collection of books and drew my attention to Ismaili philosophy, a subject which I had tended to neglect, overlooking its significance in the history of Ismailism. It was a great surprise and a great joy to hear that Mumtaz Ali from Karachi had released an article on Rāmdev Pīr's Ismaili origin at a time when I myself had just published two papers on the subject and was engaged in writing this book. Our exchange of letters was extremely fruitful and his encouragement was as precious to me as his information. Besides, the fact that his hypothesis was based on entirely different material encouraged me: from two different starting points, we had arrived at similar conclusions.

As far as French scholars are concerned, it would be unfair to think I have found no sympathy in their rank: how can I express my gratitude to Françoise Mallison (Ecole Pratique des Hautes Etudes) for her sharp acumen, critical encouragement and moral support? I also wish to thank Marc Gaborieau, Denis Matringe and Catherine Clementin-Ojha for the keen interest they have shown in my research.

In India, prolonged discussions with G.S.L. Devra, Rajendra Joshi, the late Director of the Institute of Rajasthan Studies, Jaipur, Komal Kothari and Shail Mayaram have sustained and inspired me throughout my research.

To my numerous informants who shared with me their knowledge of rituals, legends, devotional songs and other elements of their tradition, goes my deepest gratitude: Swami Ram Prakash Achyut, Mohan Lal Panda, Om Prakash Kamad, Ratan Lal Kamad, Ramchandra Jaipal, Krishna Lal Bishnoi, Surya Shankar Pareek. I cannot unfortunately thank each one, but I have forgotten none of them.

I also wish to thank Muzaffar Alam and Shereen Ratnagar (Delhi), who have read with much enthusiasm the early draft of this book and given their valuable comments. I am indebted to Francine E. Krishna (Jaipur) for her critical and kindly readings of the whole manuscript. Finally, special thanks are due to Uma Krishnan (Centre de Sciences Humaines) for having helped me fair the manuscript.

Jaipur, 1996 DOMINIQUE-SILA KHAN

Note on Transliteration

The scheme of transliteration followed in this work is the standard system internationally used for Indic and Perso-Arabic languages, with a few modifications that make the text less forbidding to nonspecialists and reflect Hindi and Rajasthani pronunciation.

These modifications are the following:

—the palatal consonant *c* and its aspirate *ch* are rendered, respectively, as *ch* and *cch.*

—nasals are represented by *n* or *m,* except at the end of a word where the sign ~ is used, as in *vaniā̃.*

—names of well-known characters and of gods like Vishnu, Shiva and so on, are given in their generally accepted anglicized form.

—in the transcription of Arabic words, the apostrophe has been omitted: for instance, Ismaili and not Isma'ili, *jamāt* and not *jama'at,* etc.

—I have retained the spoken forms of some words/expressions like 'Shiv ling' because these were the forms I heard in the course of field work.

—for names of persons, places, communities and sects, as well as titles diacritics have not been used.

Quotations have, needless to say, been left with the transliteration used by the authors.

Map 1 Routes of penetration of the Nizari *Dawa*

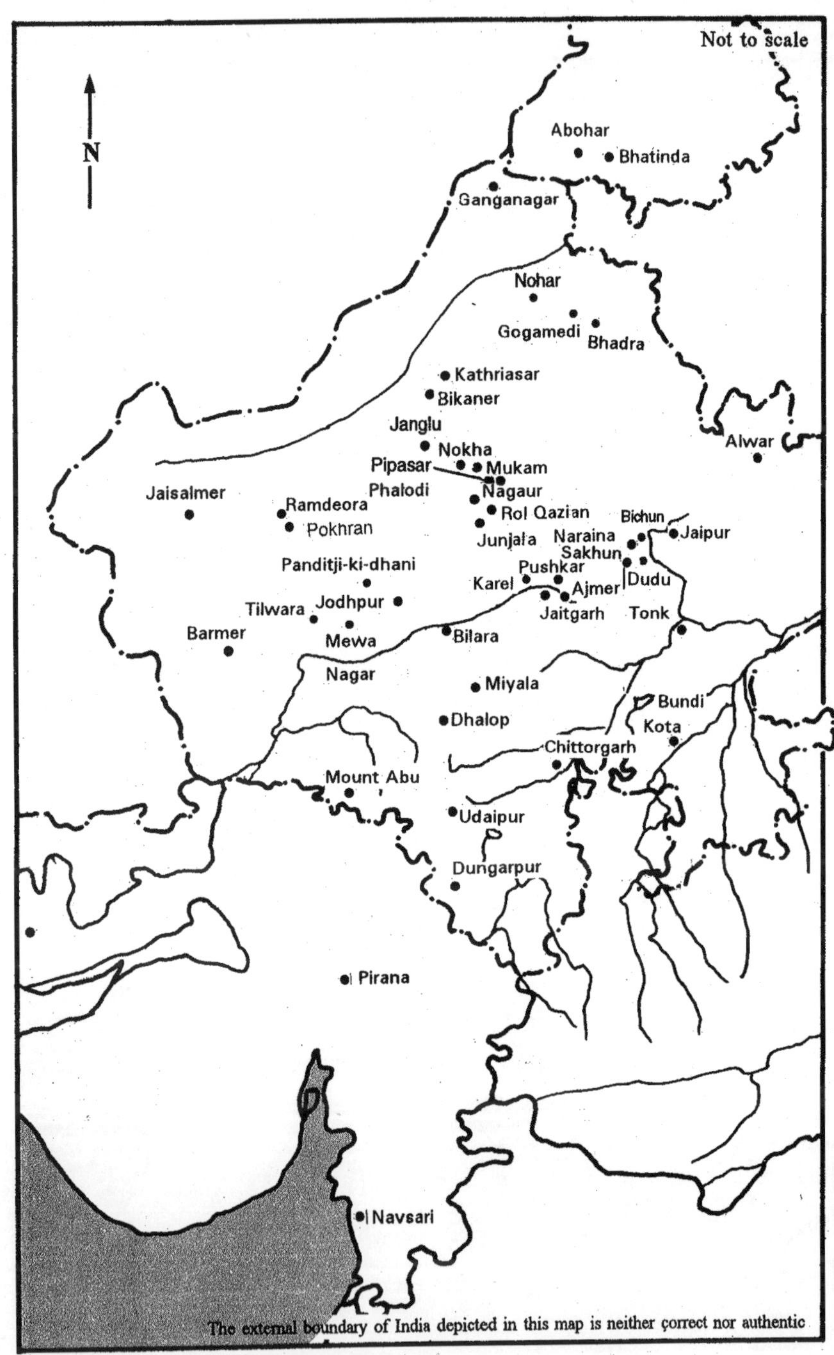

Map 2 © Centres of Nizari *Dawa* in Rajasthan

Introduction

Although the traditions connected with Ramdev, Mallinath, Jambha, Jasnath and Ai Mata, religious figures of the fourteenth and fifteenth centuries whose main shrines are in Rajasthan, can be located in the broad context of the devotional (*bhakti*) movements of medieval and modern India, they pose a number of fundamental issues for the history of Indian religions. Whether they are classified, though often arbitrarily, as folk deities (*lokdevtā*) or saint-poets (*sant*), these figures cannot fully reveal their complexity nor their originality if to describe them we resort to ready-made categories such as 'popular religion' or 'syncretism'. Their multiple personality as hero-gods, local deities and *avatārs*, their 'dual' identity as Hindu gurus and Muslim Pirs defies too simplistic an approach.

The few scholars who have attempted to study them from different points of view (anthropology, history of religions, literature) [1] have focused exclusively on the present-day perceptions of a wide range of devotees (*bhaktas*) as 'founts of power' (Grodzins-Gold 1994: 80) and/or gurus conveying a spiritual message. Although such analyses (rooted in the present) do reveal interesting trends of evolution within the broader Hindu tradition, the emphasis on traits common to the deities and Sants and on a *bhatki* type of worship transcending community and caste barriers, has prevented scholars from perceiving the historical background, in particular the process of interaction between Hinduism—in its various aspects—and Islam.

If few authors have shown much interest in the past, that may be because the absence of written documents which could help us to trace back the origin of these movements and the identity of their founders has proved an almost insurmountable obstacle. For example, regarding Ramdev it has been written, 'Because specific sources are lacking, it is not possible to do more than speculate about the role of Islam in the origin of the Ramdev cult' (Binford 1976:126).

A systematic analysis of these traditions would however reveal a number of elements which might compel the scholar to question his inability to reconstruct the past. As Benett (1993:13) has stated, 'it is only by looking at religious movements in their wide historical and cultural sweep that patterns can be discerned which are of continuing relevance in the present, awareness of which enables the anthropologist to analyze his field data within a wider temporal perspective'. By resorting to a search for 'traces' in history (Ginsburg 1989: 148) we could bring out, if not a full historical reconstruction, at least a consistent pattern capable of explaining the rise and development of these traditions, as well as the part they have played in the social and religious evolution of Rajasthan and neighbouring regions.

Whenever events cannot be reconstructed on the basis of inscriptions, learned treatises, travellogues and census reports, ethnographical data collected through the direct observation of shrines and rituals, as well as the recording of legends and songs, followed by their critical examination from an anthropological point of view may have an important contribution to make. It is to this method that I have resorted throughout this study and adding to field work the analysis of oral and written texts, I have endeavoured to reconstruct parts of a forgotten chapter of history.

Before coming to the heart of the matter I shall present briefly the religious figures I have chosen to study. Ramdev, Mallinath, Jambha, Jasnath and Ai Mata are said to have flourished in fourteenth and fifteenth century Rajasthan and their cults spread to adjacent areas as well. Although their present followers spare no effort to prove their Hindu identity, a thorough study of their traditions has shown that they have been perceived till recently (and are still perceived at times) as being endowed with a 'dual' (Hindu-Muslim) personality. The devotees generally explain this phenomenon by the fact that they had disciples from both communities and were, like many medieval Sants 'beyond castes and sects' (*jāt-panth*). Ramdev is also known as Ramshah Pir, Jambha as Jam Shah. Ai Mata's main temple at Bilara (near Jodhpur) is still referred to by her traditional female and low caste worshippers as *dargāh* ('royal court', implying a Muslim shrine sheltering a tomb or relics). The same is true for Ramdev's temple at Ramdeora-Runicha (near Pokaran, between Jodhpur and Jaisalmer). These religious teachers, were buried according to Muslim rites, although their tombs are currently referred to as *samādhis* (funeral monument of Hindu–Jain ascetics and saints). The literature connected with them, mainly in the form of devotional hymns (*bhajans, vāṇīs*), seems interspersed with Islamic terms and concepts, even as the general atmosphere is quite Hindu.

However, the current trend of development has been to expurgate these traditions of their Islamic elements which render them less and less conspicuous to the superficial observer. In the cases under study the gradual shift of emphasis and the effort to 'reHinduize' the literature and rituals may lead us to underestimate the significance of these elements. Referring to a context which is more familiar to those who have studied the medieval *bhakti* movements, one could compare these attempts to the efforts of the religious leaders of the sects founded by Kabir and Dadu (the Kabir and Dadu Panths): their reconstruction of history is aimed at proving that these Muslim sants were in reality Hindus. But it is equally important to stress, at this stage, that the search for a clear communal identity is a fairly recent trend (Frykenberg 1989:21-49).

Those scholars who have written on the religious movements studied here have missed another essential point. The rigid classification that they have generally followed has prevented them from discovering the striking similarities which exist between these various Sants: for instance Ramdev and Mallinath have been classified as folk deities (*lokdevtā*), whereas Jambha and Jasnath enjoy the ranks of *sant* and *siddh* (powerful ascetic) (Pemaram 1977:passim); Ai Mata is often regarded as a local goddess comparable to the Rajasthani *lokdevīs* Jin Mata and Karni Mata. The only feature all these figures seem to share, in the perception of these authors, is their power and their capacity to perform miracles.

The reason why Jambha and Jasnath are termed Sants is fairly clear: both are known to be the founders of specific religious traditions or sects (*sampradāy, panth*) which have subsisted to this day as well defined and structured movements, with their lineages of gurus and disciples (*guru-śiṣya paramparā*), their sacred scriptures, and their shrines. In contrast Ramdev, although portrayed as 'a great synthesizer of Hindu-Muslim differences' (Binford 1976:126), is not credited with a similar achievement. According to B.N. Sarasvati (quoted by Binford, ibid.:124), the cult of Ramdev is different from movements founded by poet-saints like Kabir or Dadu or reformers like Nanak, in as much as 'the saint-based *bhakti* cults are well-organized institutions with objectives clearly defined by their respective founders and subsequently elaborated by the corps of ascetic specialists'. Binford (ibid.:124) concludes that 'as far as we know Ramdev did not leave behind a fixed body of scripture, a set of rituals or a system of belief.... There is no central cult leader or organization. Ramdev's descendants have inherited his temple as a property, not as a spiritual legacy.'

Characteristically such statements, which are fairly common among scholars of Rajasthan (but not Gujarat), result from the lack of awareness of an older 'secret' tradition connected with Ramdev which I will describe and analyse in detail in the following chapters. Other reasons why this tradition has been ignored are, besides its secretive character, its transformation under various influences and its gradual loss of unity and identity. Nowadays only scattered fragments seem to subsist, while the movement, as a whole, tends to merge into the general stream of Hindu devotional religion.

The case of Ai Mata might help to demonstrate the extent to which this classification and the distinction between a Sant and a folk-deity can be arbitrary. Jiji Devi (otherwise named Ai Mata) is viewed as a Rajasthani *lokdevī* and she is the caste goddess of a particular group of Sirvis (the Sirvis are an agricultural community akin to the Jats, found mostly in Pali, Udaipur and Bhilwara districts). She is often compared by the local population (whether or not they worship this religious figure) to other Hindu goddesses related to regional or caste cults, which does not prevent her traditional followers from perceiving her also as a human guru, founder of a sect referred to as the Ai Panth. This claim is legitimate since the sectarian tradition bearing this name is indeed a well-structured movement whose religious leader is the 'Diwan of Ai Mata' who enjoys the rank of *Pīr-murshid* (Gahlot-Banshi Dhar 1989:110). This sect has its sacred books, its rituals and a whole network of *gaddīs* (centres or seats of a sectarian religious tradition) and shrines.

On the other hand, if the majority of non-sectarian Hindus regard Jambha and Jasnath as gurus and Sants, those who are their disciples (the Bishnois and the Jasnathis) view them as gods—in particular, as incarnations of the great God Vishnu.

From a third perspective, which is that of some Muslim devotees as well as their Hindu disciples, they also appear, as illustrated above, as Pirs (or *murshids*), i.e. spiritual guides connected with the Islamic tradition. The nature of this connection being vague (or, as we will see later, secretive) for the majority of devotees, it is but natural that the issue could not be elucidated to this day.

Before proceeding further let us place the problem in a wider context. Although the question of Hindu-Muslim interaction has attracted the attention of a number of authors,[2] the phenomena to which they gave rise have not been analysed in their empirical diversity—a diversity comprising both causes and effects. The general trend as has been stated above is to explain all these types of interaction with the help of a few hackneyed concepts such as 'syncretism' and 'folk religion'. A critical approach to these concepts will be suggested later. For the moment, it suffices to say that the exchanges between Muslim Sufis and Hindu Sants and yogis, as well as the 'natural tendency' of the indigenous population—especially in the uneducated classes and the lower caste groups—to absorb foreign elements have been proposed by the majority of authors as a kind of magic key to all doors. A more detailed analysis would reveal the existence of different modes of interaction, the causes and consequences of which cannot be put into the same category.

Without claiming to be exhaustive I would like to propose here a tentative classification of these phenomena.

- Divine power or charisma (*śakti* in the Hindu tradition, *barakat* in the Islamic one) may attract devotees regardless of their origin, around a particular religious figure. For example the worship of a Sufi saint like Muinuddin Chishti by Hindus and the cult of a goddess performed by Muslims, with the hope of securing a boon.
- There is in some situations a tendency to cling to one's former beliefs. For instance, some Muslims continue to worship a Hindu deity as they did before their conversion while 'deIslamized' Hindus (a much lesser known phenomenon) still perform a cult at the *dargāh* of the Pir who converted them. The concepts of incomplete conversion or reconversion will be examined further in greater detail.[3]
- All over the subcontinent a number of Muslim saints are still regarded as the guardians and protectors of a Hindu or Jain shrine. Let us give a few examples: Vavar is the guardian-deity of the god Ayyappa at the shrine of Sabarimalai in Kerala (Thomas 1973: 32-3), some Draupadi temples of Tamil Nadu are protected by Muttal Ravuttan (Hiltebeitel 1988:101-27), Bar Shah is worshipped at Saundatti (Karnataka) near the shrine of the Goddesss (Assayag 1992:789-813), Angar Shah at the entrance of the Jain sacred complex of Shatrunjaya, near Palitana in Gujarat, and a Muslim Pir is also the guardian of Kaila Devi's shrine in Rajasthan. In all these cases the

Hindu devotees generally bow before the Muslim saint before making their offerings to the deity, whereas Muslims occasionally come to revere the god or goddess at the site.

• The last phenomenon described in my classification would include the so-called 'syncretistic cults', i.e. where Hindu and Muslim elements seem to coexist within one single tradition and where the saints have a dual identity. This can be illustrated by the Nages *sampradāy* (Van Skyhawk 1994:255-73), the worship of Satya Pir (Roy 1963:214-17) and the celebrated cult of the *Panch Pīr* (ibid.:213-15), the Daryashah-Uderolal tradition (Carter 1918:197-208) and the Imamshahi sect (Ivanow 1938:19-70). It is important to emphasize that this phenomenon is distinct from that described in the first case: for instance, Muinuddin Chishti is not worshipped by the Hindus because he himself or his teaching 'look Hindu', nor is a *devī* revered by Muslims because they view her as an Islamic saint, whereas Ramdev is regarded by Hindus as an *avatār* of Vishnu and by Muslims as a saint of Islam.

After this rough classification of the various modes of interaction between Hinduism and Islam, let us revert to the concept of syncretism as applicable in this particular context.

As has been said above, the general tendency is to regard as 'syncretistic' different categories of religious phenomena; terms such as 'hybrid sects' (Hussein 1929:15), 'popular syncretism' (Ahmad Aziz 1964:140) and 'symbiosis' (Ivanow 1938:19), are used indiscriminately to describe a wide range of customs and traditions, without defining the concepts.

In contradistinction to this, some authors have attempted to formulate a definition before resorting to this category. As defined by Michael Pye (quoted by Kassam 1994:231) 'syncretism is the coherent yet somewhat uneasy coexistence of elements from diverse religious contexts. Even when a smooth cohesion has been achieved the various elements often seem to maintain their potential for conveying independent meanings.' Kassam (ibid.) illustrates this phenomenon with the image of a chalice and two faces; she insists on: '(1) the *coexistence* of diverse elements; (2) the *coherence* of their combined configuration; and (3) the retention of their respective *self-identities* whose prominence and recognition depend upon the viewer's perspective'.

The definition of both authors is satisfactory enough, in as much as it enables us to distinguish the phenomenon described as 'syncretism' from other apparently similar ones. Besides, Kassam's definition seems to fit into the pattern of the religious movements which I propose to study here. However this category can be questioned on the basis of one particular point: what is perceived by us as 'syncretism' can only be the result of a complex process and can by no means explain the mechanism which lies behind it. In other words, when one does not have a better understanding of the various factors that led to a contemporary phenomenon, 'syncretism' becomes a convenient term; though it remains a purely descriptive one. If we content ourselves with this reductionist approach we may not make any attempt at analysing the phenomenon as something that evolved. True, such an analysis might initially raise more issues than it could solve; for example, is the so-called 'syncretism' of a particular tradition the result of a conscious effort of its religious teachers to reconcile opposite or conflicting beliefs? Or is it the consequence of a 'spontaneous' process occurring at the unconscious level, as in the case of the so-called 'popular' cults? Undoubtedly both phenomena exist in different types of sects and cults and perhaps even within one single tradition.

In the introduction to his article on the sect of Imam Shah in Gujarat Ivanow (1938:19-20) makes a few interesting points. To begin with, referring to the gradual spread of Islam in the subcontinent he mentions the emergence of 'transition forms' between Islam and Hinduism. While M.I. Khan (1994:25) defines, as a whole, the apparent syncretism found in the Rishi movement as 'Kashmir's transition to Islam' (which is also the title of the book), Roy (1983: 72-3) speaks of religious 'mediators' consciously bridging the gulf between the 'little' and the 'great traditions', Hinduism and Islam. Khan (ibid.) questions his description of the spread of Islam in Bengal in terms of 'syncretism' and 'symbolic forms' which according to him can be attributed only a minor role. He prefers to view the so-called 'transition forms' as the 'meaningful response that Islam evoked from the Bengalis'.

Similarly, the concept of 'popular religion' as opposed to the so-called 'orthodox' or 'learned' forms of Hinduism (Brahmanical Hinduism or Sanskritic tradition) and Islam (orthodox Sunni or Shia Islam) defined by learned Koranic experts) might be a convenient term to refer to certain types of beliefs and practices (and must be preferred to the overly dualistic category Great/Little tradition). However it is, at the same time, too vague and restrictive to be able to explain some religious phenomena. Ultimately, labelling a specific movement 'popular' or 'learned' might depend more on the perception of the observer than on any objective criterion of classification. To give but one example, while the Bishnoi sect might be described as one of the local, 'obscure religious cults' Das Gupta (1962) called them, its followers view it as a part of the 'Great' Hindu tradition.

Eventually, what I propose to do here is to avoid as much as possible beginning with these categories. One should attempt to describe and analyse a particular tradition without, in M.I. Khan's words (1994:2), 'cramping it into pigeon-holes of "cultural synthesis", "syncretism", "orthodoxy" versus "popular religion..."'.

Let us come to the last point of this introduction: the quasi exclusive role ascribed to Sufis (without again defining Sufism nor distinguishing between various categories of Sufis) in the interaction with the indigenous Hindu religious traditions (Gold 1987:201-10, Ahmad 1964: passim). No one can deny the part played by Sufism, as the mystical dimension of Islam, throughout the subcontinent and one must equally bear in mind the fact that a number of Sufi teachers have resorted to Hindu doctrines and terminologies in their writings. However we will argue that it was not the only form of Islam that deeply interacted with Hinduism in its various aspects.

At this stage we again need to define clearly what Sufism means in our case: is it only Sunni Sufism (representing the majority but not the totality of Sufism)?. If so, it is still important to stress that the different *tarīqas* (lit. 'paths', orders of Sufis) sometimes had diverging opinions and practices, not to speak of the personalities of each particular Sufi Shaikh. And what about Shia Sufis, 'Qalandars' of various types, among whom we find the so-called '*be-shar*' dervishes, those who do not follow the Islamic Sunni (or Shia) law (Digby 1984:64-104)? Moreover it is obvious that the word 'Sufi' has very often been used in a vague, general sense for all types of Muslim saints.

An interesting illustration of this phenomenon is to be found in Hedayetullah (1977:45) who calls the Ismaili missionary, Sadruḍdin, a 'Sufi'. His statement leads me to formulate one of the central ideas of this study: the major role played by Ismailism, in particular by its Nizari branch (and its offshoots), in the various processes of interaction. This point has rarely been brought out by scholars, except perhaps those involved directly in Ismaili studies. As we will see, however, if Sufism and Ismailism may legitimately be described as two distinct traditions, one must not forget the existence of links between them, which have not been fully elucidated to this day.

It is also surprising that Ismailism has never been considered a potential source of influence and interaction by the authors describing various 'syncretic movements'. This may be due to the fact that Ismailism and its impact in the Indian subcontinent has not yet been thoroughly studied, in contrast with Sufism.

Despite Ivanow's remarkable contributions in this field, studies on this period of Ismaili history connected with its penetration into the subcontinent have, more than often, not been taken seriously. The phenomena to which it gave rise have generally been labelled 'folk Islam'. Not only scholars specialized in Islamic studies, concentrating mostly on its elitist forms and classical tradition, but Ismailis themselves have tended to neglect this field and, at any rate, never encouraged this type of study which was considered to be of low priority.

Besides, if a few studies have been devoted to the Ismaili tradition in this part of the world and its interaction with the local, mainly Hindu, culture, the analyses have been limited to communities who, converted at various times, remain to this day within the fold of Ismailism. The possibilities of its influence on other groups, now assuming a different religious identity, have hardly been contemplated (with the exception of Mumtaz Ali: 1994).

This is in fact what we propose to explore. As suggested by the title, the central hypothesis is that the religious movements analysed here have their roots in Ismailism, i.e. that besides the existing Ismaili communities, a number of other groups were converted at various times and these subsequently reverted to Hinduism or were absorbed into Muslim Sunni or Twelver Shia communities, while retaining in a more or less conspicuous way the elements which testify to this event. We will also attempt to prove that the elements are not the result of mere exchanges or influences between Ismailis and Hindus, but the consequence of formal conversions.

NOTES

1. These are mostly Indian authors such as Sonaram Bishnoi (on Ramdev), Hiralal Maheshvari (on Jambha), Kshir Sagar (on Mallinath), Surya Shankar Pareek (on Jasnath), Shiv Singh Choyal (on Ai Mata) and Pemaram on all of them, except Ai Mata. Among the foreign scholars, Mira Binford is, to my

knowledge, the only author to have devoted a whole article to Ramdev; allusions to the Ramdev tradition are also to be found in Parita Mukta and Carstairs.

2. This fascination for Hindu-Muslim interaction in its positive aspects has its counterpart, especially from the twenties onwards, in the efforts of some fundamentalist bodies, whether Hindu or Muslim, to demonstrate that these phenomena were caused by the ignorance of the 'genuine' form of the religion or are the result of manipulations by hostile powers.
3. Tendencies which the fundamentalists have attempted to eradicate at the beginning of our century. See the analyses proposed by Shail Mayaram (1996) and various authors such as Ghay (1990), Clementin-Ojha and Gaborieau (1995), and Jaffrelot (1995) of the processes referred to as 'reconversion' or *śuddhī* (purification)—issues taken up in a subsequent chapter.

PART ONE

Nizari Ismailism and the Nizar Panth

CHAPTER 1

The Ismailis in the Indian Subcontinent: Exchanges and Confrontations

In order to understand the type of interaction which might have occurred between Nizari Ismailism and various Hindu beliefs and practices prevailing when this form of Islam penetrated into the subcontinent, it will not be out of place to sketch a brief history and description of this tradition. Although there has been some work on Ismailism in the Indo-Pakistani context, it has somehow failed to evoke the interest of scholars involved in the study of Indian history, anthropology or literature. Besides, its importance in the religious culture of South Asia—which has little to do with the present number of its followers—has generally been underestimated.[1]

Ismailism derives from Shia Islam. It traces its origin to the succession dispute arising after the death of Imam Jafar al-Sadiq (AD 765).

> Many accepted his younger son as the next Imam, and continued to recognize his descendants until the line died out with the mysterious disappearance of the twelfth Imam, believed to be in a state of occultation (Ar. *ghayba*) until his ultimate return as the Mahdi (Ar. *mahdī* 'the guided one') who will return to restore righteousness at the end of time. Hence known as Isna Asharis or 'Twelvers' (Ar. *Isn̲ā aśara* (twelve) this group of Shias subsequently became powerful in Iran. . . . The other group of Shias believed the true succession had passed to Jafar al-Sadiq's elder son Ismail, and hence came to be called Ismailis. Since Jafar al-Sadiq is regarded as the sixth Imam, the Ismailis are also termed 'seveners' (Shackle and Moir 1992:4).

Emerging as a highly organized movement of a revolutionary sort (Daftary 1990:91-143) Ismailism achieved its greatest success with the establishment of the Fatimid kingdom; in this independent state located in North Africa and Egypt the Imams were the caliphs (AD 902-1171). Among the most striking features of this particular branch of Islam influenced by neo-platonic, gnostic and manicheistic ideas (Corbin 1986:115-51, Daftary 1990:122-3, 234-5, 241) one can mention the elaborate esoteric interpretation of the Koran.

Even before Fatimid rule the message of the Ismailis had begun to spread in different parts of South Asia like Multan and Upper Sind; in this region a small Ismaili state was later established, and despite its short duration (a little more than one century, as it was destroyed in AD 1010) it had a deep influence on the local population (al-Hamdani 1956:4). The importance of the missionary organization (*dawa*)[2] during this period, as well as the impact it had on the indigenous milieu, have been described by various scholars (Ivanow 1939:1-35, al-Hamdani 1956: 1-16, Ansar Zahid Khan 1975:36-57, MacLean 1989:126-58). Comparing the penetration of Sunni Arab Islam in Sind (a historical fact that has been much more often analysed) with that of Ismailism, the last mentioned author has argued that 'while the earlier form of Arab Islam was indifferent to conversion but supportive of rapid Islamization, the system of Ismailism initially propagated in Sind and accepted by certain segments of the Hindu population allowed the retention of basic elements from Hinduism, as a normative Sindhi variation of Ismailism' (MacLean 1989:157-8).

The expansion of the Fatimid *dawa* in the subcontinent was curbed by the attacks of the Sunni ruler of Afghanistan, Mahmud of Ghazna; and in 1010 all resistance from the Ismaili side was extinguished. Hundreds of Ismailis are said to have been slaughtered (Nanji 1978:36) and the Fatimid kingdom of Multan became a part of the Ghaznavid empire (MacLean 1989:139). Persecutions and exterminations forced a number of Ismailis to take shelter in more remote, better protected places and to conceal or abnegate their faith. 'However, in due course we find that though Ismaili sovereignty had been broken, Ismaili adherents still continued to persist under adverse conditions' (Nanji 1978:36). The controversial religious identity of the Sumra rulers might illustrate some forms of survival or transformation of the Ismaili tradition (ibid.: 36-9, Daftary 1990:180, 479).

Divergences, divisions and schisms had gradually weakened the Ismaili *dawa*. The Qarmatians (*Qarāmiṭa*) already represented a different approach to Ismailism and they did not recognize the authority of the Fatimid caliphs (Daftary 1990:116-17, 164-5); early historians have often confused them with the first Ismailis and the

Fatimids. Then the Druze community formed a separate branch (this was the first open division which occurred in 1013 (ibid.: 195-6), and finally a new quarrel of succession arose at the death of al-Mustansir (1094). Those who followed his younger son al-Mustali, the Mustalians, settled in Yemen and later, in the twelfth century, established their headquarters in Gujarat, where the converts came to be known as Bohras (Shackle and Moir 1992:5). The partisans of the assassinated Imam Nizar, the elder son of al-Mustansir, were referred to as Nizaris, and founded, in the Daylami region of Iran, the mountain fortress of Alamut (1090). They were known to medieval travellers of Europe and the Middle-East as the 'Hashishins' or 'Assassins' (Lewis 1985: 33). They reestablished the continuity of the line of Imams by asserting that Nizar's son was not dead and had taken shelter at Alamut. After the sack of the fortress by the Mongols in 1256 the Nizari Imams began to live mostly in concealment, practising *taqīyya* (i.e. hiding their true belief, as permitted by Shia Islam) (Daftary 1990:566), and taking the 'mantle' (*khirkā*) of Sufi dervishes (ibid.: 412). At that time one can notice an apparent shift of emphasis, when the development of inner religion and mysticism seems to have prevailed over political ambitions. To avoid the reprobation of the Sunni and Twelver Shia rulers, the Imams and their followers came closer to the more 'orthodox' wandering ascetics of Islam. Under the guise of a Sufi Shaikh Mustansir Billah II revived the Imamate in the village of Anjudan in Central Iran in 1498 (Shackle and Moir 1992:5). Meanwhile, probably from the Alamut period onwards, the 'new mission' (the Nizari *dawa*) had started to spread into the Indian subcontinent, where it was referred to by various names, such as the Nizari religion, the Daylami mission and the *Sat Panth* (lit. 'true path'), an equivalent of the Arabic *Dīn-e Haqq*, an allusion to the priority of inner, esoteric meaning of religion or *bātin* over the apparent one or *zāhir* (Corbin 1986: 33-6, 121) The different groups of Nizari converts were variously known as Shamsis, Maulais, Khojas, Satpanthis and Guptis. Later on they were globally called Khojas; nowadays they are called Agakhani Khojas since they revere the Aga Khan as their living Imam and leader of their community.

At this stage, it may be important to specify that Ismailism—as well as the Shia tradition as a whole—should not be analysed exclusively in terms of political and social history, but also in terms of a highly elaborate philosophy based on an esoteric interpretation of Islam, stressing the existence of a meta- or hiero-history (Corbin 1986:98-9). The concept of Ismailism as an 'extremist' form of Shiism or 'ultra-shiism' (ibid.)—of which other forms have been attested in history—(Marquet 1985 :7-13) refers us to a revolutionary ideal with socio-political implications[4] that cannot be artificially separated from its philosophical background and its strong messianic accent. Central to the Ismaili doctrine is the Imam as 'God's man' (Persian *mard-e-khodā*) or the 'Perfect Man' who is the prerequisite of salvation (Corbin 1986: 145-6), as well as the key role played, in the Persian period, by its representatives, the Pirs.

Little can be said of the transition between the two periods (the Fatimid and the Nizari phases) in the subcontinent, since no documentary evidence is available (Nanji 1978:59-61), but one can deduce from various sources the existence of a certain continuity. As briefly mentioned above, the case of the Sumra rulers of Punjab and Sind, said by some authors to have embraced Ismailism under Fatimid rule and then later to have become Nizaris, is an interesting one, although it has not been fully explored or elucidated (ibid.: 36-8, Allana 1984:15-17). Be that as it may, this continuity is clearly reflected at least in the method of proselytizing: already during the Fatimid period the system of conversions adopted by the Ismailis discloses certain typical features (Ivanow 1955: 172, Corbin 1970: 41-142, MacLean 1989: 61, 86, 167).

As MacLean points out (1989:149),

> the paradigmatic *da'i* (missionary) of conversion and initiation tale does not engage in public or mass proselytization, but attempts, incognito, to locate individuals who might respond positively to the message of the *da'wah*. Such an individual, when found, is led gradually through various pedagogical stages, each elucidated via discourse argued from the perceptual basis of the potential convert. The gradual revelation of the nature of the message culminates with the convert receiving personal instruction in the esoteric meaning (*bāṭin*) of Ismailism in an initiation ceremony conducted by a superior *da'i*. The neophyte convert subsequently becomes a subsidiary *da'i* himself and applies the same recruitment procedures elsewhere.

The same author points out two significant features of Ismaili missionary activity: the fact that it was secret and individualized and not public or mass (ibid.:149). It is also necessary to stress that if the expansion of the *dawa* was limited, it saw, nevertheless, the emergence of dynamic groups who played an important role in the social and political life of those times.

Both these elements will remain constant traits in the further development of Ismailism, as well as the process referred to by MacLean as 'embedment within a Hindu context' (1989:152)—a phenomenon which we might broadly contextualize as 'acculturation'.

While secrecy and concealment had their origin in the general Shia practice of *taqīyya*, the apparent Hinduization of the tradition might also be viewed as a way of gaining converts and infiltrating into local circles. Without contradicting the basic doctrines and primary goals of Ismailism this process resulted in bringing closer Islamic and Hindu cultures, a phenomenon which MacLean (1989:158) terms 'an innovative dynamic synthesis', particularly conspicuous during the Nizari phase of the *dawa*. While I agree that such a 'synthesis' can be perceived at various levels (cultic and textual), caution is perhaps needed in the use of this term: it may not be preferable to the category referred to as 'syncretism'. It might be of some interest, at this stage, to distinguish between at least two types of perceptions when analysing the acculturated form of Nizari Ismailism in the subcontinent.

In the perception of the Ismaili *dāīs* (missionaries) this form is certainly not intended to be a 'synthesis' or a form of 'syncretism'. As Nanji has rightly stated (1978:131-2)

> The terms generally used to categorize the Nizari Isma'ilis in the context of Indo-Muslim history range from 'syncretic' to 'heterodox'. . . . The field of Islamic Studies has still to rid itself of prejudice inherited from the works of Medieval Muslim heresiology, and terms such as 'orthodoxy' and 'heterodoxy' continue to be bandied about indiscriminately. One unfortunate result has been that 'syncretism' has come to imply the existence of a pure form which has been devalued by accommodation to other values.

The fact that the Nizari Pirs accepted a number of local traditions cannot be explained only by the desire to make converts or by customary precautionary dissimulation: the *dāīs*, it seems, attempted to convince the Hindus that the new faith they proposed was nothing more than the fulfilment of their former beliefs. Hinduism and Ismailism should therefore be neither identified nor 'mixed' (which would amount to a synthesis or to syncretism) but the new converts should understand that the message of the Nizari missionaries was actually the culmination of their own religious traditions which it encompassed, revealing deeper layers of truth.

There was also the perception of the converts, formerly Hindu (or Jain), having various beliefs and practices. Until the beginning of the twentieth century when Hinduism was tentatively given by fundamentalist thinkers a conceptual unity, compelling Hindus to acquire a new awareness as a separate community clearly opposed to other faiths, the way the neophytes viewed their new religion might have been somewhat different from their understanding of other forms of Islam, including Sunni Sufism. It is probable that in their eyes, Ismailism did not appear as something fundamentally distinct from their former beliefs—if one bears in mind the fact that, in the course of time, within the indigenous context, religious leaders have proposed a wide range of doctrines and observances often far from what we would call 'Brahmanical orthodoxy'. In particular, converts from the masses, unfamiliar with learned treatises and elaborate rituals of the Vedic type, might have perceived the Nizari religion as just another sect in which they were accepted, as the Nath Sampraday.[5]

Before entering into details and presenting the acculturated form taken by Ismailism in the subcontinent, let us briefly consider the history of the relationship between Sufis and Ismailis. Sufism, it may be recalled, is a complex religious phenomenon characterized by a variety of doctrines and practices, as expressed by different spiritual guides (*murshid, pīr*) belonging to particular orders (*tarīqa*) and forming lineages (*silsila*) of teachers and disciples (*pīr-murīd*), sometimes by wandering ascetics generally known as *fakīrs*, not affiliated to any particular *tarīqa*, and commonly referred to as *qalandars* (Digby 1984:80-108).

Consequently, we shall avoid resorting to general statements when discussing the ideologies and methods of the Sufis. For example, the majority of Sufis are clearly related to the Sunni Islamic tradition, but a few were connected with Shiism (Daftary 1990:444-6, Corbin 1986:55-7). While some were associated with the local rulers, others remained far from any political involvement. Without generalizing, one can however remark that, in most cases, with a few exceptions (the most notable being the case of the ninth-century mystic Mansur al-Hallaj), Sufis did not radically or openly challenge the legitimacy of the Islamic law (*sharīa*), even if they emphasized the need for spiritual reflection and adopted a characteristic way of life.

Yet Sufi tolerance, and in certain cases its friendly interaction with Hindu religious teachers such as the Nath Jogis, must not be overestimated in the light of many legends which testify to rivalry with these ascetics. To give an example, the Sufi Abdul Quddus made ample use of yogic terminology and ideology and even wrote under the Hindu *nom de plume* Alakh (a name of the formless God) (Rizvi 1983, I:336-48), whereas Muinuddin Chishti is said to have forced the yogi Ajaypal to accept his superiority by demonstrating his supernatural powers (Currie 1989:76-81).

In other words, the reality of friendly exchanges with Hindu yogis and Sants should not prevent us from perceiving the other side of the picture: the important role played by some Sufi *tarīqas* in converting Hindus and propagating Sunni Islam in the subcontinent. This propagation was also accompanied by a phenomenon which has not been properly analysed to this day: the attempts of a few Sufi orders to eliminate Ismailis whom they regarded as dangerous heretics and rivals. This aim is said to have been achieved by compelling the Nizari converts to embrace Sunni Islam or to revert to their old Hindu beliefs which were considered less harmful than the Ismaili 'heresy'[6] (A.Z. Khan 1980:276). In this process they also took over shrines (tombs) of Ismaili Pirs and went so far as to include some of them in the list of their own Pirs. For instance, Hasan Kabiruddin, a fifteenth century Nizari *dāī*, is listed among the Sufi Shaikhs of the Suhrawardi *silsila* as 'Hasan Daryạ' (Daftary 1990:480). The case of Lal Shahbaz Qalandar also deserves some mention, in so far as this Muslim saint is generally regarded as a figure connected with the above-mentioned *tarīqa* (Ansari 1992:19). Ismaili tradition claims that he was one of the thirteenth-century Nizari Pirs (Allana 1984:36) whom Hindus had identified with an incarnation of Vishnu. Those who among the Momnas have embraced the Sunni faith claim that they were converted to Islam by the Sufi Muinuddin Chishti (Misra 1985:64-5), while it is a well known fact in Ismaili history that the founder of this community was the Nizari Sayyid Pir Mashaikh (Shackle and Moir 1992:8).

Interesting cases may also be mentioned of some ex-Ismailis, who, having become Sunni or Twelver Shia Muslims, have attempted to modify the identity of a Pir they still revere as their *murshid*. The most striking example is probably that of Pir Shamsuddin Sabzwari, a leading figure of Nizari Ismailism: the custodians of his tomb in Multan (in modern Pakistani Punjab, one of the traditional centres of the Ismaili *dawa* in the subcontinent) have adopted the Isna Ashari faith and, for this reason, connect Pir Shams with Twelver Shia Islam (Rose 1990:546). The famous 'Aga Khan case' which took place in the Bombay High Court in 1866 (Masselos 1978:109-15) revealed the desire of some Ismaili Khojas to be regarded as Sunnis. However, they failed to prove that Pir Sadruddin (fourteenth-fifteenth century), who had converted them to Islam, and Kabiruddin his successor, had been Sunni religious teachers. According to Shackle and Moir (1992:9), the most conspicuous result of this court case was that 'for the first time in the entire history of the Khojas the Nizari Imamate was brought out of the secrecy which had hither to surrounded it. . . .'

Reverting now to the relationship between Sufis and Ismailis, we will have also to examine its positive aspect, i.e. the extensive exchanges which are said to have occurred at various periods of history (Ivanow 1959:13-17, and 1953:17). It is during the post-Alamut period that what can be termed the 'coalescence' between Persian Nizarism and Sufism took place (Daftary 1992:452-3, Corbin 1986: 142, 152-4, 156-7). According to Daftary (453), 'Nizarism became increasingly infused in Persia with Sufi teachings and terminology . . . nonetheless, the adoption of a Sufi exterior by Nizaris would not have been readily possible if the esoteric traditions had not had common grounds'. Not only did the Ismailis 'camouflage their beliefs mainly in the guise of Sufism' (ibid.:460), but the Imams (Shamsuddin Muhammad and his successors in the Qasim Shah line) adopted the dress of Sufis and their titles of Pirs, while their disciples came to be known as *murīd*' (ibid.). In the fifteenth century the Imam Mustansir Billah II revived the Imamate and, to secure his status in Iran under adverse circumstances, 'assumed the role of a Sufi Shaikh of the Nimatullahi order' (Shackle and Moir 1992:5). This trend continued for a fairly long time, as can be illustrated by the fact that under Aga Khan I, at the beginning of the nineteenth century, a Nizari Sayyid named Muhammad Sadiq Mahalahti was initiated into the same *tarīqa* of Sufis, followed by his son Muhammad Ali urf Izzat Ali Shah (Daftary 1990:503).

The 'appropriation' of Ismaili Pirs (and their shrines) by Sufis, reported earlier, curiously had its counterpart in an interesting phenomenon: the Nizaris came to regard as their coreligionists some poets of Persia whose identity as Sunni Sufis is beyond doubt (Daftary 1990:454, Shackle and Moir 1992:16), while in other cases the authorship of some texts has remained a disputed matter. Shamsuddin Tabrizi, the spiritual guide of Jalaluddin Rumi, the celebrated Sufi mystic, is sometimes believed to have belonged to the Ismaili tradition (Hollister 1953:318). Besides, a few scholars have it that Sufism as a whole, despite its later evolution towards Sunnism, has its roots in the Shia philosophy (Corbin 1986:29, 55-7, 84, 152-4 and A. Rahmatoullah, personal communication).[7]

Although the phenomenon has hardly been studied, there is good reason to believe that this coalescence—and not only the rivalry mentioned above—prevailed in the Indian subcontinent for the same reasons (*taqīyya*, a specific method of conversion, and philosophical affinities). In this particular environment, as Nanji has it (1978:68), 'the Pir emerges as a Hindu yogi or a wandering dervish, working totally with the forces current at the time'. The natural consequence is that 'in an environment permeated by Sufi *tarīqas* and *bhakti* groups revolving around religious personalities, the Ismaili Pirs must have been quite inconspicuous . . . some of these Pirs were so successful in representing themselves as spiritual teachers that till today the non-Ismailis of Punjab and Sind revere them as Sufi masters of Sunni persuasion' (Asani 1991:3).

Despite the absence of inscriptions or other documents revealing their true identity, it is logical to infer that whenever an Ismaili *dāī* appeared in a Muslim guise, he was identified with a Sufi dervish or a Qalandar. Moreover, according to Hedeyutallah (1977:45), the epithet 'Sufi' is still used in modern times to refer to a Nizari Pir: 'the Sufi who made the most valuable contribution towards the interaction between Hindus and the Muslims was an Ismaili missionary named Pir Sadr-ud-din'.

THE EXPANSION OF THE ISMAILI *DAWA*: ROUTES AND MODES OF PENETRATION

A number of documents referring to the Fatimid organization of the *dawa* (Daftary 1990:228) mention the division of the non-Fatimid world into a certain number of areas for conversion purposes; twelve *jazāir* (sing. *jazīra*, lit. island) represented the dioceses intended for missionary activity. Among those *jazāir* were *al-Hind* and *al-Sind*, two regions separated by the Indus river, corresponding roughly to modern India and Pakistani Sind. As for Sunni Islam brought by Arab and Central Asian conquerors and by Sufis into the subcontinent, Ismailism must have penetrated from Iran along the major trade routes which, before the creation of the Bombay harbour and the 1947 Partition, were mainly caravan roads crossing Sind, Punjab and

Rajasthan, to Gujarat or Delhi and the Ganges Valley. These routes enabled not only the movement of goods, but also of men and ideas.

A map of the Nizari *dawa* in South Asia—as sketched by specialists of Ismaili history (see for example Nanji 1978: map, frontispiece) — shows Sind, Punjab, Gujarat and a part of Maharasthra as the 'major' (ibid.) centres of missionary activity. Anticipating the traces of Ismaili presence in other areas, to be discussed later, we can at this stage make one more important point. Those familiar with Indian cultural, political and economic history would be surprised by the following detail: the conspicuous absence of the region now designated as Rajasthan (an area which emerged gradually and rather recently as a regional entity) (Lodrick 1994, I:1-44). From remote antiquity, due to its geographical position, this area was closely linked with Sind, Punjab and Gujarat (Vaudeville 1962:18). Rajasthan to this day shares with its neighbours a number of ethnic, cultural and religious traits which even modern travellers unaware of Indian history can perceive.

Sind was connected with various parts of Rajasthan, especially through the medieval city of Barmer; according to some historical documents, 'the invasions of the Turks and the Mughals in this country throw light on routes and roads from northern India to Gujarat through Rajasthan'. For instance, it is said that Mahmud of Ghazna's route from Multan to Gujarat went through the town of Lodarva (near Jaisalmer) (G.N. Sharma 1985:162).

When travelling from Multan to Gujarat, as any map will clearly indicate, one can pass through Rajasthan to avoid the area of Kacch (the Rann) otherwise famous for its particular breeds of horses and camels. Cities like Pokaran,[8] Nagaur, Osia, Barmer, Lodarva and Jaisalmer had been important trading centres which linked Central Asia, Sind and Punjab to other parts of India. A Punjabi tradition concerning the journey of the legendary *Panch Pirs* (Five Pirs) mentioning as their halting places Bhawalnagar, Abohar and Pokaran (the last situated in Rajasthan), throws some light on the links that may have existed between these cities and their surrounding areas for centuries. More will be said in the next chapter about these five saints.

Besides commercial exchanges which have brought into contact men and ideas as well, as far as the spread of Ismailism is concerned, one must also consider the geographic mobility of different caste and tribe groups for which oral tradition bears ample testimony.

Bhangis (sweepers-scavengers) have migrated from Punjab (especially from the Dhera Ghazi Khan region) to Gujarat and Rajasthan where they have brought their customs and beliefs; Meghvals (Meghs, Meghvars) settled in Sind, Punjab, Gujarat and Rajasthan and share a common cultural heritage. Jats (an agricultural but also martial group) moved along a line extending between Punjab and Rajasthan now cut by the border dividing India and Pakistan. I have also personally suggested that some Multani castes (among whom mainly Sunars, goldsmiths) settled in Rajasthan where they came to be known as Nyaryas (D.S. Khan 1995: 310).

These are but a few examples and the whole issue will have to be reexamined, particularly the case of the migrations of some Muslim weavers (Julahas) from western India to the Ganges Valley. This phenomenon is of particular significance, since, as stated above, according to the Ismaili tradition conversions were generally made by choosing an influential person belonging to a specific social group who would later convert his caste fellows. The result was the 'establishment of little pockets of followers' (Nanji 1978:68) functioning somewhat independently. Due to the persecution of Sunni rulers, as has been said earlier, *taqīyya* was extensively practised so that

> the identity of such groups would be extremely difficult to discover within the complex of religious trends emerging after Muslim settlement. Moreover, the groups could continue to function as a *Jama'a* [the Muslim congregation of the faithful] related to a specific profession. . . . Further the continuation of Hindu cultural traits, as well as association with a professional caste acted as a cover for Ismaili tendencies (ibid.).

We will return to this problem which is of exceptional interest for our study.

ISMAILI PIRS OF THE NIZARI PERIOD

Let us now revert to Ismaili history and examine the missionary activities in South Asia during the Nizari phase.

This chapter of history, as we said, is rather difficult to reconstruct, insofar as practically no documents are available before the nineteenth century. A tentative reconstruction has been made by different scholars, mainly on the basis of oral tradition; the literature of the Khojas has been transcribed at least from the eighteenth century onwards, which has enabled them to preserve a part of the old heritage. Although in a semi-legendary form, these texts, generally referred to as *gināns*, contain a great number of interesting details.

The first Pir to be mentioned by the Nizari tradition of the subcontinent is Nur Muhammad, also named Satgur Nur, Nur Satagur, Pir Sadat, or Sadaji. Nothing is known for certain concerning this *dāī* who is said to have been sent by an Imam from Alamut, Hasan ala Zikrihi al-Salam (at the end of the twelfth century) (Mujtaba Ali 1936:39), although various other periods, such as the eleventh or the thirteenth centuries have been suggested for this Pir, whose tomb is said to be located in Navsari (coastal south Gujarat). The shrine is now in the hands of the Imamshahis, a separate branch of the Nizaris. The information concerning this first missionary being extremely vague, he has been regarded by some authors as an 'archetypal missionary' (Nanji 1978:61) who cannot be identified with a single, real character. Some scholars like Zawahir Moir (forthcoming) however consider that he was a historical figure—a conclusion drawn from the analysis of different *gināns*. The case of Shamsuddin Sabzwari (so-called because he was supposed to have come from Sabzwar in Iran) is somewhat different. This religious figure seems to possess more 'historical consistency'. According to the Nizari tradition, he settled in Multan, an old centre of the Ismaili *dawa*, from where he propagated his message to various parts of the subcontinent. His father is said to have been Salahuddin (Lakhani 1973:87). Various dates have been proposed for his missionary activities, ranging from the twelfth to the fourteenth century (Noorally 1973:83-6). Moir (forthcoming) is of the opinion that he may have flourished in the twelfth or at the beginning of the thirteenth century. Although I am not a competent authority in this matter, I can at least suggest that the fourteenth century given by some Ismaili sources as Pir Shams Sabzwari's time seems to conform with the field data I have collected in Rajasthan (see next Chapter). The vagueness of dates is still aggravated by the fact that this Nizari missionary has been confused with other historical figures; for instance, since he is known in Pakistani and north Indian traditions as 'Shams Tabrez' (Shams-e Tabrizi), he has often been identified with the thirteenth century *murshid* of Jalaluddin Rumi; elsewhere he is mistaken for his namesake who flourished in Kashmir in the fifteenth century (Hollister 1978:353), when he is not identified with the Imam Shamsuddin Muhammad, the last master of Alamut (thirteenth century).

On the tradition connected with this *dāī* and his hagiography, Noorally (1973:83-6), Moir (forthcoming) and Mallison (1991a:117-38) have brought out many interesting and revealing features. For instance a confrontation took place, it is said, between Shams and the Sufi Bahauddin Zakariya, a famous thirteenth-century Shaikh of the Suhrawardi order (Rizvi 1978:I:190-94). This episode, interestingly enough, is also reported by the Meghval worshippers of Ramdev Pir. Another point which deserves attention is the way in which Pir Shams is said to have joined the devotees of the Goddess in Gujarat in their *garabī* dance, before gradually leading them to a new revelation (Mallison, ibid.).

Those converted by Pir Shams came to be designated as Shamsis or Shamsiyas (A.N. Khan 1983:39, 205). For the modern history of religions it is clear that this term refers to the Nizari Ismailis, who are not distinct from other converted groups, such as the Khojas. None the less, it will be interesting to note that perceptions till recently have been different. For example, Ahmad (1969:24) calls them 'a subsect of the Khojas' and remarks (ibid.:25) that 'they are a syncretistic sect even more deeply influenced by Hinduism'. By reading Rose's account of the Shamsis of Punjab (1990:402-3), one can conclude that, at least in the nineteenth century, their identity was by no means clear, although the author who regards them as 'a curious sect of followers of Pir Shams Tabriz', half-Hindu half-Musulman, 'held in abhorence by both orthodox Muslims and Hindus', has inferred a connection with the Nizari Khojas and their leader the Aga Khan (ibid.). The reason for such confused perceptions is the fact that the Shamsis (among whom one found mostly Sunars but also other artisan communities and a higher status group, the Khatris) had lived in concealment more or less until the arrival of the Aga Khans in the subcontinent.[9] Rose also mentions the fact that, solicited by their Imam, some Shamsis openly declared themselves followers of the Nizari sect for which they were 'excommunicated by the Hindu community' (ibid.), whereas others preferred to retain their Hindu identity, even if their beliefs and practises appeared unorthodox from the Brahmanical point of view.

Since they were secret followers of the Ismaili religion, Shamsis have been also referred to as *Guptīs* (lit. secret)—a designation, we must insist, for all Nizaris practising *taqīyya* and hiding their real identity, and not for a particular branch of Ismailism, as has been erroneously stated (Ahmad 1969:26).

Finally, attention may be drawn to the fact that the hagiography of Pir Shams, as presented in the ginanic literature preserved by the Khojas (Ivanow 1948, I:90-5) includes a description of his travels to regions not hitherto known to have been important in the history of the *dawa*: Malwa, the Ganges Valley and Bengal.[10] In the absence of supporting evidence these travels may be regarded as mere legends forged by missionaries to enhance their prestige by exaggerating the expansion and power of the Ismaili *dawa*. However one must not reject *a priori* the possibility that Shams himself, or his successors and/or their disciples, also converted people in these regions where no Nizari community has survived to the present day (except of course the Khoja migrants from Sind, Punjab and Gujarat). Actually, as we will see, there are hints of the influence of Ismailism in these areas in a number of elements which have been preserved in the culture of particular communities now seen as Sunni, Twelver Shia or Hindu (Allana 1984:37-54).

The most famous Nizari missionary, known even to scholars who are not familiar with Ismailism, was Pir Sadruddin (d. 1416?) (Shackle and Moir 1992:11). His fame accrues from what is often viewed as a synthetic or syncretistic approach to religion (Husain 1929:29-30, 34, Ahmad 1969:24-5). Sadruddin is supposed to be the inventor of a 'system of equivalences' between Hindu and Muslim concepts and terminologies. He is, moreover, regarded as the organizer of the first *jamāt khāna* (congregational lodge) (Nanji 1978:74). Whatever truth there may be in this assumption (some Ismaili sources point to a greater antiquity of these ideas and institutions), his major achievement has been the conversion of a group known as the Lohanas from which the community of the Khojas (in the strict sense of the word) is believed to have originated (the name Khoja is derived from *khwāja*, master, a title often given to nobles, teachers or merchants) (Daftary 1990:562). As the identity of this caste group is of particular interest for our understanding of the expansion of Ismailism, we will have to return to this issue. The Lohanas are an important merchant community of Sind, some members of which migrated to Gujarat, claiming the status of Rajputs (it is said that they were previously referred to as *ṭhākur*, an equivalent of the Islamic term *khwāja*). It is difficult to ascertain the reason for this claim, but it must be recalled that, during the period which concerns us, Rajput identity (as a caste group claiming Kshatriya status) was far from being constituted in the rigid way it would later be, after the establishment of Mughal and British rule. In the fourteenth-fifteenth centuries, as Kolff has it (1990:182-92), it was probably a much more flexible category which depended on the martial and organizational capacities of those who took service (*naukrī*) under some king rather than on real genealogical links with those described in the epics. It is probably not a coincidence if the Ismailis chose to give them the title *khojā-khwāja* which emphasized their traditional claim to a higher status.

Sadruddin is said to have been the great grandson of Pir Shams. He was succeeded by Hasan Kabiruddin (d. 1470?) (Shackle and Moir 1992:7; Nanji 1978:77-9) of whom we have said above that he had been listed in the *silsilā* of the Sufi Suhrawardi Pirs. Like Shams and Sadruddin, the name of Kabiruddin often figures among the signatures of various devotional hymns of the Khojas. In his hagiography he is described as being clad in white dress or occasionally wearing the saffron colour cloth typical of Hindu ascetics while he is believed to have become a staunch vegetarian (Upanga 1973:91-3).

The next Pir is Tajuddin, his brother, whose career was short-lived, and whose destiny after deposition by the Imam still remains a mystery (Nanjiani 1918:195-6, Nanji 1978:79). More will be indicated about him and his tradition in subsequent chapters.

Kabiruddin's son Sayyid Imam Shah (d. 1513) and his son Nar Muhammad Shah (d. 1533) are the last missionaries entitled to be called leaders of the *dawa* of Hind and Sind. The line is said to have ended because of the schism which occurred during the latter Pir's time, when he claimed the Imamship for his dead father, creating a 'dissident' branch which came to be designated as *Imāmshāhī, Pīrānā Panth* or *Sat Panth* (its centre is near Ahmedabad, where the tombs of Imam Shah and Muhammad Shah are located). The latter appellation, it might be recalled, had also been applied to the main Nizari sect. After Nar Muhammad Shah's death, Imamshahis were divided into several sects and the *dawa* suffered a serious setback. As a consequence of the schism the Persian Imam of the time is said to have, sent a book entitled *pandiyāt-i javānmardī* (lit. 'precepts of manhood') for the instruction of the faithful in place of a main *dāī* or Pir. This book, strangely enough, was included in the genealogy of the *dāīs* as the last Pir or 'Pir Pandiyat' (Shackle and Moir 1992:8). However, descendants of the previous Pirs and other disciples of the Nizaris continued to organize the community. Those who claimed descent from the main *dāīs* were referred to as Sayyids (to stress the fact that their ancestors were from the Alid family) although they were also popularly called 'Pirs'.

Another schism may be briefly mentioned here, when Sayyid Pir Mashaikh, claiming descent from Hasan Kabiruddin, formed the Momna community at the end of the seventeenth century (Shackle and Moir 1992:8, Misra 1985:64-5).

According to the Nizari Ismaili tradition (personal communication by Zawahir Moir), the period which extends from Tajuddin's activities (corresponding to the establishment of the Imam at Anjudan and the revival of the Imamate) to Muhammad Shah must have been simultaneously a period of extensive missionary work—a fact which my personal research seems to corroborate—and of confusion, due to the above mentioned schism. It seems that the Persian centre of the Ismaili *dawa* could neither fully keep the different communities under control nor collect the taxes due to the Imam (mainly the obligatory tithe or *dassondh*, levied on all members of the community). A struggle might also have ensued between the Nizari Sayyids who remained faithful to the Persian Imam (these missionaries were the Kadivala Sayyids, their main centre having been Khadi, in Gujarat) and the disciples of the 'dissident' Muhammad Shah (Imamshahis, Satpanthis) to gain control over the groups which had previously been converted to Ismailism in different parts of the subcontinent.

A brief mention must be made of the Aga Khans (a title conferred on the Imam in the nineteenth century) (Daftary 1990:505-14), the first of whom arrived in the subcontinent around 1840. Changing political and social circumstances, together with the presence of the influential leader of the Nizaris among his Indian followers, had an important consequence: the local Ismaili community gradually came out of concealment. Among those who wished to follow the Aga Khan as their Imam, those who had hidden their identity mainly under a Hindu guise, the Guptis, started to profess openly the Nizari religion and changed their Hindu names for Islamic ones (personal communication by A. Rahmatoullah). This was followed by a slow process of 'reIslamization' of the tradition, of which more will be said at the end of this chapter.

ISMAILISM PREACHED TO THE HINDUS: THE SATPANTH AS THE CULMINATION OF HINDUISM

We now move on to an analysis of the particular form Nizarism took in the Indo-Pakistan subcontinent. It was mainly known by the Hindu appellation of *Sat Panth* (lit. the 'true path' or the 'true sect'), which may be regarded as an equivalent of the Arabic *dīn-e haqq*, the true religion, as also *sirāt-e-mustaqīm*, the right path, used to designate Ismailism in other contexts and emphasizing the priority of esoteric interpretation (*bātin*) over the exoteric (*zāhir*). Rather than trying to be exhaustive (I refer the reader to various comprehensive studies made in this field), I will limit myself to stressing a number of points which appear particularly relevant for the analysis of the 'forgotten branches' of Ismailism in Rajasthan, adding a few details which derive from my personal research.

The process of acculturation is particularly striking in the literature of the Nizari Khojas, referred to as *ginān* (the word *ginān* derives from the Sanskrit *jñāna*, knowledge) (Shackle and Moir 1992:17) — a collection of devotional hymns and texts of varying content preserved as the Khoja heritage. The oldest manuscript found to this day being fairly recent (1736), it is difficult to ascertain at what time the *ginanic* tradition began. However, a number of elements point to its antiquity. There seems to be evidence for the existence of a sixteenth-century manuscript, and, most scholars specialized in Ismaili studies admit that the *gināns* must have existed even before Pir Sadruddin's time (i.e. before the fourteenth century), their language and style having gradually evolved through a long period of oral transmission (Shackle and Moir 1992:15).

As Asani has stated (1991:5-6), 'literatures in the vernacular were instrumental in explaining fundamental Islamic concepts to the native populations in terms that were familiar and accessible to them . . . in the process, the authors who formulated these literatures, indigenized the Islamic tradition to the local Indian cultural environment' (a process which is generally termed 'acculturation').

These compositions are ascribed to various Pirs and Sayyids (Asani 1991:2-3), but a thorough examination of the texts reveals that, in most cases, these can be regarded only as signatures (*chhāp*) aimed at increasing the prestige of the *gināns*, much in the same way as many Hindu devotional songs (*bhajans*) are traditionally ascribed to famous poet-saints who do not appear to be their true authors [although it is, undoubtedly, their teachings that are conveyed (Hawley 1988:269-90)]. Therefore nothing can be said with certainty on the authorship of the Ismaili *gināns* and for the moment we will assume that they represent the ancient tradition of oral religious poetry of north India with which they share, as we will see, a great number of traits.

Be that as it may, we are mainly concerned here with the terminologies, concepts and thematic contents of this literature. On discovering some of these texts, Francoise Mallison, an authority on medieval Hindu Gujarati devotional poetry, was struck by one fact: 'I had the revelation of a religious tradition very much akin to the non-sectarian Vaishnavism of the 15th-16th centuries in Gujarat' (Mallison 1991a:93). Nanji finds a similar kinship (1978:126), (96-7) and has stressed the resemblance of these traits with the *bhakti* poetry in general, and in particular with the devotional literature associated with the non-sectarian Sant Kabir. Shackle and Moir (1992:28-30) have pointed to 'South Asian parallels' with the *ginānic* tradition: the compositions of some Sufis, but also of Sants such as Kabir, Nanak and Dadu are compared with the Ismaili hymns.

However, it is not only non-sectarian Vaishnavism, whether *saguṇ* or *nirguṇ* (devotion to the 'qualified' and 'non-qualified' God), but many other aspects of the Hindu tradition which are mirrored in the *gināns*—as a result of which these texts cannot appear as a mere variant of Sant poetry, and deserve to be regarded as original creations. As Kassam has written (1994: 232a): 'The *gināns* were not an accidental by-product of contact and change between two cultures mutually influencing each other but rather the result of a specific intention to create a certain kind of literature by the *da'wa*.'

THE *GINĀNIC* LANGUAGE

A characteristic of the Ismaili hymns is the 'frequent parallel use of Sanskrit terms (actually their different regional vernacular forms) together with their synonyms of Arabic or Persian origin to express a single concept' (Shackle and Moir 1992:20). This phenomenon, which might superficially appear as an attempt at translating one idiom into another, somehow reminds us of the methods of the Christian missionaries of south India who sought out Tamil equivalents for the Christian concepts expressed in European languages. For this purpose they chose indigenous terms from the local religious vocabulary and transplanted them as such into the Christian context, without concern for the differences which existed between the two semantic universes. The case of the Ismailis is however different: the original Islamic terms and concepts 'translated' into the indigenous religious idiom are not discarded but used in tandem.

Here are a few examples of such a parallel use, of particular relevance for our subject.

- The pious believer is termed *momin*, according to the general Muslim terminology, but also designated *rikhisar* (*rikh, rikhi,* from the Sanskrit, *ṛṣi* referring to the ancient 'seers' of India) and *munivar* (*muni,* an ascetic in the Buddhist, Jain and Hindu traditions). This is evidently not a 'faithful' translation, if at all, but it appears as an attempt to redefine the identity of the believer in a local context.[11] We will have to revert to the word *ṛṣi* (*rikh*), in so far as it is an essential element of the Nizari terminology used in the subcontinent.
- Remembrance of God is referred to as *zikar* (Islamic) and as *samaraṇ* (skt. *smaraṇ*) according to the Hindu tradition.
- God is invoked by many names: *Khudā* is also *Sāmī* (Skt. *Swāmī*), *Allāh* is *Alakh, Rahīm* or *Rahmān* is *Rām,* and so on. Let us remark, by way of digression, that Hindu-Muslim equations of the names of God constitute a typical feature of Sant poetry, for example of Kabir.[12]
- The spiritual guide or *Pīr* (the Persian equivalent of the Arabic *Shaikh*) is also called *Guru* (*gur*), while the supreme Pir of the Nizaris, the Imam, as a divine epiphany, is *Gur Nar.*
- The Arabic root for knowledge *ilm* (*um*) is compared to the Hindu mystical syllable *om* (Engineer 1989:38).

The fact that the Hindu terms do not obviously try to render the original meaning of the Islamic words and concepts shows that the use of a 'bilingual' terminology was not meant to be an attempt at asserting the doctrinal identity of both traditions. Nor was it intended to create a kind of synthesis. It must be rather perceived as a pedagogical method, for, as Kassam (1994:232) has expressed it, 'since the purpose of the *da'is* was to win converts, we should find in the *ginān*s clues to their methods of effecting change. That is to say, the *ginān*s should reflect techniques of transformation that facilitate conversion.' In other words, while this 'double' terminology certainly testifies to a profound interaction between two religious cultures, the aim of the Ismaili missionaries was more to show that indigenous elements can be not only integrated into their conceptual framework, but also be reinterpreted—a phenomenon which should regarded as a genuine 'Ismaili motivation' (Nanji 1978:132) attested throughout the history of its expansion in different countries. As a consequence of this motivation the Nizari message is presented to the potential converts as the culmination and fulfilment of their religious expectations.

Without giving up their original Islamic names the Nizari Pirs also adopted Hindu ones. As has been said earlier, Nur Muhammad was equally known as Satgur Nur (from *satguru*, the 'true guide'). According to my hypothesis he was called Gusainji in Rajasthan and Matang Rishi among the untouchables of Gujarat. In Rajasthan, as my field research has shown, Pir Shams was called Samik Rishi or Samas Rishi. The Ismaili tradition tells us that Sadruddin adopted the Hindu names of Sahadev, Balram and Harchand, Tajuddin that of Prahlad, and Kabiruddin was also named Anant-jo-dhani. Similarly, I will suggest that Sayyid Bala Shah, a son of Kabiruddin, was the same person as Balmik, a saint deified by the Bhangis of Punjab. The motivations for such a two-fold identity is evidently the same as for the above mentioned Hindu-Muslim terminology. In fact the adoption of a Hindu name might be explained by cautious dissimulation (*taqīyya*), as well as by the desire of the missionaries to appear closer to the indigenous population.

HINDU MYTHOLOGY REVISITED BY THE ISMAILI *DĀĪS*

Rather than a mere borrowing of Hindu themes, one should speak of an authentic creation when considering the heritage of the *gināns*. As stated by Nanji, 'the *gināns* seized upon Hindu motifs and myths and transformed these into narratives reflecting the *da'ẉa* preaching . . . without totally rejecting the conceptual and even the social framework of the society he has penetrated', the Pir proposes ultimately 'a new life and a new thought' (Nanji 1978:101-2).

More than that, the Nizari missionaries literally infiltrate the theatre of Hindu mythology, just as science fiction characters penetrate, with the help of a time-machine, into the realm of the past and even take part in historical events by which they attempt to modify the course of history. In this way, one could say that the Nizari poets have not negated, but partially 'rewritten' and recast into a new mould the epics and legends associated with Hinduism.

The great popularity of the Mahabharata in its classical and yet more its regional popular versions (Rao 1980, Hiltebeitel 1988)—which gave rise to various local cults, and the powerful figure of the god Vishnu-Krishna, champion of the *bhakti*, inspired the Ismaili religious teachers. In this perspective they proposed to the neophytes a new revelation: the Ismaili Imam, who for his followers is divine, (Corbin 1986:71, 137)[13] had already manifested himself to the Hindus from the remotest times in the form of Vishnu. While for the Nizari Muslims he entered our cycle of time as Ali, son-in-law of the Prophet Muhammad, in the Hindu *kali yuga* he has continuously been reincarnated as the Imam, being none other than the tenth *avatār* of Vishnu, Kalki, whose advent the Hindus still await. This ever-living Kalki was also given a new name, not referring to him in the Hindu lore: Nikalank (or *Niṣkalank, Naklankī* the 'immaculate', the 'faultless one', a name corresponding to the Arabic epithet *masūm*, 'pure', 'innocent', traditionally applied to the Ismaili Imams).

The parallels drawn between the Ismaili concept of divine epiphany (*mazhar*) and the *avatār* theory of the Vaishnava tradition, of course, made sense only because a number of similarities already existed between the concept of cyclic time and of divine and human reincarnations in both traditions (Daftary 1990:394, Marquet 1973:397-400).[14]

As suggested by their Hindu names, the Nizari preachers claim to have played a role, during their former incarnations, in the Epic and Puranic history. For instance, Sadruddin may have appeared in one earlier birth as Sahadev, one of the five Pandava brothers, heroes of the Mahabharata, or as Krishna's brother Balarama (Balram) while in another era, he was Harischandra (Harchand), the famous king devotee (Dowson 1991:118-19). As for Tajuddin, it is suggested that he was Prahlad, the demon-devotee saved by Narasimha, Vishnu's incarnation as man-lion (ibid.:238-9). On the other hand in some *ginans* all the main Pirs are said to be *avatārs* of Brahma (Ivanow 1948:130-2).

Vishnu's *avatārs* and the stories related to them, will come to play such an essential part in the transformed Hindu folklore created by the Ismaili missionaries, that—although these are originally indigenous motifs—they will betray, as we shall see, the influence of the Ismaili Pirs. The doctrine of personal salvation and the very importance of the soteriological theme in the Nizari religion will be enhanced and expressed through the highly popular *bhakti* stories in which gods fight with demons (*asura, rākśasa*). It is for this reason and in order to rescue their devotees, and to grant them liberation (*mokśa*) or promise them paradise (*svarg, vaikunṭha, amarpurī*) that gods have been incarnated in our world (Hollister 1979:383).

Let us revert to the motif of the tenth incarnation of Vishnu which plays a key role in the Ismaili Indian tradition. The regular manifestation of the Imam (perceived as the leader of the Nizari community or as the Hindu god Vishnu) and his final, triumphal reappearance at the end of a cosmic era, in conformity with the Ismaili doctrine of *qiyāma* or resurrection, as the Imam Qaim[15] has a decidedly messianic flavour which also corresponds to the global Shia doctrine (Corbin 1986:61, 80), if we remember that the Isna Ashari believers expect their concealed Imam to reappear triumphantly at the end of time. In the acculturated Nizari tradition of the subcontinent this theme is further enhanced through the description of the fight between *Nikalank avatār* (Vishnu's tenth incarnation, as perceived by the Ismailis) and the demonic king Kalinga, personification of the evil of our era (*kali yuga*), referred to as Kali in the original Hindu mythology. Actually, what is most striking here is that, although the figure of Kalki appears in various Puranic contexts (Stutley 1985:138), he has not become, in the indigenous context, the focus of a messianic cult. Wherever and whenever real messianic movements emerge in India they are generally connected with tribal milieus or more recent socio-political trends influenced by foreign elements (Fuchs 1992). As Herrenschmidt has remarked (personal communication), though the Hindus had an ideal model of the messiah in the figure of Kalki, they never resorted to it for their expectations of a saviour capable of bringing them into a better world. Messianism, moreover, cannot be regarded as a dominant feature of Hindu civilization. This essential point needs to be borne in mind for one reason: whenever the Kalki motif appears in the medieval Hindu poetry in the guise of Nikalank (a creation of the Nizari missionaries), it can be considered a trace of Ismaili influence.

In the theatre of Hindu mythology revisited by the Nizari Pirs, other Hindu divine entities played a role and were compared to Muslim figures: Muhammad was equated with Brahma, Adam (and Imam Hasan) with Shiva, while Fatima was naturally identified with the great Goddess (*Śakti*). This last identification is extremely important in view of the popularity of the worship of the Devi in various forms by different Hindu or Jain communities. Similarly, the five Shia sacred figures or *panj tan*, Muhammad, Ali, Hasan, Hussein and Fatima were as a whole comparable to the five Pandavas—a detail which is particularly significant for this study.

Among the reinterpreted themes of Hindu mythology connected with the essential notion of salvation obtained by recognition of the supreme Truth embodied by the ever-living Imam,[16] we find one oft repeated motif. Based on the soteriological role of the *avatārs* during the different Hindu eras or *yugas*, this motif can be interpreted as an original pattern designed to ensure the continuity of the religious message from Hinduism to Ismailism: Vishnu in his Narasimha incarnation—so say the Nizari *dāīs*—had promised his devotee Prahlad that he would save thirty-three crores of souls (the figure representing in the original, Hindu tradition the symbolic number of gods: *teintīs karoṛ devtā*). In this way, five crores are said to have been saved together with Prahlad himself, seven in the following *yuga* with Harischandra, and nine in the third with Yudhishtira and his four Pandava brothers. In the present era or *kali yuga*, it was the Nizari Pir Sadruddin who would grant liberation to the remaining twelve crores. According to the Ismaili tradition, this is one of the reasons why the above mentioned *dāī* was also named *bār gur* (the guru of the twelve)—although this appellation might also refer to the fact that he had twelve companions or lieutenants—twelve being a key-figure of Ismaili symbolism (Córbin 1986:58-9, 132). We have, once more, a dominant theme of the Indian Nizari tradition which, albeit inspired directly by Hindu mythology, betrays its Ismaili identity in a specific form. In other words, this motif might also help us to trace hidden Ismaili influence in various contexts.

ISMAILISM AND THE NATH YOGI TRADITION

Besides the mythological epic and Puranic lore, and mention of gods, *asuras*, devotees and *ṛṣis*, the literary tradition of the *gināns* points to the fact that extensive contacts had been established with Shaiva ascetics, in particular those who came to be identified with the Nath Sampraday, the tradition of Tantric yoga, as practised by ascetics referred to as Naths, Gorakhnathis, Nathpanthis and Kānphaṭā Jogis (Briggs 1989).

There is reason to believe that this sect, or rather, in a broader framework, the religious tradition it represented in various forms, was extremely popular in the subcontinent in medieval times. It is also clear, from different sources, that at least before what can be termed the process of Sanskritization (Srinivas 1952) of the movement, it constituted a powerful alternative to the models of

Hinduism proposed by the Brahmans and the higher castes. The fact that in some medieval religious compositions of the Sants the Naths are often listed separately (one generally finds the triad Hindu-Nath-Musulman), testifies to their somewhat distinct identity. Among the most remarkable peculiarities of the Nath tradition is the absence of caste discrimination—a feature also typical of the *Sant paramparā.*

Finally one should mention certain practices in which Nath gurus did play an important role and which appeared contrary to 'Brahmanical orthodoxy' insofar as they challenged the rules of purity governing contact and commensality between individuals and castes: Tantric-Shaktic observances, such as the famous *kạula* ritual, also referred to as *chakra pūja* or *panch makāra* (Bhattacharya 1987:120, 149), as well as the curious customs connected with the Aghoris or cremation-ground ascetics (Parry 1982, R. Gupta, 1993). The strong note of social protest which it carried might have appealed to various groups of people, including the lower castes, as proved by the fact that many untouchables were attracted towards the Nath movement and adopted Tantric and Aghori practices (Gunarthi 1987:287). As has been reported (Khakhar 1878:51n.1), before the Sanskritization of the Nath Sampradāy some untouchable Meghvals had even been the heads (*mahants*) of Nath monasteries (*maṭhs*).

It has been said above that at times the Ismaili Pir emerged as a Hindu yogi. The Nizari tradition illustrates this phenomenon by way of various references. It is reported, for instance, that Pir Satgur Nur was killed by one of his disciples 'while in a state of *samādhi*' (Hollister 1978:352)—a Hindu term connected with yoga, and, as such, with the Nath Sampradāy.[17] It might also be of some interest to mention that the Khojas have preserved a daily practice of meditation (between 4 and 5 a.m.) which they refer to as *jāgraṇ* (vigil).

In his Rajasthani hagiography Pir Shams appears as an ascetic holding a sacred hearth (*dhūṇī*), typical of Nath yogis and, other Shaiva ascetics (Gokuldas 1982:156). As has been said above, Hasan Kabiruddin sometimes dressed in saffron clothes as many ascetics, and among them the Naths, do to this day. Besides, there is a *ginānic* tradition of his encounter with the yogi Kanipav, a famous disciple of Jalandarnath, who is at present the foremost guru of the untouchable householder Naths, the Kalbelya Jogis, better known as snake-charmers (V. Joshi 1991:43-8).

In the tradition of Sind it seems that a number of Muslim Pirs have been identified with yogis of the Nath lore. Pir Patho is also called

Gopichand, like the famous king-renouncer, and Lal Shahbaz is identified with Bhartrihari who, like his nephew Gopichand, is the hero of many popular ballads of north India (Grodzins-Gold 1992). In addition it may be noted here that Pir Patho, generally considered as a Sunni Suhrawardi Sufi (Ansari 1992:19) might well have been in reality a Nizari missionary, as claimed by the Ismailis (Allana 1984:34).

The issue of contacts between Nizari Pirs and Nath Jogis deserves further investigation for one particular reason: in the course of my field research into the 'lost branches' of Ismailism in Rajasthan, I have found that traces of the Nath influence regularly coincided with those of an ancient Nizari presence. We will come back to this problem in one of the following chapters.

THE NIZARI CEREMONY OF *GHAṬ-PĀṬH*: AN ACCULTURATED MODEL OF HINDU RITUALS

It is probably a free mixing of devotees of all castes, eating and drinking together—a fact hardly acceptable for the Brahmanical socio-religious ideal—that provided the primary model of the Nizari congregational ritual known among the Khojas as *ghaṭ-pāṭh* (from *ghaṭ*, pot, and *pāṭh*, wooden plank).[18] The drinking of *amṛt* (the foot-nectar of a divine image or of a guru) had its counterpart in Tantric-Shaktic ceremonies in the absorption of less 'innocent' substances, such as semen virile mixed with food offerings and wine, fish and meat (N.N. Bhattacharya 1987:108-57). This served as a model for the rites established by the Nizari Pirs: by resorting to it they could bring together the converts in a congregation (*jamā*) in conformity with the Islamic ideal, regardless of caste or sex, and make the converts taste another kind of divine ambrosia, consecrated water mixed with Kerbala clay, i.e. the holy earth associated with Imam Hussein's martyrdom (Ivanow 1948, I:35-40).

On the subject of Tantric ceremonies, a word may be added about the cult of the Goddess (*śakti*) in these types of rituals, within the broader Hindu tradition. The fact that Ismaili Pirs appreciated the importance and popularity of the cult among those whom they wished to convert, and understood that they could not simply uproot it, incompatible as it might have appeared with the Islamic tradition, is illustrated by an episode in Pir Shams Sabzwari's hagiography. The Nizari missionary, who has come to Gujarat, observes a dance (*garabī*) devoted to the Devi, then enters personally the circle of dancers and participates; it is only gradually, that, without ceasing to dance, he reveals his spiritual message to the Hindu devotees (Mallison 1991b:117-38, Kasam 1995: 320-70).

The choice of a pot (*kalaś, ghaṭ*) for the ritual of the Khojas, an object used, among others, in the worship of the Goddess (Enthoven 1989:72), might appear in this light as an attempt to replace the prohibited anthropomorphic or zoomorphic idols which the Ismailis, despite all their flexibility and tolerance, could not accept. As we shall see a similar process seems to have inspired the Pirs to resort to another aniconic symbol for which, incidentally, Muslim and Hindu traditions already had a common ground: the cult of the sacred footprint (D.S. Khan 1995:311-13).

The singing of *ginān*s, which is one of the major characteristics of the Nizari religious ceremonies, had also probably been inspired by the various Hindu devotional night sessions (*jāgraṇ*), and in particular by the Tantric secret vigils, where religious hymns (*bhajan, vāṇī*) were sung. Incidentally, the strict secrecy with which these Shaktic rituals were performed found its counterpart in the secretive character of the Nizari congregational meetings, although the motivations were obviously different. This analogy was not to be without consequences: the two ceremonies, sharing some common traits, came at times to be identified with each other by those who did not follow them. In some cases, even the Nizari rituals were mistaken for Tantric ones: for example Allauddin Khilji, the Sunni ruler of Delhi (fourteenth century) accused the Ismailis of indulging 'in free licence and incest' (Sarantal 1979:277), an accusation which was generally brought against the so-called 'left-handed' Tantrics practising the *kaula* rites. Interestingly enough, it appears that to this day a certain confusion has subsisted regarding those who practise the ceremonies established by the leaders of the various *panths* which I call the 'forgotten branches' of Ismailism.

The idea of exploiting such types of indigenous beliefs and observances connected with the cult of the Goddess seems to have occurred also for another reason: the untouchable groups (Meghvals, Regars, Kolis, Bhangis) and the Sindhi Lohanas, strongly connected with Shaktism, were apparently the major target-groups of the Ismaili Pirs and it is among them that they perhaps achieved their greatest successes (Nanjiani 1918:14-16, 22-31, 117-20).[19] And finally it was this acculturated model created in the Indo-Pakistani subcontinent which was to be adopted as the pattern of worship for the whole Khoja community, including those who migrated to other parts of the world and managed to preserve the tradition (Nanji 1982: 105-8).

REALIGNMENT: THE NINETEENTH AND TWENTIETH CENTURIES

This chapter would not be complete without the mention of another important phenomenon which might superficially appear as a process of reIslamization. Use of this term actually amounts to acknowledging the fact that the acculturated form of Ismailism is a syncretistic religion, a dissident or devaluated form of Islam, a view which has previously been rejected. Whatever the truth, the process I am alluding to in fact began with the arrival of the Aga Khans in the subcontinent (Masselos 1978:97-116; Boivin 1994:197-216). For instance, when the Nizari Imam approached the Shamsi community of Punjab its members were compelled to choose a specific identity which could be termed 'Hindu' or 'Muslim'—and within the latter category they again had the choice between three main sects, Sunni, Isna Ashari and Ismaili. Their decision, needless to say, depended mostly on the balance of the current socio-religious forces and on the influences they had undergone during their long *taqīyya* period. In any case this was not without consequence for the evolution of the Nizari tradition in this part of the world, given that such a clear-cut redefinition of religious identities hardly corresponded to the widely popular Indian non-sectarian tradition, as against what was to occur later with the emergence of fundamentalist movements.

According to Asani (1991:7-8),

> In more recent times, certain expressions in the *gināns* have also been altered so that they are more in consonance with changes in the community's religious identity. Thus, as the community identifies itself more closely with the greater Islamic world, vocabulary items of Indian and Sanskritic origin perceived to be of 'Hinduistic' origin have gradually been replaced by Perso-Arabic ones that are considered to be more compatible with an 'Islamic' character.

Similarly, the texts referred to as *Das avatār* dealing with the ten incarnations of Vishnu seen in the Nizari perspective (Shackle and Moir 1992:157-9) came to be suppressed from the sessions of the *jamāt khāna* where they had been previously regarded as an essential item. The third Aga Khan chose to support Muslim separatism in

Indian politics (Ahmad 1969:25) and Muhammad Ali Jinnah, the founder of the Pakistani state, was a Khoja. Undoubtedly this move later guaranteed the peaceful coexistence of Nizari minorities in the predominantly Sunni context of Punjab and Sind, and at the same time did not endanger them in independent India, in the framework of a secular government which, moreover, supported the minorities. Therefore the apparent 'reIslamization' of Ismailism can neither be regarded as a betrayal of earlier allegedly 'oecumenical' or 'syncretistic' ideals nor a voluntary assertion of the supremacy of Islam, whatever its form. In the light of the extreme flexibility of Ismailism which could without contradiction appear successively, or even simultaneously, as a strong ideology supported by political and military power and as a peaceful spiritual message emphasizing the need for inner religion, the process which may be perceived as 'reIslamization' should perhaps be viewed as a new phase in its history that lead to a realignment of international Islamic politics. It is precisely its open-mindedness and its capacity to adapt itself to changing circumstances, a trait shared by Hinduism, which enabled Ismailism to survive in a difficult or hostile environment; and what might appear more surprising is that the same characteristics also ensured the survival of some of its doctrines and rituals in communities that, for a long time, have ceased to identify themselves as Ismailis.

NOTES

1. For a better knowledge of the Ismaili tradition, we refer the reader to the various specialized works listed in the Bibliography.
2. The definition of the word *dawa* (*da'wa, da'wat*) proposed by Daftary (1990:559-60) is:

   'Mission or propaganda; in the religio-political sense, *da'wa* is the invitation or call to adopt the cause of an individual or family claiming the right to the imāmate; it also refers to the entire hierarchy of ranks, sometimes called *ḥudūd* . . . within the particular religious organization developed for this purpose, especially amongst the Isma'ilis. The Ismai'lis often referred to their movement simply as *al'da'wa*, or more formally as *al-dawa al-hādiya*, the "rightly guiding mission".'
3. How these terms came to be applied to the Nizaris is explained by Lewis 1985. According to the Arabic and Persian sources they initially applied only to the Nizaris of Syria, as did the name 'old man of the mountain' for their leader; later on, however, these appellations were generalized and used for the Persian Ismaili centre as well (Lewis 1985:6-9).
4. Concerning the revolutionary ideology, Maxime Rodinson, in his preface to

the French translation of Lewis (1984:34), states that 'there has been indeed an Ismaili project (which failed) which one may rightfully consider as a revolutionary one. The expectations raised by the project were actually as great as those formulated by the present revolutionaries, the upheaval which was to take place was a radical one and consisted as well in "transforming life", the fervour was as great and the mechanics of the struggle were mostly the same.'

5. The issue of whether Ismailism in the subcontinent should be viewed as a heterodox form of Islam or Hinduism is raised by Mallison (1992b:105-13).
6. Regarding the setback suffered by the Ismailis at the end of the fifteenth century, A.Z. Khan (1980:276) argues that 'one of the important reasons for their downfall was the work of the Suhrawardi and Qadiri Sufis, supported by the Chishtis. Later perhaps the Naqshbandis who opposed *hamahust* and the influence of Vedantic beliefs did much harm.'
7. According to Corbin (1986:29):

   'the idea of esoterism which lies at the very basis of Shiism, being one of its essential components, will bear fruit outside the Shia milieu (raising thus a number of crucial issues). It will bear fruit with the mystics, the Sufis, as well as with the philosophers', and (ibid.:152) 'the coalescence of Ismailism and Sufism in the post-Alamut period, refers us to the issue of its origin, which is far from having been elucidated. If one assumes, as do the Shia spiritual teachers, that Sunni Sufism is something which, at an undetermined time, has been split off from Shiism by transferring onto the sole Prophet the attributes of the Imam (thus making out of the *walāyat* an Imamless imamology), Alamut Ismailism does nothing but restore the initial order.'
8. As we will see in the chapters that follow, Pokaran has a special importance for the 'lost branches' of the Ismailis in Rajasthan—A study of the map will show that if one draws a straight line between Multan (traditional centre of the *dawa*) and Ahmedabad in Gujarat, another important area, Pokaran lies more or less half way between the two cities.
9. As A. N. Khan (1983:246 n. 27) has pointed out:

   'the Account based on original sources [the author refers here to Hollister 1978; 353, sqq] of the Isma'ilis themselves reveals the profound influence of the Hindu creed, mythology and customs so much so that the Ismailis especially the Shamsis identified themselves with the Hindus. It was only in 1911 that the Shamsis largely discarded the cover of Hinduism. This was because the Arya Samajis had started writing against the Aga Khan, their most revered Imam, their religious and spiritual leader. It is in this context, significant that Sir Edward Maclagon describes them as Hindus; *vide, Census of India Report: Punjab*, 1981, 77.'

   The probable role of the Arya Samaj will be discussed further in Chapter 5.
10. The *gināns* describing the trips of Pir Shams to various parts of the subcontinent are known as the eighteen *joḍilā*; similarly in the compositions ascribed to Sayyid Imam Shah (fifteenth century) one finds a description of Imam Shah's mission to Malwa, Gujarat, Benares and the Deccan. I am grateful to Zawahir Moir for having provided me with a version of these *gināns* in the Gujarati script.

11. Ivanow (1948:139 n.1) is of the opinion that the word *munivar* (ascetic) applied to the Nizari believers 'appears as merely a conventional literary device, "wishful hyperbolism" as it may be called. As may be seen from the contents [of the *ginans*], these rules are intended for ordinary people who have not much to do with asceticism.' The rules the author is alluding to form a kind of code of conduct and various *gināns* have been composed to list them (see Ivanow 1949:139-45 and Shackle and Moir 1992:6-67, 145-7). We will come back to these compositions which have a bearing on our subject. However, I do not agree with Ivanow when he considers the use of the term *munivar* as a mere literary hyperbole. In my opinion, the choice of the words *munivar* and *rikhisar* was dictated by the desire of the missionaries to increase the standing of ordinary people and of those belonging to the depressed classes and to impart them with a kind of self-confidence so that they should be proud of following the new religion.
12. According to Ahmad (1964:144-5):

    Such alliterative or vocal equations, which in their Arabic counterparts meant concepts quite different from what Kabīr imagined them to be, became the "lexique technique" of his Bhakti syncretism. Thus *Hari* is aligned with *Hazrat* and *Krishna* with *Karīm*. Alliteratively Muhammad is aligned to *Mahādev*, *karama* to *kalīma*. Adam, the first man is equated on the basis of confused hearsay with Brahmā the God of the Hindu Triad. His (Kabīr's) knowledge of Islam compared to that of Hinduism appears to be second-hand and very superficial.'

    A parallel with the Ismaili literature might show that what Ahmad attributes to the ignorance of the Sant Kabīr might be explained by a totally different phenomenon.
13. Corbin (1986:71) explains that the Imams are 'inspired, superhuman figures whom one will go as far as calling 'divine man or divine lord in human form', although it does not imply the idea of incarnation': the Imamate is a Temple of Light (*haykal nūrānī*) (ibid.: 137) and 'is, as such the *lāhūt* or divinity of the Imam'. It is thus clear that, according to the Ismaili philosophy, the idea of divine epiphany is somewhat different from the concept of incarnations (*avatārs*) in Hinduism, since the Imam, however deified, is not regarded as a direct emanation of God.
14. While the Hindu system is based on a division in *yugas* (cosmic eras) and *kalpas* (longer cycles of time) (see Stutley 1985:138), the Ismaili concept of cyclic time is based on heptades (the number seven being particularly sacred in Ismailism). Each cycle of prophecy is initiated by a *Nātiq* and a *Wasī* (Prophet) to whom succeed one or more heptades of Imams, and ends with a last Imam who is the *Qāim*, i.e. the Imam of the resurrection who puts an end to the former period and enables the new prophet to come. All the seven periods constitute the totality of the cycle of prophecy (Corbin 1986:135). According to the philosophy of the Ismaili *Ihwān al-ṣafā* (brothers of purity), there are not only cycles of seven thousand years, but longer ones, corresponding to astrological configurations: these can last twelve thousand, thirty-six thousand, or three hundred and sixty thousand years or more (see Marquet 1973:397-400, for more details).

15. As stated by Daftary 1990:565, in Ismaili doctrine, Resurrection (*qiyāma*) does not only refer to the last judgment, it

    'also came to be used in reference to the end of any partial cycle in the history of mankind, with the implication that the entire hierohistory of mankind consisted of many such partial cycles and partial *qiyāmas*, leading to the final *qiyāma*, sometimes called *qiyāma al-qiyāmāt*. The Nizaris of the Alamut period interpreted the *qiyāma* spiritually as the manifestation of the unveiled truth in the spiritual reality of the current Imam, who was also called the *Qā'im al-qiyāma*.'

    In the history of the Nizari Ismailis of Alamut, the *qiyāma* was once proclaimed during the reign of Hasan ala Zikrihi al-Salam (1162-66) and consequently, for this period, the *sharīa* or Islamic law was abolished (Corbin 1986:142). On the important concepts of *madhī* and *qāim* in Islamic history, and in particular in Shiism, *The Encyclopaedia of Islam* 1986: V, pp. 1230-8 and 1978: IV, pp. 456-7).
16. 'Recognizing the Imam' is an essential element of the Ismaili tradition. It has been given a mystical interpretation: those who die without knowing their Imam die in a state of unconsciousness because they have not succeeded in knowing themselves (Corbin 1986:83).
17. *Samādhi*, a state of deep meditation, is referred to by Eliade (1954:87-8) as 'enstasy (*en-stasis*) rather than, ecstasy'. According to the tradition of the Naths (and of other Shaiva ascetics such as the *Dasnāmīs*), when the yogis wish to put an end to their terrestrial mode of existence, they have themselves buried alive in a state of *samādhi*, a custom which is designated as 'living *samādhi*' (*jīvit samādhi*). The monument (sometimes a simple platform or *chabūtrā*) built over this spot is also called *samādhi*.
18. More details on this ritual will be given in Chapter 4 when comparing the *ghaṭ-pāṭh* of the Khojas to the sacred vigil of the Meghwal/Kamad worshippers of Ramdev Pir.
19. In Chapter 5 more will be said on the relationship which might have existed between Nizari Ismailism in its Indian form, Tantrism and the untouchable groups.

CHAPTER 2

Ramdev and Other Rajput Pirs: The Nizari *Dawa* in Rajasthan

Concerning the hypothesis of a Nizari *dawa* in Rajasthan and its connection with the Ramdev movement one could state, as did Iwanow (1938:22) for the Imamshahi branch of Ismailism, that 'it would be obviously useless to search for any information about the sect in general historical literature because it almost always existed as a secret community'. According to some Khoja sources, the *dāī* Satgur Nur made conversions among the untouchable Meghvals of Sind and, in the fifteenth century, following his example Ramdev, a Tanwar Rajput, converted the same communities in Kachch, Sind and Tharparkar (Hollister 1978:352, Campbell 1990:40 and personal communication by Z. Moir). Though Rajasthan is not mentioned in these sources, according to the *Khojā Vṛtant* first published in 1892, which is for the larger part based on oral tradition (Nanjiani 1918:136-7), Ramdev came from Rajasthan where his main shrine (*samādhi*) is located, a fact well known to his modern worshippers. Writing at the beginning of our century on the folklore of Gujarat, Enthoven (1989:97) suspects that Ramdev was 'one of the first Khoja missionaries who practised teachings more Hindu than Musulman in order to secure a following among Hindus'. Mumtaz Ali (1994:24-9) is of the opinion that he had embraced Islam on the teachings of Pir Satgur Nur and had been deputed among the lower castes and he argues that 'the *bhajans* of Ramdeo are rich in potential terminology, possessing strong resemblance with the *ginān*s composed by Ismaili Pirs. A comparative study will most probably reveal further important missing chains. Unfortunately, scholars have never touched this field, and more attention was focused on the Pirs and Sayyids who had been deputed to India by the Iranian Imams' (ibid.: 29), whereas 'Ramdeo was a Rajput and did not belong to the Sayyid family', yet 'he identified himself with a Nizari in his extant *bhajans*, giving ample evidence of his being a Nizari Ismaili' (ibid.:27). According to the same author, Ramdev would have left his mission incomplete or did not leave clear traces of his activities. Besides, after the schism which led to the creation of the Imamshahi sect the *dawa* suffered a setback: eventually the Ismaili origin of the Pir of Runicha was 'shrouded into mist, and it became difficult for the modern scholars to determine the part played by Ramdeo in the propagation of Ismailism' (ibid.: 29).

It is precisely to this that we will now turn. My task will first consist in showing how the Ramdev movement evolved so that it is now perceived among Hindus as a *bhakti* cult having nothing to do with any sectarian tradition (*sampradāy, panth*) and located within a purely Hindu context. Through the narration of a few orally transmitted legends, I will endeavour to trace the elements which will enable me to link this tradition with the Nizari *dawa*. I will then explain how the Ismaili mission could have operated in the social, political and religious contexts of the fourteenth and fifteenth centuries in Rajasthan. Further, I will make an attempt at analysing the process through which this tradition has been adopted, preserved and finally modified by the untouchable communities, in particular by the Meghvals of Sind, Gujarat and Rajasthan in the form of a secret sect having its own shrines, rituals and hymns. A careful study of these elements and their comparison with the Khoja Nizari tradition will enable me to demonstrate the Ismaili origin of this sect and explain how it became independent from the centre of the Nizari *dawa*. I will then try to reconstruct the 'missing links' between the past and the present, and show how the Ramdev movement can be perceived as a 'fortgotten branch' of Indian Ismailism; how its ambiguities and elusiveness are viewed by the Hindus in modern India; and the efforts made to replace it gradually by what could temporarily be defined as its 'reHinduized version'. All this would lead us to raise once more from a different perspective, the fundamental question of the nature of Hinduism and Islam in the subcontinent and their interaction throughout history.

As as been stated at the outset in our investigation into the 'forgotten' history of Ismaili communities in Rajasthan, we must not expect to find documents, inscriptions or sacred books capable of giving unambiguous information. Instead, innumerable traces can be found at various levels and if no single, isolated detail might appear convincing, it is eventually their association and recurrence that will be decisive in this matter.

As P. Mukta has said of the sixteenth-century poet Mira Bai (1994:31), one could state that the conjoining of the figure of Baba Ramdev 'to the histories of an elite literary tradition, to a high hinduism, and to a high cultural form, were all processes initiated by nineteenth and twentieth century interpreters'. The fact that Ramdev was a Rajput chieftain of the Tanwar clan, made it easier for these modern elites to forget that the Kshatriya hero-saint of Marwar had long been derisively nick-named *dhedhõ kā dev* (the 'god of the pariahs').[1] At present, in the eyes of millions of devotees from Rajasthan and other areas who flock to his main temple at Runicha-Ramdeora (near Pokaran, between Jodhpur and Jaisalmer), the Ramdev tradition is only one of the many popular *bhakti* cults centred around the figure of a local deity: it starts with Ramdev's birth or rather with his 'descent' to earth—since he is believed to be an *avatār* of Vishnu-Krishna—and ends with his *samādhi.* However his power is still manifest for those who come to visit his numerous shrines spread across Rajasthan and Gujarat to seek the fulfilment of a vow, and in particular to Ramdeora-Runicha during the famous *melā* (fair and pilgrimage) which takes place in the month of *bhādõ* (August-September).

Whether they view Ramdev as a powerful Kshatriya god or as the 'protector of untouchables' and 'saviour of the poor' (Binford 1972:120), the modern *bhaktas* do not seem disturbed by the strange aspect of his main temple-complex at Runicha, a testimony to the fact that 'faith is blind', and that Hindu 'popular' beliefs as against the Brahmanical tradition have little to do with orthodox standards and classification. Actually, as one Rajput inhabitant of Pokaran once admitted, 'this shrine looks like a Muslim cemetery (*kabristān*). It is impure, but people believe in the powers of Ramdev.'

Ramdev's alleged *samādhi* (a term referring to any kind of Hindu or Jain funeral monument) is a grave in the Muhammedan style, topped by a big half cylindrical stone[2] and cloth-covered, like the tombs of many Muslim saints and martyrs (*shahīd*). Many other graves of the same type surround it inside the main temple building and outside, in the courtyard. Some of them are sheltered by a *chhatrī* which makes them look like the *samādhis* of Rajput warriors and saints. Foot-print stones, rag-horses and clothes (*chādar*) are regularly offered to these tombstones by the devotees. The *chādars* are of various colours, including green, which is also the traditional colour of Ramdev's banner.

Examples are not wanting where Brahmans perform rites at the *samādhi* of Hindu saints, and even at the graves of Muslim Pirs.[3] The capacity of most Hindus, and not only of lower caste *bhaktas*, to worship all kinds of objects believed to be powerful, as embodiments of the Divine, is a well-known fact. This renders unconvincing S.N. Saraswati's argument that if untouchables are predominant in the Ramdev cult it is because higher Hindu castes are reluctant to perform grave-worship (quoted by Binford 1972:123 n. 13). The original meaning of the popular saying *Rāmdevjī ne milyā ḍheḍh hī ḍheḍh* 'Ramdev found only pariahs', is probably not that only Meghvals and other impure castes worship the Pir of Runicha but that a specific, historical link exists between him and these downtrodden groups.

However, even if we admit that, in the so-called 'popular religion' of the Hindus, tombs of Muslim saints may be worshipped as a fount of power and blessing (the most famous example in Rajasthan is the *dargāh* of Khwaja Muinuddin Chishti in Ajmer), the mystery of an allegedly Hindu saint buried like a Muhammadan Pir is not resolved: Hindus may be buried, but in the sitting position, like ascetics, or without erecting a tombstone, in the recumbent one, like untouchables.[4]

Who really was Baba Ramdev whom his devotees invoke as Ramdev Pir, Rama Pir, or Ramshah Pir? Contrary to a current belief, those Muslim appellations are also extensively used by Hindu *bhaktas*, mainly by his traditional followers, a majority of Meghvals: they are not creations of the Muslim devotees who, each year, are less and less numerous at the shrine of the Pir of Runicha. Nonetheless, for most people, Ramdev was a 'true Hindu', and if he is a Pir (a Muslim title also used by certain *mahants* of Nath monasteries), he must be referred to as *Hindu Pīr* or *Hinduõ kā Pīr* (Binford 1972:120, Enthoven 1989:97). According to the current hagiography, this title was conferred upon him after he had won a contest of miracles with five Muslim Pirs coming from Mecca who were forced to admit that he was more powerful than they. This story became so popular (probably because it implied the superiority of Hinduism and dispelled the doubts concerning Ramdev's identity) that it eventually overshadowed other versions of the legend (Binford 1972:125) and became a favourite subject of the popular iconography associated with the Pir of Runicha.[5]

A few Muslims are of the opinion that the saint buried at Runicha was in reality a Muhammadan Pir, and that his *dargāh* was, at an undetermined time, taken over by Hindus; but except for citing an inscription on one of the graves (Binford 1972:126), they cannot offer much to prove this fact or explain it. Other members of this community have joined the chorus of Hindu *bhaktas* and continue to worship Ramdev as a saint endowed with supernatural powers (*barakat*) whose identity, after all, is not of much concern to them, provided that he continues to shower his blessings.

By following a pilgrimage of middle-class devotees from Bombay to Runicha-Ramdeora, Binford (1972) has been able to give a detailed and accurate description of the way in which the Ramdev tradition is generally perceived nowadays among the majority of *bhaktas*, a tradition which testifies to the triumph of a modern, encompassing type of *bhakti*.[6] Viewed in this perspective, and despite a number of specificities, the cult of Ramdev does not greatly differ from hundreds of other Hindu cults all over the Indian subcontinent. Binford thinks that because of the lack of historical sources, the role of Islam in this tradition cannot be elucidated (Binford 1972:126). Like many others, she fails to understand the historical link of Ramdev with the untouchables, Tantrism and Islam, three major issues which concern us. Meanwhile, reduced to the common denominator of Hindu *bhakti*, the Ramdev tradition has been cut off from its original roots and, gradually losing its specificity, has been absorbed into what one can perceive as a dominant trend in Hinduism.

This transformation can be witnessed at various levels. Having been miraculously cured of some disease by the grace of Baba Ramdev, a wealthy Rajput whom I have interviewed admitted that, although he was a staunch devotee of the god of Runicha (seeing no difference between him and Krishna), he could not follow his example and would be reluctant to mix and eat with untouchables.[7] It goes without saying that, in the two temples he had built in his honour, the *sevā* (religious service) was entrusted to members of 'clean' castes. This example helps us to understand how Ramdev's Rajput identity has been instrumental in triggering the above-mentioned transformation.

In current hagiography (mainly in the booklets sold in the bazars and in the oral tales of the devotees) Ramdev appears as the son of a Rajput Tanwar chieftain believed to be a descendant of the celebrated Anangpal Tomar (Tanwar), ruler of Delhi, who lost his throne to the Chauhans in 1170 (M.P. Sharma 1980-1:70). Ajmal

Tanwar who held a *jāgīr* (fief) in the desert area of Pokaran, was childless. After a pilgrimage to Dwarka, the focus of Krishnaite *bhakti*, he obtained from the Lord himself the boon of two sons: the younger one would be, he had promised, his own incarnation and become famous under the name of Ramdev. The prediction came true. This divine son, however, was not born naturally (contrary to Krishna in the Puranic legends) but miraculously appeared in the cradle where Viramdev, his elder brother, was sleeping. Since his very childhood he performed numerous miracles (playing the traditional role of *avatār*), slayed the demon Bheru[8] and taught lessons to various people. He gathered around him devotees of all castes and creeds, a fact which is not viewed by present devotees as a 'revolutionary process' endangering the caste system but in the light of an encompassing *bhakti*, transcending the frontiers of communities and sects.

However, a close investigation would show that this portrayal of Ramdev as a Rajput hero-saint, an *avatār* of Krishna linked with the Vaishnava *bhakti*, emerged only gradually, probably over a long period extending from the eighteenth to the twentieth century. Mukta (1994:58) is therefore wrong in asserting a reverse process, and in declaring that 'from being a Rajput hero he was transformed into a champion of the Dalits' (the untouchable communities). Except for the short description of the seventeenth-century chronicler Munhata Nainsi (Nainsi 1968:II:349) who actually says nothing about Ramdev himself, the oldest testimony of a phenomenon which one could term 'Rajputization' (Sinha 1962:35-80) is to be found in the 'gallery of heroes' (*teintīs karoṛ devtā*) at Mandore, the ancient capital of the Rathore rulers before the foundation of Jodhpur. Amidst the various figures cut in the rock one can see Ramdev on his horse, together with other heroes of Marwar: Pabu, Meha, Harbu, Goga and Mallinath. Deprived of his usual beard (which is a typical feature of his popular iconography but obviously makes him look like a Muslim Pir) Ramdev cannot be distinguished from the other five saints. Interestingly enough, the carving of this rock-cut gallery is ascribed to Abhey Singh, the same ruler of Jodhpur who in the eighteenth century is credited with building at Tilwara (Barmer district) a temple to Rawal Mallinath, a historical figure closely linked with the Ramdev legend.

Once the *dhedhõ kā dev* was accepted among the Rajputs and other higher castes, it was but natural that emphasis was placed on heroic values, *kṣatriya dharm* and supernatural powers (the last value having been associated with the Nath tradition which became popular with some Rajput rulers).[9] The next phase could be illustrated by the efforts of the twentieth-century ruler of Bikaner, Maharaja Ganga Singh (1887-1943) who, in the twenties, attempted successfully to revive, at the cost of transforming them, old 'popular' traditions such as those of Goga and Ramdev:[10] at Gogamedi (see Chapter 9) he caused to be rebuilt in marble Goga's grave and, not daring to modify its original shape, had a hero slab carved on its side. At Runicha, he ordered a big temple to be erected at a place where (according to some sources) there was nothing but a sacred burial ground, traditionally referred to as *mukām* (Nainsi 1968, II:349). It may be of some interest to specify here that the word *mukām* which originally means 'halting place' and is of Arabic origin, is currently used to designate a Muslim *kabristān,* in particular the *dargāh* where a Pir is buried (Lalas 1988:3784). Hagiographical accounts of events said to have taken place in the eighteenth and nineteeth centuries testify that, in those times, the Ramdev cult was not particularly popular among Rajputs. To illustrate this fact one could mention the story of a Rajput queen who was accused by her royal spouse of worshipping secretly 'the god of the pariahs' (S. Bishnoi 1989:102). Maharaja Ganga Singh's religious policy was thus instrumental in permitting a greater number of devotees to join a tradition that had long been considered as 'ill-famed'. The final wave of popularity came after Independence when many temples were built in Gujarat and Rajasthan by various other communities and when the Ramdev cult was made to fit into the general framework of Hindu *bhakti.* As its specificities became less conspicuous it became increasingly like other local traditions connected with various 'folk-deities'.

It is instead among a much more limited number of devotees, mainly the untouchables of the Meghval community, that one can still perceive the traces of an ancient tradition which has retained most of the embarrassing elements gradually wiped out by Rajputization: links with the untouchables, Tantrism and Islam. In the light of this forgotten tradition, the popular saying, 'Ramdev found only pariahs' can be understood in a different sense: its meaning would be that, despite all his efforts, the 'Hindu Pir' was not exceptionally successful in winning disciples, except among the depressed classes; for them he was not only a god, but a guru, the leader of a specific religious tradition. That religion, because of its connection with such 'despicable' people, came to be referred to as *ḍheḍiyā panth* or the 'sect of the pariahs' (Mukta 1994:58). As we will see, Ramdev's traditional followers do not claim that the Pir of Runicha was the founder of their *panth*; for them it was established long before him and continues to this day, even as it is not divulged to the non-initiated and tends to dissolve its identity in the general *bhakti* process described earlier.

It is with this specific tradition, and not with the Ramdev cult in its present, popular form, that this study is mainly concerned. In spite of the fact that many modern devotees will sincerely deny the existence of any *panth* connected with their favourite deity, the Lord of Runicha,[11] Ramdev's traditional followers, especially among the Meghvals and the Kamads (a community associated with the Meghvals and with the Ramdev tradition) are perfectly familiar with this idea. One can also find references to it in various publications. The oldest mention is probably in the 1901 *Gazetteer of Bombay* (Campbell 1988:544-5), if one accepts Nanjiani's suggestion that it is connected with the sect of the Khojas (1918:136-7). But we are dealing here with works which do not contemplate the possiblity of such a connection. In his history of Rajasthani literature, Hiralal Maheshwari (1980:187) reports that 'a sect bearing names like *Pramāṇī, Viśvāsī, Bīsnāmī* and *Mahādharma* is said to exist and accept these *Pramāns* [the *chaubīs pramān*, a series of twenty-four devotional compositions attributed to Ramdev] to be its scripture'. Unfortunately, the author does not give more details. In Rajasthan, the Meghval religious leader Swami Gokuldas has made various stray references to this tradition, especially in *Meghvanś Itihās* (1982), a 'History of the Megh clan'. Finally Gujarati authors like Gohil, Rajyaguru, Shrimali, and Makran Dev have also written about it in more detail.

An examination of these sources shows that the religious tradition associated with Ramdev, elusive as it appears in these descriptions, was, and is still, referred to by numerous names. To those already mentioned by Maheshwari we can also add the following appellations: *Alakh Panth* (Skt. *alakśya* designating the formless, 'non-qualified' god, especially in the Nath tradition), *Kāmaḍiyā Panth* (the sect of the Kāmaḍiyās or Kāmaḍs), *Mahā Panth* (lit. 'the great sect') and *Bījā Mārg* (the *panth* of the *Bīj*, a word which will be explained in Chapter 4). Eventually some of our informants consented to reveal that the true name of their tradition, the most sacred and secret name, was *Nizār Panth* or *Nizārī Dharm* (the sect of Nizar, the Nizari religion),

Ramdev being still currently invoked as *Shāh Nizār* and (in *mantras* or ritual formulas) as *Nikalank Dev Nizār* (D.S. Khan 1993:43, 1995a:321, Mumtaz Ali 1994:27). According to Gohil (1987:23), in Gujarat where the name is still used and has been kept secret to this day, it is mainly known as *Nijār Panth* (or *Nizār panth*, *z* and *j* being marked by the same letter and pronounced, in Gujarat and Rajasthan, in a similar way), *Mahā Dharm, Ādi Dharm, Mahāmārg, Sanātan Dharm,* and *Dhūno Dharm.* If the Tanwar Rajputs settled at Ramdeora are reluctant to speak about their sect, preferring to cling to the Rajputized model of the Ramdev tradition, the Jaypals (a clan or *gotr* of the Meghvals) have a different attitude. They have inherited only a small part of the temple-complex, the rest being in the hands of Ramdev's descendants. They own the tiny shrine dedicated to their female ancestor, Dali Bai, said to have been the *dharm-bahan* (adoptive sister) or the *guru-bahan* (co-disciple) of the Pir of Ramdeora. The major part of the offerings being made to Ramdev's *samādhi* and pocketed by the Tanwars, the Jaypals earn their livelihood by singing *bhajans* before Dali Bai's *samādhi* and by organizing for the devotees sacred vigils referred to as *jamā* (or *jamā-jāgraṇ*, from the Arabic *jamāat*, congregation of the faithful) and *jāgraṇ*, night session devoted to the singing of devotional songs. It is through these *bhajans* and through legends, that they have preserved the memory of the past.

How came a Rajput chieftain to be the favourite god and, still more, the spritiual teacher of a group of pariahs in the fourteenth and fifteenth centuries? Before attempting to answer this particular question we will have to describe the tradition connected with his family, as told by the Jaypals of Ramdev. These legends will give us an idea of the historical context in which the movement took birth in Rajasthan and adjacent areas.

Few higher caste *bhaktas* are aware of the fact that the Ramdev tradition in fact originates two generations before him. According to legend (S. Bishnoi 1989:18-20), Ramdev's grandfather, Ransi Tanwar, who was a descendant of Anangpal Tomar, the ruler of Delhi (M.P. Sharma, 1980-1:70), had been deprived of his throne by a Chauhan prince. Although it is a historical fact that the Chauhans succeeded the Tomars (Tanwars), this event occurred in the twelfth century, i.e. much earlier, there is no proof that Ransi belonged to the direct lineage of Anangpal. But, as usual, legends show little concern for chronology and follow their own logic.

Reduced to an extreme poverty, Ransi started to wander all over

Rajasthan and took to plundering caravans with the hope of collecting riches, a method which was by no means rare among other petty rulers of various clans in medieval and later periods. The story is given in poetic form by Gokuldas (1982:151-67) who claims to have composed it on the basis of various oral tales. His version corresponds, in most of its details, with the stories I have collected from my Meghval informants at Runicha.

During his wandering Ransi comes across a strange ascetic travelling with a caravan. He is dressed as a Muslim fakir and his name is Samas Rishi or Shams Pir. Gokuldas claims that he was a Brahman (*vipr*) who had taken the guise of a Muhammedan Pir to avoid persecution at the hands of the Muslim ruler of Delhi who, allegedly, was the enemy of Hindu ascetics and made forced conversions everywhere. Actually, as my field inquiries have shown, even for the traditional followers of Ramdev, the question of his identity is more complex that it seems; some informants have even admitted the contrary of what has been stated by Gokuldas, namely that 'Samas' was a Muslim Pir in the guise of a Hindu ascetic. Despite his Muslim dress, Gokuldas describes him as establishing a *dhūṇī*, the sacred hearth of Hindu ascetics. What is more, this author presents the fakir in an ambiguous way: he has visited Hindu *tīrthas* (centres of pilgrimages) but also Muslim ones (Mecca), which accounts for the fact that he was recognized as a *dev* (deity) by Hindus and as a Pir by Musulmans: ('*pirā me pīr devā me deva donõ* [illegible] *mil dhyāyo*', Pir among the Pirs, god among the gods he reconci[illegible]oth religions).

The same story gives ot[illegible] insights into his spiritual message, apparently aimed at reconc[illegible] Islam and Hinduism, as did later the Sant Kabir: when Shams rea[illegible]ed the city of Ucch (near Multan) the worried mollahs, custodians of orthodox Sunni Islam, warned the ruler: 'a *siddh* has come to our town, his voice proclaims the two religions (*dīn*) at a time'. If he were identified with the Nizari missionary Shamsuddin Sabzwari, this figure would no longer be so amazing.

Let us however come back to Ransi Tanwar's story as preserved in the Meghval oral tradition. After the throneless prince has plundered the fakir's caravan (the modern version would specify that he dared attack the saint only because he had mistaken him for a Muslim), Shams cursed him with disease. Struck by leprosy which transforms men whatever be their status into outcastes, Ransi experiences innumerable sufferings until he reaches a village called Dudu (between modern Jaipur and the city of Ajmer) where he meets Khivan Balai, a poor untouchable weaver. As a leper, the erstwhile Rajput chieftain has become the equal of this pariah. Eager to help, Khivan reveals that he is the disciple of a guru endowed with miraculous powers. None but he is able to cure this disease. When both men reach the ascetic's *dhūṇī* amidst the hills, not very far from Dudu at a place called Bichun (a name said to be derived from *bīch*, 'between') Ransi immediately recognizes Shams who, however, does not identify this disfigured leper with the plunderer he had once cursed. The ascetic's disciple is required to prepare a bowl of milk. Shams drinks it and asks both men to swallow the rest, which they readily do. As soon as he has absorbed the content of the bowl Ransi is cured and recovers his former appearance. The story goes on with a second curse from the Pir, this time directed on both Ransi and Khivan: the deceived saint condemns them to a violent death. As his untouchable disciple protests his innocence and falls at his feet, and tries to explain the facts; 'Samas' then consents to make the curse milder as he cannot, according to a Hindu belief, abolish it all together. If both men are to escape the violent death predicted by him they will become famous saints and die performing miracles. After this prediction Shams prepares to leave for Multan (an interesting detail if one remembers that this was the centre of the *dawa*). Ransi and his untouchable companion start to preach their spiritual message throughout Rajasthan. Although nothing is said of the tenets of their doctrine (according to our Meghval informants, it was the 'Vaishnava faith' or simply '*Hindu dharm*' or '*Sanātan dharm*'), we find that the ruler of Delhi puts them in jail. Subsequently he attempts to test their alleged miraculous powers in the presence of his own Pir (who, logically, must be a Sunni Sufi Shaikh). The prisoners are condemned to be executed by the saw if they are defeated. Knowing they cannot escape the death foretold by 'Samas Rishi', Ransi and Khivan put above their head a miraculous saw made of margosa (*nīm*) leaves.[12] Their bodies are instantaneously cut into two pieces, but at the same time their blood and bones are turned into milk and flowers (according to the Hindu tradition flowers are symbolic of the bones left after cremation). After having witnessed this supernatural feat the Muslim ruler eventually admits that both saints are more powerful than his Pir and their religion superior to his own. He confers on them, *post mortem*, the title of Pir and gives grants of land to their descendants. In Delhi their graves are revered as those of Dudh Pir (Milk Pir) and Phul Pir (Flower Pir). However, according to the same legend only half their mortal remains were buried in the capital of the Sultanate; the remainder, miraculously flying in the air, reached the saints' respective villages, Naraina for Ransi and Dudu for Khivan (although it has not been specified earlier that the Tanwar chieftain was in some way connected with Naraina). In both places cenotaphs were erected, which are simultaneously referred to as *samādhi* and *dargāh.* We will come back to these shrines which, being important centres of pilgrimage for the Meghval community, constitute two local seats (or *gaddīs*) of the Nizar Panth.

But we must proceed with the story of Ransi and Samas Rishi. Although the episode described above seemed important for my informants, most of them insisted that there was no link with the Ramdev cult. Ransi simply happened to be Ramdev's ancestor, a Tanwar Rajput of the lunar clan (*chandravanś*) the descendant of Arjun (one of the five Pandavas), and a staunch devotee of Vishnu who was later incarnated as his grandson. According to them, it was for an entirely different reason that Ransi had received the title of Pir, and the fact that Ramdev also came to recognized as such was viewed by the Meghvals as a mere coincidence. When asked if the Tanwar chieftain had become a disciple of 'Samas' they replied that there was nothing of the kind: the saint by whom he had once been cursed, had cured him and eventually cursed him again, and that was all. Khivan alone was his disciple. Despite these assertions a closer examination of the legend and its comparison with the statements of other informants affiliated to the Ramdev movement, have shown that these stray fragments can be put together to form a more coherent image.

Let us first examine critically the episode of the bowl of milk. Related to Shams/Samas, whom I have tentatively identified with the Ismaili missionary of this name, it reminds us of a *ginān* in which the Pir preaches among the Hindus in some unidentified country. When the Nizari *dāī* finally convinces the Raja of the superiority of his faith:

By the order of the Pir the *bhagat* [his ex-Hindu, faithful disciple Vimras] brought water; Ganga water was sprinkled upon everyone.

Then Vimras brought a cup and going to the cow, milked her. He brought the milk before Pir Shams.

Sat Gur Shams handed the cup to the raja, bidding him to give some milk out of it to everyone.

The raja issued an order that no one in the town of Bhot should go without partaking of the milk given by the Pir (Ivanow 1948:95).

In a footnote Ivanow explains that 'this story may be an aetiological myth showing the "foundation" of the drinking of milk at religious assemblies which was probably in course of time replaced by consecrated water'. There is little doubt that, despite the denials of our informants, the episode where Ransi drinks the milk from Samas Rishi's bowl is an allusion to the fact that he was, at that time, initiated by the Pir: 'taking a cup', *piyālā lenā,* is, moreover, the usual phrase referring to the initiation into a Sufi order. Evidently, this detail accounts more logically for his title of Pir than the stories forged by the Meghvals. This is further confirmed by the fact that, at Naraina, where his shrine is located (I could find no trace of his grave in Delhi) there is still a lineage of *mahants* occupying the local *gaddī* who are known as Pirs. It can also be suggested that it was by spreading Shams Pir's message that the Tanwar chieftain had to die as a martyr. Such cases of martyrdom, when the Ismailis, considered dangerous heretics, were put to death by Sunni rulers, are testified to in historical records. For example, during the reign of Alauddin Khilji (fourteenth century, a time at which my Ramdeora informants generally located the events for which Gokuldas gives a much earlier date) it was discovered that 'certain Shia sects, like the Carmathians and the Ismailis indulged in free licence and incest....[13] As soon as Allauddin came to know of the existence of such shameless people he ordered them to be severely punished. The saw of punishment cut them down after searching them in towns and cities, so that these incestious tribes were altogether extirpated' (Sarantal 1979:277). The case could well apply to Ransi Tanwar, and many others who, in the subcontinent, had embraced the Nizari faith, before and after Allauddin.

Coming back to the figure of Shams Pir, we see that his Rajasthani hagiography, as preserved by the Meghvals and the Kamads, is perfectly consistent with the legends spread elsewhere, for instance in Punjab. It must be recalled here that the Pir's tomb is located in Multan (at the boundary of Sind and Punjab) and that he was, and is still, popularly known as Shams Tabrez, having been confused with the spiritual teacher of the Sufi Jalaluddin Rumi. Like some of my informants of the Kamad community, Gokuldas reports the same episodes as does Temple in his Legends of the Punjab (1993:89-91).

Arriving at Ucch the Pir resuscitates a dead young man when all other saints and miracle-mongers have failed. Unfortunately, the Pir who, in Gokuldas's poem is significantly described as reciting only 'one half of the *kalima*' (the divine word of Islam expressing the unity of God) (1982:151), resuscitates the boy in his own name and not in the name of Allah, which displeases the mollahs. Consequently, viewed as a heretic, Shams is condemned by them. Much in the same way as Ransi and Khivan inflicted upon themselves the torture before being given into the hands of the executioner, the Pir shows one more miracle in flaying himself alive. Finding neither food nor shelter he wanders through the town until a merciful person (in the main version told by Temple, by Muslim communities of Rajasthan and by the Kamads, he was a butcher) offers him some raw food, meat in the Rajasthani and the Ismaili versions, but fish in Temple's account, and bread (*roṭī*) in Gokuldas' poem, in keeping with his portrayal of Samas as a Brahman.

Shams asks the sun, his alter ego, to cook his food (*shams* in Arabic means 'sun') thus bringing it closer to the earth. In the local folklore, this episode is supposed to account for the scorching heat of Multan. In the Meghval tradition it is said that, after this new miracle, the Pir's skin grew again and that he continued to perform supernatural feats in the area. The legend of Shams resuscitating the boy and flaying himself alive is also known, as mentioned above, to other communities of Rajasthan, in particular to the Muslim artisan castes such as the Julahas (weavers) and Nyarias. However, it may be suggested that a *ginān* ascribed to Pir Shams (Ivanow 1948:97-8) may reflect the initial source of inspiration.

Another episode reported by Gokuldas (1982:162) deserves to be mentioned: on reaching Multan, Shams finds a number of other Pirs. *Bhāval pīr ke sang me pīr auliā lār,* 'in the company of Bhaval Pir came other *auliā* (saints) and Pirs'. To signify that he is not welcome 'Bhaval' offers Shams a bowl full of liquid to the brim: in the same way as the bowl cannot contain any more milk, the celebrated and sacred town of Multan cannot give shelter to one more Pir: *suī ek kaṭore ḍārī ūpar phūl tirāyā* (Gokuldas ibid.: 162). 'So he gave him a bowl, but he (Shams) made a flower float on top of it', meaning that his presence would not make a difference.

Incidentally the same event is reported in Pir Shams' hagiography preserved by the Nizari Khoja tradition. 'Bhaval' Pir may be identified as the thirteenth century Suhrawardi Sufi Bahauddin Zakariya who figures in a similar episode (Nanji 1978:54). This saint may not have been a contemporary of Shams, but here it is the symbolic meaning that matters, and it is a remarkable fact that this story has spread and been preserved to this day among the Meghval followers of Ramdev in Rajasthan.

Gokuldas's account of the Pir's life culminates with his 'living *samādhi*' in Multan, while the resuscitated boy, who has become his disciple, goes to Rajasthan to inform Khivan and Ransi (not yet martyred at that time). At this stage, let us make one important point: the fact that 'Samas', elsewhere called Samik Rishi, the name of a legendary Hindu seer (Vettam Mani 1989:680), is portrayed as a Hindu ascetic holding a *dhūṇī* and taking *jīvit samādhi*, must not been perceived exclusively as an attempt of modern devotees to disguise the old Ismaili tradition into a Hindu one, albeit this effort would be perfectly consistent with the present aspirations of the Meghvals for a clear Hindu identity. If one remembers the parallel use of Muslim and Hindu terms, names and concepts prevalent in the Khoja *ginānic* tradition (Chapter 1) one could come to the conclusion that words such as *ṛṣi*, *samādhi*, and *dhūṇī* were already part of the acculturated Nizari tradition. This constituted one of its peculiarities even before the reHinduized groups thought of using them as evidence for the Hindu origin of their tradition. The essential issues of 'Hinduization' and 'reHinduization' related to the development of the Nizari communities will be discussed later.

For the moment attention will be drawn again to the personality of Ransi Tanwar, and his link with Shams Pir and the Ramdev tradition. In Rajasthan the existence of a coherent pattern connecting the three figures and making of this episode something more than a 'family story' full of strange coincidences (for instance why should Khivan's descendants be particularly staunch devotees of Ramdev?) is not denied everywhere. Bichun, the very place where Ransi met Shams for the second time, is an important centre of pilgrimage for the Meghval community, being a *gaddī* of the sect connected with Ramdev. Its present *mahant* (the 'Pir') made a number of interesting revelations to me. He said that, in the fifties, the devotees had transformed this shrine into a 'mere temple of Ramdev', whereas its original founder was Pir Shams. As a testimony of this neglected heritage which he found unfair to push into the background, stands the following inscription painted over the main gate: *samas ṛṣi ki gaddī sthān—Bichun* (seat of Samas Rishi's order, Bichun). Shams, claimed the *mahant,* flourished long before Ramdev, albeit both belonged to the same tradition, a tradition which, however, the Pir of Bichun did not care to define. According to him, Shams whom he once described as a Brahman in the guise of a Muslim fakir and once as an Islamic Pir dressed as a Hindu, had initiated Ransi Tanwar who subsequently became himself a Pir; later on Ransi passed on this title to his son Ajmal, and Ajmal did the same for Ramdev. 'Thus', concluded the *mahant* of Bichun, 'Pir Shams came first, then Ransi, then Ajmal, so that Ramdev was the third Pir of the Tanwar lineage.'

Before proceeding with this tentative reconstruction of the 'Rajput Pir' stories, a few words must be said about the political situation of north India in the fourteenth and fifteenth centuries. According to Gujarati and Rajasthani sources, the beginning of the fourteenth century was the period during which Pir Shams, settled in Multan, acting as the main *dāī* in charge of the *dawa* of 'Hind and Sind'. To 1306 the Mongols had been a continuous threat. The most powerful ruler of that time was Allauddin Khilji of whom it has been said above that he tried to extirpate the Ismaili 'heresy'. He would perhaps have been successful in establishing an empire after his various conquests (among which one may note the famous fortresses of Ranthambore and Chittorgarh) if his power had not been weakened by political intrigue. He was followed by rulers belonging to the Tughlag dynasty, Ghiyasuddin, Muhammad, and Firoz Shah. In 1398 the Delhi sultanate was shaken by Timur Leng's onslaughts which had previously dismantled the fortresses of the Nizaris in Persia (Daftary 1990:452). The Turkish conqueror left the subcontinent and placed in power in Delhi the Sayyid dynasty (1414). Meanwhile, various provinces of the Sultanate had become independent under local Muslim dynasties. In 1451 the Sayyids were succeeded by the Afghan Lodi princes. In 1526 at Panipat Babar put an end to Lodi rule and, a year later, at the battle of Khanwa, checked the ambitions of Sangram Singh (Maharana Sanga) the Rana of Mewar. Mewar had been to then the most powerful state in western Rajasthan. Throughout this period, independent kingdoms had subsisted in the region, Mewar (the capital of which would later be Udaipur) and Marwar (Jodhpur) being the most important (R.C. Dutta 1990:326-60).

Sunni rule was not always accompanied by intolerance towards Hindus and Jains (Thapar 1986:279-80). Nonetheless ruthless moves against all kinds of 'heretic' sects had taken place at various intervals, as reflected in the accounts of the Muslim historians of the time

(Elliot and Dowson 1867-77:335-6, 377-8). It is therefore understandable that Ismaili missionaries and their converts should have extensively resorted to the Shia principle of *taqīyya*, as they had been doing in similar circumstances. For this reason, if, as I believe, the Nizari *dāīs* penetrated into Rajasthan by one of the trade-routes linking Sind-Punjab-Gujarat to Delhi,[14] they must have operated with the utmost discretion, without leaving any direct traces of their presence. In accordance with established methods, the nature of their strategy would have depended on the milieu and region selected for the mission. In Rajasthan, among a majority of Hindus, they might have appeared as Hindu ascetics, for instance as Nath Jogis, who must have been popular at that time, and elsewhere as Sufi Pirs or Qalandars (incidentally in some *gināns* Pir Shams is called 'Qalandar' see Shackle and Moir 1992:110-11). It may be added that while these various groups were largely heterogeneous, many of them shared at least one significant trait: a capacity to challenge the more orthodox Brahmanical Hinduism or 'legalistic' Sunni Islam. We have seen previously that Shams, for example, in the Rajasthani tradition transmitted by the Meghvals, appears in both guises as a Hindu ascetic and a Muslim fakir. One more point must be borne in mind: the epithets 'Hindu' and 'Muslim' cannot be applied to all medieval communities in the same way as they are now currently used in India. In other words, the religious identity of certain groups was obviously fluider than it is at present. For example, in his religious compositions, Kabir, like other Sants, mentioned 'Hindu-Turk', these terms probably referring to 'Brahmanical' Hindus and Sunni Muslims. Other devotional poets distinguished three main religious groups, Hindus, Muslims and Naths. As can be inferred from various historical documents, the 'impure' castes were not considered Hindu by the higher castes. Buddhists and Jains, once regarded as heretics by the Brahmans, came so close to the Hindus that they are now treated as members of Hindu society. On the other hand, the Muslim conquerors had initially forged the term Hindu (from Hind-Sind, the Indus river and the regions around them) to designate all the 'original inhabitants of Hindustan', regardless of their beliefs.

But it is time to come back to Ransi Tanwar and analyse his story in its setting. If we accept that his son Ajmal was a contemporary of the Rathore ruler Mallinath, whose reign began around 1375, Ramdev's grandfather may have expired during the reign of Sultan

Firoz Shah Tughlaq (1357-8). Incidentally this ruler is also said to have been intolerant towards heterodox Muslims (Eliot and Dowson 1867:377-8), so there would be nothing surprising if Ransi's martyrdom would have occurred during his reign.

The portrayal of Ransi as a landless warrior and a throneless prince, plundering caravans and wandering from town to town with which the Meghval version of the legend of Ramdev's ancestors starts, is in conformity with a Rajasthani tale (*bāt*) transcribed from the oral tradition in the eighteenth century and preserved in one of the libraries of Bikaner (S. Bishnoi 1989:531-6). Ramdev's grandfather appears as the chieftain of a minuscule principality, probably consisting of a few villages. He goes to Delhi in order to take *chākrī* (service) at the court of some powerful ruler, a fairly common occurrence in medieval times (Kolfe 1990:74-85). According to this *bāt*, Ransi serves the Padishah of Delhi (whose name is not mentioned) before going back to his (equally unidentified) village. While going through a forest, he encounters an anonymous ascetic who imparts to him some of his special powers. Later a quarrel ensues with the ruler of Delhi and Ransi has to fight against his army. Eventually both men become reconciled and the Padishah gives to his *ex-chākar* (servant) a grant of land (*jāgīr*) at Pokaran. Ransi entrusts it to his elder son Ajmal (Ajay Singh) who settles there, while he himself 'takes the *kāśī karot*', an allusion to the episode of the miraculous saw made out of margosa leaves. We notice that this tale differs in a few aspects from the legend told by the Meghwals: according to the untouchable worshippers of Ramdev it is not from the Muslim ruler of Delhi, but from the Hindu Rathore king Mallinath that Ajmal, and not Ransi, obtains the *jāgīr* of Pokaran which is said to have been a part of the Mallani kingdom during that time. Even if both tales are far from reproducing accurate historical facts, the Meghwal version appears more in conformity with the historical truth, at least for this particular detail.

On the other hand, legend connects Ransi to Naraina (where his shrine is located). According to S. Bishnoi (1989:21-2), Ramdev's grand-father was the ruler of this village (located between Phulera and Ajmer) which, he thinks, was a part of the historical kingdom referred to as Tunwarawati or Torawati (land of the Tanwars). However, in his detailed historical study of the region, M.P. Sharma (1980-1) does not include the area of Naraina in the province referred to as Torawati.

The description of the changing fortunes of Ransi first a landless advendurer then the servant (*chākar*) of a mighty ruler, and eventually *jāgīrdār* of Naraina, fits quite well into the socio-political pattern of the times (Kolff 1990:74-85). According to various historical sources (Jain 1972:378), after the defeat of Prithviraj Chauhan III in 1192, the ancient city of Naraina came under the rule of the Delhi sultans until the sultanate disintegrated after the death of Firuz Shah Tughlaq (1388). In this case Ransi would have been the vassal of the Muslim ruler—a fact which may be reflected in the Rajasthani *bāt* where he becomes his *chākar.* If, as I suppose, he had embraced Ismailism, he would, following the principle of *taqīyya,* have kept his Hindu name and a number of indigenous customs. In other words, Ransi Tanwar may be regarded as a Gupti, one of those Nizari converts who chose to cling to a Hindu exterior as a method of precautionary dissimulation.[15]

This did not prevent him having himself buried according to the Islamic rite; *mazārs* (Muslim tombstones) were erected for him and his successors on the *gaddī* of Naraina (here not in the sense of a royal throne but as one of the seats of the sect). Later these graves were replaced by modern *chabūtrās* (platforms) in the Hindu style and the sacred complex where they are enclosed is now called a *mandir.* In despite of these recent efforts to modify the 'religious identity' of the shrine, a row of ruined *mazārs* located in the courtyard (the cylindrical stones of which seem to have been deliberately broken as if in an attempt to conceal their Muslim origin), two graves outside the compound still testify to the original mode of burial. It might be interesting to note however that the Khoja Guptis, at least most of them, were cremated so as not to betray their real faith in public rituals and functions. The case of Ransi and his disciples is, as we have seen, different, owing to the coexistence of Hindu and Muslim customs.

As for other events mirrored in the legends, it is not possible to tell if Ransi was initiated and appointed the head of a local *gaddī* (as a subsidiary *dāī*) by Pir Shams himself, or by one of his disciples or successors. However, for us names and dates are less important than the analysis of the causes and circumstances which led to the conversion of Hindus to Ismailism in the socio-political context of the fourteenth century.

In accordance with the method applied by the Nizari missionaries, conversions were focused on some influential person in the area chosen for the *dawa* (Maclean 1969:149); it was assumed that the neophyte would proceed to convince others to embrace the new religion. In the case of a local chieftain, this strategy would have been particularly successful since he could easily convert not only his clan or caste-fellows, but most of his subjects. The episode connected with Ransi Tanwar may be profitably compared with the better known historical example of the conversion of the Sumra rulers (Rose 1990, III:488) of Punjab and Sind to Ismailism, an event which must have had some impact in that region (Daftary 1990:189, 479, Allana 1984:15-17).

The case of the chieftain of Naraina, who acted simultaneously as a ruler and as the head of a religious community, reminds us of an important characteristic of Ismailism and of the Muslim tradition as a whole, the ideal association of political and spiritual powers. Even if, in Ismailism, the period of triumphant rule was replaced by what has been termed a shift of emphasis from political ambitions to more mystical ideals caused by historical circumstances, there is no reason to doubt that the original ideal subsisted, albeit on a more modest scale.[16]

The question of what attracted these chieftains towards the new religion must be linked with their personal ambitions and cannot be answered easily. Although Ransi Tanwar, and later his grandson Ramdev, seems to have been more successful with untouchables than with other communities, his power had probably a real weight in the area. The fact that he may have been despised by those Rajputs associated with Brahmans did not negate his influence.[17] Khoja and Imamshahi sources give numerous examples of princes like Siddhraj Jaysingh in Gujarat who supposedly converted to Ismailism (Nanji 1978:50-1), as well as of Nizari Pirs marrying local Hindu princesses (Shackle and Moir 1992:126-9, Nanjiani 1918:196).

Whatever be the historical truth, the phenomenon is worth mentioning insofar as it testifies to its embeddedness within the socio-political context of the subcontinent. According to the Meghval tradition, Ransi had to fight a battle against the Sultan of Delhi, during which most of his sons were killed. Only two of them survived, Ajmal and Dhanrup (Rupji, Dhanraj). Both, it is believed, abandoned the paternal *jāgīr* taken over by the Sunni ruler and fled. Although no historical record of this event has been found to this day, it seems to confirm the legend of Ransi's martyrdom and to account for the fact that his descendants had to settle elsewhere (in the Pokaran area) while the religious *gaddī* of Naraina was attended to by Khivan Balai's descendants (Gokuldas 1982:176-8). The story goes on with Ajmal, Ransi's elder son, going to meet Mallinath Rathore, the Mahuwa king (around 1373-8)—an independent Hindu ruler who is said to have fought battles with the ruler of Delhi. His kingdom, Mallani,[18] was but a vast tract of arid land crossed by the river Luni which, during a great part of the year, flows underground. According to the devotional literature of the Ramdev tradition, Mallinath is said to have stated, 'I am only a king, you are an emperor because your son will be the tenth *avatār*' (from a *bhajan* attributed to Harji Bhatti, an eighteenth-century poet-saint, transcribed by S. Bishnoi 1989:302).

The connection of Ajmal and his son with Mallinath is full of implications. In folk legends, even beyond the circles of their traditional followers, the king of Mallani and Ramdev Tanwar are inseparable; for instance, they are portrayed as two allied and friendly rulers playing *chaupar*, a popular Indian game (S. Bishnoi 1989:539) or singing *bhajans* together during a sacred vigil. There are several allusions to the fact that they are affiliated to a mysterious, rather ill-famed sect, the Kunda Panth or Kamadiya Panth (Munshi and Munshi 1895: 529, 534, 536-7). It would have been founded by a certain 'Gusainji' (a Shaiva ascetic who figures in the Mandore 'gallery of heroes'). Nainsi, the seventeenth-century Jain chronicler, reports that one of Ramdev's daughters was married to Jagmal Rathore, a grandson of Mallinath, so that the Pokaran *jāgīr* ultimately returned to the hands of the rulers of Mallani (Nansi 1969:291).

A tradition preserved by the Jaypals of Ramdeora has it that when Dhanraj, Ransi's younger son, became a widower, he left his two children (two daughters) with Ajmal and, after having taken the vow of *sannyās* (renouncement) went to Mewar. It is said that later on, to imitate his nephew, he took 'living *samādhi*'. The structure erected on the spot of his alleged *samādhi*, once more a *mazār* in the Muslim style, can still be seen at Miyala, a village located between Bhim and Deogarh on the Udaipur-Ajmer road. It is also an important place of pilgrimage for Ramdev's traditional worshippers although it is unknown to the modern *bhaktas* who recently started to participate in the cult. A group of Tanwar Rajputs settled in the area, main *pujārīs* and owners of the land attached to the shrine, claim to be Dhanraj's direct descendants (which contradicts the above-mentioned legend according to which he became a renouncer and had only two daughters). The Tanwars, the Meghvals and the

Kamads of Mewar give a more elaborate version of Dhanraj's life. Their version of the legend is of particular interest, owing to its association with kingship.

It is said that Mokal Singh (1419-20 to 1433), (Somani 1976:116) the ruler of Chittorgarh, the former capital of Mewar, was childless. Since Ramdev Pir had the reputation of a miracle-maker, he thought of inviting him to his kingdom and asking him the boon of a son. However, instead of coming himself, the Pir of Runicha delegated his uncle whom he invested with supernatural powers. There, Ransi's younger son, referred to in the local Mewari tradition as Dhanraj Pir, established his *dhūṇī* in front of the seventh gate of the fort, now called *Rām pol*, where a shrine dedicated to Ramdev was later built. From there he summoned the queen, so that he could 'fill her lap'— a common Rajasthani phrase alluding to the 'pouch-filling' ritual of fertility (Grodzins-Gold 1989:150-4). Unfortunately, her royal spouse refused. The Rani, being a Rajput, lived in seclusion (*pardā*) and could not leave the palace. Angry, the Pir decided to go away. In great distress, the queen sent her servants to stop him, declaring that she would come to meet him secretly. While she sat at his feet, the infuriated Rana arrived on the spot and, sword in hand, threatened Dhanraj: if he could not prove his supernatural powers by giving him a son immediately he would kill them both. The Pir invoked Ramdev who gave him special instructions. At his command an earthen pot (*kalaś, ghaṭ, kumbh*) was brought and put inside his *dhūṇī*. With these objects he performed worship to Ramdev (reference is made implicitly to an important ritual of the Nizar Panth, which will be described in Chapter 4). At once the pot burst and out of it came a child whom Dhanraj Pir put into the queen's lap. Because he had been born from a pot (*kumbh*) the heir apparent of Mewar was named Kumbha. Maharana Kumbha, one of the most famous kings in the history of Rajasthani kingdoms, was to rule between 1433 and 1468 (Somani 1976:121-45). After having witnessed this miracle Mokal fell at the feet of the saint and granted him five *bīghās* of land (about three acres) which was confirmed by a copper-plate (*tāmrapatra*). At the place where the miracle had occurred, and where the present village of Chanderia is located, a shrine was later built. It functions like a temple with a Kamad *pujārī*, and the village has been renamed 'Ramdevji ki Chanderia'. Today a local *melā* commemorates the event.

Incidentally, Mokal's reign coincides with the dates traditionally ascribed to Ramdev Pir by the bhajniks (*samādhi* in 1458). However, in this case it is not the adequacy of facts and dates, but the association of a Rajput Pir with the royal power that will hold our attention. Contrary to Ransi and to Ramdev, Dhanraj appears as a mere ascetic; he is portrayed neither as a religious leader nor as a ruler. However he is credited with a considerable deed, ensuring the continuity and legitimacy of the local lineage of Mewar rulers. Another interesting point is the key role played by Maharana Kumbha in various hagiographical traditions. The Meghvals describe him as a worshipper of Ramdev (S. Bishnoi 1989:98-9, Gohil 1987:73 and passim). On the other hand for the Hindu leather-workers referred to as Raidasis or Regars, Kumbha's queen Rani Jhali became the disciple of Sant Ravidas (Mukta 1994:105-6) later to be followed by the king himself who had witnessed his miracles, among which, incidentally, was the episode of the *Kāśī karot* (see note 12 above). In the Bishnoi tradition the same ruler becomes a devotee of Jambha. The three saints Ramdev, Ravidas and Jambha are supposed to have flourished in the fifteenth century, which, does not necessarily support the historicity of the episodes related above but draws attention to a significant fact: the mutual exchanges and influences which seem to have taken place in the medieval world of *bhaktas*, Sants and Pirs. In this respect the figure of Maharana Kumbha plays a leading role, as does Sikandar Lodi (1489-1517) associated with Kabir by his followers, with Jambha by the Bishnois and with Jasnath by the Jasnathis (see Chapters 7 and 8).

Having performed the miracle, Dhanraj Pir is said to have remained in Mewar and won many disciples among whom, apart from untouchable Meghvals and Regars, were to be found Mers (Rawats) (Gahlot and Banshi Dhar 1989:237-8) and Oswal Jains. Bhils (ibid.: 209-22) who are still numerous in this hilly region of Rajasthan also became his followers; some of these tribesmen established their *dhūṇīs* in the Aravallis and became ascetics of repute (personal communication by Ratan Lal Kamad).

Considering our basic hypothesis we can suggest, for all these events, the following pattern of interpretation. Pir Shams Sabzwari (or any other Ismaili Pir) converted a petty Rajput ruler settled in the region of Naraina after having initiated the untouchable leader of the neighbouring Balai-Meghval community of Dudu (Khivan). Both men spread the Ismaili faith, for which they were charged with propagating a heresy and condemned to death. Subsequently, helped by the independent Rathore King Mallinath who had also become an Ismaili, Ajmal established a small principality and a diocese in the Pokaran region, while Ransi's younger son, Dhanraj, spread the *dawa* in Mewar. In this perspective it is logical that not only Ransi, but Dhanraj should have been traditionally referred to as Pirs, as would be the case for Ramdev. Although Ajmal is not portrayed as a Pir in the local folklore, the popular iconography presents him wearing a sort of high cap of the Sufic type, tentatively disguised as a royal crown. The reason why, ultimately, Ramdev was given more importance than his ancestors or relatives and became the most famous among the Rajput Pirs of his lineage, will be explained in Chapter 5.

While Dhanraj was busy spreading the new faith in Mewar, Ajmal who was issueless was deeply worried. The version of Ramdev's birth which is current in the present 'reHinduized' context of his cult as performed by all castes and communities, has already been given above. It is now necessary to introduce another variant prevalent among some Nizarpanthi worshippers of Ramdev and generally kept secret. Instead of going to the Hindu sacred town of Dwarka, Ajmal in this version goes to the Muslim holy city of Multan where he prays to Shams Pir (presumably on his tomb) to give him the boon of a son. The Pir declares that he will fulfil his wish and predicts that his son will become as powerful as himself: he will be, in fact, his own reincarnation (personal communication, Komal Kothari and Swami Ramprakash).

As if to confirm this prediction, Ramdev became so famous that he eclipsed the glory of other Rajput and Sunni Muslim Pirs. According to the Rajasthani legend, this fame would have passed to his direct descendants, but for an unfortunate event which occurred shortly after he had taken his *samādhi*. Ramdev had requested his relatives not to dig up his grave on any account and they had acquiesced. However, one day, Harbuji, one of the famous 'five Pirs' of Rajasthan, going through a forest, met the Pir of Runicha riding on his mare; he was surprised since he had heard that Ramdev had recently taken *samādhi*. 'People are telling all sorts of stories', answered the saint, eluding the question when Harbuji asked him to explain the mystery. He then gave him a few items to take to Ramdeora. When Harbuji reached the place he was still more amazed to see that the whole village was in mourning. When he showed them the objects given by Ramdev, people were shocked:

they knew these things had been buried together with the Lord of Runicha. Devoured with curiosity, they wanted to see if the Pir was still sitting in his *samādhi* (this term referring to the pit where ascetics are buried in the posture of meditation) or if he had escaped from it, a suspicion which, incidentally, reminds us of a famous trick performed by the Madari magicians of Hindustan (Siegel 1991). While they were digging up the grave a celestial voice was heard; because they had disobeyed him, said Ramdev, no other 'great Pir' would appear in the Tanwar lineage. Ramdev's curse is supposed to account for the fact that his descendants were far from being as powerful as himself and left but few traces in history and legend. In the Ramdev tradition it is believed that his two sons, Sadaji and Devji, inherited the *pīr gaddī* from their father (Vaishnav:148). According to Nainsi who wrote in the seventeenth century, in the region of Pokaran, near Ramdeora, one finds another settlement called Viramdeora, after Viramdev, Ramdev's elder brother, and a third, Sadaji-ro-was, so named after one of his sons (Nainsi 1969:349-50). Although he does not give any detail of Ramdev himself, the Jain chronicler of Marwar mentions their descendants (at Ramdeora, Viramdeora and Sada-ro-was) whom he calls 'Rajput *paṇḍits*' and to whom the land attached to the shrine belonged. Nanjiani (1918:137) refers to the Tanwar Pir's descendants in Rajasthan as *Rāmdev pautras* although he claims that they were the sons of Viramdev, the Pir of Runicha having been childless; the same *Rāmdev pautras* are still found in Gujarat (Enthoven 1990, III:50), and it is said of both that they levy a special tax on the Meghvals, a detail which can be interpreted, in the light of their former Ismaili affiliation, as the customary tithe (*dassondh*) collected from all the believers of the Nizari community (Nanji 1978:52, 75).

Though occasional references are made to the *pīr gaddī* of Ramdeora, in the current hagiography, the present descendants of Ramdev at Runicha do not refer to themselves as Pirs. The lineage ended in 1982 with the death of the last direct descendant of Ramdev, Rao Rirmal Singh whose *chhatrī*, in the Rajput style, is located inside the sacred complex of Ramdeora. The Tanwars who have not yet chosen their new *mahant* (it is said that they are expecting Baba Ramdev's decision in this matter), do not claim to be Pandits: they have entrusted the *pujā* to local Brahmans whom they pay for these services, vivid testimony of the process referred to as 'Sanskritization'. For this reason they may simply appear as hereditary owners of a shrine (Binford 1972:124) where hero and ancestor worship is performed. The Tanwars of Runicha are now a well-off group, enjoying a fairly high status in the caste hierarchy. But before the Ramdev cult became popular among the 'twice-born' (high caste) devotees, they were regarded as Rajputs of low status with whom other Rajputs would neither dine nor intermarry. Reduced to extreme poverty (as if the curse of their ancestor had been effective), the Tanwars of the Ramdev lineage lived on alms until recently, especially during the periods of drought which are so frequent in the region of Pokaran. A few texts describe them as leaving the village begging, with Ramdev's rag horse on their shoulders, and coming back to Runicha only after collecting a sufficient amount of money and other offerings (Pemaram 1977:56).

The case of Mallinath Rathore, ruler of the Mallani kingdom, will now be discussed. According to a tradition (which seems to be denied by historical facts) the Rathore clan originated among the Gahadaval Rajputs of Kanauj. Rao Siha is said to have been the great grandson of Jaichand, a famous ruler of that kingdom. His son Asthan left Kanauj and settled at Khed, in west Rajasthan. His direct descendant in the sixth generation was Kanhad Dev whose brother Salkha's eldest son was Mallinath. The latter is said to have become the ruler of that region known as Mahuwa around 1374 (Raghuvir Singh and M.S. Ranawat 1988:26-7 of Introduction) after killing his uncle. Although Mallinath Rathore occupies an important position in the history of Marwar, many of his battles and heroic deeds being described in various sources, he has become famous in Rajasthani folklore (as well as in Gujarati popular tradition) as a hero-saint and a deified *siddh puruṣ* (a man endowed with supernatural powers). Like Ramdev, with whom he is supposed to have been closely linked, he is said to have taken 'living *samādhi*'. Unfortunately his funeral monument cannot be found and my informants attempted to solve the mystery by declaring that both Mallinath and his spouse Rupande had vanished in the sky. However the saintly ruler of Mallani has a temple at Tilwara on the Luni river. This shrine is believed to have been erected by the eighteenth-century Jodhpur ruler, Abhey Singh, who allegedly popularized other hero-gods such as Ramdev, Pabu, Goga, Meha and Harbu. It looks like any Hindu *mandir* dedicated to some heroic ancestor; in the sanctum (*garbhagṛha*) one can see a memorial stone representing him as a horse-rider, while at his side a rough stone figures his wife Rupande clad in red clothes.

Householder Naths are the regular *pujāris* of this shrine. They claimed that it was Maharaja Abhey Singh himself who entrusted the *sevā* (religious service) to their ancestors. Besides these functions, they also organize *jamās,* and sing *bhajans* with the accompaniment of the five-stringed instrument called *tandurā,* typical of Ramdev tradition. Meghvals, Regars, Kamads and Bhils also participate in these vigils.

It is in what may we call the 'Hinduized' or 'Rajputized' version that the legend of Mallinath-Rupande has become popular all over Rajasthan and Gujarat, but older layers of the tradition have been preserved in the form of devotional songs and tales. The most interesting one is a Rajasthani *bāt* transcribed in the eighteenth century and entitled *Mallīnāth panth mẽ āyo* or 'How Mallinath became member of the sect' (S. Bishnoi 1989:536-8).

For the sake of comparison and comprehension of the process termed 'Rajputization', the current, Hinduized version of the legend will first be given. Rupande, a poor Rajput girl, marries the ruler of Mallani. He does not know that, in her native village, she has an untouchable *dharm-bhāī* (adoptive brother) Dharu Megh, a Meghwal. The latter had invited her a few times to participate in *satsangs* (devotional sessions) organized by his Rajput guru Ugam Si (Ugam Singh) Bhatti.

When I asked to which tradition (*sampradāy*) he belonged, my Nath informants, the *pujaris* of Tilwara, answered as follows: 'It was *bhakti,* only *bhakti, satsang*. . . no particular sect, and because it was *bhakti* there was no difference between castes.' Ugam Si, they specified, was not a Nath like themselves, nor was Mallinath, thus named because he had been born through the blessing of a yogi. Let us come to the conclusion of the plot. One night, out of jealousy, Mallinath's first wife discloses that Rupande has secretly left the palace to participate in some devotional gathering in which members of unclean castes are present—a severe blow to the *kṣatriya dharm.* Ready to kill the culprit, the ruler of Mallani goes out, at dawn, sword in hand. On the way he meets his young wife who has just left the *satsang* and is returning to the palace, holding in her hand a tray full of *prasād* from the sacred vigil. A miracle happens when Mallinath orders her to remove the cloth which covers them: the offerings have been transformed into flowers which Rupande can claim to have plucked for the morning cult in the domestic temple. Impressed, the ruler of Mallani begs her for forgiveness and asks to be brought to her guru, Ugam Si Bhatti. Both husband and wife subsequently become famous *siddhs*, without, it is specified, renouncing the throne.

This version emphasizes a number of points. The miraculous powers of saints and *siddhs*, the non-sectarian *bhakti* equated with the Sant *paramparā* in which there is no caste discrimination, and the leading role played by Rajputs (Ugam Si Bhatti, Mallinath Rathore, Rani Rupande). Allusions to the existence of a sect are, unwittingly or not, concealed. However, as has already been stated, the older tradition has not been totally lost, and traces can be found in the literature connected with Mallinath. The 1901 *Gazetteer of Bombay Presidency* (Campbell 1988:544-5) also gives interesting details on the sect referred to as '*Bījpanthī* or *mārgī* sect'. The Rajasthani *bāt Mallīnāth panth mẽ āyo* describes in a very suggestive way the initiation of Rupande, her relationship with Kamads who were important figures in the sect, and Mallinath's acceptance as a disciple (S. Bishnoi 1989:535-8). Many devotional songs are common to the Ramdev and Mallinath traditions, but in the latter one also finds compositions ascribed to a certain Qutbuddin, a Muslim devotee who, incidentally, appears in the Khoja *ginānic* tradition as well (Nanjiani 1918:120, Shackle and Moir 1992:72-4). In a book entitled *Heroic Songs of Mallani* (S.S.S. Shekhawat 1992:16) we learn that 'the disciples of Mallinath were both Hindus and Muslims, and he is worshipped as a Pir' (a detail which is generally omitted in the Mallinath folklore of Rajasthan). In Qutbuddin's *bhajan* (ibid.:16-17) one finds the mention of the same type of ritual (*pāṭh-kalaś*) prevalent in the Ramdev tradition as among the Khojas, a ritual which will be described in Chapter 4.

This leads us to a fundamental issue connected with the spread of the Nizari *dawa* among communities who no longer identify themselves with the Ismailis. Mallinath as a mighty ruler and Nizari subsidiary *dāī* meeting Ramdev Tanwar, the Pir and chieftain of Pokaran-Runicha, both men 'going to Multan to see the great Pir', as stated in a Rajasthani *bāt* (M. Sharma 1977:51), all conjure up the image of a period when the local non-Sayyid Pirs commissioned to make conversions in Rajasthan and elsewhere, were part of a single united organization which later collapsed and split into a number of 'parochialized' cults and movements. This theme will be illustrated throughout this study.

In the last section of this chapter another important figure of the Ramdev tradition will be introduced: the eighteenth-century Rajput

Harji Bhatti to whom many devotional songs are ascribed. He was not a ruler, but a saint and a poet. His *samādhi* is located in a village called Panditji-ki-dhani, near Osiya (Jodhpur district). He seems to have revived the tradition, at least on the literary level, since no important poet of Rajasthan connected with the Ramdev movement is remembered before him. The hagiographical compositions ascribed to him deal with Ramdev's life and miracles, and if one supposes that he is the real author of at least some of them, they may be the oldest songs describing the career of the Pir of Runicha.

Harji Bhatti's story helps us to understand the evolution of the tradition during the last part of the reign of emperor Aurangzeb. (Rather than accept the dates ascribed to Harji by the tradition, I have relied here on an inscription found in his shrine.) The Bhatti saint is said to have been a staunch devotee of Ramdev. Popular iconography represents him standing in front of his horse and waving a fly-whisk, though at least three centuries separate the two saints. His *bhaktas* claim that he had no human guru, but that Ramdev himself, in a vision, instructed him to spread his faith. Once more, older sources reflected by oral traditions give a different picture: they connect Harji with a Pir named 'Samīk Rishi' and his *gaddī* referred to as *Samsāṇī*. I was told by my informants that this 'Samīk Rishi' is the same as 'Samas Rishi', in other words, Pir Shams, whose shrine is located in Multan. From this interesting detail one can infer that Harji Bhatti belonged to a guru-disciple lineage which started with Shams.

The shrine of the Bhatti saint deserves a detailed description. In front of the temple proper one can see a row of *chhatrīs* in the Hindu style, each sheltering a tiny *mazār*. These monuments are said to be the *samādhis* of a lineage of Pirs, in the local tradition named *Paṇḍits*. All of them were celibate renouncers but were invariably chosen among local Bhatti Rajputs to succeed Harji on the *gaddī* of Panditji-ki-dhani (the name of the village deriving from their title). The temple itself (defined by the present Bhatti *pujārī* and holder of the *gaddī* as *Rāmdevji kā mandir*) has some interesting peculiarities. It contains a recess facing west which, obviously, functions as a *mihrāb* showing the direction of Mecca, but also as a *garbhagṛha*. Instead of the *murti* (whether an anthropomorphic or zoomorphic image, a stone or a symbol) which would be typical of any Hindu shrine, it shelters a replica of Muhammadan tombstone, cloth-covered, perpendicular to the recess. Clothes (*chādars*) of different colours are regularly offered to this miniature grave, as is generally done for Sufi saints, whereas rag horses (manufactured by one of the untouchable communities of the village) and foot-print stones are also donated by the devotees. Curiously enough, some of these stones combined the foot-print symbol with a tiny replica of *mazār*, a type of *ex voto* which I have found in some older shrines connected with the Ramdev tradition. However the grave symbol does not figure any more on the modern foot-print stones sold nowadays during the *melās* in the bazars of Ramdeora or other places.

Coming back to the strange *murti* found in Harji's temple, I was told that it is not the saint's grave: it lay outside the shrine, in a separate *chhatrī*. My informants insisted that it was not a funeral monument but just a sacred image (*murti*). When I asked whose image it was, they explained that it was a 'model' of Ramdev's *samādhi* at Runicha.

If the erection of *chhatrīs* outside the temple testifies to a more recent rajputization of the tradition, the *mazārs*, and in particular the main replica inside the shrine, immediately call to mind the popular worship of the 'Five Pirs' (Panch Pirs, Panch Piriyas). According to D. Coccari (1989:254-6), in the shrines dedicated to these figures, the image can be either a replica of a grave, or a mound or five wooden pegs. The paintings which are to be found on the walls of Harji's shrine (even if they are not very old) seem to confirm the analogy. On one side of the gate we see five horse-riders, the Panch Pirs of Rajasthan, whose names are written as Ramdev, Harbu, Mallinath, Goga and Pabu. On the other side the five Pandavas are figured. The presence of the heroes of the *Mahābhārata* is characteristic. Some authors (Crooke 1978:202-3) are of the opinion that the folk concept and cult of the 'Five Pirs', which spread over north India and Pakistan particularly among low castes, might have evolved under the influence of the worship of the five Pandavas, itself connected with the development of the popular versions of the epic. It is possible that the similarity between the words *pīr* and *vīr* or *bīr* (hero, god, spirit in the Hindu tradition) has inspired the folk imagination which proposed innumerable variants of the series of five Pirs, in which Muslim saints, as well as Hindu heroes, gods and goddesses are listed. Among the Muslim Pirs one finds renowned Sufi saints, such as the Suhrawardi Bahauddin Zakariya, but also, remarkably enough, Pir Shams of Multan, the Nizari *dāī*. Among the Hindu figures, Bheru or Bhairon, a folk-deity linked to the classical Bhairava, a gruesome aspect of Shiva (incidentally Bhairava is said to be one of the fifty-two Virs in Puranic mythology) and the Goddess are generally found. In the regional tradition of Rajasthan, as we have seen, along with Ramdev and Mallinath (sometimes replaced by Meha), we find Goga, Pabu and Harbu. All of them, as may be stressed here, are Rajputs. Besides, only two of these figures, Pabu and Meha, can be identified with a 'pure' Hindu tradition, i.e. one without Islamic components.

We have said that, from the Hindu prespective, the cult of the Panch Pirs may have been inspired by the worship of the five Pandavas. Its Islamic source of inspiration is, interestingly enough, a Shia one: the reverence for the *panj tan i pāk* or 'five sacred bodies', the Prophet Muhammad, his son-in-law Ali, their two sons Hasan and Hussain, and Ali's spouse Fatima. In the light of these combined elements most authors have viewed this popular cult as a syncretistic phenomenon (Hussain 1929:30-2) where various traditions, Hindu, Shia and Sunni, overlapped 'spontaneously'.

While I do agree that the subsequent developments of the Panchpiriya tradition are of an organic nature (as is the case for most religious ideas when they are not checked by guardians of the orthodoxy), I doubt that its initial stage was 'spontaneous' as alleged. In the Khoja Ismaili tradition we come across a revealing detail: among the numerous parallels which the Nizari Pirs attempted to establish between Islamic and Hindu concepts and terms, occurs the identification of the *panj tan* with five Nizari Imams of the Alamut period (the Imam of the time was regarded as the Supreme Pir) and the five Pandava brothers. As has been remarked above, the shrines dedicated to the Panch Pirs contain only one grave (wherever they use this particular symbol). They can be regarded as Hindu or Muslim places of worship, but in all cases devotees of both communities gather at the same place without wondering about its 'religious identity'.

A *dargāh* located at Abohar in modern Indian Punjab is considered to be the main shrine of these five Pirs. Abohar, incidentally, is not far from the present border of the Rajasthan state and is now in the hands of Qadiri Sufis. In this local tradition the five Pirs are Khwaja Khizr (Uderolal, Darya Shah see Chapter 9), 'Zikariya' (Bahauddin Zakariya), Shakarganj (Baba Farid Ganj-e Shakkar), two Sufi Shaikhs, Mundra (?), and Lal Shahbaz (the disputed Qalandar claimed by Suhrawardis and Ismailis alike). The legend describing the travels of these five Pirs deserves mention in so far as it has a direct bearing on our subject: as suggested in Chapter 1, it seems to be connected with the spread of the *dawa* along particular trade-routes. Character istically, this tour starts in Multan, the abode of the Pirs (and traditional centre of the Ismaili mission). From there the five saints intend to go to Abohar, the ruler of which has stolen their five horses. On their way they stop near Pokaran, where they meet Ramdev. They perform miracles in front of him by throwing on the ground their five tooth-brushes out of which grow five Pipal trees. This particular episode is common to the Ramdev folklore, with the difference that the Pir of Runicha eventually proves his superiority by performing a still more difficult 'trick': he brings instantaneously in front of them their five bowls which had remained inside a locked room in Mecca. We need to specify that in the older devotional tradition, for instance in a *bhajan* by Likhmoji Mali (eighteenth-nineteenth century), these five Pirs are said to have come from Multan: *mahimā sun multān mulk rā āyā pīr milān tāhi* . . . ('hearing of his glory, from the country of Multan the Pirs came to meet him' quoted in J. Solanki: 24). In Ramdev's hagiography it is said that one of the Pirs who had acknowledged his superiority and given him the title *hinduō kā pīr* decided to remain in the kingdom of Pokaran. His *dargāh* is known as *Panchpīpalī* and forms a part of the Ramdeora sacred pilgrimage. The legend seems to have been forged to account for the fact that, once more in a shrine obviously connected with the Panch Pirs, only one grave is to be found. This is a tombstone covered by a green cloth, to which offerings of foot-print stones and rag horses are made, as they are to Ramdev in his shrine of Runicha. It is interesting to note that this grave, which is believed to be the *mazār* of a Muslim Pir, is in fact perfectly identical with the alleged *samādhis* located in the sacred complex of Ramdeora, often covered with green *chādars.* At Panchpipali, in front of the grave and inside the enclosure a Hindu temple has also been built in which *pujā* is regularly performed.

Reverting to the legend of Abohar, we will follow the five Pirs in their travel: from Pokaran they go to Jalandhar, then to Firozpur, and finally reach Abohar, where they try to get back their horse. However, the king does not behave well and the Pirs curse his city which immediately falls into ruins. Later on, a grave was built at this place to commemorate the five Pirs; each year, during the *melā,* on the fifteenth of the Hindu month of *sāvan* (July-August) hundreds of Muslims and Hindus flock to the shrine in the hope that their vows will be fulfilled. This Panch Pirs story, which has a distinct Ismaili 'flavour', seems to be a 'tale of the mission' highly coloured by popular imagination. A look at the map will immediately reveal that the five Pirs' itinerary is not at all logical: the choice of Pokaran as a halting place when going from Multan to Abohar is not exactly what one would call a short-cut and much more than a simple detour. However, it may be an allusion to certain important centres of the *dawa* which, though fairly distant one from the other, were once presumably linked, as in the legend of the secret tunnel of Balinath's *dhūṇī* (see note 8).

Coming back to Harji Bhatti after this long digression, one could regard his association with the Panch Pirs as a later folk development, whereas the *mazār* replica functioning as the image of his shrine may have had its historical origin in an interesting local custom connected with the cult of Pir Shams in Rajasthan, the *chillā dargāh.* This custom will be described in Chapter 3.

To conclude, a few words must be said of Harji's successors. He had three main disciples. The first was a Bhatti Rajput, the second a Meghval, and the third a Gurra (or Chamarwa Brahman, a domestic priest of the untouchable castes) of the Sahni clan. From them sprang three lineages of Pandits (as they are referred to) which continue to this day and form three separate *gaddīs,* albeit with the Bhattis in the leading role. Another interesting detail of Harji's hagiography is that he is believed to have been arrested by the Jodhpur (Hindu) ruler for trespassing the *kṣatriya dharm,* i.e. mixing freely with all sorts of low caste people and performing 'unorthodox' rites. However, impressed by a series of miracles, the king released the saint from his prison.

The last episode I propose to report has been narrated to me at Panditji-ki-dhani. In it figures the last 'Rajput Pir' of our series. Once, in a village located near Jaitaran (Jodhpur district) lived a Rathore chieftain who was afflicted by a terrible skin disease. In a dream he saw a mysterious *sādhu* who put his hand on his shoulder and blessed him. When he woke up he was cured. After he had revealed his vision to his kin and friends, they suggested that the hermit was none other than Ramdev himself. Then he was told that the successor of the Pir of Runicha was the saint Harji Bhatti who was at present living somewhere near Osiya, in a modest hut. Grateful, the *ṭhākur* sent a good amount of gold, silver and precious stones loaded on a camel and ordered a temple to be erected on the spot. The inscription above the gate reads Samvat 1857-67, which corresponds to AD 1800-10. We can also surmise that the curious object of worship chosen for this temple, a replica of a Muslim grave, was intended to represent Ramdev's *samādhi* if, as the tradition claims, the shrine of Panditji-ki-dhani is indeed dedicated to the Pir of Runicha. But still more amazing is the fact that the *ṭhākur* seems to have secretly embraced the faith of Ramdev and Harji and acquired some of their special powers; in any case, at his death, instead of being cremated as all twice-born householders should be, he was buried and a *mazār* was erected outside the walls of the fort.[18] Imagine my surprise when, going to that village after my visit to Panditji-ki-dhani where I had heard this story, I was told that the present *ṭhākur's* ancestor who was a devotee of Ramdev, had never had any *samādhi*, though I had been careful enough to express the whole thing in the purest Hindu terminology. At Ramdeora, experience had told me that it was enough to refer to Ramdev's *mazār*, or those of his parents, relatives and disciples, as *samādhis* to be shown, with enthusiasm, as many graves as I wished. This time, obviously, it did not work. I was prepared to leave the village when it occurred to me that I should be more obstinate. I asked if there was not, in the village, any other *samādhi* belonging to some saint or *sādhu*. In reply I was told of a *chhatrī* of some *mahātmā* of the Kumhar (potter) caste. Before I rather reluctantly consented to visit this monument, suspecting that it had nothing to do with the Rajput devotee of Ramdev, my husband asked all of a sudden, 'is there, by chance, in your village, any *dargāh*, the tomb of a Muslim Pir?' The response was clear. There was one and it was very famous. We were immediately taken to the *mazār*, in a place where the outbuildings of the palace are now located. It was a simple cloth-covered grave but the Pir, we were told, was very powerful. Every morning the Rathore family established in the village started the day by offering *pujā* to him. Numerous devotees also came to make their offerings and many Hindu women asked for the boon of a son. Who was this Pir? Nobody knew; he was simply called 'Bapji', an appellation which was rather Hindu. I inferred that the mysterious 'Bapji' was none but the *ṭhākur's* famous ancestor who had been cured by the grace of Baba Ramdev, and buried like him — like all devotees of Ramdev. However, at a certain time, which may not very remote, it became difficult for the Hindu lords of the region to acknowledge the 'Gupti' style of their forefather. On the other hand, according to a pan-Indian belief, ancestors, Pirs, and Virs, whether Hindu or Muslim, can be dangerous if they are not propitiated. Therefore the traditional worship continued, but a story was forged to explain why the Hindu chieftains of the village revered a Muslim *mazār* located in their land: the saint buried in the compound was an Islamic Pir who had once found shelter in the palace of the *ṭhākur* who was, of course, exceptionally tolerant. There was no shame in worshipping a powerful saint of the Muslim tradition, as was current all over India.

The new legend had, however, an unexpected momentum: it spread among the Muslim communities of the village who started to believe in it. Subsequently, they began to claim the *dargāh* for themselves. At the time of writing they are still offering to the present *ṭhākur* thousands of rupees to buy the land and the grave of this powerful Pir whom they want to appropriate. To date it is only a tombstone with a sacred tree located among the crops; they want to build an enclosure wall, erect a few subsidiary structures, repair the tomb and, naturally, organize a *melā*.

But how could the Rathores 'sell' their ancestor without incurring his wrath? Buried with his secret, the 'mysterious Pir' of the village testifies to another interesting fact: the 'Rajputization' of Pirs of the Rajasthani Nizari tradition has its limits. Whenever and wherever they cannot be Rajputized in a convincing way they have to change their identity.

NOTES

1. The word *ḍheḍh* normally refers to all the untouchables who remove the carcasses of dead cattle. It was applied, in particular, to the Bhambis (Balais, Meghvals) with a distinctly derogatory meaning.
2. This piece of stone 'resembling the hump on a camel's back or the back of a fish . . .' is normally erected for men; in some places the segment of the cylinder is much smaller and is called *qalamdān* (pen-box) (Herklot and J. Sharif 1972:102).
3. The most striking example is perhaps that of the shrine of Diggy Kalyanji (south of Jaipur). For a long time in an underground hall, worship was performed simultaneously to an image of Vishnu and to the grave of a Pir. Recently the underground chamber has been closed to the public and the Brahman *pujārīs* even try to deny the existence of the tomb. However, they still secretly perform worship to it twice a day, for fear of incurring the wrath of this powerful Muslim saint. (This information was gained from my field research.)
4. The saint Sai Baba of Shirdi who has been buried according to the Muslim rite represents a similar case. In his shrines, one finds, together with his

anthropomorphic image, a small replica of a grave. This peculiarity is in conformity with the saint's message—he consciously refused to assume a clear-cut religious identity (Ruhela 1994:19, 85).

5. As we will see further, this tradition seems fairly recent since the nineteenth-century *bhajans* mention that the Pirs came from Multan.
6. S. Bishnoi's study *Bābā Rāmdev, Itihas evam Sahitya* (Baba Ramdeo, History and Literature) has been entirely conceived from this point of view, which is that of most modern devotees.
7. According to the Meghval tradition, Ramdev ate with the untouchables, and sang *bhajans* in their company. For this reason, his cousin Sugana Bai's in-laws, the Rajputs of Pugalgarh, broke all relationship with him and called him derogatorily a 'Kamadiya' (Kamad) (see the ballad transcribed by S. Bishnoi, 1989:403).
8. There are many legends connected with this episode. The Meghvals of Ramdeora show a cave which is supposed to be the place where Ramdev killed Bheru, a blood-thirsty, man-eating *rākśas*. According to a legend, there is a secret passage linking this cave to the *dhūṇī* of the yogi Balinath, Ramdev's alleged guru. I was told by the Nath priests of Balinath's temple that this tunnel is even longer: it would connect Pokaran to Naraina, Dudu, Junjala (near Nagaur) and even Junagarh in Gujarat. This seems to be an allusion to the 'secret tradition' associated with Ramdev Pir of which the above mentioned towns or villages were important centres (see Chapter 3).
9. At the end of the eighteenth century, owing to the patronage of the Jodhpur ruler Maharaja Man Singh (1782-1843), the Nath yogis gained considerable power in Rajasthan (P. Sharma 1972). This contributed, no doubt, to their elevation in Hindu society, after they had long been regarded as ascetics of a low category (up to a certain period which must be fairly recent, even untouchables could become *mahants* of Nath monasteries).
10. I thank Professor Deora for reminding me of the key role played by Ganga Singh in the 'Rajputization' of Ramdev and Goga cults.
11. It is curious that most Rajasthani scholars hold the same opinion, although their Gujarati colleagues 'next door' have recently written so much about the sect connected with Ramdev.
12. This miraculous saw is referred to as *kāśi karot*; it also plays a role in the legend of the untouchable Sant Raidas Chamar who, with its help, demonstrates his supernatural powers and convinces the ruler of Chittorgarh: cut by this *kāśi karot* he caused milk to spurt out from his body (personal communication by Komal Kothari).
13. This charge reminds us of what has been said about the Syrian Nizaris: they were accused (in the twelfth century) of the worst debaucheries and sins: they drank, did not respect their mothers nor their daughters, women were dressed as men, and so on (quoted by Lewis 1985:111).
14. Interestingly enough the Rajasthani legend of Samas Rishi/Shams Pir shows him travelling with a caravan (Gokuldas 1982:152).
15. I am grateful to A. Rahmatoullah for having given me a detailed account of his own family story. His ancestors lived outwardly like Hindu merchants, keeping a vegetarian diet and following other such customs. They took names like

Gopal Das, and Gur Das. In the nineteenth century, under the influence of the Aga Khan, Ram Das, for example, changed his name to Rahmatullah.

16. It seems that after the fall of Alamut the Ismailis did not forsake all political ambitions, even if, for a long period, they had to live in concealment. The permanence of the association between political and spiritual powers is testified by the attempts of Aga Khan I and of some of his successors to acquire political control over certain regions. Aga Khan III (Sultan Muhammad Shah) was appointed president of the Indian Muslim league (1906), he wished to become the head of the entire Muslim community of the subcontinent and dreamed to conquer a part of Persia. He later declared himself ready to reside in Baluchistan, on the condition that he should be regarded as the ruler of this province which would then become a legitimate kingdom (Bose 1984: 258).
17. This is, at present, the case of the leader of the Ai Panth (see Chapter 6): he has claimed the status of a Rajput, succeeded in marrying into a Rajput family, and is a Congress member of the legislative assembly, but high caste people still refer to him as the 'chief of the Gurras' (the Gurras are the domestic priests of the untouchables and are themselves classed as untouchable).
18. The suffix—*āṇī* is obvioulsy not Rajasthani; the usual suffix is—*vāṭī*: Shekhawati, Torawati, i.e. the kingdom of the Shekhawats, of the Tanwars, etc. On the probable Sindhi origin of this ending, see the next chapter. If one accepts the fact that Mallinath was an older contemporary of Ramdev, it is possible to determine the approximate time when he flourished (around AD 1400) on the basis of inscriptions connected with the ruler of Mallani.

CHAPTER 3

Hindu and Muslim Pirs: The Community Fragmented

From the innumerable legends preserved in the traditions of Ramdev's worshippers, it has appeared that, despite recent efforts to present the tradition as some kind of Rajput ancestor worship, the story of these noble Pirs cannot be separated from that of their 'pariah' (*ḍheḍh*) brothers. In the folklore spread by Meghval devotional singers, Rajputs and untouchables are frequently associated: Harijans can be the disciples of Rajputs, but also their gurus or their co-disciples (*guru-bhāī*). This constant, rather 'unorthodox' association of members of clean and unclean castes has been a characteristic feature of the Ramdev tradition illustrated in a famous *bhajan* composed by Likhmoji Mali (J. Solanki: 29-30):

> Ransi ahead, Khivan Rishi follows . . .
> Shri Ramdev ahead, Dala Bai follows . . .
> Malde-Rupa ahead, Dharu follows . . .

If, in modern times, most untouchables prefer to join the chorus of higher caste devotees in worshipping Ramdev as a universal pan-Hindu god rather than the guru of a particular sect, a few of them still cling to what they regard as their original cultural heritage. Furthermore, today they are ready to unveil a part of their secrets, a recent phenomenon which may be connected with the acquisition of new rights in independent India. It is probable that, by disclosing this hidden religious heritage, presented as a very ancient Hindu tradition, they hope to demonstrate to the world that their alleged 'backwardness' is but a historical misunderstanding.

The Meghvals, who constitute the majority of Ramdev's worshippers, form a specific community divided into a number of regionally variable sub-castes. Their traditional occupations have been weaving and leather work as well as the removal of dead cattle, which earned them the derogatory nick-name of *ḍheḍh*. Under the influence of their religious leaders and reformers (the most famous having been Swami Gokuldas), they now tend to give up the professional activities which are a source of ritual pollution. The Meghvals are known under various names according to the region where they live, but also their status. For instance, they are popularly designated as Bhambis (from *bhāmb*, forced labour), and Balais nearly all over Rajasthan (Balai-Balahi being also used in Madhya Pradesh), and Salvis in Mewar. They can contemptuously be named Chamars (applying to all types of leather-workers) or still worse, Dhedh. Instead, anybody wishing to treat them with respect will have to use the name Meghval (Munshi and Munshi 1895:527-35, Briggs 1990, Mathur 1969:4-9, 16-17, 38-9, 42-3, Gokuldas 1982:58-65).

By seeking to revive their half-forgotten religious heritage the Meghvals, of course, did not intend to acknowledge their former allegiance to Ismailism. Recent social and religious trends, combined with the influence of Hindu revivalism, prompted them to reinterpret their history. The results of these efforts, which can be perceived during discussion with Ramdev's traditional followers, are also reflected (as has been said in the previous chapter), in a few publications in Hindi and Gujarati. In Rajasthan, Gokuldas' work gives a rather confused idea, as if the author dared not express himself in clear terms for fear of disclosing too much. Instead, the books of Gujarati authors such as Gohil, Shrimali, Rajyaguru, and Makrand Dev may be regarded as a conscious attempt to redefine, in the Hindu idiom, the religious tradition to which many people still claim affiliation. If one can therefore view the Ramdev cult as a pan-Hindu *bhakti* movement, its practice among untouchables must be regarded as a separate phenomenon engendered by its own process of evolution.

In the general folklore of Rajasthan (as also Gujarat and Sind), Ransi, Khivan, Ramdev, Mallinath, Megh Dharu, Jaisal, Devayat, Ugam Si and others are considered gods or saints who share nothing in common except their virtue, mainly their capacity to help devotees and perform miracles. But among the untouchables connected with the Ramdev tradition they are all members of a secret sect (Gohil 1987:24-9, 74-5 and passim). In this sectarian tradition, usually designated the Nizar Panth, the Harijans are supposed to play the main roles, although a few Rajput and other higher caste devotees have occasionally joined them. In other words, according to some authors, the Nizar Panth is essentially a religious heritage of the

Harijans. One might define this claim as a tendency to 'Meghvalize' the tradition, as there has been a 'Rajputizing' trend. We can surmise that by 'appropriating' the sect, sifting and sorting out the elements which can be made to fit into their pattern, the untouchable worshippers of Ramdev have preserved but a small part of the Nizari Ismaili tradition of Rajasthan, namely that which is linked to their caste. The existence of other convert groups, now perceived as separate communities, will be discussed subsequently.

THE NIZAR PANTH IN GUJARAT: THE LINEAGE OF MATANG

The present members of the Nizar Panth usually insist that the sect is eternal (*anādi*), in so far as it was created by the god Shiva himself (a claim shared with the Nath yogis with whom the Nizarpanthis seem to have many affinities) (Gohil 1987:34). Its origin on the human or historical plane is described in legends transmitted by Gujarati untouchables of Kacch and Saurasthra (mostly the Maheshvari Meghvals) (Bahadur 1981:20-1).

According to one of them a certain Brahman, son of a famous astrologer, stole the books of his deceased father and ran away. Chased by his three brothers, he took shelter in the hut of a poor Meghval family who, subsequently, gave him their daughter in marriage. The Brahman's son (according to other versions his grandson) became the famous saint Matang. Thanks to the sacred books he could impart to the Harijans total magic and spiritual knowledge. Matang was later deified and worshipped as an *avatār* of Shiva. His son Matei Dev was equally powerful and regarded as a divine incarnation. In legends he is also called Jakh Dev (skt. *yakśa deva*, object of an ancient fertility cult). His *murti* as a horserider is still revered in Kacch and Sind, while toy horses are offered to him as they are to Ramdev.

According to the same tradition, Matang had helped the local ruler of Sind, Jam Lakho Dhuraro, obtain victory over the Muslim conqueror Mahmud of Ghazni. In this way, he and his descendants, all designated Matangs, became the *kul-gurus* (clan gurus) of the Jam kings of Kacch, Junagarh and Sind (Shrimali 1993:222-30).[1]

In another legend Matang had two sons, Lunangdev and Monand; Matei Dev would then have been Lunang's son. However, in all versions the two powerful gurus and Pirs of the Maheshvari Meghvals,

Mamei Dev and Devayat Pandit (Devayat Pir) were the sons of Matei. Incidentally, whereas the Matang lineage as a whole seems to be unknown in Rajasthan, the Ramdev tradition in *bhajans* ascribed to Devayat are famous in this area. The *samādhis* of Lunang, Mamei and Matei in Sind are still important places of pilgrimage for the Maheshvari Meghvals of Kacch. Further enquiries among these communities in Gujarat would show if they still, at least symbolically, function as *gaddīs* or centres of the Nizar Panth, despite the fact that they are now in Pakistan.

In conformity with the spirit of our times, all these gurus appear as Hindu figures and further as saviours and protectors of the Hindus. However, the strength of the tradition is such that it was not possible to erase all traces of their former affiliation to the Nizari sect of Ismailism. Thus another version of Matang's legend makes him an incarnation of Ali (Bahadur 1981:20) and such typical Nizari terms as Alamut, Daylam, Ali, Qayam, etc., are still repeated in the devotional songs ascribed to Devayat Pir (Nanjiani 1918:123-7).

Let us compare the 'Hinduized' version of Matang's story with the tradition of the Nizari Khojas. One of their legends has it that the first missionary sent to Hindustan by the Imam of Alamut took the form of a parrot. Satgur Nur preached among the Meghvars (Meghvals) of Sind, Tharparkar and Kathiawar (personal communication by Z. Moir), where he was known as Matang. According to another variant, closer to the Meghval story of Matang's birth, Chach, disciple of Satgur Nur and servant of his wife, Rani Palande, murdered his master while he was in a state of *samādhi* (Nanjiani 1918:133-6); running away with his sacred books, he found shelter among the Meghvals to whom, under the name of Matang, he brough the Nizari Ismaili faith. In both traditions, Meghval and Khoja, Satgur Nur is also known as Sadaji. Whether he should be identified with Satgur Nur himself or his disciple (or with the son of the Brahman who escaped with the books), Matang was deified and considered an *avatār* of Shiva, Vishnu and Ali, but more particularly, he was an incarnation of Kalki renamed *Nikalank avatār.*

From this amalgam of colourful and intricate legends the minimal inference is that before Pir Shams himself converted the Meghvals (as did later Ramdev) some sections of this community seem to have already come into the orbit of Ismailism through Satgur Nur or of one of his successors and disciples.[2]

THE NIZAR PANTH IN RAJASTHAN: A NETWORK OF *GADDĪS*

If Ramdev's traditional followers were indeed, at one time, part of the Nizari community like the present Multani Shamsis and the Khojas of Sind and Gujarat, we should find traces of an organizational structure. This could be decisive evidence, for as Ivanow has it (1948:20), 'the only branch of Islam in which the preaching of religion, da'wat, was not only organised, but even considered of special importance, was Ismailism. It must be noted, however, that the Ismaili da'wat, though religious in form, was mainly political in substance.' As mirrored in the history of Ismailism, the corollary of such a phenomenon was a strong organization.

In Chapter 1 we saw that the world to be converted had been divided into a number of dioceses (*jāzir*, pl. *jazāir*) during Fatimid rule. During the Nizari period, Multan and nearby Ucch were again chosen as centres of the mission in the subcontinent. The Imam appointed there a main Pir in charge of the local *dawa.*

Gokuldas (1950:8) makes an indirect allusion to the connection of the so-called Hindu Nizar Panth with the Ismaili Nizari *dawa* when he claims that the oldest *gaddī* or seat of the sect, referred to as the Samsani and established by Shams Pir, is located in Multan.

In Rajasthan the other main *gaddīs* are said to be Mallani, Ramdevani and Harchandani. Gokuldas attempts to explain the ending -*āṇī* found in all these names as deriving from *dhūṇī* (ascetic hearth or *gaddī*) and *vāṇī* (voice, devotional poem). Needless to say, these etymologies do not hold. My informants, instead, declare that the suffix -*āṇī* refers to 'lineages' or 'disciples'. Mallani being mentioned in the histories of Rajasthan as the ancient kingdom of Mallinath Rathore, the ending -*āṇī* has often been interpreted as a geographic designation—an explanation we have already rejected (Chapter 2, n.18).

It will be suggested instead that -*āṇī* represents a Sindhi, or rather a Siraiki (the language of Multan area) genitive ending. It is still used for local family names: for instance, the sons or descendants of Tola are named Tolani, those of Lalu Lalwani, etc., whereas in Rajasthan the sons of Jagmal would be called Jagmalot, those of Shekha Shekhawat. The names Samsani, Mallani, Ramdevani, and Harchandani should logically derive from those of their founders, and therefore be translated as 'disciples' or 'lineages' of Shams,

Mallinath, Ramdev and Harchand, which would be in conformity with the interpretation of my informants. The use of the Multani ending could indicate that the original organizers of these local seats were indeed the Pirs of Multan.

The whole network of main and subsidiary *gaddīs* established around the *samādhis/dargāhs* of the founders or some sacred relic, presents similarities with the Nath monasteries (*maṭhs*) and with the *gaddīs* of various sects derived from the *Sant paramparā*, as well as with the *dargāhs* (and *gaddīs*) of different Sufi *silsilas*.

In these shrines there are *dhūṇīs* (here ascetic hearths), platforms (*chabūtrās*) with footprints (*charan, pagliyā*), temples (*mandirs*), *samādhis* and *mazārs*. Each of these sacred places is endowed with land, as is the case with Hindu temples and monasteries and Sufi *dargāhs*. In the Nizarpanthi tradition the head of a *gaddī* is designated Pir, occasionally *mahant* or *paṇḍit*. It may be remembered once more that, despite Muslim terminologies, the religious leaders and the sect they represent are now perceived by the devotees as purely Hindu, one reason why I have referred to them as 'Hindu Pirs'.

The Pir of a particular *gaddī* is said to have, under his authority, a number of village *dhūṇīs*. The heads of these local centres are called Kamadiyas or Kamads and play a significant role in the Ramdev tradition. For instance, the Pir of Bichun, an important *gadaī* we will describe below, claims to have 485 village *dhūṇīs* under his authority, which corresponds, at present, to an equal number of temples dedicated to Ramdev. (The last detail reflects the transformation of the sect into a cult centred on the figure of the God of Runicha). Between the main Pirs and the village Kamads intermediary units are also found, in the form of subsidiary *gaddīs* held by Pirs of a lesser rank, who depend on the *mahant* of a main *gaddī*.

For certain ceremonies, like the annual *melā* and special *jamās*, the initiation of a new *mahant* or Kamad, and their funerary rites, the main Pir must be present and receive his share from the local *dhūṇī* (Gokuldas 1982:181).

However, in the present state of affairs, this structure, described by Gokuldas and various informants, looks rather like an ideal, theoretical framework; in many cases, owing to recent historical developments the authority of the main Pirs is questioned by the heads of subsidiary *gaddīs* and even by the village Kamads who constitute the lowest unit, and shares are no more regularly distributed. These shares, perhaps the vestiges of an ancient tithe system, must have played an important part in the functioning and cohesion of the whole network of *gaddīs*.[3] Recent changes possibly occurred because a majority of Pirs of the Hindu Nizar Panth are of Meghval origin, and because the Kamads, who in the course of time have formed a separate caste, refuse to admit the superiority of these *mahants* at the village level. The Meghvals constitute the *jajmāns* of the Kamads and are their disciples. Whereas Pirs fight among themselves for power and money, Kamads, with a similar aim, claim to be independent gurus and priests.

A description of these *gaddīs* will enable us to grasp the complexity of the situation in its historical dimension.

SAMSANI: THE DISCIPLES OF PIR SHAMS

The *gaddī* referred to as Samsani will first be described in detail. Its main seat, Multan, being now in Pakistan (Pir Shams Sabzwari's *dargāh* is at present in the hands of Twelver Shias who claim to be his descendants), it has retained only a symbolic value for the Rajasthani Nizarpanthis. According to Pir Gojit Das, the *mahant* of Bichun, 'nobody among us any longer goes to Multan'; because of this, he declared, the main seat of the Samsani must be considered Bichun. As explained in one of the legendary traditions reported in Chapter 2, it is from that once desert place in the Aravalli hills that 'Samas Rishi' had spread his message, initiating the untouchable leader Khivan and the Rajput chieftain Ransi, who was to become Ramdev's grandfather. The nearby hamlet of Sakhun is said to have been another place of ascetism and meditation of Shams, but it is now deserted and its two small temples are in a state of disrepair.

Bichun, Sakhun, Dudu and Naraina are believed to be the four original *gaddīs* linked with Shams, the first centre being considered as the main one by its Pirs. As a matter of fact, when asked to which lineage or main *gaddī* they were affiliated, the *mahants* of Naraina and Dudu unhesitatingly answered that they were 'of the Samsani', even if they would no longer acknowledge the authority of the Pir of Bichun. The village Kamads living in the area of Sikar (province of Shekhawati) also stated that they belonged to the Samsani, as did the three lineages of *mahants* at Panditji-ki-dhani, and the Tanwar Pandits of Miyala, owners of the shrine dedicated to Ramdev's uncle, Dhanraj Pir.

From the above-mentioned points it should be clear that the

designation Samsani does not correspond to a regional unit or diocese but rather, as its etymology suggests, to *gaddīs* and lineages established in various places by a particular Pir. In this respect Samsani must be indeed the oldest lineage, since Shams most probably came before Mallinath, Ramdev and Harchand.

Dudu and Naraina are important shrines for the traditional devotees of Ramdev (mostly Meghvals) and, as has been said, commemorate the martyrdom of Ransi and Khivan for whom *samādhis* (*dargāhs*) have been erected. Bichun, however, is distinct. It does not shelter a grave or a relic, but claims to have preserved the *dhūṇī* of 'Samas Rishi'. In front of the temple gate one can see a small, brand-new square-shaped marble slab, referred to as the *samādhi* of Shams and understood to be a replica of his original grave in Multan. It is difficult to imagine how the shrine looked before its transformation which is said to have started in the fifties. It has now been converted into a temple of Ramdev by a simple device: the installation of an image in the round representing the Pir of Runicha riding on his mare. The inner portion of the shrine seems to be older than its outer structure. In fact, the recess which is supposed to be the *sanctum sanctorum* looks very much like the *mihrāb* of a mosque facing Mecca. In the courtyard vestiges of ruined graves which have the appearance of Muslim *mazārs* can be seen. At present only two *samādhis* are in good condition; they are in the form of rectangular *chabūtrās*, deprived of any symbolic ornament and are said to belong to the Pirs who preceded Gojit Das on the *gaddī* of Bichun.

The lineages of the *gaddī* of Bichun and those of Naraina and Dudu must now be mentioned. According to the Meghval tradition (Gokuldas 1982:163), Sankar Das, the resuscitated boy from Ucch, who had become a disciple of Pir Shams, would have been the first *mahant* of Bichun (after his guru). Following his spiritual teacher's *samādhi*, he would have left Multan to inform Ransi and Khivan (not yet martyred) and remained in Rajasthan.[4] Later he himself 'took *samādhi*' there. Gokuldas states that it is Khivan Balai who subsequently organized the four *gaddīs* established by Samas. He was himself at the head of Sakhun and, after Sankar's death, entrusted the leadership of Bichun, Naraina and Dudu to his descendants and disciples. The reason why Naraina is no more in the hands of the Tanwars was that, after the battle against the ruler of Delhi, the two surviving sons of the Rajput chieftain fled from the village and settled in the area of Pokaran (Chapter 2). Although we cannot rely entirely on the lists provided by Gokuldas (1982:174-80), nor treat them as reliable historical documents, they at least illustrate the continuity of the tradition through an uninterrupted chain of disciples. In the lineage of the Pirs of Dudu, for instance, starting from Khivan's son Hadmal and ending with the present *mahant*, thirty names are given, which would roughly correspond to a period of six hundred years; this confirms, though undirectly, Khivan's period as being the middle of the fourteenth century. The *mahants* of these *gaddīs*, it must be specified, were not always descendants of previous Pirs but also their disciples; they were both householders and celibate renouncers (*sannyāsīs*). Besides, if one finds Kumhars (potters), Malis (gardeners) and Dasnami Gosains (Shaiva ascetics) as holders of the *gaddī*, the majority of the *mahants* would probably be of Meghval origin.

After the Khivan lineage became extinct, Seva Das Rishi, a Meghval from Dumara (a village near Ajmer), disciple and adoptive son of Gokuldas, succeeded, probably owing to the prestige of his guru, in having his twelve-year-old son appointed the new Pir of Dudu. According to Seva Das, Naraina should also be in the hands of Meghvals and of *mahants* of Khivan's lineage, but various disputes had arisen in the past, as a result of which this *gaddī*, together with its substantial resources in the form of land and offerings, had now passed into the hands of Rajputs.

Without entering into details we may conclude this section by pointing to the profound, but probably recent, transformations that seem to have occurred in the appearance of the shrines and in the structural organization of the *gaddīs*. Khivan's cenotaph seems to have been built or rebuilt in the eighteenth or nineteenth century, though, interestingly enough, in a purely Islamic style (the cusped arches were introduced by the Mughals in the seventeenth century). In contrast, the shrine of Naraina has undergone more drastic changes (see Chapter 2). Yet these places became new foci of the Ramdev cult, at least for the Meghvals. Devotees of higher caste who joined the movement recently 'from outside', do not even know of their existence, whereas the inhabitants of this region simply refer to them as 'temples of Ramdev'.

These four seats of the Samsani are the centres of an annual *melā*. Each of them takes place separately but at the same time, starting on the *dūj* or *bīj* (second day) of the bright half of the Hindu month of Asoj (*Āśvin śukl pakś* or *Āsoj dūj*). A *jamā*, also called *jamā-jāgraṇ*, takes place during the previous night, followed in the morning by the *melā*. On that day, sitting in a *rath* (chariot) and with his royal paraphernalia (staff, fly-whisker and banner) accompanied by musicians, the Pir circumambulates the sacred area which extends beyond the shrine. Most devotional songs sung during the night session are related to Ramdev, whereas traditional *bhajans* ascribed to Khivan, Ransi and Devayat are occasionally sung by older devotees.

The second day of Asoj, during which other important *melās* are held, seems to be of special importance for the Nizari tradition. For the Khojas too it is auspicious, as illustrated by the fact that the Khoja Pir Hassan has his fair at Ganod (Gujarat) on that date (Enthoven 1989:59).

A description of the Samsani lineages would be incomplete if we do not mention other communities of Rajasthan who acknowledge Pir Shams as their guru but who, instead of having assumed a Hindu identity, claim to be 'orthodox' Muslims. They represent another side of the 'forgotten tradition'.

The fascinating shrine of Junjala (mentioned in the *bhajans* of Ramdev and Mallinath traditions) gives us an idea of the extreme complexity of the subject. It will help us to understand how the original Nizari community of Rajasthan has been split into innumerable units which now function separately, with the identity of a caste group or under the banner of a spiritual guide. In this regard the Nizari *dawa* in Rajasthan may be compared with a large and imposing river which gradually branches into smaller and smaller tributaries, until the tiniest rivulet gets lost in the sands.

According to a legend reported by Meghvals and Kamads, before initiating Khivan and Ransi and settling at Bichun, Shams had visited other places in Rajasthan. There, he had established, or better reestablished, the ancient faith (believed to be eternal or *anādi*) brought by his predecessor, a certain 'Gusaiṇji', probably the archetypal missionary of the Nizaris in Hindustan, Satgur Nur. In the Khoja tradition, Ramdev is said to be related to Satgur Nur, as he is associated with Gusainji for the Nizarpanthis.

As a symbol of this religion in which idol worship was strictly prohibited (whether it is perceived as a principle of Hindu *nirgūṇ bhakti* or as a Muslim prescription), Shams would have brought a sacred foot-print stone. In the Islamic idiom it was considered a relic of Muhammad or Ali (*kadam sharīf, kadam rasūl*) found in Mecca, whereas in the Hindu context, it was supposed to be a foot-mark of

Alakh (the formless god of the Jogis) or Vishnu (the Nirgun Lord). The first place where this foot-print is said to have been installed was Junjala, a village located on the Merta road, at a distance of 40 km from Nagaur.

Then Pir Shams would have continued his trip to Jaitgarh, a village situated between Pisangan and Osiya, 60 km from Pushkar, where he enshrined a replica of the sacred foot-print. He proceeded to Karel, near Pushkar. As Ramdev's traditional worshippers still repeat in their songs:

> Junjala, Jaitgarh, original shrines, Karel,
> First the pilgrims go there and make their
> offerings in the cauldrons of the *dargāh*. . . .

As indicated in the *bhajan*, these places were originally a part of the pilgrimage to Ramdeora. Junjala is still visited by many Meghval devotees going to the *Bhādõ melā* of Runicha; Jaitgarh and Karel are centres of local fairs related to the Nizar Panth. In these three villages one finds temples referred to as *Alakhjī* or *Gusāīnjī kā Mandir*. The foot-print installed by Shams at Jaitgarh has somehow been lost (an interesting tradition has it that it was stolen and brought to Ajmer where it was enshrined in the famous *dargāh* of Muinuddīn Chishti). However, the *mahants* and priests of the shrine, who are Kamads by caste and designated Pandits, still remember the story of 'Samas Rishi'. In front of the newly built shrine which now shelters two *murtis* (a slab representing Ramdev as a horserider and another with 'Mataji', Durga killing the bufallo-demon, Mahisasuramardini), is an old mango tree. Legend has it that at this very spot the Pir once threw a mango stone which instantly grew into a full-sized tree. This demonstration of yogic or fakiric powers strikingly reminds us of the famous 'mango trick' performed by the Madari-caste magicians. Incidentally, as we will see, these Muslim jugglers claim to be the *murīds* of Pir Shams.

Karel, or rather the near-by hamlet called Manjhevla, has another similar temple but its sanctum still contains a foot-print stone enshrined in a recess which, here too, looks like a *mihrāb*. The sacred object is regularly bathed and offerings are brought to it once or twice a day. Another family of Kamad Pandits are the caretakers of the shrine. At Jaitgarh and Karel annual *melās* also take place on Asoj *bīj*.

The shrine of Junjala being the most important of the three and its history being of a great complexity, I have left its description for the last. Here lies the foot-print presumably brought by Shams. The priests are Nath Jogis but, like the custodians of the shrines at Jaitgarh and Karel, are traditionally referred to as *ek pāv ke pujārī* ('priests of one single foot').

A few comments on this curious appellation will be in order. In Rajasthan Meghvals and Kamads claim that their tradition was first strictly *nirgūṇ* and that image worship was prohibited, though the symbol of a single foot-print was used. After Ramdev it became *sāguṇ* and the single foot was replaced by a pair of feet engraved on a stone, an object currently offered at Ramdev's temples. This transformation within the transmission of the tradition is metaphorized in a devotional song: *pahlo pāv junjālo, dūjo devrā* . . . (the first foot at Junjala, the second at Ramdeora). My informants commented on this verse as follows: the formless god, Alakh, made the first step at Junjala, where he manifested himself as Gusainji; the second step was at Runicha-Ramdeora, where he became incarnated as Ramdev. Ultimately, both Gusainji and Ramdev were *avatārs* of the same god. It is tempting to interpret this as a metaphor of the transition from the original Muslim Nizari tradition acculturated in the subcontinent to the so-called 'Hindu Nizar Panth'.

It is difficult to imagine how the shrine of Junjala looked before Independence. Everyone agrees that the structure in its present form is new. However, like the temples of Jaitgarh and Karel, it has retained the rough shape of a Muslim *dargāh,* a detail which must not be given too much importance considering the fact that Hindu shrines, like palaces, have sometimes imitated the Islamic style of architecture. Of more relevance, however, is the main object of worship: it is a foot-print engraved on a rectangular stone of red colour (which reminds us of the famous *kadam rasūl* enshrined in the Jama Masjid in Delhi). By its side lie Ramdev's *pagliyā,* on a square stone. a picture representing the Pir of Runicha hanging behind it on the wall transforms the shrine into a temple of Ramdev. The wall of the *sanctum sanctorum* which takes a semi-circular shape, functions once more as a *mihrāb* facing Mecca.

The legends told by the present *pujārīs* who claim to be householder Naths (but have a low status in the eyes of higher caste people) reflect the ambiguities of a shrine which, despite recent efforts, cannot yet assume a 'perfect' Hindu identity. According to these the sacred foot is ascribed a double origin: it is at the same time the trace of Vishnu's foot during his famous incarnation as Vamana-Trivikrama, when he vanquished the *asura* Bali (Vettam Mani 1989:104) and a *kadam rasul*, a mark of the Prophet's (or Ali's) foot that Pir Shams would have brought from Arabia. These references to an Islamic heritage are still a part of the oral heritage, as testified by a famous *bhajan* of the nineteenth-century poet and disciple of Ramdev, Likhmoji Mali (J. Solanki:14):

dargāh mẽ pīr makkā mẽ allāh junjālā mẽ gusāīn
nāv dirāy dhokai ghaṇī dhamā kadmā rasūl kevāī. . . .

No longer understood by most Kamad and Meghval singers, these verses are still repeated mechanically. They may perhaps be translated as follows: 'a Pir in the *dargāh*, Allah at Mecca, Gusain at Junjala, this (shrine) has gained much fame as the pilgrimage place of the Prophet's sacred foot-print.' These words seem to be the last echoes of a slowly disintegrating heritage.

Attempting to correlate the two different stories of the origin of the sacred foot-print, which now appear as conflicting versions in the light of modern aspirations to a clear religious identity, the Nath *pujāris* declared that 'Vishnu, as Gusainji, had made the first step at Mecca, the second in Uttarkhand and finally a third stride at Junjala'. This parochialized version of the pan-Hindu myth of Trivikrama, tinged with Muslim folklore, appears once more as a limpid metaphor of the penetration of the Nizari *dawa* into the subcontinent; we almost see the personified mission, with its supreme leader the Imam, locally represented by Pirs, striding from the original Mecca where Ali had manifested himself to the mountains of Hindustan and then to a tiny village in Rajasthan.

Following Nanji (1978:51), Mallison (1991a:101 n.35) reminds us of an interesting fact: in the local Hindustani context the missionary Satgur Nur (whom I have identified with Gusainji) was understood to be the master of the three worlds (*tribhovara rāya*) by the Gujarati king Jayasimbha whom he is supposed to have converted. Mallison thinks the epithet may be a reference to Shiva as well as Vishnu in his Trivikrama *avatār*. The defication of Pirs, sometimes nearly equated with the Imam who was regarded as the supreme Pir and guru (*satguru*),[5] seems to be illustrated in the Junjala tradition where 'Gusainji' has come to refer to God, as Vishnu and Shiva, as well as to a particular human guru.

Considering the importance of the shrine connected with Shams

Pir's first halting place in Rajasthan,[6] I was surprised to see that it had not been listed as a main or subsidiary *gaddī* of the Nizar Panth. Instead, as I found out later, it was referred to as one of the four *chaukīs* (lit. posts) of the sect. Besides, Nath Jogis did not appear to be Pirs or *mahants*: they were simply the *pujārīs* of the temple. Subsequently I heard that, because of the above described ambiguity, the sacred complex of Junjala had been (at a time which I could not determine) the object of a communal conflict between Hindus and Muslims, both claiming the shrine as their legitimate heritage.

To start with, the Naths would not explain what the nature of their relationship to the shrine was. (I rather expected Meghval Pirs or Kamads to be its custodians, because of what I had observed for the other *gaddīs*.) But one day their secret was unveiled. The eldest among the Naths admitted that, four generations earlier, his ancestor had been born as the son of a Muslim fakir and of a *gṛhastha* (householder) Nath lady whom he had married against the will of his coreligionists. The couple had had another son who had remained within the Muslim community and become the Pir of some *dargāh*. This Muslim family had been, before the Naths, the custodians of the shrine of Junjala and the owners of the land attached to it.

It occurred to me that the mystery could not be completely elucidated without meeting these Muslim Pirs. Unfortunately, no Hindu devotee would reveal their existence; some of them denied that the shrine had ever had any connection with Islam, whereas others pretended not to understand the question. It was finally a Muslim Teli (oil-monger) who told me that the 'Sayyid Pirs' of Junjala (Sayyid, it may be recalled, designates a descendant of the Prophet's family) could be found in the nearby village of Kuchera.

It is there, 10 km from Junjala, on the Merta road, that I had my first encounter with the Sayyids. There I learned that the Pir's elder brother, who was more knowledgeable, resided in a distant town, at Fathepur in Shekhawati. A series of visits coupled with many painstaking inquiries at Kuchera, Fathepur and Jaipur, resulted in the disclosure of a multitude of new facts and details.

We have seen that the Pirs of all the *gaddīs* supposedly established by Shams, could trace their links with this Pir through a lineage of guru-disciples. Only the Naths of Junjala could not do so. In fact, the Sayyids of Kuchera-Fathepur were to be regarded as the legitimate custodians of the shrine of Junjala, as they claimed descent from Pir Shams himself. At some undertermined time, however, their authority was questioned by the traditional worshippers of Ramdev who, having chosen a Hindu identity, could no longer acknowledge Pirs who had assumed a Muslim one. After a long dispute, the details of which I was not able to reconstruct in a satisfactory way, the shrine was ceded to the Hindus.

The Sayyids said they had lost the *dargāh* in the following circumstances: as *gaddīnishīns* (holders of a *gaddī*) of this sacred shrine[7] they had entrusted its custody (cleaning of the buildings, washing of the *kadam rasūl,* etc.) to a family of householder Naths settled in the area. They did not specify the date nor explain why it had been necessary to resort to Hindu ritual specialists, when any of their numerous *murīds* could have easily performed the same task. The most logical explanation would be that, though 'reHinduized' like the Meghvals and the Kamads, these Jogis were traditional devotees of Pir Shams, related to some guru-disciple lineage of the Samsani. The case of intermarriage reported above probably testifies to a traditional link between the two communities, the Sayyids and the Naths, and, in my opinion, must not be regarded as a scandalous or unusual incident.

It is possible that, claiming descent from the Sayyid *gaddīnishīn* and adopting a Nath Hindu identity, one of the sons of this intercaste couple was prompted by the Meghvals, Regars, Kamads and other Hindu devotees of 'Samas' and Ramdev, to conduct the *pujā* according to their requirements, and, of course, claim the *gaddī* for himself, whereas his brother had to renounce it and remain within the fold of the Muslim community to which his father belonged. It seems also probable that during that period, the Hindu communities linked to the Nizar Panth became gradually aware of the benefits they could draw from a shrine whose popularity was increasing, as Ramdev's *samādhi*-temple at Runicha was acquiring an unprecedented fame. The Nath *pujārīs* say that the dispute was solved by the ruler of Jodhpur Raja Man Singh (1803-43) who would have entrusted the *sevā* to these Jogis. Till further inquiry can bring out more reliable historical data concerning this dispute, it cannot be proved that the incident happened during the first half of the nineteenth century, as the intermarriage reported above is said to have occurred more recently, at the beginning of our century. The connection with Man Singh is however interesting if we recall that the king of Marwar allowed the Nath Sampraday to gain considerable influence during his reign (see Chapter 2, note 9, Grodzins-Gold 1993:45 and P. Sharma 1972).

Be that as it may, the reality of the dispute cannot be questioned and from the perspective of an ancient Nizari *dawa* in Rajasthan, may be interpreted as follows. During the nineteenth century the emergence of clear-cut religious identities led to confrontations between groups which, though they had originally belonged to the same Nizari tradition, had subsisted in various guises or with a 'liminal identity' (Mayaram 1996) owing to the necessity of *taqīyya*. Anticipating the discussion proposed in Chapter 5, it may be suggested that, after having severed their links with the Persian Imam and his local representatives (the Pirs of Multan and Ucch, then the Kadivala Sayyids), they had gradually drifted away. We could also surmise that the final confrontation and reconstruction of their religious history (Hindus claiming that 'Samik Rishi' was a Brahman, Muslims that he was a Sunni or Twelver Shia fakir) was less a spontaneous process than the result of the activities of Hindu and Islamic fundamentalist organizations.

Like the Meghvals, Kamads and other 'Hindu Nizarpanthis', the alleged Rajasthani descendants of Pir Shams did not claim any connection with the Ismaili *dawa.* They introducted themselves as orthodox Sunnis. Shams was their ancestor, but he was, like them, affiliated to the Sufi Qadiriya *tarīqa* whose founder was Abdul Qadir Jilani (1077-1166) (Rizvi 1975, I:84-5).

According to these Sayyids, at a time which they could not specify (the events were said to have occurred in the fourteenth, the seventeenth or the eighteenth century), Shams Pir's Rajasthani lineage had been divided into three branches: three brothers had established their *gaddīs* respectively at Junjala, Fathepur and Kishangarh. Tajuddin who had settled at Junjala later went to Fathepur where he gave the boon of a son to the childless Kayamkhani ruler Alif Khan. He was buried there, like his brother and their descendants, in a small *dargāh* of Fathepur, the *Pīrjī kā Rauẓā.* The miracle could have occurred in the seventeeth century, as Alif Khan is said to have lived during the Mughal emperor Jahangir's rule. However, neither D. Sharma (1983:25) nor Mishra (1994:88-96) mention the event in their histories of the Kayamkhanis of Shekhawati.

At our request the Pir of Fathepur showed us a genealogy (*shajarā*) of their family. It is however full of contradictions. The names occur in a confused order and various *silsilas* are mixed; the number of generations between Tajuddin and the present Sayyid do not tally either. On the top of the chart is named their order, 'Naqshbandi-

Qadiriya', associating thus two separate *silsilas*, a phenomenon which reminds us of the fact that some Sufi Shaikhs were, at times, initiated into two different *tarīqas*. As for all the Sayyids, the lineage started with the Prophet Muhammad himself. Below the usual names of various Alids (descendants of Ali) is mentioned Abdul Qadir Jilani, founder of the Qadiriya order of Sufis. After a few generations appears, curiously enough, the name of Muhammad Nur Baqsh[8] the alleged founder of the Nurbaqshiya sect (Daftary 1990:462-3) which was first established in Persia, and later spread in Kashmir, with one other Shams as its leader (Nanjiani 1918:143-6, Nanji 1978:64). Still further, the Ismaili missionary is mentioned, rather unusually, as Shams al-Haq. I would have doubted that he is the same as the Nizari *dāī*, if the Sayyids had not spontaneously declared that their Pir and ancestor came from Multan where he had his shrine and that, though he was popularly known as 'Shams Tabrez', his real name was Shamsuddin Sabzwari, which is indeed the full name of the missionary recorded in the Ismaili tradition (Noorally 1973).

A comparison with the *shajarās* of some Imamshahi Sayyids as analysed by Ivanow (1938:25) might be useful. In studying the genealogy of a branch of the Pirana sect (see Chapter 1) Ivanow remarks:

> the sequence of names is completely confused, it is said that the Pirs of the line are the descendants of the Itna Ashariya Imam Ali Rida, while in the next fragment quite a different genealogy is given. Sadruddin [a Nizari Pir believed to be the great grandson of Shams] is confused with Satgur Nur of Nawsari etc. No dates, no history [occur]. . . the second fragment the just over two pages and contains the beginning of the genealogy of the line not from Ali Rida but from Imam Ismail whose name is however omitted, together with the name of his son and successor Muhammad (founder of the Ismaili branch of the Shias so named after his father). These perversions, as also those in the preceding fragment, show that these works were intended for the general public and that the author tried his best to dissociate himself and his ancestors from all connection with Ismailism, by suppressing some facts and names in the sectarian tradition, which were scarcely known outside the sect.[9]

Actually, the tradition of Junjala can be compared with the Imamshahi branch of Ismailism from many other points of view as both have undergone a similar evolution towards the rejection of their past religious heritage. For instance, in the Pirana Panth, the headmen of the converted Hindu community known as *kākās*, became custodians of the *dargāh* where the graves of Pir Imam Shah and his son Muhammad Shah are located. The reason why they clung to it is obvious: they do not wish to be deprived of the substantial benefits derived from the shrine (ibid.: 55, 65). None the less, the phenomenon of Hindu priests wearing ochre-coloured turbans, like the Naths of Junjala, and doing the *sevā* of a Muslim shrine, is worth analysing, and one can consider that, in this respect, the cases of Pirana and Junjala are not different. Living as Guptis (concealing their Ismaili affiliation in the guise of 'orthodox' Hindus) the *kākās* who were permitted to comply with the prescriptions of Hinduism, in conformity with the principle of *taqīyya*, eventually retained this Hindu identity without wishing to dissociate themselves with the Imamshahi Pirs. Their position is somewhat comparable to that of the present Nath *pujārīs* of Junjala vis a vis the Sayyids. Ivanow (ibid.: 60) explains that the phenomenon was typical of Ismailism: 'the Hindus converted to the Pirana faith remained (outwardly) Hindus and members of their corresponding castes'.

How did the Sayyids of Junjala come to be connected with Sunni Sufism? Here also, a comparison with the diferent branches of the Imamshahi sect will be helpful: some of them became Sunnis, other Twelver Shias. As far as the Sayyids of Rajasthan are concerned, one can surmise that, at a certain time they came under the influence of Sufis (mainly the Qadiriyas, but also the Naqshbandis) when these *tarīqas* became powerful and attempted to erase the Ismaili 'heresy'; the *gaddīnishīns* of Junjala were thus made Sunnis. In attempting to dissociate themselves from the sect of the Ismailis, but not with their illustrious ancestor who was one of its *dāīs*, they forged a new genealogy where the name of Shams, which could not be eliminated, was somehow made to coexist with that of the founder of the Qadiriya order of Sufis. Characteristically, the other *shajarā* which was shown to me at Kuchera differed from that of Fathepur in many details.

The Sayyids of Junjala claim to have numerous *murīds* belonging to different Sunni caste groups. When asked who among them revered Shams as 'their' Pir, they replied that the majority of them were Madari magicians (or Bazigars, Maslets), as distinct from the Madari wild animal tamers also referred to as Qalandaris (Siegel 1991). Pir Sayyid Hussein said that these Madaris were converted by Pir Shams himself and that was the reason why these people would take solemn oaths only on his name. According to Siegel (ibid.:32), the Madaris tell the story of their conversion to Islam in the following way. While they were on their way to the Ganges to take a holy bath, a Muslim fakir appeared who demonstrated his miraculous powers by causing the sacred river to flow in front of them. The name of the fakir is not mentioned. Significantly, my field research shows that the Sayyids of Junjala have a similar legendary tradition concerning the conversion of the Hindu Bhambis (Meghvals) by Pir Shams. The same legend is also reported in Imamshahi hagiography concerning Sayyid Imamshah and the Gujarati Kanbis (Enthoven 1990:150). Reverting to Pir Shams, the miracle of the Ganges was known equally to the Isna Ashari community of Rupangarh (Ajmer district). Although Muslims, the Julahas whose traditional occupation is weaving, have nearly the same low status as the Hindu Meghvals and are treated with contempt even by their coreligionists. When they tell the story of the conversion of the Hindu Bhambis by Shams one cannot help suspecting that they were themselves these Bhambis before conversion. Though they have come into the orbit of Twelver Shia Islam, they still worship Pir Shams as their true *murshid*, and will not take initiation with any other Pir.

In Ajmer and Rupangarh two separate communities of Nyariyas, the former being Sunni, the latter Isna Asharis, also narrated how Shams had converted the untouchables by causing the Ganges to flow in front of them so that they could bathe without having to travel a long distance. These Nyariyas trace their descent from various Multani communities (they have kept different caste names) among which the Sunars (goldsmiths) may have been the majority.[10] They still rever Pir Shams as their *murshid*, without acknowledging any connection with Ismailism.

It is remarkable that, whether affiliated to Shia or Sunni Islam, these communities have preserved the same legendary heritage and the same reverence for Shams. As was probably the case of the Sayyids of Junjala, the activity of Sufis and the religious leaders of the Isna Asharis must have been instrumental in absorbing them into Sunni or Twelver Shia Islam, without being able to dissociate them from their original Pir.

Owing to the fragmentation of the former Nizari community of Rajasthan the network of *gaddīs* had obviously been shattered. It was interesting to know how the Muslim Pirs, for instance, perceived the shrines which are now kept by Hindu Pirs. Did Sayyid Hussein know anything about Bichun? Was it also a sacred place connected with Pir Shams? Curiously enough the answer was given spontaneously by the Pir's son: 'Bichun is at present in the hands of Hindus . . . but for a long time it had been abandoned. There was a great confusion, as nobody knew if it was a Hindu or a Muslims shrine . . . certainly, this is an important place connected with Shams's *chillā*.'[11] The word *chillā* (M.I. Khan 1994:265), normally referring to a period of meditation of forty days in the Sufi tradition and to the place where it is performed, had, it appeared, another meaning. As everybody could not go to Multan to visit the shrine of Pir Shams (after Partition that became still more difficult), a commemorative structure called a *chillā* was installed at Bichun, as was sometimes done in private houses for the worship of any Muslim saint. These words immediately reminded me of the symbolical *samādhi*, which the Hindu Pir of Bichun had shown us in front the temple. It is not impossible that, before the *murti* of Ramdev was installed in the sanctum at a fairly recent date, its image had been such a *chillā mazār* in the Islamic style. In fact, the establishment of such *chillā* graves (a custom for which I could not find references elsewhere in the Islamic tradition except in Currie 1989:121) was described as follows. The pilgrim who went to the real tomb of the Pir (in our case the *dargāh* of Shams in Multan) took from there a few roses and a cloth (*chādar*) which had been offered to the *mazār*, together with a little earth. Having come back to his village he buried these three items in some clean place and erected over it a replica of a grave which was intended for regular worship. These *chillā dargāhs* evidently recall the famous shrines dedicated to the five Pirs (see previous chapter) and the custom among Ramdev's worshippers of installing a model of the *mazār* in a temple or in the courtyard of a house, for the cult.

Considering the perception of Bichun by the alleged descendants of Pir Shams in Rajasthan, it can be inferred that the evolution of this shrine shows striking similarities with that of Junjala, though no communal dispute has been reported. Once more, this phenomenon attests the imperative for clear-cut religious identities, emerging probably during the late nineenth and early twentieth centuries after the gradual drifting away of various groups who, formerly affiliated to Ismailism, had come under the influence of more powerful religious currents, both Hindu and Muslim.

While Sunni Sufis and Isna Ashari leaders apparently succeeded in absorbing Nizaris into their respective communities, the Ismaili converts who were subsisting under a Hindu Gupti identity could secretly preserve their tradition in adverse circumstances. This leads us to raise a fundamental question: how can one explain the fact that the Hindu Nizarpanthis were more successful than their ex-coreligionists who had adopted other forms of Islam in preserving a great part of this tradition?

The answer lies in the very nature of what is usually referred to as Hinduism and Islam. While the Ismaili form of Islam was extremely flexible in its acculturation programmes and methods, the numerous and complex socio-religious trends gathered under the label 'Hinduism' were themselves remarkable for their fluidity and capacity of absorbing various currents, whereas the Sunni or Isna Ashari forms of Islam tended to show a much greater doctrinal rigidity. The following conclusion may thus be suggested, before the discussion is resumed on a larger scale. Before certain forms of Hinduism became more and more inflexible in this century, a process which is still going on (as is demonstrated by the present dynamism of the Ramdev tradition), the Nizari groups who lived outwardly as Hindus found it easier than their ex-coreligionists who had become Sunnis, to preserve elements that did not comply with 'orthodox' Muslim models. Nothing was 'heretical' for Hindus who had always developed composite models of religious beliefs and practices.

Concerning the *gaddīs* occupied by Pirs of Shams' lineage (Samsani) one must mention two other important centres, Miyala and Bilara. Miyala is a village located in Mewar, between Bhim and Deogarh. Here lies the shrine of Ramdev's uncle, mentioned in the previous chapter. The interesting evolution of this *samādhi*-temple deserves our attention. The oldest elements seem to be the cloth-covered grave of Dhanraj Pir. Over it the *Rāmdevjī kā mandir* has recently been erected. The sacred complex also includes a *dhūṇī* and a *dharamśālā*. Whereas the Tanwar Rajputs who claim to be descendants of Ramdev's uncle own the shrine and its land, as *mahants* of the *gaddī*, the *sevā* of the *dhūṇī* is entrusted to a *nāgā* (celibate renouncer) Kamad. It might be of some interest to specify here that the *dhūṇī* holders of Miyala can be selected from any caste and become Kamads only after having been initiated into the order by the previous Kamad of the shrine. In other words, they form a group which should be distinguished from the householder Kamads who form the majority and constitute an endogamic sub-caste.

Among the four Kamads of Miyala whose graves are located just outside the shrine, three were from the Meghval community and one was a Mali (gardener). The *dharamśālā* has been built by the local Mer (Rawat) community among whom many traditional worshippers of Ramdev are to be found, but the temple itself has been erected with funds from the Jain community settled in a few nearby villages. As a testimony to this fact the donors caused a small figure of a sitting *tirthankara* to be carved inside a recess above the gate. The people of this community also regularly visit the shrine, as do members of other castes. They belong to the Oswal group said to have originated from Osiya (K.C. Jain 1990:180-4). Legend has it that, converted from the Hindu Shakti Panth to Jainism, they fled from the town to avoid the wrath of the local goddess Sachiya Mata. Deprived of her alcohol and meat offerings once her devotees had become vegetarians, she swore to exterminate them if they stayed overnight in the village. But how did the Oswal Jains come to be linked with the Nizar Panth and its local Pir Dhanraj? In Nanjiani's *Khojā Vṛttant* (1918:137) it is written that Ramdev Pir had won disciples among the Oswals. In this respect we may note that to this day many Jains flock to the shrine of Ramdeora during the annual *melā*. It is therefore possible that this group had, at one time, been formally converted to Ismailism, retaining, as a precautionary dissimulation (*taqīyya*) their Jain identity which they subsequently fully reassumed after having severed their links with the Imam.

Besides Oswal Jains, Meghvals and Malis, the major disciples of Dhanraj Pir and his successors seem to be the Mers and the Bhils. As stated earlier, Ramdev's uncle had made many disciples among the Bhils who reside to this day in the Aravalli hills where they have estalished their *dhūṇīs*, held by religious specialists called Kamads or Kamadiya Jogis. Further inquiry among the Mers, who share with the Meos of Mewat many similar traits, among them a 'liminal' religious identity,[12] the former being now Hindus or Muslims and the latter only Muslims, would probably reveal another segment of the fragmented Nizari community which, together with some common elements (e.g. reverence for Dhanraj and Ramdev) has preserved a separate tradition regarded as the religious heritage of the caste. Like the Meghvals, the Hindu Mers worship their own Pirs.[13] Jaitgarh, one of the places where according to the legend a sacred *kadam rasūl* brought by Shams was earlier kept, is inhabited entirely by Mers, except for a Bhil and a Kamad Pandit family, the latter in charge of the shrine.

As for Bilara, like Junjala, with which it seems to share a number of pecularities, it is not usually mentioned as a *gaddī* of the Samsani lineages; but this important centre of pilgrimage is clearly related to Pir Shams disciples in Rajasthan. A number of *bhajans* attest that it is a sacred place also for Ramdev's traditional worshippers. In a *vāṇī* ascribed to Ramdev Pir, where the ultimate triumph of the new religion (the Nizari faith) is couched in symbolic terms, as the wedding of God, *Nikalank avatār*, with the pariah virgin Meghri,[14] one reads (Gokuldas 1982:143):

chittoṛ chanverī delhī derā
ābū toraṇ bhānīje
bīlaṛa mẽ ferā firsì

which can be translated as:

The wedding altar will be in Chittor, the bridegroom's party will establish its camp at Delhi, the nuptial arch will be hung at Abu, the sacred fire circumambulations will be performed at Bilara.

The ritual of this cosmic wedding will extend, as presumably the Nizari *dawa* hoped, between the capital of the sultanate ruled by the Sunnis, the main city of Mewar connected with Dhanraj Pir and Maharana Kumbha, Mount Abu (an old Hindu and Jain sacred mountain, once a part of Kumbha's kingdom) and Bilara, a city near Jodhpur.

The 'Kamads of Ramdev' residing in the villages located in this particular area, according to what I have learned during my field work, go to the shrine of Bilara to receive the customary *pagṛī* (turban) and *chādar* (shawl) at the time of their investiture, implying that they are under the authority of this *gaddī*. The shrine, perceived as a *dargāh* and a temple of the goddess, is however the main seat of a different sectarian movement. At Bilara, therefore, one can observe another type of fragmentation of the former Nizari community. At Junjala it had been split into two groups assuming respectively a Hindu and a Muslim identity; here the original tradition seems to have been divided into two different sects, both assuming a Hindu exterior: the Nizar Panth connected with Ramdev, Dhanraj, etc., and the Ai Panth related to Ai Mata, led by a religious figure known as the Diwan. The latter is an important sect and will be described in more detail in Chapter 6. For the moment, suffice it to say that its founder, Ai Mata, is believed to have been a disciple of Pir Shams.

MALLANI: THE DISCIPLES OF MALLINATH

The other *gaddīs* mentioned by Ramdev's traditional devotees must be briefly examined. If it could be adequately reconstructed, the history of the *gaddī* of Mallani would certainly reveal many missing links in the developmental sequence of the tradition. I hope one day to be able to complete my enquiries in the region extending from Jasol and Barmer into Kacch (Gujarat) where the legends and songs connected with Mallinath Rathore have been preserved.[15]

The legend of Mallinath and Rupande having already been sketched in the previous chapter, the discussion will now focus on other specificities of the tradition that show a remarkable tendency to embed itself within particular caste groups. Here it has been split into two major segments. The shrine of Mallinath, commemorating the ruler of the Mallani kingdom, is clearly a high-caste or Rajput place and as such is visited today by all the devotees of Ramdev and Mallinath, regardless of status. Its annual *melā*, which takes place from the eleventh day of the dark half of Chaitra (March-April) to the eleventh day of its bright fortnight, has become one of the famous cattle-fairs of Rajasthan. Though the Nath Jogis and higher-caste groups attempt to refer to the temple as the only sacred place associated with Mallinath (thus, from the point of view of the Nizar Panth, as the main seat of Mallani), the fact is that the *gaddī* is now represented by two separate centres.

If the higher castes recognize only the temple dedicated to the Rathore ruler, the Meghval community, joined by the Bhils, the Regars and other low caste groups, have gathered under the banner of another saint, Megh Dharu. He can be said to belong to the Mallani tradition, in the broad, regional sense of the word, in so far as he was (like Mallinath and Rupande) the disciple of Ugam Si Bhatti. According to one of our informants, all traces of Dharu's *samādhi* have been lost (which curiously enough is also the case for Mallinath's grave). Recently, probably in the fifties, the Meghval community who was in search of its own forgotten religious heritage, decided to establish another shrine near Mewa Nagar (Mahuwa), former capital of the Mallani rulers. The sacred complex, of a very modest size and appearance, includes the reconstructed *samādhi* of

Megh Dharu (which I could not see as it was locked) and, in the same enclosure, a rather inconspicuous building referred to as a 'temple of Shiva'. In fact it was a naked cube of masonry enshrining a *lingam* installed on top of a small platform. Just in front of it, one could see the *samādhi* of the previous (and probably first) *mahant*, a celibate Nath, a *chhatrī* sheltering a *shiva-lingam*, the usual funeral monument of these Shaiva ascetics. The present *mahant* was also a Jogi who originally belonged to the Meghval community; his disciple and successor also seemed to be a Meghval. I could not get much out of the frightened Nath who, in any case, seemed to know very little about Dharu and his tradition. He explained that in the village religious night sessions (*jamās*) regularly took place during which mostly Meghvals and Bhils, playing the traditional *tandurā*, sang *bhajans* related to Dharu, Mallinath-Rupande, Ramdev and others.

A few comments have already been made about these devotional compositions and a particular author named Qutbuddin, also found in the Khoja tradition, has been mentioned. Unfortunately practically nothing is known about Ugam Singh Bhatti, Mallinath's and Dharu's guru; according to some sources (Campbell 1988:544) he came from Benares. Another interesting fact is that a legendary tradition of the Meghvals connects Megh Dharu with Jambha, the founder of the Bishnoi sect which will be introduced in Chapter 7.

Before further inquiry into the Mallani tradition, it may be temporarily concluded that little seems to have been preserved of its past heritage and that, in comparison with the Ramdev movement, it is characterized by a more advanced stage of 'Rajputization' accounting for the fact that Mallinath, as a Kshatriya hero-saint, has completely overshadowed Dharu, Ugam Si, Qutbuddin and other religious figures related to this lineage. However, owing to its geographical position and its proximity to Sind, the region of Mallani which might also have corresponded to a specific diocese or *jāzir*, has probably been an important centre of the *dawa* of Rajasthan.

RAMDEVANI: THE DISCIPLES OF RAMDEV

As its name indicates, this *gaddī* has been established by Ramdev Pir and its central seat is located at Runicha. The shrine and its various legendary traditions, having been described in the previous chapter, we will limit ourselves to a brief comment. As for the Samsani (but not the Mallani), this *gaddī* does not refer to a diocese but to various lineages of guru-disciples beginning with Ramdev and located in different areas, from the region of Pokaran to the Aravalli hills. A shrine apparently affiliated to the *gaddī* of Ramdevani is the sacred complex of Jergaji situated in the mountains near Gogunda. It is dedicated to a famous devotee of Ramdev Pir, an untouchable Gurra of the Sahni clan, who is believed to have been the horse-groom of the Pir of Runicha. According to one tradition originally the name of the place was not 'Jergaji' (which is supposed to be the name of the devotee) but Dargahji alluding to the fact that it was formerly a Muslim shrine (*dargāh*). During the annual *melā* Meghvals, Regars and Bhils flock to the newly built temple.

HARCHANDANI: THE DISCIPLES OF HARCHAND

The main seat of this *gaddī* is located in the Aravalli mountains, at Dhalop, not far from the famous Jain temples of Ranakpur (near Ghanerao). A systematic inquiry might shed more light on its still confused history. Gokuldas (1982:187-8) says it was founded in the seventeenth century by a disciple of Khivan's lineage, a Kamad named Harchand. If this is true, it would like the Ramdevani be a sub-*gaddī* of the Samsani. One of Harchand's successors, a certain Raghunath Pir, became so famous for his miracles that he overshadowed the founder of the *gaddī*. The local Meghval community responsible for repairing and enlarging the shrine established at this place a kind of *maṭh* referred to as *Raghunāth Pīr kā āśram*. An annual *melā* also takes place at Dhalop. The Pirs of this *gaddī* appear to have always been Meghvals, and they have been both householders and renouncers. Most Kamads of the surrounding villages admit that they are under the authority of the Harchandani.

The *āśram*, which is the rallying centre of the community, is a vast compound enclosed by a wall and sheltering different structures. Besides a small temple dedicated to the Pir of Runicha (recent and unpretentious as it is, it testifies to a gradual transformation of the tradition into a Ramdev cult), and the various buildings serving as kitchen, resting place for the Pir and for special guests, the main part of the shrine is located within a smaller enclosure. It contains two structures, the grave (*mazār*) of Harchand protected, together with a *shiva lingam*, under a large stone canopy, and a separate building containing the tombstone of Raghunath Pir. This structure possesses a recess facing west in which Ramdev's *pagliyās*, tiny metal horses and *murtis*, have been installed in the usual attempt to transform the *mihrāb* into a *garbhagṛha* and the *dargāh* into a temple. Incidentally, this shrine is related to the sacred complex of Jergaji mentioned earlier.

Both Harchand and Raghunath's graves regularly receive offerings of coloured clothes (*chādars*), as do the Sufi Pirs. In the courtyard, behind this shrine, one can see the graves (*samādhis*) of the different Pirs who succeeded Raghunath on the *gaddī* of Dhalop. As in the case of Ramdeora, they illustrate the evolution of the tradition towards a 'normative' form of Hinduism. Full-sized graves in the Islamic style were no longer erected after Raghunath Pir (or were not preserved). There are small replicas of *mazārs* under the stone canopy of a classical square *chhatrī*, which results in a curious if typical association of Hindu and Muslim elements. The same structure, it may be recalled, has been observed at Runicha. The last grave represents a further step towards 'normalization', or reHinduization: like many Hindu ascetics and saints the predecessor of the present Pir has only a square *chabūtrā* embellished with a pair of feet in relief. The *mahant* of Raghunath Pir's *maṭh* solemnly sits in front of a *dhūṇī* near which a pair of *chimtās* (iron tongs) and a trident have been placed, which makes him look like any 'ordinary' Shaiva ascetic.

We conclude by mentioning that in the Meghval and Kamad tradition, frequent references are made to the existence of other types of *gaddīs*. These are perceived as being originally of the same tradition (the Nizar Panth) from which they would have separated. For example there is Jalani, which I first mistook for a corrupted variant of Mallani, as I had heard some Kamads related to a local Aghori *math* claim that as the name of their *gaddī*, (Samsani, being derived from the word *samsān* meaning 'cremation ground')! This *gaddī* is said to have been founded by a certain Jalansi Pir whose main disciples would have been the Regars, a group of leather-workers who also form a major part of Ramdev's worshippers.[16] A systematic enquiry among these people may shed more light on this *gaddī*, about which not much more can be said at present.

Nāthānī, 'disciples of the Naths' referred, according to our informants, to the centres where Nath Jogis acted as *mahants* (Pirs) but had been initiated and initiated others into the Nizar Panth. The interesting issue of the coalescence between the Nizar Panth and the Nath Sampradāy will be discussed in Chapter 9.

Eventually, Ramdev's traditional worshippers, especially Meghvals and Kamads, acknowledge the fact that 'Jambha Pir', the Panwar Rajput saint born at Pipasar near Bikaner and buried at Mukam (same region) who was a younger contemporary of the Pir of Runicha, founded a sect known as Bishnoi Panth or Prahlad Panth which they consider to be a detached branch of the Nizar Panth. Eventually as illustrated by legend it became a rival movement. Jambha, who is integrated in the legendary heritage of Meghval devotees of Ramdev, has what might be called a *chillā samādhi* inside the sacred complex of Runicha; this is supposed to be one of the *mazārs* situated in the row of graves located just behind Ramdev's *samādhi*.

To conclude, a word on the financial organization of these *gaddīs*. Nowadays they function separately, each shrine deriving benefits from its land and from the offerings of devotees, disciples and villagers belonging to the Nizar Panth, wherever they acknowledge the authority of the Pirs. It can be inferred from various sources that what must have once sustained this now disintegrating network of *gaddīs* was probably a system of tithes similar to the *dassondh* and other taxes prevalent in the Ismaili Nizari tradition. Collected from each member of the community, it was presumably forwarded to the Pirs who in turn would given it to the main *dāī* of Ucch-Multan who entrusted it to the Imam in Persia.[17] We will see that if very few traces of the *dassondh* system have been preserved in the Nizarpanthi tradition, its existence can easily be attested in other related sects, such as those connected with Ai Mata, Jambha and Jasnath.

NOTES

1. According to the Pir of Bichun, Hari Singh, Hindu king of Junagarh (Gujarat), also became a disciple of 'Samas Rishi'.
2. According to Z. Moir (personal communication) it is not certain that Satgur Nur belongs to an earlier date than Shams; both might even have been contemporaries. In the tradition of the Nizarpanthis of Rajasthan, and, it seems in the Khoja Gujarati sources, Satgur Nur (if my hypothesis that he must be identified with Gusainji is right) is supposed to have preceded Shams; one of our Kamadiya informants told us that Gusainji spread his message exclusively among the Hindus, especially among the untouchables whom gurus associated with higher castes refused to initiate, whereas Shams had both Muslim and Hindu disciples. This statement corresponds to what has been said of both Pirs in the Khoja tradition: 'One item of interest in the case of Pir Shams is that he is represented as working within both Muslim and Hindu groups as contrasted with the accounts of Satgur Nur whose activities were directed only at Hindus' (Nanji 1978:66).

3. As already said in the previous chapter the descendants of Ramdev apparently levied a tax on the Meghvals in Gujarat and Rajasthan. According to Enthoven (1990, III:50): 'these descendants of Ramdev had a certain poll-tax, a kind of slavery tax, on the Meghvals, but of late they get through the State a fourth part of the income which accumulates through fines, etc., from the Meghval caste instead'. In my opinion the author's interpretation is erroneous: the *Ramdev pautras* acted as Pirs and the taxes they levied on the Meghvals, as their major disciples, was actually a vestige of the *dassondh* system.
4. In a *ginān* ascribed to Pir Shams (Ivanow 1948:99), the boy who was brought to life by him becomes his disciple and follows him after the Pir has left Ucch.
5. As Shackle and Moir (1992:6) have it, 'These Pirs are depicted as personages with spiritual powers of an exaggerated nature, and overshadow the Imams living in obscurity in the distant land of Iran.' Also (ibid.:22) 'it is indeed in many contexts not always possible fully to distinguish the Pir from the Imam, who are often merged in such doublets as the "Guide and Lord" (skt. *gur-nar*) or "Lord and guide" (Persian *pīr śāhā*)'.
6. According to Z. Moir (personal communication), 'there are various places along the Indus way where Shams *derās* (*astān,* stopping places) are found'.
7. The Sayyids of Junjala claim that the Mughal emperor Alamgir (Aurangzeb) presented them with a *farmān* confirming that they were the legitimate custodians of the *kadam rasūl dargāh* of Junjala.
8. Interestingly enough, we learn from Nanji (1978:64) that

   'Another layer of confusion was added in the modern sources by seeking to relate Pir Shams to the leaders of the Nurbakhshiya sect in Kashmir. The beliefs of the Nurbakhshiya Order were introduced into Kashmir by one Shams al-Din who eventually became the representative of Shah Qasim, the son of Sayyid Muhammed Nurbaksh. Shams al-Din started his work in Kashmir in 1502. Since Pir Shams according to the Tradition is said to have travelled through Tibet and Kashmir before coming to India, it appears that an attempt was made to identify the two sets of names, particularly in view of the "Mahdawi" beliefs that the Nurbakshiya are alleged to have held in Kashmir.'
9. Another example is the Imamshahi branch of Burhanpur; one of its seventeenth-century leaders and saints, Muhammad Shahi Dula, is said to be a Sunni. As Ivanow explains (1938:52), concerning a book on this lineage of Pirs

   'As it was rather awkard to include the name of an Ismaili saint in a book devoted to notes concerning the most orthodox saints of the ancient city, he (the author) made him a Sunnite also. *Taqiyya* is often practised by sectarians; but the present *sajjadanishin* and his family really are Sunnites, there is no doubt about this.'

   The same could be said of the Sayyids of Junjala who have really become Sunnis.
10. The Nyariyas have different professions but one of their traditional occupations consists in separating 'the precious metal from the refuse of the working of the Sunars. They were employed in melting gold and silver ornaments' (Gehlot and Banshi Dhar 1989:264). In D.S. Khan (1995:310), I have expressed the opinion that the word *Nyāriyā* is a corrupt form of the original *Nizāriyâ* (Nizari)

which referred to religious affiliation rather than to occupations which were of various types; some Nyariyas, as I was told, were traditionally *kasāīs* (butchers).

11. I am grateful to Z. Moir for having accompanied me to Fathepur and helped me in my field inquiries. Her deep knowledge of the Islamic tradition, and in particular of Ismailism, enabled her to ask different questions which triggered new types of answers so that she could also interpret in an interesting way, making up for my lack of competence in Islamic studies.
12. On the Meos, see Mayaram (1996). She has tackled in an interesting way the issue of what she calls the 'liminal identity' of some groups which had to face up to pressure from fundamentalist bodies of both religions.
13. Gunarthi (1987:187) mentions one Pir Harraj who would have ruled at Bednore (Mewar). Further inquiry would show if he was in some way connected with Dhanraj.
14. This important theme will be discussed in the next chapter, where it will be compared to a *ginānic* motif.
15. Many of these devotional hymns have been collected in Kshir Sagar (forthcoming).
16. The Regars or Raidasis generally claim to be the disciples of the fifteenth-century Sant Raidas (Ravidas, Rohitdas). Neither his legendary tradition nor the devotional songs attributed to him display any kind of Muslim influence. It seems that many Regars had become Nizarpanthis under the influence of Ramdev or other earlier Ismaili Pirs. At a later date it seems that Raidas' popularity overhadowed Ramdev's fame among the Regars, a reason which might have prompted them to claim that the untouchable Sant was also a Nizarpanthi, a claim which does not hold good but probably reflects the aspirations of untouchables to a broad religious heritage.
17. For the *dassondh*, see Enthoven (1990, II:228). I am grateful to Mumtaz Ali Tajddin who supplied me with detailed information about the Ismaili tithe. I quote here but a short extract of his letter:

    'In past times, it was difficult to remit the funds of *dasond* to the Imam, living in Iran. Therefore, Pir Shams had authorized persons (each called *musafir* "traveller") to collect the funds in different villages. The *musafirs* hence collected and deposited them at the central treasury at Multan, and thence the whole fund was remitted at an appropriate time to Iran. It may be noted that during the Indian *dawa* period, the dasond collected from each person was 12.50 per cent, 10 per cent of which was separated for the Imam, and the rest (2.50 per cent being the zakat) was retained by the Pirs as per the instructions of the Imam. With the income of 2.50 per cent, the Ismaili Pirs could sustain their lives.'

    Mumtaz Ali explains the difference between the *dassondh* proper (tithe, ten per cent of the monthly income). The *zakat*, paid as charity by all Muslims and the *ushr* (also a tithe) levied upon the Muslims as a land revenue. The above-mentioned three taxes were prevalent among the Ismailis.

CHAPTER 4

Hymns and Rituals: A Comparative Study of the Nizarpanthi and Khoja Religious Literatures and Ceremonies

RITUALS

To prove that the secret tradition centred around the worship of Ramdev Pir is connected with the Nizari *dawa* in one way or another a number of common elements in the legends, and observations regarding shrines and *gaddīs,* have been brought out in previous chapters. If our hypothesis has substance, similar elements should be found in the devotional literature and the religious ceremonies of the studied communities.

The similarities which exist between the rituals of the Imamshahi sect (a 'dissident' branch of the Nizaris) and those of the Nizar Panth have already been examined by a Gujarati author (Rajyaguru n.d.) who, however, comes to the opposite conclusion from ours. He infers that the allegedly Hindu sect propagated by Ramdev Pir has influenced the tradition of the Khojas. Before demonstrating that this assumption is baseless, and clearly biased, we will have to describe and analyse the main elements that led me to examine the characteristic features of certain rites connected with Ramdev's sect (D.S. Khan 1994 and 1996).

To begin, we stress the fact that even though the modern cult of Ramdev is characterized by image worship and by a simplified form of *pujā* (Binford 1972:130-1), the traditional worshippers of the Pir of Runicha admit that their gurus, Ramdev, and his predecessors 'Gusainji' and 'Samas Rishi' had strictly prohibited idol worship (Pemaram 1977:54). In a chapter of his book on the Hindu Nizar Panth, Gohil (1987:39) states that the Nizarpanthis originally worshipped the formless God without the help of any image, whereas after Ramdev this *nirgūṇ* tradition took a *sāguṇ* turn.

Field work among the traditional devotees and priests of Ramdev and among untouchable Meghvals and Kamads, revealed that the traditional religious ceremony connected with their *panth* did not include image worship; it was, as has been mentioned earlier, a sacred vigil referred to as *jamā*. Although this type of night session might call to mind vigils like *jāgraṇs* and *rāti-jagās*,[1] it differs from them in a number of specific traits. Actually, the description of a traditional *jamā* for Ramdev is not an easy task, owing to various recent accretions and modifications, as well as the emergence of modern variants in which pan-Hindu features are prevalent.

For the traditional followers of Ramdev Pir, especially for Meghvals and Kamads, the *jamā-jāgraṇ*, as it is currently termed constitutes the sole authentic cult of the Nizar Panth. It is perceived by them as the worship of the formless, non-qualified (*nirgūṇ*, *niranjan*) God (Gokuldas 1982:97-9). The public and open form of *jamā*, as it is organized nowadays for all devotees of Ramdev, including the higher caste groups who have recently joined the cult, begins in the evening and ends at dawn (it can be organized any day, though the second day of the bright half of the month and Fridays are considered particularly auspicious). Characteristic elements are as follows:

- First there is a *pāṭh* or wooden plank symbolizing the royal throne (*gaddī*), here the seat of the invisible God (Alakh)—as image worship in the form of an anthropomorphic or zoomorphic *murti*, is forbidden.[2] This plank is covered by two cloths, a red one above which symbolizes the *śakti* (or manifested female energy of the Absolute), and a white cloth below, said to represent the formless God. All these elements, it may be specified, seem to derive from the tradition of the Nath Jogis. Various patterns are drawn on the *pāṭh* with raw paddy grains and/or mungo beans, an operation which is referred to as *pāṭh pūrnā* (lit. to fill up the throne). Among these drawings can be seen a variety of common indigenous symbols such as the sun, the moon, the *svastika*, '*Om*', and so on. Moreover, symbols which are particular to the Ramdev tradition are frequently used: a pair of foot-prints (*pagliyās*, a common aniconic symbol of Ramdev), a riderless horse and flag (or rather banner on top of a spear, *nejā*), as well as Ramdev's grave in the form of a Muslim *mazār*. This last element tends to be omitted in recent practice.

> Then there is a *kalaś* or earthen jar filled with water, decorated with green leaves and topped by a coconut encircled by a red and white cotton thread (*molī*).

We may note here that the combined use of wooden plank and earthen pot is typical of certain forms of worship of the Goddess in some folk cults (Enthoven 1989:49) and during the Durgā Pūjā (Kinsley 1987:111). Besides, thrones and jars have long been symbols of the Divine in various indigenous traditions and practices.

Informants stated that the *kalaś* was the symbol of *śakti*, whereas the coconut, functioning as the *Śiva lingam* on top of a *yoni* (the Godess's womb) was meant to represent Alakh, the god of Shaiva ascetics.

The *jyot* (light), another important object of worship during the *jamā*, was represented by a clay lamp fed with clarified butter (*ghī*). This lamp stood for the eternal (*akhaṇḍ*) light (*jyoti*) of Alakh, a concept also expressed by the Arabic term *nūr* in some devotional hymns (Gokuldas 1982:98). The installation of these objects is accompanied by the chanting of various *mantras*, each one supposed to correspond to a particular phase of the *pūjā* (for example, the *kalaś mantra* is used when installing the water pot).

The central part of the ceremony consists however in a kind of *satsang* (here, the singing of devotional compositions) in which all present take part. One or more Kamadiyas devoted to Ramdev (in some cases replaced by Meghwals, gurus of other castes, Naths or Dasnamis) accompany these songs on the traditional five-stringed *tandurā*, now often discarded in favour of the harmonium, an instrument of 'higher status' which, despite its foreign origin, has become very popular with devotional circles and folk musicians. Two ritual specialists are supposed to lead the ceremony: the Kamadiya (also called Kamad or Kambariya) who is generally a householder belonging to the caste bearing this name, but sometimes an ascetic from any community initiated into the order of Kamadiyas (D.S. Khan 1995 and 1996), and the Kotval (custodian).

THE *JAMĀ* AND ITS VARIANTS

Owing to the recent popularity of the Ramdev cult in wider circles of devotees who are not traditionally linked with the Nizar Panth, a number of changes have taken place within the public form of the *jama-jagraṇ*. For instance, any devotee who is familiar with the basic ritual may conduct one of these sessions. In this case the *mazār* motif drawn on the *pāṭh* will be generally omitted and a poster representing Ramdev as a horserider will be sometimes installed; though it goes against the prohibition of image worship, it testifies to the evolution of the sect.

According to a still prevalent tradition no *jamā* may be organized without inviting at least one Rikh (Rajasthani for *ṛṣi*), whereas in other cases their minimum number is said to be four. The Meghval followers of Ramdev claim that the title is applicable to their caste as a whole, as they consider themselves to be the direct descendants of one Megh Rishi (Bhanawat 1963:183). However, according to some of our informants (mainly the Kamadiyas) the term *ṛṣi* (*rikh, rikhi,* etc.) did not refer exclusively to the Bhambis-Meghvals, but to all those who were initiated into the *panth,* regardless of caste. This was confirmed by the fact that a number of traditional devotees of Ramdev affixed this title to their name after initiation. It is probable that, at least in certain areas, the Meghvals being the majority of adherents of this sect, they have attempted to claim this title as an exclusive mark of their community in the same way as they have tried to appropriate the heritage of the Nizar Panth.

Two other forms of sacred vigils practised among the Nizarpanthis may now be described. Before doing so, however, attention may be drawn to a few elements which seem to be analagous in the Nizarpanthi and Khoja traditions. The word *jamā* (Rajasthani *jamo*) derives from the Arabic *jamā'at* or congregation of the faithful in Islamic tradition. As has already been noted, the Nizaris of the subcontinent do not say their prayers in a mosque (or at home) by placing themselves in the direction of Mecca but gather in a special place known as *jamāt khāna,* whether it be a separate building or a secluded room in some private house (Hollister 1976:384-9). For the Khojas, the most auspicious dates fall on the New Moon and on the night following it, referred to as *bīj* (second day here of the bright half of a Hindu month, corresponding to the beginning of a month in the Islamic calendar). The two leading figures of the ceremony are the Mukhi (leader, lit. 'main person') and his assistant the Kamadiya.[3] During the ritual an earthen pot (*kalaś, ghaṭ*) filled with water and a low wooden table or *pāṭh* are used (Ivanow 1918:36-9, Nanji 1982:105-8).

The two forms of secret *jamā-jāgraṇs* practised by Meghvals, Regars, Kamads and other disciples of the Nizar Panth, regardless of their caste or other openly admitted sectarian affiliation, can be perceived as Tantric rituals (Ivanow 1948:36-9). Both are referred to as *kuṇḍā panth*. Its allegedly 'complete form' which is more secretive and does not seen to be approved by all the leaders of the Nizar Panth, is called *bīsā panth* (lit. sect 'twenty') and its milder form *dasā panth* (sect 'ten'). This latter ceremony is regarded as one of the central events in the life of the Nizarpanthis and accepted by all members of the sect. (D.S. Khan 1994:443-62).

As described by my informants, the *bīsā panth* is clearly a local variant of the well-known 'left-handed' Shaktic-Tantric ritual referred to in specialized literature as *kaul mārg* or *vām mārg* during which the *panch makārs* (five substances starting with the letter *m*) are partaken: meat (*māms*), fish (*matsya*), wine (*madya*), grain (*mudrā*) and the product of ritual copulation (*mithun*). In this type of ceremony men and women must be in equal numbers (Briggs 1989:171-5), Bhattacharyya 1987:121-3, Bhanawat 1986:32-7). This ritual has also been referred to as *cholī mārg* or *kanchlī mārg*, as each sexual partner is selected at random by picking up, out of an earthen vessel, the *cholīs* or *kanchlīs* (bodices) of the female participants (Bhanawat 1986:32, Nanjiani 1918:22-9). According to my informants, it is *mithun*, one of the five *makārs*, which supplies the main offering to the deity (here supposed to be the Tantric Goddess revered by the Nath Jogis, Hinglaj Mata). After the ritual copulation each woman must collect in the palm of her hand the semen virile of her partner, which she deposits into a round flat earthen vessel called *kuṇḍā*. At the end of the ceremony all the sperm is mixed with *churmā* (a traditional food offering made of millet, *ghī* and sugar) and partaken as *prasād* by all the members of the sect. It is named *pāyal*.

Before proceeding it might be worth nothing that in popular belief, the word *nizārī* and its variants *nijārī* and *nejārī* have come to be regarded as synonyms of *vāmmārgī* rituals; the sect connected with Ramdev is believed by some to be connected with left-handed Tantrism (Carstairs: 67). In contradistinction to this, the people of the Nizar Panth claim that the term *nizārī* alludes to chastity and sexual abstinence and that the rituals of the *bīsā panth* are not connected with their sect (S.S. Pareek, personal communication and Gohil 1987:29). One of my Meghval informants explained that these Tantric practices had nothing to do with Ramdev, but that his followers, particularly among the untouchables, had not been able to discontinue them; in his eyes this was a token of their ignorance and backwardness. Another informant, belonging to the Kamad community, did not deny the value of the *vāmmārgī* rituals which according to him, could help the initiated to obtain supernatural powers (*siddhīs*); however he simultaneously stressed that the real purpose of the *Panth* (and the true meaning of the word *nizārī*) was to overcome one's instincts and become pure in order to obtain salvation.

Actually the association of Tantric elements with the Nizari Ismaili rituals is an interesting and complex issue. My hypothesis is that by borrowing certain elements from the Shaktic rituals the Ismaili Pirs resorted to their usual methods: they accepted a part of the religious heritage of the people to be converted and by transforming it, led them onto the new path. On the other hand, it is quite possible, as stated by my Meghval informant, that despite their efforts, the older *vāmmārgī* rituals have either continued or resumed under the influence of other religious teachers such as the Nath Jogis. Moreover, the secretive character of the Nizarpanthi ceremonies may account for the fact that, in the opinion of the non-initiated, they were related to Tantrism, which was a familiar model of secret religious gatherings.

Let us now come to the first ritual referred to as *dasā panth*. Despite its present interpretation, in a Hindu Tantric context, as an incomplete, 'milder' form of the *kuṇḍa panth*, it seems to be more directly related to the former Ismaili affiliation of Ramdev's worshippers. If the *bīsā panth* ritual can be performed at any time of the year (the most auspicious date falling on Shivaratri, a festival in honour of Shiva) (Bhanawat 1986:33), in Rajasthan at least the *dasā panth* is organized only on the twelfth (in some cases the third) day following the death of any member of the sect. As for the *bīsā panth*, initiation is required to take part in this religious ceremony, and it is regarded as compulsory among the Nizarpanthi communities. Thus, those who have not been initiated are derogatorily termed *nugrās*, a word which literally means 'without guru', 'wicked' and has come to refer, in the sect, to all non-initiated. Only *sugrās* (those who have a guru, here, the initiated) are considered to be pure and full-fledged members of the community. According to my informants initiation into the *dasā panth* can be given at any time through a simple ceremony during which the guru whispers a secret *mantra* into the ear of the candidate (a reason why he is termed *kān guru*).

Another important feature of this ritual is that men and women, referred to as *jatis* and *satīs* (chaste, virtuous men and women) must participate and sing together devotional songs. The Kotval or custodian of the *jamā* will let them penetrate into the secluded place selected for the ceremony only after they have uttered the right *mantra* in answer to his question (Bhanawat 1986:125). On entering each member is required to wash his feet in an earthen *kuṇḍā*—a gesture which reminds us of the Muslim custom of doing ablutions before praying in a mosque. This *kuṇḍā* full of polluted water is kept till the end of the ceremony. A *pāṭh* has been installed, on top of which five burning lamps are placed and around which five persons sit: the guru, two members of the sect referred to as 'Bhairavas' (the name of a god, usually the gruesome aspect of Shiva in his role as a custodian), a 'witness' and the son of the deceased. A puppet has been made with sacred grass (skt. *darbha, kuśa*) together with a miniature ladder symbolically supposed to link the earth to the heaven. By moving the puppet along the ladder the guru imitates the ascent of the soul into the celestial spheres. The ceremony goes on more or less like the usual devotional session dedicated to Ramdev where hymns are sung. At the end, the water in the earthen vessel is offered to the devotees who have to drink it as *charanamṛt.* In common Hindu rituals *charanamṛt* refers to the water or sacred liquid with which a divine image or the feet of a guru have been washed. Here the water of the *kuṇḍā* is also called *pāyal.* The *pāyal* ceremony of the *dasā panth* incidentally recalls a Sikh custom which consists in drinking the water where the ordinary devotees have washed their feet before entering a *gurudwārā*: like the various types of *amṛt* used for their initiation, this water is referred to as *pāhul* (the issue raised by the similarities which exist between Sikh and Nizarpanthi customs will be analysed in Chapter 10).

On the other hand, a comparison of the above described ritual with a similar ceremony performed by the householder Naths as a funeral rite and referred to as *śankā ḍāl*[4] would show that the *dasā panth* of the Rajasthani Ramdev tradition, as reported by my informants, differs from it mainly by two points: the initial ceremonial washing of the devotees' feet before entering the sacred precints, and the drinking of this water as consecrated liquid called *pāyal.*

Before proceeding to a comparison with the Nizari Khoja rituals, let us briefly mention the existence of similar rituals among the Nizarpanthis of Gujarat, in connection with the Ramdev tradition and the Harijan religious heritage (Gohil 1987:46-53). Despite a considerable number of analogies, the *dasā pāṭh* and *bīsā pāṭh* described by Gohil are substantially different from the Rajasthani *dasāpanth* and *bīsāpanth* insofar as they are, at least in this description, devoid of Tantric features. Other common elements, however, deserve a mention as having a direct bearing on our subject. In both Gujarati rituals the *prasād* is referred to as *pāval* or *kolī pāval*[5] (Gohil 1987:60). Also mentioned is the use of a *pāṭh* and a *kalaś*, the terms *sugrā* and *nugrā* applying to initiated and non-initiated persons, and the tying of a sacred bracelet called the *kānkan*.

We have now a sufficient number of elements for beginning a short comparative analysis. Each element will be examined separately and its purport and meaning in the Khoja tradition will be evaluated.

JAMĀ, JAMO, JAMEYO AND *JAMĀT, JAMĀ' AT*

While presenting the Sat Panth as the Indian form of Nizari Ismailism preserved among the Khojas, Ivanow (1948:36) has pointed out that

> it is determinately iconoclastic in its tendencies and outlooks. Prohibition of idolatry is the most prominent motive in the *gināns* . . . *Satpanth* knows no priests and its prayer is congregational, in which even women and children also participate. In Hinduism such features are exhibited only in Tantric cults. Such prayers take place three times a day in *Satpanth*, namely morning, evening and before going to bed, in a special praying hall called *jamā'at khāna*.

The importance of the *jamāt khāna*,[6] also called by other ex-Nizari communities, for example the Imamshahi Kanbis, the *dharamśālā* (Enthoven 1990, II:157) must be stressed. In some *bhajans* of the Nizarpanthis it is announced, in the form of a prophecy, that 'mosques will be destroyed and *dharamśālās* built in their place' (Nanjiani 1918:119). If one assumes that the word *dharamśālā* does refer here to the Ismaili *jamāt khāna* (and not to a resting place for pilgrims which is the primary meaning of the term), it is the triumph of the Nizari religion over the Sunni *sharīa* which has been foretold.

PĀṬH, KALAŚ, JYOT, AND *MANTRAS*

The use of a symbolic throne in the form of a low table and an earthen pot (*ghaṭ*) (Shackle & Moir 1992:13) is attested among the Khojas and Imamshahis (Ivanow 1948:36). In the jar is stored holy water referred to as *ami* (skt. *amṛt*), *pāval* or *ghaṭ-gangā*, the last term being also used by the Gujarati Nizarpanthis (Ivanow 1948:79-139, Gohil 1987:64).[7]

Rajyaguru (n.d.:6), in describing the ceremony of the Pirana sect, mentions the use of a 'small wooden table' covered by a white cloth and a water pot (*kalaś*). The importance of the *pāṭh* in the Nizarpanthi tradition is attested by the fact that the whole ritual is sometimes referred to as *pāṭh-upāsnā* (lit. worship of the throne), whereas among the Khojas it is generally known as *ghaṭ-pāṭh* (pot-throne).

Another significant trait is the use of a sacred lamp, a powerful and universal symbol of Divine light. If the light (*jyot*) is an important element of Hindu worship, the concept of light (*nūr*) in Islamic tradition, and its particular significance in the Ismaili religion must also be noted. Similar formulas are used during the ceremonies of the Khojas, the Imamshahis and the Nizarpanthis (Rajyaguru n.d.:505-8). They have been established on the model of indigenous *mantras* and contain Hindu as well as Islamic references.

ṚṢI, RIKH, RIKHISAR, MUNI AND *MUNIVAR*

In the first chapter it has been said that, in the *ginānic* tradition, these words were used in tandem with the Islamic term *momin* referring to the believers. *Ṛṣi* or *muni* were obviously not meant to be faithful translations of the Arabic *momin*, but must have been a creation of the Pirs. Whereas in Puranic and later Hindu lore *ṛṣi* was exclusively used to refer to certain ascetics or hermits endowed with special powers (generally Brahmans by caste), the term applied to all the followers of the Nizari Ismaili sect, regardless of their rank and caste, as in the Ramdev tradition to all members of the Nizar Panth. As has already been said, this was probably meant to give ordinary devotees, and among them untouchables, an importance which they could not dream to have obtained in Hindu society.

NUGRĀS AND *SUGRĀS*

It was another *ginānic* phrase (Shackle and Moir 1992:163) drawn from Hindu usage. In both Hindu and Ismaili contexts, *nugrās* referred to the impure and sinful ones, but in the Nizari tradition it also had a specific and restricted meaning, as it distinguished those who did not belong to Sat Panth from those who did. Inquiry among the Nizarpanthis of Rajasthan has led me to the hypothesis that these opposite terms were also used as a kind of secret code to designate the members of the sect and differentiate them from the outsiders.

KĀMAḌIYAS

Whereas I have found no trace of a religious functionary referred to as Mukhi among Ramdev's followers, Kamadiyas are dominant figures of the Nizarpanthi *jamā* in Rajasthan (Gohil does not mention them in Gujarat). Their assistants, the Kotvals, correspond more or less to the Khoja Kamadiyas. Their complex characteristics in the Rajasthani tradition probably testify to a long historical evolution, the major phases of which are still shrouded in mystery (D.S. Khan, 1996). Considering the fact that they appear as householder ascetics, mainly Shaiva yogi holders of a sacred hearth (*dhūṇī*), priests of Ramdev and leaders of the village *jamās* (including the *dasā* and sometimes the *bīsā panths*), they hardly look like their Khoja homonyms; the latter are generally portrayed as accountants and treasurers of the *jamāt khāna* (Hollister 1979:401), though they also discharge certain religious functions (Shackle and Moir 1992:13). However, both their homonymy and their indispensable presence during the *jamā* or congregation of the faithful point to a common origin.

PĀYAL/PĀVAL

In the two compared traditions this term seems to refer to different kinds of consecrated liquids. For the Nizaris, it is generally water mixed with earth from Kerbala (a sacred place connected with the history of Shiism). In the Tantric rituals of the Nizarpanthis, it may refer to the water where devotees have washed their feet or to the sperm obtained after ritual copulation. In the Nizari Ismaili tradition *pāval* seems to be a word attested in some older *gināns* (Ivanow 1948:66), whereas *ami* (*amṛt*) has later been used more extensively (Shackle and Moir 1992:148), representing 'the regular term for the holy water of the *ghaṭ-pāṭh* ceremony'.

Ivanow (1948:37) makes a few interesting remarks about the *pāval* ritual, pointing to its Islamic Persian origin: 'it is the *piyalā* (cup) which is offered at the initiation of the darwish into the *tarīqāt*'. He alludes to its probable Tantric connotations (at this ceremony men and women participated) and mentions, remarkably enough, the partaking of sperm diluted in water (ibid.:30).

The author also notes the obscure etymology of the word *pāval* which, in this form, does not correspond either to a Persian or Arabic substantive nor a Sanskritic one (ibid.:38). As a matter of fact, neither the Sufi custom of *piyalā* nor the Hindu *charanamṛt* are referred to in literature and current usage as *pāval*. If we leave aside the homonym derived from the root *pāi/pāv* and designating an anklet, the word is not found in any Hindi, Sindhi, Punjabi or Gujarati dictionaries, with the exception of the variant *pāhul* connected with Sikh rituals on which we will comment later.

Different etymologies are proposed by the Nizarpanthis, but most agree on one point: this term is an equivalent of *charanamṛt*. One of my informants provided an explanation which might appear convincing, namely that *pāyal/pāval* was, like its homonym, formed on the root *pāy pāv* (foot) to which the suffix *-al* was added. Therefore both as 'anklet' and as *charanamṛt*, *pāyal* referred to 'something related to the foot', whether divine nectar or an ornament. Even if this etymology were correct, the question remains as to why this word has not been used in other indigenous traditions to designate the consecrated water. It is equally possible that the term has been coined by the Ismaili Pirs on another existing model: *pāyas*, which refers to a drink made of water or milk. According to Kinsley (1987:194), the water of the Ganges which is used for the cult of the Goddess is sometimes compared with milk or *amṛt*: 'the stream of the river carries *pāyas*. The word *pāyas* stands for both water and milk.' This analogy might not seem too farfetched if we remember that *pāyal/pāval* is also called *ghaṭ-gangā* (the Ganges from the sacred water pot), and that milk seems to have been used during the earlier rituals of the Nizaris. As will be shown in Chapter 6, among the Aipanthis the *amṛt* partaken by the devotees and termed *pāyal* is made of milk or curds mixed with different substances and sacred water.

KĀNKAN

The word generally refers to a ritual bracelet used in *pūjās* and initiation rituals of various kinds. In the *jamā* of the Gujarati Nizar Panth it plays a similar role. In the Khoja tradition it is performed when the guru dips his finger into holy water and passes it round the wrist of the person to be initiated, indicating the form of a bracelet (personal communication by Z. Moir).

At the end of this brief comparative study we may once more raise the issue of the origin of these similarities, in other words, of the nature of the influence which each sect had on the other. But before drawing any conclusion it is necessary to establish the same kind of parallels between motifs and terms found in both literary traditions.

LITERATURE

As has been noted by most authors who have written about Indian Ismailism (Nanji 1978, Asani 1991, Mallison 1991 a and b, Shackle and Moir 1992 and Kassam 1994), the *ginānic* literature displays many features which are typical of medieval devotional poetry. *Gināns* are of various types; there are devotional and ritual songs, hymns of instruction, eschatological compositions and 'tales of the mission' (Shackle and Moir 1992:xii-xiii). The texts also vary in length and are generally meant to be sung during the sessions of the *jamāt khāna*. As we said at the outset, they are the products of oral transmission, even if the texts have been transcribed at various periods, possibly from the sixteenth century onwards.

The oral literature of the Ramdev cult seems to have been transcribed much later, namely after Independence, although an eighteenth-century manuscript is said to exist (Maheshwari 1980:187). Until this text can be found and examined it must be assumed that the compositions of the Nizarpanthis have been preserved mainly by religious singers who transmitted them down the generations. These texts include various *vāṇīs* ranging from short devotional poems to longer ballads of the hagiographic or popular type. As in the *gināns*, eschatologic and messianic themes are also found; in the Nizarpanthi tradition these songs are called *āgam vāṇīs* (Gohil 1994).

In the study of the religious literature of both communities one of the main issues concerns the authorship of the various compositions. Maheshwari (1980:186-7) states that the *padas* of Likhmoji Mali or Narain Panchoji (two Nizarpanthi Sants) have acquired the form of folk songs and should consequently be treated as such. In his opinion, the *bhajans* of Harji Bhatti and Rupande are also folk songs and 'names of famous saints are attached to them to ensure their acceptance and popularity'. The problem of signatures and their relationship to 'real authorship', however, does not concern solely folk literature: it is a crucial issue of the Sant tradition as well. In his analysis of the signature of devotional songs of the *bhaktas* of medieval northern India, Hawley (1988:269-90) provides a keen insight when he argues that 'such signatures register more, and at the same time rather less, than the name of a poem author . . . they say less about the authorship side of "author" than about the author's authority' (ibid.: 270).

As for the Nizari literature of the subcontinent, Asani (1991:4-5) has written:

> Indeed for many *gināns* the traditional attribution of authorship can be challenged on linguistic and literary grounds (Asani-1984). Ivanow feels that in some cases the attribution of a *ginān* to a certain *pīr* may, in fact reflect that it is a work written by later devotees about the *pīr,* rather than by him (1948:41). Azim Nanji suggests that sometimes the actual composition of a *ginān* may have been the work of a later disciple (1978:62). It is therefore quite possible that composers of some *gināns* may have attributed them to their favourite *pīr* as a way of spiritually identifying themselves with their mentors.

Concerning the *chaubīs pramāṇ*, twenty-four devotional songs on various subjects (Maheshwari 1980:187), it may be suggested that they are too diverse in form and content to be the work of a single author, leave alone Ramdev himself, as is traditionally believed. The important issue of signatures (*chhāp*), as related to the Nizari and Nizarpanthi traditions, will be briefly resumed in Chapter 6 and a clue suggested.

BHAJANS AND *GINĀNS*

When analysing the contents of *gināns* and *bhajans* and stressing the numerous similarities which exist between certain terms and concepts found in both literary traditions, the general tendency has been to think that the presence of many common elements belonging to the indigenous religious tradition can be explained by the influence of Hindu *bhakti* on the Nizari sect established in the subcontinent (Nanji 1978:14). Proceeding to a detailed comparative analysis of a religious lyric shared by the Ismaili Khojas and the Tantric *Mahapanthis* (Nizarpanthis), Mallison (forthcoming) leaves the discussion open and prefers, until further evidence is found, to treat this strange case of similarity in terms of 'exchanges and mutual influences' typical of the devotional circles in medieval times. As far as I am concerned, I doubt that such exhanges may have easily occurred, for one specific reason: while the *bhakti* and *sant* movements developed in an open manner, the Tantric and the Nizari traditions have always been secretive by nature. As a consequence, their ritual and literature could not have spread freely outside the circles of the initiated unless people broke away from the sect. Besides, if the Nizaris of the subcontinent actually accepted a good number of indigenous terminologies and concepts, they did not introduce them in their original form into their religious compositions, but transformed them, so that they could fit into their own ideology. This point of exceptional importance having been overlooked, much misunderstanding has arisen which must be made clear: not the original motifs borrowed from the local Indian traditions, but the recast models which for the sake of convenience, will be henceforth referred to as 'Ismailized Hindu patterns', are found in the devotional songs of Ramdev's traditional worshippers. To give the example already mentioned in the first chapter, the motif of the thirty-three crores is inspired from the old indigenous symbolic number of deities, but it has been applied by the Pirs to the number of souls to be saved and used with a different meaning. In other words, to start with, Hindu elements have influenced the Nizari literature and were then reworked into different patterns, and it is these 'Ismailized' motifs which have in their turn affected the contents of the *bhajans* of Ramdev tradition. When the Nizar Panth began to claim a purely Hindu origin, many of these elements removed from their original context could easily be regarded as evidence of this claim. Conversely, other terms and concepts, which primarily belonged to the Islamic world, were given indigenous etymologies and meanings by the reHinduized communities. One could say that 'Hinduized Ismaili patterns' were thus created. This phenomenon must also be taken into consideration when proceeding to a comparative analysis of both literary traditions.

For this purpose a number of characteristic terms will be selected and examined separately as examples illustrating the earlier-mentioned phenomena. Before doing so, it may be important to note that the motifs which I have termed 'Ismailized Hindu patterns' do not betray the influence of any particular tradition, but are mostly eclectic by nature. Actually, it seems that the Nizari Pirs have borrowed freely from the Nath and Tantric traditions, as well as from Vaishnava, Jain and popular religions. If my hypothesis is founded, each Ismailized Hindu pattern, as well as the Islamic motifs, whatever has been the effort to 'Hinduize' them, when found in the literature of Ramdev-Mallinath tradition can be regarded as vestiges of Nizari missionary activity.

NIKALANG (NAKLANK, NAKLANGI, NISHKALANKI)

In Hindu mythology, the coming of Kalki or Kalkin, the tenth *avatār* of Vishnu, is expected at the end of our cosmic age. In the Nizarpanthi literature he appears quite often, though he is renamed Nikalank (or Nikalang). For instance, in one of the twenty-four compositions ascribed to Ramdev and known as the *chaubīs pramān* (Bishnoi 1989:217): *Nikalang dev nem jhelai* (The 'immaculate' god has promulgated his law). Actually the name is found in numerous *bhajans* of the tradition, for example in the poems of the nineteenth-century Likhmoji Mali (Solanki 7, 8-9): *nikalang rūp ramiyā* . . . and the *nikalang hoy so* ('He has taken the form of the Immaculate'. . . and 'being the Immaculate'). In the Ramdev tradition the importance of this name is such that the most popular *bhajans* start with the invocation, *khamā khamā nikalang avatārā* ('I bow to you, O Immaculate incarnation') and that it is a part of the main *mantra* of the sect, *om nikalang dev nizār.*

Before considering the parallel use of this name in the *ginān*, an important point must be made: if the tenth *avatār* of Vishnu is to be seen as Hindu, his role in the Ismaili tradition is slightly different, as he is supposed to have already manifested himself as the Imam. Besides, the name 'Nikalank' does not appear in the Hindu literature on Kalki.[8] According to Ivanow, this name, as choosen by the Nizari Pirs (Ivanow 1948:58), is the faithful translation of the Arabic term (also used in current Hindu-Urdu) *masūm* meaning 'innocent', 'pure' (*niṣ-kalank*, 'stainless'). The term *masūm* was commonly used as an epithet for the Imam, as was, probably later, its indigenous equivalent *nikalank.*

This name and its linguistic variants are often found in the *ginānic* literature. In a fragment of the *Dasavatār* ascribed to Sadruddin (Shackle and Moir 1992:158), *eji pachāme pātr naklangi nārāyan* ('in the West as the vessel immaculate and divine'). Here it is clear that Narayan, one of Vishnu's names, connects the '*masūm*' Imam with this particular god. Another example might be cited from Ivanow

(1948:58): 'In your worship you must invoke the name of Naklangi, the Lord of the time' (the last words referring to the concept of the 'Imam of the time').

NIZĀR (NIJĀR)

As we have argued, this word which is coupled with *nikalang* is a part of the invocatory *mantra* of the Ramdev tradition, *om nikalang dev nizār.* However, in the Nizarpanthi literature, *nizār* has sometimes been Hinduized as *nijār* (chaste, viceless) (Gohil 1987:29 and personal communication by S. S. Pareek), *nijī* and *nijīā* (personal, inner, when applied to the faith of the Nizarpanthis: *nijī dharm* or the 'inner religion') and *nejārī-nejādhārī* (he of the spear-banner, this small flag or *nejā*, Skt., *dhvaja* being indeed one of the attributes of Ramdev). But it is interesting that it also appears in its original form in the Meghval-Kamad tradition which has given to its secret sect the name Nizar Panth or still more accurately Nizari Dharm.

One of Ramdev's twenty-four *pramāṇs* bears the title *Nizār pramāṇ* (sometimes Hinduized into *Nijīa pramāṇ*). In the third *pramāṇ* (*Sojī pramāṇ*) (S. Bishnoi 1989:225) we read, *sādhu jakhai bhajan khojai dhyavai dharam nizār hai* 'the *sādhus* who remember God's name follow Nizār's religion', and in Likhmoji Mali (Solanki:41), *sant nijārī śyām dharm śarsā sāchā sivaraṇ sāre* ['the saints, they all truly remember the Nizari religion as that of the Lord Shyam' (one of Krishna'a names)].

In Devayat Pir's famous *bhajan* entitled *Daylamī arādh* (Shrimali 1993:240) we read, *tene che nijārī dharm nā vasmā nim* 'She keeps the rules of the Nizār religion.'

In all these examples *nizārī-nijārī* is an adjective used with the substantive *dharm.* Finally, it must be mentioned that in the Meghval tradition, Ramdev himself is often called *Shāh Nizār* ('King Nizar'). *Nizār/ nizārī* are terms which primarily belong to the Ismaili tradition, a branch of which, first established at Alamut, in the Daylam region of Iran, had been named after the followers of Imam Nizar. Ivanow (1948:59) presents a *ginān* ascribed to Pir Shams which says, 'His name as the Imam at present is *Shāh Nizārī.*' The author expresses his embarassment in determining if this formula applies to one particular Nizari Imam named Shah Nizar II (d. 1722) or to all the Imams of the Nizari branch. Considering the fact that the deified Ramdev, identified by his worshippers as the Imam of the time or, in the acculturated terminology, as the tenth *avatār* Nikalank, was referred to as *Shāh Nizār*, I am inclined to think that the words *nizār* and *nizārī* apply here to the sect and to this founder rather than to the eighteenth-century Imam.

QĀIM-KĀYAM

This term which is primarily a Muslim one (it refers in particular to an important Shia concept) applies to the Imam as *Nikalank avatār*, in his role as the messiah (*Mahdī*) whose full manifestation will appear at the end of our cycle.

In a *bhajan* called *Mehdī Purāṇ* Devayat Pir refers to the Saviour as *kāyam rāye* (Nanjiani 1918:121/122). The some appellation occurs in other songs of Ramdev tradition.

Daftary (1990:565) has defined *qāim* as:

> riser, the eschatological *Mahdī*. In pre-Fatimid Ismailism the terms *Madhī* and *Qā'im* were both used, as in Imami Shi'ism, for the expected messianic Imam. After the rise of the Fatimids the name of al-Mahdi was reserved for the first Fatimid Caliph-Imam while the eschatological Imam and seventh *nāṭiq* still expected for the future was called *Qā'im* by the Isma'ilis.

Shackle and Moir (1992:110,182) who also explain the particular meaning of *Qāim-kāyam* in the Nizari tradition, quote a *ginān* in which one reads (ibid.:110): *Pīr Śamas kalandar iyun kaheā āyā kāem śāhā kā vārāji.* 'So says Pir Shams the Qalandar, the time of the Qaim has come'.

In the Nizarpanthi tradition, *Kāyam rājā* may also be considered as an 'Ismaili Hinduized pattern'. Insofar as recent efforts have been made to reinterpret these words in conformity with the new trends, *kāyam* would thus mean 'stable', if one refers to the Urdu/Hindi verb *kāyam rakhnā*, 'to establish firmly' derived from the same Arabic root. In this way, *Kāyam rājā* could be translated 'eternal king', that is, God. However, it appears as a recent reconstruction, if one bears in mind the fact that the name is modelled on the *ginānic* appellation *kāyam shāh*, as used when referring to the manifestation of God in future times as the restorer of order and justice on earth.

Finally, it may not be out of place to mention that the Mahars of the Berar region (an untouchable group akin to the Meghvals, living in Madhya Pradesh) (Russel and Hiralal 1993:138) share with the Rajasthani, Gujarati and Sindhi Meghvals the expectation of an avenger God called *Kāyam rāi* who will marry a Mahar girl, as in the

Rajasthani Ramdev tradition the Meghval virgin Meghri will be united with *Nikalank avatār* or *Kāyam rājā* in the prophetic *āgam vāṇīs* (Gohil 1993:19-20).

KALING(A)-KALINGO

When the names *Nikalank avatār/Kāyam rājā* are mentioned, reference is also made to his enemy whom he will destroy at the end of time, another prominent motif found in the Nizarpanthi *āgam vāṇīs*. This demoniac king named Kalinga is but the personification of the evil of the *kali yuga* (Rajasthani *kal jug*) who, in the Hindu lore connected with Kalki is known as *Kali yuga* or simply *Kali* (Bhatt and Remy 1982:111-12, 115-16). Let us quote a *bhajan* attributed to Devayat Pir (Shrimali 1993:233): *prabhu kālingā ne mārśe naklang darśe nām* ('the Lord will kill Kalinga and as such will take the name of Naklang').

In the *ginānic* tradition, Kalinga (Shackle and Moir 1992:191) is also an important figure connected with the *Qāim* as *Nikalank avatār*. He is, like the Puranic Kali, the personification of *kali yuga* and its evil, with the difference that his character has been further elaborated. In the Hindu tradition he hardly appears more than an allegory, whereas the Ismailis have given him a new name and a human personality; his wife Surja Rani (who appears in the Jasnathi tradition examined in Chapter 8) and his son, are even portrayed as having been converted to the Sat Panth and as playing an active role in the *dawa*.

In a prophetic *ginān* ascribed to Pir Sadruddin (displaying many similarities with the Nizarpanthi *āgam vāṇīs*) one reads (ibid.: 30), *tian kalinge da sir dhaiengo*. ('He the *Nikalank avatār*—will break Kalingo's head') reminding us of its Nizarpanthi counterpart in a composition ascribed to Devayat (Shrimali 1993:238): *ne tarat kālingā nū śir chhedśe* ('and He will pierce the head of Kaling').

THE TEN *AVATĀRS*

Numerous *bhajans* of the Ramdev tradition enumerate the ten main incarnations of Vishnu. Though it may appear as a purely Hindu motif,[9] we have seen that a special position and signifiance are given to the tenth *avatār* renamed Nikalank. Devotional songs centred on the *das avatār* theme have been composed, for example, by Likhmoji Mali.

The linking of Vishnu's nine incarnations with the tenth, Nikalank, who is identified with the Imam, constitutes a prominent Ismaili motif. Its significance is attested to by the fact that a *ginān* called *Dasavatār*, listing the ten Divine manifestations (Shackle and Moir 1992:158-9) was, till recently, the main prayer of the Khojas in the sessions of the *jamāt khānas*. It has now been replaced by a different text including only its final section on the tenth manifestation, the nine Vaishnava figures having been discarded (Nanji 1988:72).

Let us quote a fragment of a hymn ascribed to Pir Sadruddin (Shackle and Moir 1992:88) where the appellation 'tenth incarnation' occurs:

Hāṇe sahi āyo so indo munjo dharami rājā daśame śāha asavāri

('Soon my righteous sovereign will surely appear, the mounted Tenth Lord').

Hooda's translation of a *ginān* in Ivanow (1948:112) is still more striking in view of its Hinduized form: 'God has incarnated Himself as the glorious Tenth *avatār*', a formula which seems to imply the identification of the Imam with the Supreme God.

THE LORD OF THE WEST ('*PAŚCHIM DHARĀ SE*')

Reference to the fact that the *Qāim* or *Nikalank avatār* (Ramdev) came from the West are found in the devotional compositions transmitted by the Meghvals and Kamads of Rajasthan. For this reason he is known as the 'Lord of the West' (*paśchimādiś*). For example, in a few *bhajans* collected by S. Bishnoi (1987:4333, 325, 477) one finds the name *paśchimādiś* which is also the title of a famous composition ascribed to the eighteenth-century poet Khemraj. A song attributed to Harji Bhatti (ibid.:325) says, *Pīr avatār picham mẽ liyo*. . . ('the pīr has incarnated himself in the West').

Recently the Nizarpanthis and other worshippers of Ramdev have made out of this prominent Nizari motif a 'Hinduized pattern' by giving it a new interpretation: Ramdev (identified with the *Nikalank avatār*) was born in Marwar, in western Rajasthan. However this is not convincing as the notion of Rajasthan as a separate State is recent, and, before partition, the western part of the subcontinent would have corresponded to Sind.

In the Nizari tradition, one finds the typical formulation (Shackle and Moir 1992:70-1): *Eji āvā pācham dise sāmi rājo āveā* ('Thus has the

Royal Master appeared in the Western quarter'), which as Shackle and Moir (1992:155) comment, 'as always in the *gināns* the West indicates the promised land of Iran where the Imams resided', from where also came the Sayyids and main Pirs, such as Shams, and Sadruddin.

THE COUNTRY OF DAYLAM (DAYLAM DESH)

It refers precisely to this 'promised land', a region of Persia where the famous fortress of Alamut was located. Since it is a precise geographical denotation its mention in the Nizarpanthi *bhajans* can without hesitation be regarded as evidence of direct Ismaili influence. A composition ascribed to Devayat Pir and entitled *Daylamī arādh* (prayer of Daylam) has already been mentioned. In this text the poet has written (Shrimali 1993:239), '*deśnũ nām dailam deś*' ('The name of that country is Daylam' that is, the region from where the Saviour, *Nikalank avatār,* the *kāyam rājā,* will come).

For the sake of comparison, an example of the *ginānic* tradition will be quoted; it is a fairly recent *duā,* dating to the nineteenth century, the time of Aga Khan III (Shackle and Moir 1992:178):

> In the land of Dailam, in human guise, in the western quarter, in the realm of Iraq, has appeared the seventy-seventh vessel, the forty-eighth Imam, the tenth immaculate manifestation Nur Maulana Aga Sultan Muhammad Shah, the Generous one and Present Imam.

ALAMUT

The first centre of the Nizaris, the fortress situated in the region of Daylam, quite naturally found a place in the Nizarpanthi tradition, as testimony to the historical connection of the sect with the Nizari branch of Ismailism. In the *Daylami arādh* of Devayat Pir (Shrimali 1993:239) it is said, '*pachī bāvo ālmod pāṭaṇ padhārśe*' a sentence which is followed by the earlier quoted *deś nũ nām dailam deś* and means, 'after that The Lord will come from the city of Alamut'. In the *Mehdī purāṇ* cited by Nanjiani (1918:121) we also read, '*Ālmot pāṭaṇ vājantr gām Hari avatārśe nikalankī nām reṇ*' ('Hari-Vishnu will take incarnation in the city of Alamut, in the village of Vajantr').

This is paralleled, in the *ginānic* tradition, by such formulae as '*gaḍh ālamot śāhā dekhāḍeo*' ('The Lord has appeared in the fortress of Alamut') (Shackle and Moir 1992:86).

THIRTY-THREE CRORES

In the first chapter, reference has been made to this important Ismailized pattern. The usual sequence of five, seven, nine crore souls saved in the past and of the twelve remaining crores is found quite frequently in Ramdev traditions (S. Bishnoi 1989:218; Solanki:23). The same motif is traceable in a *bhajan* ascribed to Qutbuddin (Nanjiani 1948:120), the Ismaili figure also connected with the Mallinath tradition. This theme is linked to another one, also referring to the four *yugas*, their gods and devotees, and plays an important part in the Nizar Panth, the four sacrifices of the four cosmic ages. The basic belief is that the Nizar Panth already existed at the beginning of the world with its distinctive ritual practices. It is said that during the first *yuga* an elephant was sacrificed and that the *pāṭh* and the *kalaś* of the *jamā* were made of gold. In the second era, a horse was sacrificed and the *pāṭh-kalaś* were of silver. The sacrificial animal of the third age was the cow and the *pāṭh-kalaś* were of copper. During these three *yugas* five, seven and nine crores of souls were respectively saved. In our era, a goat is to be sacrificed and the *pāṭh-kalaś* made of wood (the symbolic throne is indeed a wooden plank or low table, as has been said earlier). The remaining twelve crores of souls will also obtain salvation in this *yuga*. The main difference with the previous three ages is that the sacrificed animals were resuscitated, whereas the goat cannot be brought back to life, as a result of the evil influence of *kali yuga*. It might be of some interest to note that goats were sacrificed until recently by the Kamads of Ramdev as a part of their ritual observances connected with the *jamā*.[10]

The theme of the thirty-three crores can also be cited from various Nizari *ginān*s with the same arrangement of five, seven, nine and twelve (Ivanow 1948:66-7). According to the Nizaris the remaining twelve crores have been saved by Pir Sadruddin who, for this reason, is known as *bār-gur*, (the guru of the Twelve), although this title is more logically explained by the fact that he had twelve faithful companions and 'lieutenants', twelve being one of the key numbers of Shia and Ismaili esoterism.

Besides this, another series of crores are referred to in a few *ginān*s, supposedly older, which are among the saved souls ninety-nine crore Yaksas, fifty-five crore Meghs and thirty-two crore Kinnaras are mentioned (Ivanow 1948:66). If Yaksas and Kinnaras can be explained with reference to Hindu lore (Stutley 1985:147, 345-6), the Meghs, tentatively interpreted as the clouds (Skt. *megha*) of Kalidas' *Meghadūta* (Shackle and Moir 1992:176), still remain a mystery. Till further evidence can be given, I would like to suggest the slightly different interpretation that Yaksas, Kinnaras and Meghs might have alluded to various converted tribes, the last being the Meghvals (also occasionally termed Meghs), who were purposely compared with mythical supernatural beings, much in the same spirit as the devotees had been globally equated with *ṛṣis*; their status was thus raised and emphasis was laid on the better fate reserved for those who had embraced Ismailism.

RSI, RIKH, RIKHISAR, RUKHI

As has already been said, the word *ṛṣi* (like *muni*) was used as an equivalent of *momin* (believer, member of the Nizari sect) in the Khoja tradition. In the Ramdev tradition the Pir of Runicha who has been identified with God himself, as *Nikalank avatār* and *Kāyam* is called *ṛṣi ro rāj*, the king of *ṛṣis* (Bishnoi 1987:218). A similar formula is found in the *ginãns*, for instance in a *Dasavatār* ascribed to Sadruddin (Ivanow 1948:113): 'He will grant the kingdom to the *rakhisar* devotees who will rule over it eternally.' Shackle and Moir (1992: 64,148) comment on the term, one more example of which is, '*ari pari keni na karavi, rukha*' ['do not stir up trouble with anyone, o believer', where *rukhi* (*ṛṣi*) is a term of address to the faithful].

PĀYAL-PĀVAL

In a Rajasthani song of the Ramdev tradition (S. Bishnoi 1989:440) it is said: '*paglyā dhoy pāyal pīyo*', 'wash your feet and drink the *pāyal*'. The last word being correctly glossed by S. Bishnoi as a synonym of *charanamṛt*.

In a Gujarat *bhajan* one reads (Shrimali 1993:243): '*āo bhāī jatyā āo bhāī satīyā, ochro kōlī pāval*', 'come, virtuous brothers and sisters, partake of the *kōli pāval*'. As far as the Nizari tradition is concerned, in a *ginān* attributed to Pir Shams it is written (Ivanow 1948:66), 'You also faithfully drink *pāval* now, says Pir Shams.'

RECOGNITION OF THE LORD

As already said, the 'recognition of the Imam' essential for salvation, insofar as it implies the knowledge of the inner truth and of one's inner self. This Ismaili term, translated in the Ramdev tradition as '*olakhno*' (the Rajasthani equivalent of the Hindi '*pahchānnā*') has sometimes been Hinduized by equating it with a prominent *bhakti* motif: God, in the guise of some religious mendicant, comes down on the earth and hides his identity in order to test his devotees, but is recognized by the best among them. Both the Hindu theme and the Ismaili concept are expressed in an important *bhajan* of the Meghval tradition entitled *Meghṛi purāṇ* (S. Bishnoi 1987:412): '*uṭho meghṛī var ne olakho*', 'Wake up, o Meghri, recognize your fiance') Meghri, a virgin pariah girl, is the embodiment of the Meghval community; the fiance whom she has recognized and whom she will wed is God. This powerful theme which is crucial to the Rajasthani and Gujarati Nizar Panth in its connections with the Harijan castes, corresponds to a prominent Nizari motif: the marriage of the Lord with the virgin earth symbolizing the converted people of the world.

As for the concept of recognition, a single example will be cited from the *ginānic* literature (Ivanow 1948:65): 'Those who recognize the Lord of the Time acquire immortality.'

DĪDAR, DEDĀR

This word of Arabic origin, used in Hindi-Urdu, is nearly a synonym of the indigenous *darśan* (sacred vision of the Divine through the vision of a god's image or of a guru). *Didār* is also a term found in the general Islamic tradition, but it has been endowed with a particular meaning and significance in the Nizari religion, associated as it is with the above-mentioned concept of 'recognition of the Imam'. The devotees who have recognized him can have the sacred vision of the Lord and of their inner selves, and subsequently be granted salvation (Shackle and Moir 1992:165).

The word *didār* is of frequent occurrence in the Nizarpanthi literature; Devayat Pir (Shrimali 1993:237) uses it in the characteristic combination: '*gurujī kā dedār*', the vision of the Guru which can be compared to the *ginānic* (Shackle and Moir 1992:82) '*yā ali didār lene kun āe śāhā teri hindi jamāet sāri*', ('O Ali, to gain vision of you, Lord, your entire Indian community has come'). The parallel is accurate if one remembers that for the Nizaris the Imam, reincarnation of Ali, is also the supreme guru or guide.

Various other words, names and concepts are similarly used in both the Nizarpanthi and Khoja traditions. If Islamic references to God, the Prophet and Ali, are but natural in the Nizari *ginānic* heritage, their mention in the literature connected with Ramdev can be viewed as a further evidence of Ismaili influence. For instance, the name of Ali occurs in one *bhajan* ascribed to Ramdev, as cited by Nanjiani (1918:131); those of Allah and Nabi Rasul (the Prophet Muhammad) in Likhmoji Malis' poem (Solanki: 18), '*ab tum sinvaro nabī rasūlā* ' ('now remember the Prophet . . .') and (ibid.:26), '*allā alekh doy mat jāṇo*' ('do not think that Allah and Alakh are two different gods')—i.e. Allah, the God of the Muslims and Alakh, the formless Absolute worshipped by the Nath Jogis are but one. The last formula strikingly brings to mind the so called 'syncretistic' Sants of northern India, Kabir, Nanak and Dadu about whom more will be suggested in the final chapter of this book.

Before concluding this comparative analysis, which is, of course, far from exhaustive, it might not be out place to mention a few more patterns shared by the compared traditions. The parallel use of the couple *nugrā-sugrā* to refer to non-initiated and initiated persons; of the term *amārpuri* (a vernacular word modelled on the Sanskrit, meaning 'city of the Immortals' or 'Immortal city') in reference to the Paradise promised to the faithful, otherwise called, as in Hindu tradition, *svarg* or *vaikunṭh* (the paradise of Vaishnavas); *Atharved* or *Atharvaved* (the latter word is the name of the fourth sacred Vedas), the former being transformed to mean 'the stable, eternal Veda', referring to the real and secret knowledge of the Nizari Ismaili religion, also designated as the 'true path' Sat Panth or Sat Dharm (the true Law).

At this stage, granting this comparative analysis to be a convincing demonstration of the influence of the Nizari sect on some communities now claiming a Hindu identity, the exact nature of this influence and the subsequent evolution of the the Nizarpanthis are issues which deserve a separate treatment. A few hints have been given in the previous chapter; the next will be devoted to a broader discussion of the problem.

NOTES

1. According to Komal Kothari, whom I thank for this important information, *jāgraṇ* is a generic term referring to all kinds of sacred vigils organized for various purposes: ancestor worship, the curing of a disease, the building of a well, etc. The word *rātī-jagā* applies to the special night sessions held for the birth, marriage and funerals of an individual. In the former only women participate, whereas for death ceremonies both men and women join in and in the singing of devotional songs.

2. The worship of an empty throne, in cases where images are forbidden, has been a characteristic of earlier Buddhism; it is interesting to note that in this tradition, as will later be the case for Ramdev, the cult of foot-prints and of a riderless horse have been associated with it.
3. Zawahir Moir (personal communication) is of the opinion that the word *kāmaḍiyā* stems from the north Indian vernacular *kāmdār* (functionary, from *kām*, work). However, if one follows the Rajasthani tradition connected with the Kamadiyas of Ramdev, leaving aside various fancy etymologies, it is possible to propose a different explanation. The original term from which Kamad has evolved would be *kāmbaṛiyā* which in turn became *kāmaḍiyā*. The original root, in this perspective, would be *kāmb*, meaning 'staff', and the Kambaṛiya—Kamadiya would be the 'man with the staff' (Lalas 1988 I:606) a synonym for the word *kāmbdār* or *chaṛidār*. Incidentally this object is an attribute of the Rajasthani Kamads.
4. For this funeral ritual, as performed in a Nath community of Nepal, see Bouillier (1986:153-7). The ceremony of *śankā ḍāl* organized on the third day after death among the Meghvals of Rajasthan, as described by Bhanawat (1986:121-7) is similar to the Nath ritual but differs from the *dasā panth* practised by my Nizarpanthi informants (D.S. Khan 1994).
5. It must be remembered that the syllable *-ya* is a vernacular equivalent of the Sanskrit *-va* also found in a number of north Indian languages. For example *rāv/rāy* (king), *pāval/pāyal* (anklet) *gav/gāy* (cow), etc.
6. The *jamāt khāna* is also a Sunni Sufi institution, though it has a different function as it simply refers to the place where the faithful, the Pirs and their disciples can gather.
7. This cannot but remind us of an important Hindu symbol: during the festival of the Goddess referred to as Naurātrā (the nine night devoted to the nine forms of the Goddess), a water pot (*ghaṭ*) representing Durga is used for the *pūjā*, and it is supposed to contain water from the Ganga which is equated with divine ambrosia or *amṛt* (Kinsely 1987:111-12). Curiously enough, Nanji (1988:66) alludes to the possible Islamic roots of the *ghaṭ-pāṭh* ceremony of the Khojas, roots which I also believe to have existed, but does not say a word about the striking similarities which can be noted between the *ghaṭ-pāṭh* and the earlier-mentioned Hindu ritual, on which it seems to have been partly modelled.
8. According to Bhatt and Remy (1982:192), the original meaning of the name Kalki would be 'the Immaculate', although its etymology seems to point to the contrary, if one assumes that it derives from *kalank* meaning stain. In this case, it is interesting to see that the Ismaili name 'Nishkalank', otherwise used by the Nath Jogis to refer to the Nirgun God would be a more literal and correct appellation.
9. Among the famous Hindu poems devoted to the ten *avatārs* of Vishnu, one can quote the ninth-century Tamil poet Nammalvar's verses (Ramayan 1992:413). The tenth-century Sanskrit work by Kshemendra, *Das avatār charitra* must also be mentioned, as well as the famous verses in praise of the ten incarnations of Vishnu which form a part of the *Gīta Govinda* composed in the twelfth century by the Bengali author Jayadeva. As has already been stressed, the main difference with the *ginān*s and the songs of the Ramdev tradition is that in both

these traditions, the tenth *avatār*, as Nikalang, plays a distinct and prominent role.

10. This detail, as reported by one of my informants and alluded to in an oral composition sung by the Rajasthani Kamads (a variant of the Gujarati *Daylamī arādh* ascribed to Devayat Pir), is also found in an old Rajasthani *bāt* transcribed in the eighteenth century (S. Bishnoi 1989:536) where Rani Rupande, wife of Mallinath Rathore, is initiated into the '*panth*' and participates in a *jamā* where a goat is sacrificed. This particular sacrifice may have served as a bridge between the Hindu tradition of goat sacrific (*bali*) to the Devi and Bheru-Bhairava and the *kurbānī* custom of the Muslims associated with the Bakra Īd festival. It must be also specified that the comments of Nanjiani (1918: 160) concerning the acceptance of allegedly Hindu 'four sacrifices of the four Ages' by the Ismaili Khojas, are erroneous, as the author fails to see that the pattern, though inspired by indigeneous beliefs, is an original one typical of the Nizari tradition.

CHAPTER 5

Ismailism and the Harijans

Assuming that my hypothesis is well founded, a number of issues remain to be discussed: what could have been the beliefs and practices of the Meghvals and other untouchable groups before their supposed conversion to Ismailism? How was this conversion made (can one term it an 'incomplete conversion')? How do we account for the fact that these communities nowadays identify themselves with the Hindus? Although these issues have come up briefly in previous chapters, a broader and more detailed discussion is undertaken here.

The appropriation or 'Meghvalization' (as one might term it) of the old Nizari tradition by the untouchables, in the form of an allegedly Hindu sect referred to as Nizar Panth, could in itself testify to the exceptional role played by the Ismaili Pirs in the religious history of these communities. We have already mentioned Ivanow's statement concerning the nature of the Nizari *dawa* (1948:20); he explains that Ismaili propaganda could be successful because it thrived in particular circumstances, using 'the hard conditions of masses, economic distress, bad administration and acute discontent with the established order' to attract people into its orbit. The phrase 'hard condition of the masses' could certainly apply to the 'depressed' classes, in particular the untouchables.

It is a well known fact that, until recently, more precisely until Independence, untouchable castes were not given access to Hindu temples nor could they receive initiation from high caste gurus. (Even today their rights have not been recognized everywhere.) Like the Shudras, they also were excluded from Brahmanical ceremonies. It can thus be inferred that they had their own beliefs and rituals. Though it is difficult to reconstruct their religious history owing to the absence of written documents, one can assume that they worshipped different deities symbolized by stones, sacred trees or other objects, rivers, and mountains, reverence to which was shared by the twice-born. It is only in the fifties that the down-trodden communities could start to build their own shrines, imitating the temples erected by higher castes, and were gradually allowed to enter Brahmanical temples.

It can also be assumed that, at various times, these groups had embraced 'heterodox' religious movements such as Buddhism and Jainism, insofar as the preachers of these movements accepted them as their disciples. Later on, Sunni and Twelver Shia Islam may have played a similar role. Besides, among other sectarian traditions, the various movements and orders broadly classified as Nath Sampraday seem to have played an important part throughout their history. As has been said, in the past the religious teachers of this tradition had accepted initiates of all castes, including the untouchables, and they were closely connected with Tantric-Shaktic rituals, as well as with Aghori practices.

These particular observances, including the 'left-handed' rituals described in Chapter 4, might have prompted the Ismaili Pirs to create an alternative model which could appeal to the converts without betraying the Nizari ideals. In the absence of other documents it is this fact which leads us to infer that before the *dāīs* started their propaganda most untouchables were already Shaktipanthis.

One of the main characteristics of these Tantric movements was that, until more recent developments towards Sanskritization occurred, they were open to people of all castes and creeds. Much more, as has been stated by a few authors (Bhattacharyya 1987:343), low caste people were given a special place in the left-handed rituals; '*Tantras* like *Vāḍavānalīya* categorically say that Dakṣiṇācāra (right-handed practices) is meant for the *Dvijas* (twice-born), and Vāmācāra (left-handed ones) for the lower *varṇas.* The same is also stated in texts like Mahākālasaṃhita in which Vāmācāra and Kaulācāra are prescribed exclusively for the śūdras and persons belonging to the lower order.' Further, the fact that the *śakti* (female divine energy identified with the Goddess, in our context mainly Hinglaj Mata) was symbolically referred to as *Chaṇḍālī* and *Ḍombī,* names suggestive of untouchable castes might be another testimony of the preeminence acquired by pariahs in these rituals (ibid.: 295). According to these *vāmmārgī* beliefs, through a reversal of values (from the 'orthodox' Brahmanical point of view), impurity which is said to lie in the very nature of untouchables, was given a soteriological function and the lowest ranked beings, for instance outcaste women, could conduct these ceremonies as gurus.

In Chapter 4 two types of Tantric ceremonies were described as belonging to the tradition of the Meghvals associated with Ramdev and Mallinath and claiming affiliation to the Nizar Panth. We saw that if the *bīsā panth* was a pure Shaktic *vāmmārgī* ritual having nothing to do with Ismailism, the other ceremony referred to as *dasā panth*, supposed to be the obligatory form of the *kuṇḍā panth* for all Nizarpanthis, showed distinct features, insofar as the Nathpanthi practice of *śankā ḍāl* had been associated with a different kind of ritual. This ritual, and in particular the drinking of water from the *kuṇḍā* in which all devotees have washed their feet, could be viewed from two perspectives. If from a Brahmanical point of view one regards this unusual *prasād* as a polluted substance, for only the *charanamṛt* of gods and gurus is pure, it can be construed as a Tantric ritual. On the other hand, bearing in mind Islamic analogies (the custom of washing one's feet before entering a sacred place), the *dasā panth* could be an original creation of the Nizari Pirs who purposely combined Islamic and Tantric elements. As has been said by Nanji (1988:66) about the *ghaṭ-pāṭh* of the Khojas, it could have served as 'a transition from a Hindu world view to a Muslim one'. Commenting further on the main characteristic of the Khoja ceremony, which could well apply to the *dasā panth*, this author writes that

> the ceremony fulfilled several important functions. It affirmed a notion of purity but also revised it, through a ritual form that had indigenous Indian roots. In the new and changed order, however, purity and impurity were projected as representing a new order which sought to integrate a number of castes (ibid.:67).

It is interesting that the same process of converting impurity (from a Brahmanical viewpoint) into purity in an initiation ritual has been observed among the Lalbegi Bhangis of Punjab (Rose 1990, II:192). The ceremony is meant as well for the integration of the candidate into the profession of scavenger, as for his affiliation to the Lalbegi sect:

> Over a rectangular pit is put a *chārpāī*, and beneath it, the candidate is seated in the pit, while the Chuhṛās [a broad caste category including, it seems, Bhangis, scavengers and Chamars, leatherworkers] sit on the *chārpāī*. Each bathes in turn, clearing his nose and spitting, so that all the water, etc., falls on to the man in the pit. He is then allowed to come out and is seated on the *chārpāī*. After this all the Chuhṛās wash his body and eat with him (ibid.).

The last detail recalls a custom of the Nizarpanthi Meghvals. They do not eat with *nugrās*, i.e. those who have not undergone the *dasā panth* initiation.

If in undivided Punjab the name Chuhra, as stated earlier, can refer to various untouchable groups, otherwise called Bhangi, Chamar, Dhedh, Meghval or Khatik (ibid.:182), it refers in a more restricted sense to sweepers and scavengers. Besides, attention must be drawn to the fact that the Lalbegi sect, to which most Bhangis claim affiliation, displays more than striking similarities with the Nizar Panth. Rose (ibid.:182-214) was struck by the curious combination of Hindu and Islamic elements prevalent in their religious tradition but failed to see that they could have been related to Nizari Ismailism. Given the importance of the fact that another untouchable community, in a different area of north India, namely Punjab (from where members migrated into Haryana, Gujarat and Rajasthan) might have been at one time affiliated to Ismailism, it will not be out of place to describe it briefly. As one more detached branch of the Nizari religion, having subsisted in the form of a particular caste and sect, it could provide additional illustration of the phenomena to which this study is devoted.

If they worship all Hindu gods, and in particular the Devi, the Bhangis also rever a deified guru: Lal Beg (Lal Pir) is known under the dual appellation of Bala Shah and Balmik (Valmiki) (sometimes Balmik Rishi). The shrines dedicated to this deity viewed as the primeval guru or ancestor of the Lalbegis, do not contain any image, the divine light being represented by a lamp. The devotional songs, which appear to Rose (ibid.:187-8, 200-3) and Temple (1993:539) as an incomprehensible and 'confused jingle', display most of the Ismaili patterns described in the previous chapter, whatever distortions and alterations they may have undergone: the four sacrifices of the four ages with the *pāṭh-kalaś* made of gold, silver, brass and finally of wood, the extensive use of the term *ṛṣi* (*rikh*), and a number of other elements. But none of these is as convincing as the name of their god and guru himself: Bala Shah, said to have hailed from Dera Ghazi Khan in Punjab. Incidentally, as indicated by the genealogies of Nizari Ismaili Pirs (Moir 1980:163), Bala Shah, one of the sons of Pir Hasan Kabiruddin (fifteenth century) was a local missionary operating in Punjab, from Dera Ghazi Khan. If this identification is correct, we are faced with one more striking example of an Ismaili *dāī* who, having been deified, subsequently becomes the tutelary deity of an allegedly Hindu sect after that community has severed its links with the central authority of the Imam.[1]

The particular significance of conversion to Ismailism for untouchable groups is also attested to by the powerful figure of Meghri. For these subjugated communities, the Tantric and Ismaili model, according to which they could be equal partners (even sometimes leading figures) in multi-caste ceremonies, must certainly have had a deep impact. Meghri is supposed to be a pariah girl whom God, as *Nikalank avatār*, has promised to marry at the end of *kali yuga*; thus God, portrayed as a Brahman and/or a Kshatriya in Hindu mythology, will unite himself to a woman of the lowest category outside the *varna* system (Gohil 1994:19-20). This belief, as already said, is shared by the Mahars of Madhya Pradesh (Russell and Hiralal 1993, IV:138). Gokuldas (1982:141) calls her a Chuhri, which, incidentally, is the broad category in which Bhangis are classified. Note that Meghri's wedding has also been described and accepted by non-untouchable Nizarpanthi saints. If S. Bishnoi (1989:414) has, perhaps not unwittingly, misinterpreted Meghri as the daughter of a Brahman *ṛṣi*, the Meghval singers of Ramdeora (but also the Gujarati authors who have written on the Harijan literary heritage) and the Nizar Panth (Gohil 1994:52-4), like most traditional worshippers of Ramdev, have stressed the fact that she was born in an untouchable family. Actually her name indicates that she was viewed as the embodiment of the Meghval community. Gohil (ibid.) points to the importance of this theme: Meghri has been chosen by God, already in the first *yuga*, as expressed in a *bhajan* entitled *Meghṛī pramāṇ* or *Meghṛī purāṇ* (S. Bishnoi 1989:412-14; Gohil 1994:20-30); but it is only at the end of the *kali yuga* that the Lord, *Nikalank avatār* (*Kāyam rājā*), will fulfil his promise and marry her; this marriage will result in the raising of the status of untouchable communities, insofar as untouchability will be uprooted and the Meghval caste granted liberation (*mukti*) (Gohil 1994:52) As has been said, the names *Nikalank* and *Kāyam* (*Qāim*) betray an Ismaili origin, from which one can deduce that the motif has been inspired by the Nizari Pirs, in accordance with their ideal of equality and brotherhood, in which caste discrimination and untouchability had no place. Moreover there was also their transformed version of the purity-impurity concept inspired by Tantric and Shia ideals. This view is supported by the fact that, in the *ginānic* tradition, a similar motif plays a prominent part: this is the wedding of the virgin Mother-Earth called

Visav Kunvari to the Lord. In a *ginān* ascribed to Sadruddin, it is said: '*eji vīsav kunwārī sacho sāmī rājo parṇe*' ('the Virgin Goddess Earth will wed the true Lord and King'). In some devotional songs of the Prahladpanthis (Bishnois) as we shall see, she is referred to as 'Vasudha Kunvari'.[2] If the 'Virgin Earth' is to be interpreted as a symbol of the converted community (which ideally, should extend itself, in the future, to the whole planet) the fact that among the Nizarpanthis she has been given a specific caste identity could be evidence of the impact of Ismailism among untouchables and of their expectations of a brighter future.

If one considers the exceptional signifiance of these expectations, as illustrated by the fact that the Nizarpanthi Harijans have preserved the tradition of singing the *Meghṛī purāṇ* and the *Āgam vāṇī* related to Meghri's divine wedding, a new question arises: when and why did these communities sever their links with the Nizari centre and dissociate themselves from Ismailism? Before answering this question, one point must be made. If the communal and congregational forms of prayers, *bhajan* singing, complex religious rituals and organizational setups, in conformity with Nizari ideals, contributed to the development of the social life of the converts, it did not, ultimately, improve the lot of the depressed groups who continued to practise leather work, scavenging and other menial tasks. The spirit of militancy which impregnates some of their religious hymns was checked and all ambitious plans were postponed to a remote future.

Nanjiani (1918:14) has explained the reHinduization of the Shaktipanthi worshippers of Ramdev (Nizarpanthis) as a consequence of 'incomplete conversion'; the teaching of the Nizari Pirs is said to have been conducted in an imperfect or insufficient way and then interrupted before they could be 'properly Islamized'. Mumtaz Ali (1994:27) is of the opinion that Ramdev left his mission among untouchables incomplete because as was customary for the Ismaili preaching, the people to be converted were only gradually led onto the 'right path' (Sat Panth). The author perceives his activities as beginning with social reform towards equal social rights of the lower castes. In the second stage Ramdev would have imparted moral and ethical teachings. Perhaps it was only after this that he was to have preached Nizari Ismailism but his age did not permit him to do so (ibid.:27). I would like to challenge both Nanjiani's and Mumtaz Ali's views on the basis of the numerous Ismaili patterns observed in the Nizarpanthi devotional compositions, as described and analysed in the previous chapter. If the preaching had not gone on well and if Ramdev had left his mission unachieved, how could one explain the presence of so many Nizari motifs in their literature? A. Rahmatoullah (personal communication) tries to solve the issue in a different way. He thinks that the Nizari Pirs, by placing emphasis on the esoteric and mystical interpretation of religion, had become the gurus of many Hindus without demanding from them a formal affiliation or conversion. I cannot agree with this theory either, insofar as the regular practice of the *pāval/pāyal* ritual, the *ghaṭ-paṭh* ceremony and the concept of the *jamā/jamāt* itself, not to speak of the *dassondh* system and organizational structure of the *gaddīs*, point, much on the contrary, to a systematic affiliation to the sect as well as to a formal allegiance to its supreme leader and representatives in the subcontinent.

In analysing the syncretistic Islamic tradition of Bengal, Roy (1983:6-7) gives an interesting clue to the issue which may have a wider application. He quotes the words of Mallick (1961) who regards incomplete conversion a 'channel through which unislamic practices passed into Indian Islam . . . long years of association with a non-Muslim people who far outnumbered them, cut off from the original home of Islam and living with *half-converts* [italics mine] from Hinduism, the Muslims had greatly deviated from the original faith and had become Indianized' (ibid.:6). According to this author, 'these arguments are contradictory since degeneration does not follow from a situation of incomplete conversion. On the other hand, to call a Muslim something less than a Muslim is a value judgment and not a description or analysis of the condition of being a Muslim from the believers' own point of view.'

I will not resume the discussion concerning the particular nature of Nizari Ismailism embedded in Indian culture and the strategy of the missionaries to prompt conversions, nor the rule of *taqīyya* which helped disguise the identity of the communities. However it was necessary to recall briefly these points before proceeding with my own theory regarding the fate of the ex-Nizari communities connected with the tradition of Ramdev's disciples.

A close analysis of the *ginānic* tradition and legends and literature connected with the Nizarpanthis would show that the periods of extensive activity of the Ismaili missionaries, roughly between the thirteenth and fifteenth centuries, were characterized by coalescence as well as rivalries between the Nizari *dāīs*, the Sunni Sufi Pirs and the

Nath yogis. This crucial issue which has been briefly raised in the first chapter will be discussed in greater detail later. All these traditions seemed to have had equal chances to gain disciples among the depressed classes, owing to their particular religious ideals. At the beginning of the fifteenth century, the Nizari *dawa* of the subcontinent was gradually reaching its peak. But then it suffered a serious set-back. The Imam residing in Persia had lost control over some local communities and the Imamsahi schism considerably weakened the *dawa*. The Imamshahis and the so-called Kadiwala Sayyids (those who had remained faithful to the Persian Imam) started to fight for control over the various Ismaili communities and to win new converts. This period was characterized by a great confusion (personal communication by Z. Moir). It is not impossible that certain communities of Rajasthan have also come under the influence of the Pirana Panth as my field data seem to indicate.[3] One can also infer that, at some undetermined time, the links of the Nizarpanthis and the representatives of the Persian Imam had been severed and that the community in which Meghvals and Kamads played a leading role, started its independent existence. This phenomenon can be compared with Daftary's observation (1990:468) that 'some dynasties of Pirs had become largely independent of the imams whose precise whereabouts were often unknown to the bulk of their followers. The hereditary pirs had become particularly autonomous in the areas farthest removed from the residence of the imams; notably Afghanistan, Badakhshan and other localities in Central Asia, as well as the Indian subcontinent.' Once the various lineages of Nizarpanthi Pirs were becoming independent, it was natural that the worship of the 'Imams living in obscurity in the distant land of Iran' (Shackle and Moir 1992:6) was replaced by that of the Pirs. It has already been said that there was a strong tendency to identify the Pirs with the Imams, by exaggerating their powers and deifying them (ibid.: 6, 22). This natural bias would but increase when the Pirs ceased to pay direct allegiance to the Imam or to forward to him the *dassondh*. We have seen that in Gujarat Matang, Mamei Dev and others were believed to be divine incarnations. In Rajasthan and Gujarat, it seems that of all the Pirs who could have been deified Ramdev emerged as the most powerful. This is illustrated by the fact that the devotional songs of the Meghvals and Kamads (and other similar groups) identify Ramdev himself is identified with the *Nikalank avatār* and *Kāyam rājā*, in other words with the Imam. In the absence of appropriate evidence, it is unfortunately impossible to say during which period this event, which could be defined as a kind of schism, comparable if not identical to the Imamshahi dissidence, occurred. If one considers that after an undetermined period of confusion and rivalries local Pirs and their disciples, mostly among the untouchables, had gathered under the banner of Ramdev (which may not necessarily have happened immediately after his death), it is possible to view this process in terms of dissidence. However, considering the loose structure of the *gaddīs*, the absence of a strong religious leader (Ramdev's descendants seem to have had less authority over the other centres of the Nizar Panth), it cannot be ascertained if this phenomenon was comparable to the Imamshahi schism (which itself has a checkered history) or if one should rather perceive it in terms of reHinduization, in so far as the emphasis shifts from a sect to a cult of Ramdev.[4]

Actually, the evolution of the Nizarpanthi communities constitutes a more complex phenomenon. The fact that Nizarpanthi Pirs and Kamads, while still claiming affiliation to their secret sect (and being initiated into it), have formally become members of other sectarian traditions, such as the Dadu Panth, Kabir Panth, Nanak Panth, Nath Sampraday and Ramsneshi Sampraday calls for explanation. The Pirs and their disciples may have continued their secret practices and transmitted their literary heritage in strictly closed circles where *nugrās* (non-initiated people) were not admitted, while simultaneously coming under the influence of gurus whose teachings they could openly follow.

The Ramanandi movement was founded in the fifteenth century, but if two generations after Ramanand, Krishnadas Payhari had already established a *gaddī* at Galta (Maheshwari 1980:106), it seems that it is not before the eighteenth century that its Ramsnehi branch (ibid.:108, 133-45), gaining a foot-hold in various places of Rajasthan, became popular among lower castes including untouchables. It is said that Hariramdasji, the founder of the Sinthal branch of this movement was a Gurra (domestic priest of the untouchables) by caste, whereas Ramdasji who established the Khedapa branch was a Kamad. The Kabir Panth did not spread in Rajasthan before the seventeenth century and Nanakpanthis and Dadupanthis were not found in this region prior to the sixteenth century.

Although from its very beginning, the Hindu *bhakti* current, as reflected in the *Bhagavad Gīta* and in the tradition of the seventh-ninth century Tamil saints, stressed the fact that devotion is a path for all, women and Sudras included, one does not find at such early dates traces of organized religious institutions which encouraged the free mixing of all lay devotees. The Shaiva ascetics were probably the first to present a serious challenge to Brahmanical ideals and among them the gurus connected with the various orders of the Nath Sampraday the Kabir, Nanak and Dadu Panths transmitted, at first, ideas very similar to those of the acculturated Nizaris. But the Ismaili Pirs, it must be emphasized, clearly antedate the founders of these movements. It seems that a good number of Meghvals traditionally associated with Ramdev became Kabirpanthis. This fact was confirmed, curiously enough, by one of my Muslim informants, a Julaha (weaver) who, though affiliated to the Isna Ashari sect, recognized 'Shams Tabrez' as his sole Pir. I have already alluded to this episode in Chapter 4: according to the weaver, Shams had converted the Bhambis (Meghvals) by causing the Ganges to flow in front of them; but, at present, he explained, they were mostly followers of Kabir. The connection which might have existed between Pir Shams, the Bhambis, Kabir and the Julahas (Kabir himself belonged to this community) will be discussed in the last chapter. For the moment, suffice it to stress that in accepting new sectarian affiliations, the Nizarpanthis did not discard their former beliefs and practices. For instance the *mahant* of Bichun is a staunch Kabirpanthi, while he continues to act as the Pir of the *gaddī* established by Shams Sabzwari in Rajasthan. The head of the Ramanandi *maṭh* at Ramdeora acts as a guru of the Ramsnehi Sampraday but he still regularly initiates his caste-fellows, the Meghvals, into the *dasā panth* ritual which is considered obligatory among the Nizarpanthis. This phenomenon is all the more striking since this type of Tantric ritual is totally adverse to the Vaishnava ideals of the modern Ramanandis whose concern for purity is inspired by the Brahmanical model. The fact is that from a certain period onwards, which may have stretched between the fifteenth and the eighteenth century, most Meghvals and Kamads started to receive a double initiation and follow two separate traditions. This case of dual sectarian affiliation is, of course, far from unique in the history of religions. However, in this context, owing to the secretive character of Nizarpanthi beliefs and rituals and the slow disintegration of the network of *gaddīs*, the scales have gradually been tipped in favour of the various Sant movements and the Nath Sampraday. Ultimately, the impression we get from the

Nizarpanthis is that either they have started to forget about their old tradition or still attempt to conceal it.

One can surmise that, until about the nineteenth century and the emergence of Hindu and Muslim fundamentalist bodies, the secret tradition was able to endure because there was no necessity for Meghvals and Kamads to define clearly their 'religious identity' in present day terms, so long as they were able to preserve their beliefs and practices. Instead, those among the Nizarpanthis who were attracted into the orbit of Sunni Sufi or Twelver Shia religious teachers (in our case the Sayyids of Junjala, Madaris, Julahas and Nyariyas), had more difficulty in keeping their former heritage owing to the greater doctrinal rigidity of these forms of Islam which were, besides, so hostile to Ismailism.

The existence of numerous communities once characterized by a 'liminal' religious identity, which are now viewed as either Muslim or Hindu, has been stressed as a major issue in a study devoted to the Meos of Mewat (Mayaram 1996). The question of how this liminality was replaced by clear-cut categories appears indeed a crucial problem of Indian society. According to Mayaram the emergence of these labels might date back to the 'categorizing' activities of British census report officers. They tended to perceive these groups as 'imperfect' Hindus or Muslims with 'confused practices', in contrast to Christians who, despite their own sectarian divisions, follow more monolithic religious ideologies. The epithet 'liminal' proposed by Mayaram would certainly be more appropriate because it emphasizes the heterogeneous characteristic of the social mosaic and the absence of theoretical categories for people who are in between and outside conventional modes of classification.

It might not be out of place to recall briefly that the indigenous movements which have been labelled 'Buddhism', 'Jainism' and 'Hinduism' have probably never constituted perfectly homogeneous blocks and that, in the category now termed 'Hinduism', a wide range of sects with a great variety of observances and doctrines had been continuously emerging in the Indian subcontinent. Their relationships to the Brahmans and to their socio-religious models have also been greatly divergent, ranging from alignment to aloofness and even total rejection.[5]

Dismissing the idea (cherished by fundamentalists) that the various phenomena connected with Hinduism and Islam in the subcontinent should be understood in terms of opposite, conflictual religious categories, Joshi and Josh (1994:44, 46-7) have proposed a new and interesting concept. Admitting that 'religious ideology could produce both, cultural contest as accommodation' that religious and cultural accommodation referred to as 'syncretism' or 'overlapping identities' was a significant fact of Indian history, acknowledging equally the 'polythetic' nature of what we call 'Hinduism', the authors have argued that the issue ought to be tackled not in terms of religious but of cultural categories. Therefore, while denying the existence of monolithic and opposed religious blocks, they introduce the concept of a 'cultural faultline' between the Hindu and the Muslim, whom they view as separate 'cultural enclosures'.

It is difficult for me to agree with this theory. I will not deny the existence, in the past, as in our times, of groups with clear-cut religious identities—a fact which can also be deduced from the Sant poetry, with its reference to 'Hindus' and 'Turks'. But it is equally obvious that these categories did not include the groups which we have termed, following Mayaram, 'liminal'. Certainly, the concept of 'cultural enclosures' cannot apply to them, nor would the term 'cultural faultline' adequately mark the difference between the Ismailis and the people they wished to convert, in spite of Joshi and Josh's opinion on the matter (ibid.:47). Actually, without denying their Islamic roots, the Nizari preachers have, to repeat what Joshi and Josh have said of Hindu groups, 'fostered inclusive strategies of incorporation' which, coupled with the necessity of *taqīyya*, gave birth to communities characterized by a liminal identity: in this way, the Nizarpanthis, and the Bishnois, the Aipanthis and the Jasnathis, like the Shamsis and the Khojas, cannot be said to represent 'cultural enclosures'.

Turning again our attention to the emergence of clear-cut religious identities, it may be stated that the nineteenth and twentieth centuries, which saw the rise of Hindu and Muslim revivalist movements, were characterized by more drastic transformations. While the Nizarpanthis had come under various influences, whether of the Nath, Sant, Sufi or Twelver Shia religious teachers, some Khojas and Shamsis were drawn into the orbit of Sunnism or Shiism, whereas others became members of the Hindu Swami Narayan sect; a few continued to live, rather inconspicuously, in the guise of 'orthodox' Hindu merchants or artisans, without interrupting their own secret practices in secluded *jamāt khānas*: these groups, as has been said, later came to be known as Guptis.

This situation began to change with the arrival of the Aga Khans in the subcontinent. The famous 'Aga Khan case' which was heard by the Bombay High Court in 1866 provided an opportunity for the first significant transformation and, as Nanji has it (1988:68), the new social and historical context created by the presence of the Nizari Imam among the communities of the subcontinent, triggered 'the need for a re-evaluation of the community's identity and future direction'. The group was identified with a particular branch of Shias and the use of *taqīyya* discarded (ibid.:69): 'In the face of this need for a specific commitment and self-identification with Isma'ili Islam, a minority felt strongly about the loss of their earlier ambiguous status. Conflict ensued; some people who resisted the imam's position filed for litigation, wishing either to be recognized as Sunni Muslims or, in some cases, as Hindus'. Later on, in 1905, the Constitution established by Aga Khan III 'provided for rules and regulations in matter of personal law, rooting them within Shi'a Isma'ili Muslim tradition and eliminating Hindu practices' (ibid.:70). These changes, as has been explained, also concerned ritual and religious life.

However, this development would not have taken place if Indian society had not been gradually influenced by various revivalist movements. Mayaram (1996, passim) and Jamous (1995:48-9) have tackled the interesting issue related to the efforts of fundamentalist Islamic bodies such as the Tablighi Jama'at (created around 1930 in Delhi) to 'reIslamize' the Meos of Rajasthan.

Before the Rashtriya Swayam Sevak Sangh (RSS) and the Vishva Hindu Parisad began to propagate a new uniform version of Hinduism, the Arya Samaj (founded in 1875 by Dayananda Saraswati) had already started its proselytizing efforts, aiming at creating a cohesive society among Hindus, Sanskritizing lower caste rituals and expurgating the culture of these communities of their Islamic influences (Mayaram 1996). Muslim reaction immediately followed, as illustrated by the creation of similar movements (Jaffrelot 1994:77).

By 'inventing a ritual of re-(conversion)' to Hinduism (*Śuddhī*—Clementin-Ojha 1994) the leaders of the Arya Samaj movement were able, towards the beginning of our century, to reorientate their efforts towards the lower castes and the untouchables. This ritual was supposed to transform them into 'twice-born' (ibid.:101). Meghs (Meghvals) and Chamars were thus 'purified' in great number between 1901 and 1912 (Jaffrelot 1994:78-9). Muslims were also converted in this way. The case of the collective *śuddhī* of the untouchable Bhangis of Punjab is mentioned by Jaffrelot (ibid.:77). Besides, groups characterized by a liminal religious identity (among whom, no doubt, were the Bhangis) were also urged to give up Muslim practices. Gunarthi (1987:187) reports the interesting case of the Mers of Ajmer-Merwara. During a great assembly of Mers, including Merats and Rawats, it was decided that Islamic customs should be discontinued among Rawats and '*śuddh hindutva* accepted'. This was followed by a modification of their social status when they received the new name of Rawat Rajputs.

Before returning to the fate of the untouchable Nizarpanthis, it is necessary to mention a remarkable fact concerning the Imamshahis, insofar as the evolution of their tradition displays remarkable similarities with that of the worshippers of Ramdev Pir. According to Ivanow (1938:59), the Pirana sect 'is rapidly declining, not only due to the unceasing quarrels and litigation between the rival parties of Sayyids and the *kākās* [the former appearing with a Muslim identity, the latter with a Hindu one, as said in Chapter 4], but also, in a greater degree, owing to the "modern spirit" of India'. The author mentions the 'aggressive propaganda' of various Hindu organizations, and among then the Arya Samaj 'which draw a great number of the followers of Imam Shah back to Hinduism. . . .'

One can surmise that a similar process occurred with the Nizarpanthis in Rajasthan, Gujarat and elsewhere, inasmuch as traces of the activities of the Arya Samaj can be found in the Ramdev movement, particularly among the Meghvals. It is not impossible that the dispute which has taken place at Junjala for the appropriation of the shrine and its religious identity has been a result of their propaganda. However, no conclusion can be drawn till further evidence is available.

The present discourse of the Meghval followers of Ramdev clearly indicates that (probably under the influence of the Arya Samaj), they were made aware of their ambiguous position and prompted to adopt a clear-cut Hindu identity. If the Arya Samajis did not succeed in eradicating from their hearts the faith in Ramdev and other similar Pirs, nor in preventing them from worshipping their *mazārs*, they encouraged the untouchable devotees to reconstruct their own religious history. According to the new interpretation, Ramdev was not called a Pir because of being Ismaili but because he had shown his superiority over Muhammedan Pirs. Through a fantastic projection in time, the Lord of Runicha was even portrayed as a champion of *śuddhī* among untouchables—before the term had been coined. He was credited with the meritorious tasks of 'purifying' these pariahs who, it was believed, had been forcibly converted to Islam, and of bringing them back into the fold of Hinduism. The worship of Ramdev as an incarnation of Vishnu helped them to redefine his movement as a Vaishnava one. Besides, they gave up the custom of erecting *mazārs* for their Pirs and religious teachers and replaced them by Hindu *chabūtrās* and *chhatrīs.* This was accompanied by a change of vocabulary. Previously Muslim-Hindu doublets were used, such as Pir-Pandit, and *dargāh-samādhi.* The terms *mahant, paṇḍit, samādhi, mandir, jāgraṇ* (instead of *jamā* or *jamā-jāgraṇ*) started to be used extensively. In order to explain the strange aspect of the *samādhi* -temple of Ramdeora, it was said that it had been purposely disguised as a Muslim *dargāh* to prevent its desecration at the hands of Muhammadan invaders. However, the Muslim elements of the old tradition were not entirely discarded: in some cases Ramdev was compared to the great 'synthesizers' of Hindu-Muslim differences, such as Kabir, Nanak, Dadu or even Mahatma Gandhi.

The reconstruction of the figure of Ramdev, according to the new revivalist ideals of the Arya Samaj, was instrumental in bringing about the most significant transformation of the tradition. Perceived as a Rajput hero, an *avatār* of Vishnu-Krishna, a Sant, the Pir of Runicha could appeal to all devotees, including higher caste Hindus. It is this gradual process which led to the present form of the Ramdev cult and obscured the old tradition connected with Islam, Tantrism and untouchables.

As has been rightly stated (Clementin-Ojha 1994:101, Jones 1976:134, 202-15), the *śuddhī* campaign of the Arya Samaj did not succeed in rehabilitating the untouchables. As a consequence of this failure, the Meghval worshipper of Ramdev developed a feeling of frustration which encouraged them to disclose some of their secrets and present the Nizar Panth, in its new Hinduized version, as a powerful religious movement in which they had played a leading role.[6]

NOTES

1. It is tempting to interpret a passage of one of their religious songs as an imitation of the Nizari Ismaili prayer (*duā*). The Lalbegis repeat: '*Awwal Pīr Asā/Dom Pīr Khasā/Som Pīr Safā/Chāram Pīr Giljhapṛā* ' (the first Pir is Asa/the

second is Khasa/the third is Safa/the fourth is Giljhapra) (Temple 1993:531) and the Khojas recite: '*Awwal Pīr Nabī Muhammad Mustafā Rasūl, sallā'Illāhu alāhi wa sallām* 2. *Pīr Hazrat Hasan* 3. *Pīr Qāsim Shāh* 4. *Pīr Jafar Shāh.*'

2. In Hindi and Rajasthani *vasudhā* is a synonym of *pṛthvī*, *bhūmi* (earth) and sometimes applies to the Goddess Lakshmi, *vasundharā* is another form of the same word.
3. This is suggested by a few elements of the tradition. In certain areas of Rajasthan, for instance in the region of Nimera (on the Jaipur-Tonk Road, near Fagi) the holders of *gaddīs* are named Piranas. But the most striking evidence is found in the Prahladpanthi-Bishnoi tradition: the story of Jambha's disciple going to paradise (referred to as Amarpuri, a *ginānic* term) and bringing gold from there is identical to the Imamshahi legend of a similar trip to Amarpuri (see Chapter 7).
4. The process has been exactly the same for the Lalbegis for whom Balmik/Balashah is now regarded as a Hindu god, although he does not seem to have been identified with *Nikalang avatār*. In this case, we are apparently faced with a phenomenon of reHinduization rather than with a 'dissident' movement.
5. The Kabir Panth is now viewed as a Hindu sect, which was certainly not the case at the beginning. The case of the Nanak Panth and of the Sikhs is still more characteristic in this respect: the Arya Samajis have perceived it like a Hindu sectarian tradition, but the Sikhs have claimed (in a famous pamphlet): 'we are not Hindus'.
6. One of the most curious attempts made recently in this direction has been the thesis of the Meghval origin of Ramdev fostered by the Ramanandi *sādhu*, Ramprakash Achyut, in his Hindi booklets (1969, 1985). This theory spread like wildfire among the Meghvals and other untouchable communities of Rajasthan and was accepted by a majority of them. The pariahs had always been proud of the Rajput origin of their god, which proved that higher caste people could ban caste discriminations. However, after the Ramdev cult was appropriated by the twice-born they felt deprived of their right to claim his tradition as an exclusive Harijan heritage.

1. Graves in the shrine complex of Ramdeora

2. Dudu: the grave of Khivan Balai

3. The sacred *kadam rasūl* at Junjala

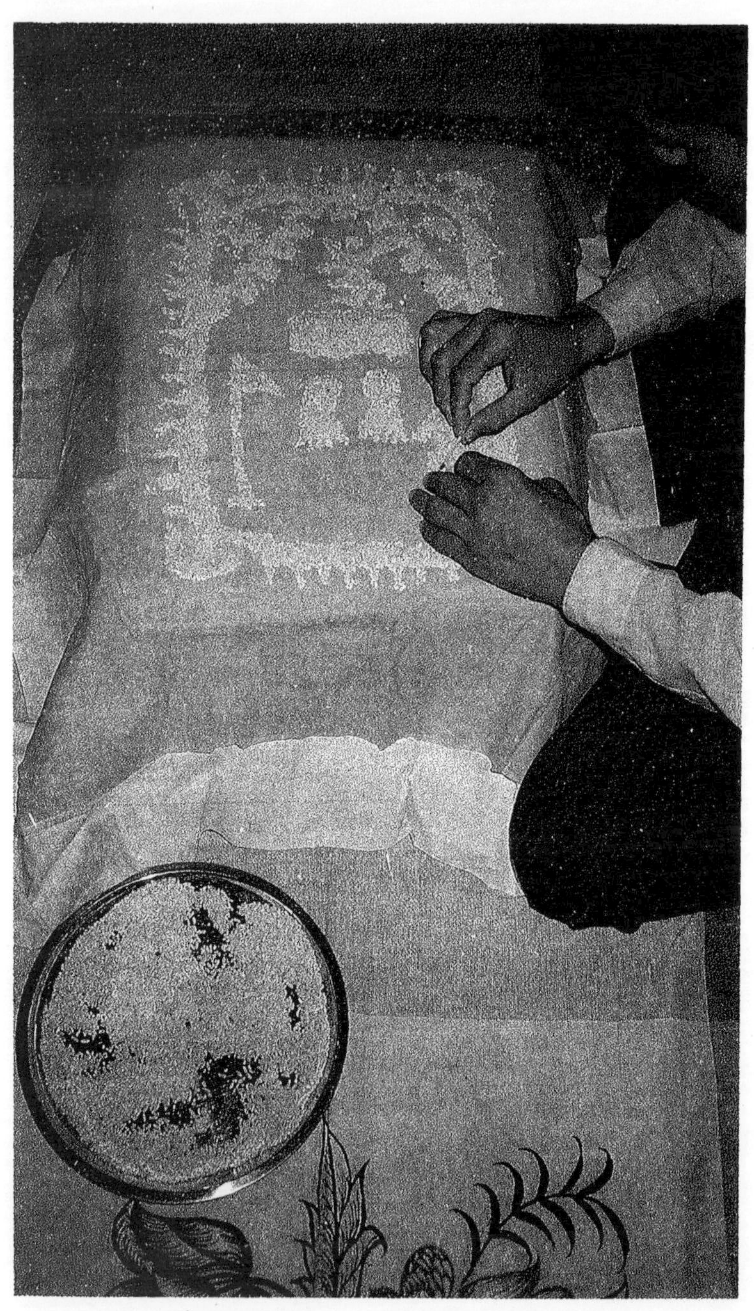

4. *Pāṭh upāsnā* in the Nizarpanthi *jamā*

PART TWO

Other Forgotten Branches of Ismailism: Secession and Dissidence

CHAPTER 6

Ai Mata and the Ai Panth of Bilara

An innocent visitor who might stop at Ai Mata's main temple at Bilara (80 km from Jodhpur on the Jaipur road) would probably not notice any peculiarity distinguishing this shrine from a hundred others dedicated to a local goddess. He might also not notice the absence of an ordinary *murti* in the form of an anthropomorhic statue, stone or trident. Ai Mata's image is replaced by a square shaped low table, hidden under an ornate cloth, which is said to be her *gaddī* or throne.

However, if our visitor has enough curiosity to read the marble slab affixed on the right wall, just at the entrance of the temple, he will be surprised to learn that this Hindu shrine is called 'the *dargāh* of Ai Mata'. Interestingly enough, educated male devotees generally mention this place as a temple (*mandir*), whereas women and naive villagers, in particular Meghvals, prefer to use the traditional appellation of *dargāh*.

In Chapter 3, we have seen that the Kamads of Ramdev considered Bilara as one of their *gaddīs* and that those who lived in this area received their initiation at this place. According to one of my informants, himself a Kamad, this *gaddī* is the seat of the Ai Panth, which, like the Nizar Panth, is believed to be a branch or an off-shoot of the Nath Sampraday.

This view, which is not supported by the members of the sect themselves, is probably inspired by the fact that among the various orders of Jogis one branch is the Ai Panth. Briggs (1989:67-8) reports that 'the Aipanthis of Hardvar say that they were followers of Pir Parsnath, and that they separated from them through the worship of Ai Devi. They trace their origin back to a female disciple of Gorakhnath, now known as Bimla Devi. They explain this by saying that Ai means Mai (Mother, Goddess). Previously, they used Ai instead of Nath in their names.'[1] Further investigation alone will indicate whether there is any historical link between the Ai Panth of the Jogis and the Ai Panth of Bilara. For the moment, suffice it to say that, as in the case of the Ramdev movement (the Nizar Panth), elements connected with the Nath Sampraday can be traced in the tradition.

Before discussing the probable connection of the Ai Panth of Bilara with Nizari Ismailism, the present perception of the sect by its followers will be briefly analysed. In the same way as Ramdev, for a majority of modern devotees, appears as a warrior-saint and a divine incarnation, Ai Mata is for her worshippers a manifestation of the great Goddess Durga. She is exclusively worshipped by the followers of the Ai Panth, which does not prevent other Hindu devotees from recognizing her as one of the innumerable goddesses of Rajasthan. Her popularity, however, is not comparable to that of Ramdev Pir whom a great number of non-Nizarpanthis have started to worship.

As retold by most followers of the Ai Panth, and as illustrated in the 'official' booklet sold at the shrine (Sirvi 1990), Ai Mata's legend can be summed up as follows. Miraculously found in a garden, a little girl was adopted by a childless Rajput, Bika Dhabi. (According to another version, Lalas 1939, Jiji Devi, as was her name, was born at Ambapur in 1415, her parents having migrated from Marwar to Gujarat.) Modern hagiography insists on the fact that, at that time, the sultan of Malwa was persecuting the Hindus and taking by force their daughters into his harems.[2] Legend has it that having heard of the exceptional beauty of Jiji Devi the Muslim ruler wished to marry her. The young girl pretended to consent and asked her parents to invite him to come to their village for the nuptial ceremony, as is the custom in Hindu marriages. On his arrival Jiji revealed to him her real form as the Goddess Durga mounted on a lion and caused him to give up his plan.

It is believed that, since her childhood, she had proved the reality of her divine nature by performing all kinds of miracles. From Gujarat she went to Sojat (modern Rajasthan) and then settled in Bilara, before having stayed for some time in two villages of Mewar, Narlai and Daylana. In both places she might have established an *akhaṇḍ jyot* (eternal light) and erected a temple to the Devi. At Bilara Jiji Devi, assuming the name of Ai Mata, organized her teachings into a *panth* and instituted specific rituals. As her successor she appointed the son of her favourite disciple, a Rajput whom she had compelled to marry a Sirvi girl, and gave him the title of Diwan. In 1504 she decided to 'take her *samādhi*'. Before doing so she explained to her followers that her light (*jyoti*) would henceforth be manifested in her Diwan, Govind Singh, to whom she had transferred her *śakti*. She then remained locked for seven days in her *pūjā* room (*pāṭh sthān*). On the seventh day, when the door was opened by the worried disciples, Ai Mata had become invisible and in her place the devotees saw an intense light. As the 'Diwan of Ai Mata', Govind Singh assumed the leadership of the sect and was, strangely, considered the male manifestation of the Goddess. The hereditary line of Diwans (also traditionally referred to as Pirs-Murshids) continues to this day. Madho Singh, claiming the status of a Rajput, is the present leader of the Ai Panth. He has received a higher education, travelled abroad, and is an active member of the Congress party. Among the Aipanthis there is a belief that this Diwan, who is the forty-fourth of the line (twenty-four is another traditional number of Vishnu's *avatārs*) will be the last one.

As in the case of Ramdev, older legends which have been eliminated from the 'official' hagiography of modern times, give a quite different picture of the tradition. The most famous of them has been reported by Munshi and Munshi (1893:103) in the section devoted to the Sirvi caste (a branch of this agricultural community akin to the Jats which forms the bulk of the Aipanthis):

> many people say that Aiji was the disciple of Shams Pir. The water of the *kuṇḍī* of Raidas *Bhagat* (the polluted liquid from the vessel in which the Chamar saint was dyeing his leather), fell on his robe and could not be washed out. So Aiji sucked the stain and it disappeared and Aiji's heart (as a result of this operation) opened (she obtained spiritual knowledge). Then she left Sind and went to Bilara where she founded the Ai Panth. In keeping with the customs of the Pir she gave the name *dargāh* to her house and to her *kāmdār* (her representative and successor) the title of Diwan. She ordered her followers to tie a cotton bracelet around their neck and to be buried after their death.

The references to Sind and Shams are particularly interesting. The encounter of Shams, Ai Mata and Raidas may appear anachronistic or absurd (Shams certainly flourished before the fifteenth century and Raidas did not live in Sind), but its symbolical meaning is of great importance. This episode appears like a denial of the traditional Brahmanical values based on the pure-impure dichotomy; what is considered impure by the twice-born is actually, here, a means of purification and salvation. The water of Raidas

Chamar's *kuṇḍī* strikingly recalls the role played by a similar polluted substance (the water where all the devotees have washed their feet) in the *dasā panth* ritual, and also the initiation ceremony of the Lalbegi Bhangis (see Chapter 5). According to the tradition, Ai Mata would have converted together with the Sirvis lower caste groups such as Darzis (tailors), Sunars (goldsmiths), Kumhars (potters), Lohars (blacksmiths), Nais (barbers), Dhobis (washermen), Mochis (cobblers) Meghvals and Sargaras (untouchables of tribal origin) who are still members of the Ai Panth. Some of my Sirvi informants stated that, at a time when caste discrimination and untouchability were prevalent, Ai Mata warmly welcomed the untouchables to her fold and compelled the other devotees to eat food and *prasād* with them.

Ai Mata's connection with Pir Shams is nowhere mentioned in the official booklet sold at Bilara, nor is it recognized by most Sirvi members of the *panth.* Curiously enough, one of my informants who denied that Shams had been Ai Mata's guru, gave me, though with much reluctance, a collection of *bhajans* in which the author of a good number of compositions is 'Shams Pir' or 'Shamsuddin'. Other Sirvi informants went so far as to admit that Shams, a Muslim Pir, had been a very close friend of Jiji Devi and her father.

It was clear that, as in the case of Ramdev, a recent trend which might have started with the activities of the Arya Samaj and similar Hindu revivalist movements, had caused the Aipanthis to be ashamed of their religious heritage and to deny it, at least partially. A similar move is the introduction of coloured posters representing the goddess in shrines dedicated to Ai Mata, though her followers still claim that image worship is strictly prohibited in the *panth.*

The structure and rituals of the sect will now be examined. I could not gather many details on the network of *gaddīs,* but it seems that all the shrines dedicated to Ai Mata are under the authority of Bilara and the Diwan who acts as the religious leader or *mahant* of the sect. Two other important *gaddīs* are Narlai and Daylana. All the followers still regularly make offerings to the Diwan in the form of raw grain and money; the untouchables give only a quarter of the amount paid by the Sirvis. Before Independence the sum was one-tenth of the income, which corresponds to the tithe (or *dassondh*) system as observed for the Khojas. Besides, to receive a consecrated *dorā* (*kānkan*) which must be regularly replaced (men wear it around their wrist, women around their neck) each Aipanthi, referred to for this reason as *dorābandhī,* must give two rupees to the Diwan. Followers of the *panth* are also found in Malwa and Gujarat.

Each shrine of Ai Mata, now commonly known as a *mandir,* is traditionally called *baḍer* or *dargāh.* The main *pujāri* is still called a Pir, although educated Aipanthis do not use this title. The *baḍer* of Ai Mata seems to have been originally a rather inconspicuous place where all the Aipanthis of the village could gather in front of the cloth-covered *gaddī* (the main object of worship), and sing devotional songs. In modern times more imposing structures began to be built as 'temples of Ai Mata'. In villages where Aipanthis are Sirvis and Meghvals, there are generally two *baḍers.* The main shrine, where worship is conducted by a Pir-*pujāri* and a Kotwal (custodian of the vigil) belonging to the Sirvi caste, is visited by all Aipanthi communities, whereas the shrine located in the Meghval quarter is avoided by 'clean' castes. This distinction, which might be a recent development, is, of course, contrary to Ai Mata's principles. The main shrine is known as *baṛī dargāh* and the *baḍer* of the untouchables as *choṭī dargāh.*

The ritual, which one author (Gunarthi 1987:131) curiously refers to as *kuṇḍā panth,* takes place during a sacred vigil on each *dūj* when devotional compositions are sung. This auspicious date brings to mind Ramdev's *jamās* and the Khojas' *jamāt khānas* sessions. The secrecy with which the ceremony has always been conducted has led non-initiated people to infer that is was a *vāmmārgī* ritual (Munshi and Munshi 1815:106, Lalas 1938:1, Gunarthi 1987:131).

The Kotwal of the *baḍer* which seems to function as a *jamāt khāna,* plays a role analogous to the Kotwals of the Gujarati Nizarpanthi tradition (Gohil 1987:55). All the participants must tie on a cotton bracelet (*Kānkan, dorā, Ai Mata ki bel*) when initiated, and wear it until it breaks and is replaced. After having kept a fast (*bīj vrat*), on the *dūj* of the bright half of each month, the followers of Ai Mata who are *dorābandhīs* bring cooked food in the form of *churmā, lapsī* or *khīr* (preparations with rice or millet, *ghī* and sugar). All the food is put into a large *kuṇḍā.* The *gaddī* of Ai Mata, actually similar to the *pāṭh* used by Nizarpanthis and Khojas during their ceremonies, is covered with a white and red cloth and used for worship together with an earthen pot (*kalaś*) filled with water and topped by a coconut. The devotees sing devotional songs and all of them have to eat the offerings in the same *kuṇḍā.* They are also requested to take *pāyal,* a consecrated liquid which, according to my Meghval Aipanthi informants, was made of milk and curd mixed with water.

The elements which appear to be similar in the Aipanthi, Nizarpanthi and Khoja rituals are the auspicious date of the vigil (*bīj*); the secretive character of the ceremony in which only the initiated (*sugrās*) may participate; the tying of a sacred bracelet, the partaking of food offerings by devotees of all castes, including untouchables; the partaking of *amṛt* referred to as *pāyal* (*pāval*); the singing of devotional songs; the use of a *pāṭh* (or *gaddī*) and *kalaś* (pot) for worship; and finally, the prohibition of idol worship.

We now turn to the literature of the Ai Panth. Ai Mata is said to have brought with her (from Gujarat or Sind) a few sacred books which were kept at Bilara (Lalas 1938:7). One or all of them are now said to be at the Diwan's residence in Jaipur. An interesting detail mentioned by Lalas and confirmed by some of my Sirvi informants is that despite all efforts, it has been impossible to this day to decipher the secret script in which they are written. Until scholars are allowed to examine these texts, nothing can be said for certain. However, my suspicion is that it might be a secret script similar to Khojki. Khojki, it may be recalled, had been derived from commercial shorthands and is believed to have been introduced in the fifteenth century by Pir Sadruddin (Shackle and Moir 1992:34-5). Unfortunately the Diwan has imposed a ban on public access to these books, as also on some sacred objects kept in the shrine of Bilara, to which *pujā* is done once a year; only the Diwan and the main *pujāri* (a Gosain Dasnami '*Bābā*') are allowed inside the secret chamber where worship is performed. It is difficult to ascertain what role Sadruddin must have played in what appears to have been a local branch of the Nizari community, but, an important figure of the Ai Panth, said to be the *bhakta* Sahadev (Sahadev was one of Sadruddin's Hindu names), is credited with the introduction of the *bel-kānkan* ritual.

Otherwise, the literature of the Ai Panth mainly consists of devotional songs sung during the vigils. A close examination of the themes and terminologies of these hymns has shown that they are nearly identical with the compositions of the Nizarpanthis (Ramdev and Mallinath traditions). Not only do they share specific motifs and words, but, in many cases, bear the same signatures (*chhāps*): Dharu Rikhio (Megh Dharu, disciple of Ugam Si), Rupande (co-disciple of Dharu, Mallinath's spouse), Khati Harkha, Raju Teli (all of Ugam Si's lineage), Devayat Pir (of the Matang lineage) and Harji Bhatti (Ramdev's *bhakta* affiliated to Shams Pir's lineage). I have not found, however, any *bhajan* ascribed to 'Ramdev'. In the Aipanthi compositions Ai Mata appears to be a central figure, and Nizarpanthi devotees, such as Rupande-Mallinath, Jaisal-Toral, etc., are frequently mentioned, but as far as I know Ramdev name's does not appear. This probably reflects a later stage of the tradition when the Nizar Panth and the Ai Panth had separated and, their followers gathered under the banner of Ramdev and Ai Mata who were regarded as distinct gurus. However, an Aipanthi *bhajan* of the *āgam vāṇī* type amply testifies to the fact that Ramdev and Ai Mata disciples originally belonged to one and the same sect. Alluding to the symbolic wedding of the holy community with the Lord, it describes it in terms of a cosmic *ghaṭ-pāṭh* ceremony, *Pokhran pyālo Bilārā pāṭh*... ('the cup at Pokaran, the *pāṭh* at Bilara') that united the two *gaddīs.*

Besides the compositions ascribed to devotees who are also claimed by the Nizarpanthis, many *bhajans* of the Ai Panth are ascribed to Muslim saints who clearly appear to be the alleged authors of the Ismaili *gināns,* a trait which I have not found in the Ramdev traditional literature.

The most frequent signature is that of Pir Shams or Shamsuddin. A long composition entitled *Pīrāvalī* has a refrain which says: '*Pīr Shams mhārā boliyā*' ('My Pir, Shams, has said').

The name 'Sunderdin' is most probably the corrupt form of Sadruddin, also mentioned in the Ai Panth as Sahadev. Additionally, 'Pir Kamaldin' might be indentified with Sayyid Kamaluddin, son of Pir Nasiruddin and grandson of Pir Shams (Moir 1980:132). As for 'Sayibdin', he is perhaps the same as Pir Shihabuddin, Kamaluddin's brother. There is also 'Pir Muhammad Shah' who may be identified with Imam Shah's son who settled in Gujarat and is said to have founded the dissident branch of the Imamshahis at Pirana.

One of my Aipanthi informants admitted that Shams was indeed related to his tradition and, interestingly enough, added that this was the case of Sant Raidas Chamar. We have seen that the Nizarpanthis too claim Raidas as a member of their sect. I have not been able to trace any Aipanthi *bhajan* ascribed to 'Raidas', but *chhāps* of other Sants were found, namely Kabir and Namdev Chhipa. We could surmise that 'Kabir' actually refers to the Nizari Pir Hasan Kabiruddin, but the same cannot be said of Raidas or Namdev. The explanation, as suggested earlier, could be a desire to link the Ai Panth to the prestigious figures of the north Indian *Santparamparā* with which, no doubt, it shared so many ideals. Moreover the leather workers who became the disciples of Raidas had probably been earlier converted to Ismailism, in the same way as the Chhipas who later gathered under the banner of the Maharasthrian saint Namdev, the 'dyer'.

Actually the crucially important issue of *chhāps* should be tackled in a broader context. A few lines written in a booklet of the Aipanthis (Lercha 1990:20) throw a new light on the question: 'In the temple of Ai Mata and during the vigils (*jāgraṇs*), *bhajans* of Ai Mata are sung. These *bhajans* have been composed by Jati Shri Baba Bhagaji.' The explanation of my Sirvi informants is that the true author of the devotional poems was the Aipanthi saint Bhagaji who lived in the nineteenth century. The *chhāps* found at the end of these compositions, such as *Samas bhaṇe, Sahadev kahe,* meant, according to them, that Bhagaji was in fact repeating their words and religious message. It is therefore not absurd to suppose that a similar process may have occurred in the Ramdev and Khoja traditions, where devotional texts ascribed to Ramdev, Mallinath, Devayat, the Ismaili Pirs and Sayyids betray a much later origin, while conveying older teachings.

Let us now return to the themes found in the Aipanthi literature, and its specific terminology. The motif of thirty-three crore souls is conspicuous; as in the Ramdev tradition, twelve crores are said to be saved by one Bal or Balchand (let us recall here that Balram was another name of Sadruddin). The name of Satgur Nur often apprears, as well as the epithet *nizārī*; God figures as Nar Nizar, Nizar Shah or Kayam Shah, Kayam Vishnu and Dasavatari. He is said to reside in or to have come from the west (*picham, paśchim*) Initiated devotees are called *sugrās* and non-initiated, *nugrās.* The demon-king of *kali yuga* is named Kalinga, the ritual bracelet is designated by the word *kānkan,* the assembly of the faithful *gat,* as in the Nizari tradition. Auspicious dates are *bīj* and *amāvas* (new moon). Recognizing (*olakhno*) the Lord is also a prerequisite for salvation, as in the *ginān*s. The sect is sometimes referred to as Sat Panth (the 'acculturated' name of the Indian Nizari tradition) and the faithful as *momino*; many *bhajans* start with the typically *ginānic* address '*jago, momino*!' ('awake o faithful!').

THE ELEVEN OR FORTY-FIVE PRINCIPLES OF THE AI PANTH

As a kind of manual of conduct comparable to the Nizari Khoja *So kiriā* and the Imamshahi *Śikṣāpatri* (Shackle and Moir 1992:145), it is an arrangement of Aipanthi rules. Incidentally, one of my Kamad informants showed me a similar text related to the Ramdev tradition comprised of eighty-four principles. More will be said in next chapter on this type of composition which plays a major role in the Bishnoi tradition.

The eleven principles (said to correspond to the eleven sacred knots in the *Ai Mata kī bel* or ritual bracelet), like the forty-five rules, deal with prescriptions recommending purity, honesty and other virtues. We will mention only a few of these rules from a list provided by Sirvi (1990:49-50).

(1) This sect has existed in the four *yugas*. (The Nizar Panth has a similar claim concerning the timeless character of the tradition, which corresponds to the Ismaili idea that the *dawa* has existed also in previous eras.) (3) 'Do not talk of this *panth* to the foolish ones' (allusion to its secretive character; the members of the sect are requested not to disclose anything about their tradition to those who are not initiated.) (43) Observe the *bīj* of Saturday of the bright half of the month. (44) On the *bīj* day distribute milk and curd to the *sādhus* and *sants*. (45) Take the *pāyal* of the guru (*charanamṛt*).

FAIRS OF THE AIPANTHIS

The *melās* following the all-night sessions of devotional singing are colourful events where hundreds of Aipanthis gather, regardless of caste, around Ai Mata's main shrine at Bilara. As in the Ramdev tradition, here too the *jāgraṇ* takes place on the night of *ekam* (first day of the bright half of the month) and the fair on the *dūj*. On this occasion the Devi's *rath* circumambulates the city. The procession actually consists of a few bullock-carts or, according to the taste of modern times, of tractors and trucks. They are all decorated with symbols and images of Ai Mata. Aipanthi *sādhus* don their yellow dress, including a broad skirt, tie *ghunghrūs* (small jingling bells) around their ankles and dance in the streets, between the various *raths*. The main *melā* takes place in Bhado, when the *jyoti* is renewed in the shrine and *pūjā* offered to the secret objects and books kept in the sanctum. The other two important fairs are held in Magh and Baisakh. The Nausatī kā Melā ('fair of the nine satīs') is also a significant event which takes place near the river Banganga (a few kilometres from Bilara) in front of a big cemetery where many Sirvis are buried, in conformity with the rules of the sect. This place is said to be the original site of the town of Bilara which, before Ai Mata, would have been referred to as Balipura, the city of Bali. Bali, the same as the demon-king vanquished by Vishnu in his incarnation as Vamana-Trivikrama, is believed to have lived and performed his sacrifices at this very spot. The 'nine *satīs*' (*Nausatī*) are supposed to to be the nine spouses of Bali's father who became *satīs* after his death.

The aspects which have been just described may be considered original developments within the particular tradition of Ai Mata. Even when they are, at least symbolically, linked with Ismailism, they can be defined as 'folk traditions' or better, as popular, local developments of an originally Islamic tradition, at the stage when it became reHinduized. In other words, whereas I would not be prepared to speak of Ai Mata's movement in terms of 'folk religion', I would not hesitate to apply these words to the more recent aspects of the tradition.

THE MAKING OF A DEVI—*SATĪS* OF THE AI PANTH AND THE ROLE OF WOMEN IN THE NIZARI TRADITION

The deified religious teachers of the Nizarpanthis, such as Ramdev and Mallinath, constitute an interesting phenomenon related to the Hindu concepts of Guru and God as well as to the Nizari perception of the Imam as Vishnu, and of the Pirs as incarnations of Hindu deities, in particular Brahma. However, the fact that Ai Mata was a female saint posed the problem in somewhat different terms: deified by the ex-Hindus who embraced her *panth*, she could but be compared to the Goddess. After it became reHinduized the tradition automatically evolved towards a cult centred around Ai Mata as a form of Durga.

We have seen that in converting different groups among whom the worship of the *śakti* was prominent (this was the case of the untouchables, but also the Lohanas who came to be referred to as Khojas) the Nizari *dāīs* had borrowed from them a certain number of concepts, terms and rituals which could help converts during the transition from their old beliefs to Ismailism. The worship of the Shia *panj tan* enabled them to compare Fatima to the Devi. The name of Bibi Fatima appears more than once in the Aipanthi *bhajans*, as in some devotional compositions of the Nizarpanthis (Choyal 1992:16). A few hymns of both traditions develop an interesting motif: the incarnations of the Goddess in the four *yugas*. This theme has been made to coincide with the motif of the four *bhaktas* of the four ages, each one saving a specific number of souls (five, seven, nine, twelve crores) with the help of his faithful wife or *satī* (here in the original sense of a virtuous spouse). The important role played by women in the Nizarpanthi tradition is illustrated by the fact that both *jatis* (men) and *satīs* (their wives) were summoned to the *jamā*. The same is true of the Ai Panth and might derive from the Nizari Ismaili tradition where women enjoyed a comparatively high position and were to be found in equal number in the *jamāt khānas*. Women could become *mukhiānīs* (leaders of the congregational lodge) and *kāmaḍiyānīs*. Moreover it must be recalled that Fatima is an important figure in Ismaili history, as she gave her name to the celebrated dynasty of the Fatimids which she legitimized. The *ginānic* literature does not lack references to pious women who play a significant part in the spread of the *dawa* (personal communication by Z. Moir). There is Rani Palande, Satgur Nur's wife; Surja Rani who, contrary to her husband the demoniac king Kalinga, embraces the 'true path' and actively participates in the sessions of the *jamāt khāna*; and Emna Bai, who, by her virtue, chooses the same path and obtains the paradise (*Amarpuri*). Finally, mention must be made of Sayyida Imam Begam, the author of *gināns* who died in Karachi around 1866 (Shackle and Moir 1992:8).[5]

In the Nizarpanthi tradition female saints and gurus play a prominent role: Rani Rupande, Dali Bai, Sati Toral, Mata Devu are but a few names found in devotional songs and oral tales. Therefore, it was natural that Jiji Devi, who, according to my hypothesis, could have been a Nizari *dāī* related to the guru-disciple lineage of Pir Shams, should be compared simultaneously with Bibi Fatima and Durga Mata, and later (when the tradition became reHinduized) rose to the status of a full-fledged Goddess. A few original traits nevertheless remained, such as the worship of the *pāṭh*, the low, square table, reinterpreted as Ai Mata's *gaddī*. Similarly, the Aipanthis have developed their own version of the sacrificed *satī* (the virtuous spouse who immolates herself on her dead husband's funeral pyre). According to the traditional followers of Ai Mata, a *satī* is endowed with certain supernatural powers, owing to the strength of her virtue—an idea which is in conformity with the Hindu belief. However, for the Aipanthis, these powers are directed towards a most original goal: their *satīs* are believed to be able to predict their husbands' death a few months in advance. When this occurs they announce their decision to follow them. However, since in Ai Mata's tradition the dead are not cremated but buried, another solution has to be found: these *satīs* are said to work themselves into a state of profound meditation (*samādhi*) before having themselves buried alive. *Chabūtrās* and *chhatrīs* dedicated to these *satīs* are found in Aipanthi cemeteries. They are known as *Satī kī pol* (*pol* is here a synonym of *kabr*, or *mazār*), which testifies to the fact that the burial custom, far from being similar to the *samādhi* of Shaiva ascetics, is a typically Islamic one. The worship of buried *satīs*, as will be mentioned in Chapter 8, is also attested to in the Jasnathi Sampraday.

Further inquiry among the Aipanthis alone will reveal more about the connection of the sect with Ismailism, its later evolution under the influences of Hindu revivalist movements, and its internal conflicts. Similarly, a detailed study of its literature, structure and rituals might shed new light on the history of Nizari Ismailism itself.

NOTES

1. Bimla (Vimla) Devi is a Tantric goddess who is, among others, worshipped at Puri. Ai is indeed an equivalent of *māī* (mother) and refers currently in Gujarat to the powerful goddesses of the Charans (personal communication by Indardan Dheta and Catherine Weinberger-Thomas whom I both thank for this valuable information).
2. This is an obsessive theme, like the allegedly forced conversions of the Muslims, which has become popular under the influence of revivalist movements.
3. It may be of some interest to note that the title of Diwan has also been used in Sufism to refer to the successor of a Pir, for example, in the tradition of Baba Farid, a famous Shaikh of the Chishti order (Matringe 1995:184). The title of Diwan is not unknown in the Hindu religious context, as illustrated by the fact that the rulers of Mewar, from Bappa Rawal onwards, are referred to as the 'Diwans of Eklingji' the ministers of Shiva. Bappa Rawal is believed to have been initiated into a Shaiva sect and blessed by his guru who foretold that he would found a powerful kingdom.
4. Curiously the followers of Mastnath, a Jogi of the Aipanthi order of the Naths, form two divisions known as *baṛī dargāh* and *choṭī dargāh*, the latter apparently comprising Chamars and other untouchables (Briggs 1989:68). Although more evidence is required before drawing any conclusion, this would support my view that there is some connection between the Ai Panth of the Naths and Ai Panth of Ai Mata at Bilara.
5. I am mentioning here, with her permission, a few points of Zawahir Moir's lecture on the role of women in the Nizari Ismaili tradition, with the hope that her fascinating comments will soon be published.

CHAPTER 7

Jambha Pir, the Prahladvanshis and the Bishnoi Panth

As already pointed out, the Nizarpanthi followers of Ramdev consider Jambha, whose *chillā mazār* (*samādhi*) symbol is worshipped in the main shrine of Ramdeora, as a Pir. He must have established his own separate *gaddī*, and his disciples, as illustrated by a popular legend of Ramdev's hagiography, became the rivals of the Nizarpanthis. As in the case of Ramdev and Ai Mata, the movement connected with Jambha has undergone, probably in the same period, a series of significant transformations as a result of which Jambha's disciples, the Bishnois, now consider themselves full-fledged Hindus, worshipping a guru whom they regard as an incarnation of Vishnu-Krishna. Before discussing the historical link which may have existed between Jambha's sect and the Nizari Ismaili *dawa*, a brief summary of his modern 'official' hagiography will be given. This version of the legend has been expurgated of its Islamic elements. Mentioned in the nineteenth-century gazetteers and census reports, they have been denounced by the Bishnois as regrettable distortions and calumnies (Maheshwari, 1970: I, 442-3).[1]

The Hindus who are not members of the sect generally regard Jambha as an exponent of *bhakti*, similar to Kabir. This is also the current perception of modern Rajasthani scholars and journalists who have written articles on the Bishnoi community and their tradition of nature protection. A few documentary films on the subject are also available. For the Bishnois, however, Jambha is much more than a Sant and an 'ecologist'; he is an *avatār* of the formless (*nirgūṇ*) Vishnu (Bisen, Visen), a reason why they have been called Bishnois. According to their tradition, Jambha was born in 1415 at Pipasar, a village in the area of Bikaner, in a Rajput family of the Panwar (Skt. Paramara) clan. He probably lived and taught in the arid region extending between Nagaur and Bikaner. Legend has it that his parents, Lohat and Hansa, were childless; once, wandering in the jungle, Lohat met a mysterious *sādhu* who gave him the boon of a son. According to a popular etymology, having performed many miracles in his childhood Lohat and Hansa's son might have been named Jambha from the word '*achambā*' (marvel). I could not trace the true origin of this unusual name.[2]

Jambha's parents were worried, as their son grew without ever uttering a single word nor taking any food. Thinking that he was possessed by an evil Pirit, they invited a Brahman to perform special rituals in order to exorcise him. The priest was not successful, but after having shown a miracle, the child eventually uttered a few words which were the first couplets (*dohās*) of a long series of a hundred and twenty *sabads* (sayings, *vāṇīs*) constituting the main bulk of his teaching. Significantly, his first words were as follows: '*Om*: Recognize the Guru!' (Gyanprakash 1992:17).

Recognizing his divine nature, his devotees accepted him as a form of Krishna and as the promised tenth *avatār* of Vishnu, Kalki, renamed *Nikalank avatār*: '*jug chaute dasvo visen santā kāraṇ sambhāl*' 'During the fourth Age the tenth (incarnation of) Vishnu has come for the benefit of the pious' (K.L. Bishnoi 1992:2).

The necessity of his manifestation is explained by the promise, once made to the devotee Prahlad, that during the first *yuga*, thirty-three crore souls would be saved after him. Five were granted liberation with himself, seven in the following Age with Harishchandra, nine with Yudhishtira. Jambha had incarnated himself to save the remaining twelve crores. For this reason, they would be also referred to as Prahladvanshis (descendants of Prahlad) and Prahladpanthis (members of Prahlad's sect).

At this stage, three prominent Ismaili motifs may be identified: the recognition of the Supreme guide (guru), the tenth *avatār* as Nikalank, and the thirty-three crores. In suggesting that the Bishnoi Panth is one of the lost branches of the Nizari Ismaili sect, I am inclined to propose a different etymology for the appellations Prahladvanshis and Prahladpanthis. These names, which probably have little to do with the mythological figure of Prahlad, the demon-devotee, would rather suggest that the Bishnois belong to a sect founded by a saint named Prahlad, some of them being his descendants. Incidentally, we learn from the Ismaili tradition that the fifteenth-century Pir, Tajuddin (son of Sadruddin and brother of Hasan Kabiruddin), was also known as Prahlad (Nanjiani 1918:196, Rajyaguru 1980:302). As we have seen earlier, it was by no means uncommon for the Ismaili Pirs to take a double Hindu-Muslim name. According to Nanjiani (ibid.:196-7), Tajuddin-Prahlad would have married a Rajput Sodhi princess of Tharparkar, and their descendants, who continued to act as local Pirs of the *dawa*, came to be known as 'Prahladpautras' (descendants of Prahlad). The Sodhas, it must be specified, form a particular branch of the Panwar (Paramara) clan. It is not difficult to see that the words Prahladpautra and Prahladvanshi are synonyms. It may then be suggested that Jambha was one of Tajuddin's sons by the Sodhi princess, and that he had established himself, as usual in an anonymous way, under the guise of an ascetic. As will be illustrated by the following legend, his 'religious identity' was by no means clear, contrary to what some modern authors are attempting to prove.

According to the tradition, the raja of Bikaner, Lunkaran, and the governor (*subedār*) of Nagaur, Muhammad Khan, had become disciples of Jambha. Both are historical figures who have flourished during the period ascribed to Jambha. One day, while they were praising their spiritual guide, they started to quarrel. Bika's son (Bika, Lunkaran's father, was the founder of Bikaner kingdom) argued that Jambha was a Hindu guru and *avatār* and, to support his view, quoted a number of prescriptions of the sect: ritual purity, bathing daily, doing the *jāp* (repeating God's name). On the other hand, the Muslim governor insisted that he was an Islamic Pir. Had he not ordered his devotees to grow a beard, bury their dead and abstain from idol worship? Unable to solve the dispute, both men went to see Jambha and asked him whether he was Hindu or Muslim. However, refusing to choose between the two faiths the saint answered that he was 'above all distinctions of sects (*panth*) and castes (*jāt*)' (Gyanprakash 1992:38). A number of *sabads* ascribed to Jambha (among them *sabad* 6 to 12 (ibid.:33-45) criticize both Hindus and Muslims for their hyopocrisy, in a sharp tone very much reminiscent of Kabir.

'If you are Hindus why don't you repeat the name of Hari?'

and:

'O Qazi, cease to invoke continuously the name of the Prophet Muhammad, since you do not follow his precepts!'

In Jambha's hagiography a number of episodes related to kingship play a prominent role. Once more these episodes illustrate the part played by Gurus and Pirs in the legitimatization of local power. While Var Singh and Duda Rathore (two sons of Jodha) were quarrelling over the kingdom of Merta which both desired to rule, Duda was blessed by Jambha whom he met at Pipasar. As a token of his blessing, the saint would have given him a 'wooden sword' made of a dry branch of *khejṛā* (*śamī, prosopis cineraria*): thanks to this magic weapon he would dissuade his rivals and rule over Merta as long as he would keep it. Legend has it that, laughed at for giving so much importance to this ridiculous sword, one of Duda's descendants threw it away. The kingdom of Merta, needless to say, declined and was eventually conquered by the ambitious Maldev of Jodhpur. However, the precious talisman was found by one of Jambha's devotees, repaired, cast into a steel frame and enshrined at Rotu (near Nagaur). Today the miraculous sword is on display inside a newly built temple and *pūjā* is regularly offered as if to a consecrated image.

Similarly, Jambha is said to have offered to Duda's father, Jodha, the ruler of Marwar, a miraculous drum called *berīsāl nagāṛā* the sound of which, as indicated by its name (*berī*: enemy, *sāl*: drive away) was capable to of putting all enemies to flight. This sacred object is in the museum of Junagarh Fort in Bikaner.

Another legendary tradition has it that, after having witnessed a series of miracles, the famous king of Mewar, Maharana Kumbha (associated, as seen in Chapter 12, with Ramdev's uncle, Dhanraj Pir) and his spouse Rani Jhali, became devotees of Jambha and elected him their *iṣṭdev* (favourite deity, freely chosen for worship, in contradistinction to the *kuldev* or clan deity). Whereas in the Nizarpanthi tradition Kumbha is regarded a member of Ramdev's sect, in the medieval hagiography of Raidas, Rani Jhali, and subsequently her royal spouse, is said to have received initiation at the hands of the untouchable Sant.

Finally, mention must be made of an interesting episode concerning the encounter of Sultan Sikandar Lodi (1489-1517) and Jambha (1451-1536). The saint of Pipasar miraculously appeared in his palace in order to save two of his Muslim devotees, Hasim and Kasim, who had been put to jail by the Sunni ruler. Impressed by this miracle, he immediately released the prisoners and promised henceforth to rule with justice. The story evidently recalls Kabir's famous confrontation with the same ruler (Keay 1995:20-21).

Jambha's travels also constitute an important feature of his hagiography. The saint is said to have performed miracles and made conversions at Mecca, in Afghanistan and in the region of Multan. He also went to Mewar, Malwa, the Ganges valley and even Karnataka. In all these areas he made disciples among Hindus and Muslims alike. Although travelling with the aim of spreading a spiritual message is a common component of the hagiography of saints, whatever their religion or sect, the trips made by Jambha are strongly reminiscent of those made by Guru Nanak who preached during the same period in neighbouring Punjab (also a stronghold of the Bishnoi sect). Similarly, the reply given by the Rajasthani guru to Lunkaran and Muhammad Khan reminds us of the famous declaration of the Sikh saint, 'there is no Hindu nor Musulman' (Banerjee 1983:76).

Tradition has it that Jambha took his 'living *samādhi*' at Janglu, near Bikaner, on the seventh day of the dark half of *Mārgaśirṣa*, in 1593 Vikram Samvat (AD 1536). Despite this phrase, which is a clear reference to the custom of Shaiva ascetics, his body is said to have been enclosed in a *sandūk* (coffin) and buried in a recumbent position. It seems that a quarrel arose regarding the place where his body should be buried: the inhabitants of the Hindu kingdom of Bikaner wanted to keep the remains within their territory, whereas those who lived in the principality of Nagaur (a province of the Delhi sultanate) wished to have it in theirs. As a result of this dispute (reminiscent of the famous Buddhist 'war of relics'), a few disciples built a *samādhi* (actually a tomb) near Phalodi, at a place called Jambholav, whereas another monument was erected near Bikaner. The latter shrine, considered to be the main *samādhi*-temple of Jambha, is known as Mukam (*mukām*), an Arabic term originally meaning 'halting place', actually a reference to a *dargāh* or *mazār*.

Jambha's imposing mausoleum is said to have been built by the famous Muslim artisans, the Silavats of Rol (Rohal Sharif) village who became reputed for its stone-carvers in the eighteenth-nineteenth centuries.

Before proceding to an analysis of the structure of the sect, its ritual and literature, we bring attention to the perception that the Rajasthani Nizarpanthis have of Jambha and his sect. It has already been said that they consider him a guru of their *panth* who founded a separate *gaddī*. They view him only as a powerful Pir whereas Ramdev is believed to be an incarnation of Vishnu (the tenth *avatār*). For the Bishnois it is their guru who is a divine incarnation (*Nikalank avatār*). I have not heard them speak of Ramdev, but, when visiting some Bishnoi hamlets, I became aware of the fact that many of them revered the Pir of Runicha. The only Rajasthani scholar to have written a detailed study of the Ramdev tradition is himself a Bishnoi (S. Bishnoi 1989).

An interesting legend told by the Meghvals and Kamads reports the encounter between the two saints and their miracle contest. Even if the episode is an anachronism (Ramdev has most probably preceded Jambha) it seems to reflect the rivalries between the members of what had become two separate sects. The fact is that the core areas of the Nizarpanthi and Bishnoi sects were located near each other, the boundary between both territories being situated near Phalodi.

When Jambha decided to dig up a tank, at a place now named Jambholav (near Phalodi), Ramdev Pir came with the aim of demonstrating his superiority as a miracle monger. He cursed the *tālāb* to remain dry for the major part of the year, a miracle which is supposed to account for a natural phenomenon. Later, as Ramdev started in turn to dig a tank at Runicha-Ramdeora, Jambha Pir arrived to retaliate and caused the place to be full of sand for eight months in the year. His success is attested by the numerous sand deposits observed in the water tank, especially during the periods of drought. This legend may well be an illustration of the process of fragmentation described in Chapter 3; once a part of the vast Nizari *dawa*, the different communities must have split after having severed their links with the Imam and, consequently, evolved as distinct and rival sectarian traditions.

What is important is that the memory of an old link between Jambha and the Nizar Panth has been kept by Meghvals and Kamads in the form of legends which constitute alternative versions of Jambha's birth. Worried by a long period of drought in his kingdom, the sultan of Delhi had invited to his court Dharu Megh and Mallinath (both disciples of Ugam Si Bhatti) who had acquired the reputation of *siddhs*. For some reason the Muslim ruler found fault with Dharu and put him into jail. The sultan's daughter (in another version she becomes Akbar's *dāsī* or female servant) who was sympathetic to the untouchable saint secretly went to visit him in his prison. She fell in love with him, as a result of which she soon became pregnant. In due course she gave birth to a male child whom she abandoned in the jungle. The little boy was fed by a female antelope, till one day, Lohat and Hansa Panwar from Pipasar found the little boy and, being childless, decided to adopt him. According to the Meghval Nizarpanthi tradition, this was the reason why Jambha's disciples revere and protect the black buck.

According to another version, Jambha was born as the son of Swartha Kathi (a carpenter) and Rupawati, disciples of Ugam Si Bhatti. While going to a *jamā* to which they were summoned, the carpenter's wife gave birth to a son in the middle of the jungle. The couple was worried because the formal invitation to the secret Nizarpanthi ceremony was for two people (the *jati* and his *satī*) and the mother had to abandon the new-born child on the spot. Her husband who had gone to fetch some water to drink witnessed an amazing scene: a she-ape tightly held against her bosom the corpse of an infant which had apparently died a few days ago. No sooner had he described the scene to his wife that her heart broke and she died. The desperate carpenter wrapped both mother and child in a big cloth and walked towards the place where the *jamā* was held. Reproached for arriving late and without his wife, and asked what he was carrying in his big bundle, the carpenter untied the knots and to his surprise, both mother and child emerged alive. Grateful for this miracle, Swarthi gave him the boy who was to become his disciple and eventually would obtain great fame as a guru and Pir named Jambha.

It is intriguing that a similar theme is developed in a *ginān* ascribed to Pir Shams. After having been summoned to a gathering of the *jamāt*, a king and his spouse experience great distress because the queen has just given birth to a child and as there was no one to look after the new-born baby, they were obliged to leave him alone in his cradle. On their way through the forest the lady happens to see a deer suckling her fawn. At this sight the queen's breasts become full of milk while the breath left her body (Shackle and Moir 1992:102-3):

> The summons, O brother had come for two people. How could he go alone? Spreading a sheet, he tied it up in a knot, and took it to the Divine Lord's abode.
>
> Lamps of gold were shining before them. The Lord of the three worlds was sitting there.
>
> 'Arise, Queen Heart, and drink the nectar. Suckle the child in your lap.'

This motif is of great significance, insofar as it is closely connected with the rituals of the Nizari community of the subcontinent, during which both husband and wife must be present, as in the Nizarpanthi *jamā*, where they are referred to as *jatis* and *satīs*.

Reverting now to Jambha's birth, according to the Meghval hagiography, it can be said that both legends appear to be an attempt to connect the founder of the Bishnoi Panth with the Nizar Panth through Ugam Si and his lineage. However, no more can be said till the origin of this lineage is traced and connected with the Nizari Pirs of Ucch-Multan.

ORGANIZATION OF THE BISHNOI PANTH: STRUCTURE, SHRINES AND RITUALS

According to the Bishnoi tradition, Jambha would have founded the sect in Vikram Samvat 1542 (AD 1485) at Sambharatal, near Mukam, by 'establishing the *kalaś*', uttering the *pāhal mantra* and ordering his disciples to partake of the consecrated water referred to as *pāhal* (S.K. Bishnoi 1991:28). Before taking his *samādhi*, Jambha had organized the *panth* by creating three main seats or *gaddīs* and appointing, at their head, three *mahants*: Rero became the head to the *kālī pauśak* order (thus designated because its *sādhus* were originally wearing black clothes), Nyaldas was appointed *mahant* of the *lal pauśak* order ('red robe'), whereas Randhir was told to direct the *gheruā pauśak* section of the sect ('ochre robe'). Later on, succeeding Nathoji who was a disciple of Rero, Bilhoji became the *mahant* of the *safed pauśak* ('white robe') order, the main seat of which is located at Mukam around Jambha'a *samādhi*. Each *mahant* was entrusted with the collection of *dasbandh* (tithe, a vernacular variant of the word *dassondh*) from all lay disciples, members of the community. At some time in the past this custom was replaced by voluntary offerings of grain to birds, and other charitable gifts. The tithe system is referred to in the Bishnoi devotional literature, sometimes in the form of an injunction as: '*dasbandh kharcho*' (give the tithe . . .) which is a prominent Ismaili motif, as in the *ginānic* 'they will all partake of the *pāval* drink and pay tithes' (Ivanow 1948:67). In one of his *sabads* Jambha himself predicts that at the end of *kali yuga*, when the evil forces will reach their peak and everything be upside down, even the devotees will cease to pay the *dasbandh*, a fact which actually occurred much earlier than the Sant had foretold! (Sabad 60, Gyanprakash 1992:243).

Originally, the Bishnoi Panth was open to people of all castes and faiths. The Bishnois were generally encouraged to remain householders and continue their professional activities. Only those who had a real vocation for ascetism became *sādhus*. It seems that in Rajasthan and Punjab (here 'undivided' Punjab, comprising Indian and Pakistani Punjab, parts of Himachal Pradesh and Haryana) the majority of Jambha's disciples were Jats traditionally involved in agriculture and cattle breeding. According to the Bishnoi tradition, Rajputs, Shudras, and untouchables also became members of the sect. A few Meghvals are said to have embraced the new religion preached by Jambha. Quoting Crooke, Russell and Hiralal (1993,II:341) mentions that Brahmans, Banias (merchants), Sunars, Ahirs (a pastoral community) and Nais had become Bishnois. Jambha's devotees are found also in Madhya Pradesh and, according to one of my Bishnoi informants, ancient communities are found as far as Afghanistan.

At an unknown time in the past the sect ceased to recruit members and, as the result of inter-marriages, evolved into a caste.[3] However, many followers of Jambha have kept their caste names and still avoid marriage with other communities, especially when they belong to the twice-born groups. Some members use a Rajput *gotra* (clan) as their surname (for instance Panwar), but many have chosen the surname Bishnoi. To be considered as a full-fledged Bishnoi one must be born in the community and have received initiation by partaking of the *pāhal*.

As has been said, Jambha's followers are traditionally buried after death. According to Russell and Hiralal (ibid.:343), 'the practice which formerly prevailed among the Bishnois of burying their dead in the courtyard of the house by the cattle stalls has now fallen into disuetude as being insanitary'. Most Bishnois, however, continue to bury their dead. According to one of my informants, those who live in the region of Haryana generally cremate them.

The centre and main *gaddī* of the sect is Mukam, where Jambha's shrine is located. Although it is currently referred to as *samādhi* and *mandir*, it looks like a Muslim mausoleum of the Lodi style (Lodi tombs, as seen for example in Delhi, are square or octagonal massive monuments). The shrine has recently been enlarged into a gigantic structure reflecting the social aspirations of the enriched Bishnoi community, but the original shape has been preserved, namely, it is a square tomb topped by a huge round dome. However, since dome-shaped temples are also found in the 'pure' Hindu tradition, this feature cannot be regarded as evidence of the Islamic origin of Jambha's sect. More interesting is the fact that, till recently, it was, like Ramdev's shrine, referred to as *dargāh* and *mukām* (a synonym of *dargāh*), the latter name being now used for designating the hamlet where the shrine is located.

The interior of the monument which has remained unaltered (except the walls which have been covered by a fresh layer of pink coloured paint), is similar to a Muslim tomb; it is a square chamber sheltering a *mazār* with the characteristic north-south orientation while the western wall is provided with an arch-shaped recess which evidently looks (and functions) like a *mihrāb* indicating the direction of Mecca. Above it a coloured picture representing Jambha has been hung with the probable aim of transforming the *mihrāb* into a Hindu *garbhagṛha.* One of our informants stated that it was a recent innovation, since this went against Jambha's prescriptions. As attested by the 1961 *Census of India* (C.S. Gupta 1966, vol. XIV:50) this 'lifesize portrait of Jambheswarji' was already there at that time and it is probable that it has been installed in the fifties. In the same report, one finds the interesting mention that 'the real vault in which the body of the saint was buried, is said to be some 30 m underground'. This detail is reminiscent of the Mughal custom of keeping the real grave in an underground chamber and building its replica at an upper level, which visitors of the famous Taj Mahal have certainly observed.

When I visited Mukam I found that the grave was covered by an ochre-coloured cloth, another interesting detail, as this colour is the symbol of Hindu ascetism, particularly associated with Shaiva *sādhus,* such as the Nath Jogis. However, on lifting this cloth, it was not difficult to see that the *mazār* was adorned with another *chādar* of dark green colour.

It is clear that an attempt has been made to 'Hinduize' the shrine in various ways. Two Bishnois clad in white clothes (their head covered, as is still compulsory for men and women before entering a Bishnoi temple) receive the offerings of the devotees (generally a few varieties of sweetmeets), although the *prasād* custom has not been fully introduced. However no *pūjā* or *ārati* is conducted in the Bishnoi sacred places; this is replaced by the *hom* (*havan*) ritual performed in the assembly hall in front of the sanctum: a small portable *havan kuṇḍ* is placed in the middle of the hall and all the devotees who enter the shrine have to sit around it, bow to the ground and repeat 'Vishnu! Vishnu!' before throwing three spoonfuls of *ghī* into the sacred hearth. The ritual, which is said to have been prescribed by Jambha himself, is evidently inspired by the old Vedic fire oblations which on certain auspicious occasions are still practised by the Hindus.

In the Bishnoi tradition, the ritual of *havan* which has replaced the regular *pūjā* associated with idol worship, must be connected with the particular ideals and way of life of this community. In the areas of Jodhpur, Nagaur and Bikaner, the agriculturist members of the sect do not live in villages but in isolated farms (referred to as *ḍhāṇīs*, a word usually used to designate a hamlet). Each house is separated from the other by a large tract of cultivated land and 'jungle' in the original meaning of dry land (Zimmerman 1982:7). Within the Bishnoi territory, killing animals (especially the black buck, *antelope cervicapra*, typical of this landscape) and cutting green trees are said to have been strictly forbidden from Jambha's time. The episodes of the sacrifices of Bishnoi men and women embracing the *khejṛā* trees which the Rajput rulers had ordered cut, are well-known scenes of the Bishnoi martyrology (Pemaram 1977:101-2), which has inspired the modern green movement *Chipko āndolan*. Though this tradition of protecting nature has attracted the attention of a few Western journalists and film-makers, the phenomenon has not been properly explained in its Indian context.

The tradition appears to have been inspired by an old indigenous utopian model attested in Sanskrit literature: the *abhayavana* ('forest of protection') (Zimmerman 1982:63). These protected zones, as one would describe them in modern language, would have extended around the hermitage of ancient *ṛṣis*. In these zones, even the kings were supposed to respect the rules and abstain from killing animals and cutting green trees. In Rajasthan, the tradition later gave birth to the concept of *auraṇ* (Skt. *araṇya*) according to which hunting, slaughtering animals for butchery, eating flesh and drinking alcohol, cutting green trees, etc., are prohibited in a delimited zone around certain Hindu or Jain shrines.

However, the Bishnoi model appears to refer directly to the *ṛṣi* tradition, rather than having been derived from this later development. Each Bishnoi living with his family in a isolated house surrounded by a kind of *auraṇ*, seems to imitate the mythic *ṛṣi*, who was generally a householder, residing in his hermitage and, like him, performing the *havan* ritual in place of image worship. Although I have not heard that the term *ṛṣi* (*rikh*) was used to designate the disciples of Jambha, contrary to what I had observed in the Nizarpanthi tradition, it may be recalled that this was a standard *ginānic* word referring to the faithful or *momins.* Incidentally, according to a Bishnoi author, Kabir like Jambha 'belonged to our Rishi tradition' (*ṛṣi paramparā*) (Krishnanand 1990:80). The fact that the Bishnoi Panth, like the movement connected with the weaver saint of Benares is called the *ṛṣi* tradition, seems to confirm my hypothesis. If my theory of the Ismaili origin of the Bishnois is correct, this would mean that the *ginānic* appellation *ṛṣi,* referring to the believers, was not a mere name given to them through hyperbole, but could, at least in certain cases, be applied to a specific way of life. It might also correspond to the Ismaili teaching concerning the necessity of working; in the arid environment of Marwar and Jungaldesh, rational methods of agriculture and husbandry, associated with the protection of nature may have been encouraged by the Nizari Pirs as a means of improving the conditions of the converted communities.

Coming back to the Bishnoi rituals, the main religious ceremony is a sacred vigil referred to as *jamā* (Rajasthani *jamo, jammo*). These night sessions devoted to the singing of hymns should be held at least at each new moon (also an auspicious date for the Khojas, as has been said earlier). A *pāṭh* and a *kalaś* are used for worship. However the pot is not topped by a coconut nor decorated with leaves, as is the case for the *jamās* dedicated to Ramdev Pir. It contains only consecrated water which will be partaken of by all members of the sect (the same water which is used for the initiation ritual). This *amṛt* which is called *pāhal* is generally distributed while chanting the *pāhal mantra* (S.K. Bishnoi 1991:36-7). Among other formulae the *mantra* comprises characteristic words such as *'Kāyam rājā āviyo'* and *'Nikalank kī pāhal'* ('Come, O King Qayam and the *pāhal* of Nikalank').

As far as the word *pāhal* is concerned, it is not mentioned in Hindi or in Rajasthani dictionaries. A few etymologies have been proposed; S.K. Bishnoi writes that it derives from the Hindi *pāl* meaning 'edge', concluding that the phrase *pāhal lenā* (take *pāhal*) means taking refuge in Jambha (1991:39). Maheshwari (1970; I:460-1) argues that 'the word *pāhal* comes from *pāṭhal, pāṭh* meaning *jal* (water) and the suffix *-al* expressing "sweetness" '. Besides remarking the striking resemblence of this ritual with the initiation ceremony of the Sikhs, where consecrated water is called *pāhul,* the same author (ibid.:144) states that 'Nanak started his sect in Samvat 1554 or later (AD 1497) whereas Jambha did it in Samvat 1542 (AD 1485) therefore the *amṛt* of the Sikhs seems to have been inspired by the *pāhal* of the *Biśnoī*

Sampradāy'. Even if both saints operated in neighbouring areas during the same period, it is somewhat ridiculous to assume in the absence of any strong evidence that the obscure religious leader known as Jambha has influenced the famous Sikh guru, as there is absolutely no mention of this sect in the Nanakpanthi tradition. It might be suggested instead that both Jambha and Nanak had borrowed from another, older tradition, namely the Nizari *pāval* ritual, a view which may be supported by the fact that consecrated liquids referred to as *pāyal* and *pāval* are also used in the Nizarpanthi and Aipanthi sects.

THE BISHNOI LITERATURE

According to the tradition, the core of Jambha's teaching is contained in his *sabads* or sayings. Each *sabad* consists of a series of *dohās* (couplets). A poem consisting of eight couplets and entitled *Untīs niyam* (twenty-nine principles) is also ascribed to the founder of the *panth* and contains the main religious prescriptions of the sect. These tenets are also grouped in different arrangements, for instance, in the *Battīs ākhaṛī* (thirty-two rules) attributed to the sixteenth-century poet Bilhoji (K. L. Bishnoi 1993:230-5).

The Bishnoi literature also comprises various devotional compositions in the form of ballads, *sākhīs* and *vāṇīs* in the Rajasthani language. The *sākhīs* sung during the *jamā* (*jumle kī sākhiā*) present striking similarities with the *gināns*. They are signed by various authors with either Hindu or Muslim names who are all considered to have been disciples of Jambha. A critical analysis of these texts shows that they should be considered works of oral literature and that the *chhāps* are not a garantee of authorship. The first manuscript transcribing the poems is said to have been the work of the Bishnoi guru, Parmanandji, around 1761, thus relatively late, during a period which, incidentally, corresponds to the establishment of the oldest Khoja manuscripts now available.

Examined critically, these texts reveal a number of interesting features. First, it is not certain if the *sabads* are faithful reproductions of Jambha's sayings, in view of the fact that Jambha is called *Nikalank avatār* and claims to be God's incarnation, a belief which I personally consider to result from a later development. As has been said, deifying a guru is a natural process in the indigenous traditions and transferring the name *Nikalank avatār* from the Imam to a Pir may have been a way of claiming the autonomy of the community vis a vis other rival groups, after they had severed their formal links with the Persian centre of the Nizari *dawa*. This is obvious if one remembers that for the Nizarpanthis it is Ramdev who is the *Nikalank avatār*, whereas Jambha is only a powerful Pir. Similarly, considering that one of the prescriptions concerns the prohibition of tobacco, it is not difficult to assume that the twenty-nine principles, at least in their present form, cannot have been composed earlier than the eighteenth century when the use of tobacco became widespread in the subcontinent. A similar remark is made by Ivanow (1948:142) when examining one of the Khoja principles dealing with the same ban.

Actually, although the Bishnois claim that these types of prescriptions constitute the exclusive heritage of their sect, it is not difficult to see that the *Untīs niyam* or *Battīs ākhaṛī* are analogous, in spirit and content, to a type of *ginānic* composition called the *So Kiriyā* (Shackle and Moir 1992:145-7) or 'hundred deeds'. One of these texts is signed Pir Sadruddin (ibid.:62-8).

We will now proceed to a systematic comparison of the Bishnoi principles (*Untīs niyam, Battīs ākhaṛī*) with the Khoja *So kiṛịa*. For this purpose I will select, from both traditions, a few verses where the parallel is the most striking. The Khoja rule will be marked 'K' and the Bishnoi one 'B'.

—K: Do not drink water without filtering it, do not knowingly kill living creatures (Shackle and Moir 1992:65).
B: Use water, other liquids and combustibles only after having filtered them,
Show pity for living creatures (S.K. Bishnoi 1991:9).

—K: Do not cut a green tree, O creature! (Shackle and Moir 1992:67).
B: Do not cut a green tree (S.K. Bishnoi 1991:9).

—K: Bathe at dawn before going out (Shackle and Moir ibid.).
B: Bathe every morning before sunrise (S.K. Bishnoi ibid.).

—K: Do not consume asafoetida or tobacco, O creature! (Shackle and Moir ibid.: 64).
B: Keep away from opium, tobacco, cannabis, flesh and alcohol! (S.K. Bishnoi ibid.)

—K: Do not sell animals you have reared (Shackle and Moir ibid.: 67).
B: Avoid selling your own calves and oxen (K.L. Bishnoi 1993:232).

—K: Do not wear clothes dyed with indigo, O brother (Shackle and Moir ibid.:65).

B: Do not cover your limbs with indigo coloured cloth; avoid them when you see them (S.K. Bishnoi ibid.).

—K: Never castrate an animal (Ivanow 1948:142).

B: Do not castrate the male calves (S.K. Bishnoi ibid.).

—K: Do not wear your turban crooked, O brother (Shackle and Moir ibid.:65).

B: The unpious wear their turban crooked (S.K. Bishnoi ibid.:69, drawn from a *sākhī* sung during the *jamā*).

The last parallel will involve an Imamashahi principle (I) contained in the *Śikṣāpatri*, a composition similar to the *So kiriyā* associated with the 'dissident' Pirana Panth:

I: If thou remainest in the state of *sūtak* (without purifying thyself) [after birth and death] thou will harm thyself, ending in great misery (Ivanow 1948:141).

B: Observe the *sūtak* for three days (S.K. Bishnoi ibid.)

It is not difficult to notice that a good number of prescriptions have to deal with ritual purity according to indigenous ideals associated with Vaishnavism and Jainism rather than Shia Islam: non-violence to living creatures, morning ablutions, prohibition of the dark blue colour, etc. The ban on blue clothes is particularly interesting and seems to be related to Brahmanical and Vaishnava ideas concerning the impurity of black and indigo. However, they have been adopted by Ismailis and even modern Agkhani Khojas wear neither dark blue nor black (R.H. Thomas 1993:648). According to Zawahir Moir (personal communication), dark blue, being similar to black, has long been abhorrent to the Shias, since the rule of the Ummeyad caliphs who were responsible for the martyrdom of Hussein and whose banner was black.

While we were discussing the possible origin of the *So kiriā* and similar types of compositions in the Ismaili tradition, the same scholar expressed the opinion that they were probably the creation of the Imamshahis who have composed analogous texts concerning diverse rules of conduct (*Śikṣāpatri*). As their headquarters were located in Gujarat, they may have been inspired by the Jains who were particularly numerous in this area. Much later, towards the end of the nineteenth century, the Agakhani Khojas would have imitated them with the *So kiriā*, to which they attempted to give the prestige of tradition by ascribing it to the fifteenth-century *dāī* Pir Sadruddin.

Whatever the truth, I would personally suggest that the initial model for the *So kiriā* is a type of classical composition in Sanskrit referred to as *Śataka* ('century'). Some *Śatakas* consist in a series of strophes on virtuous behaviour, the first part of which proposes a rule or a maxim, whereas the second seeks to validate it through some famous example drawn from the epics or Puranas (Piovano 1988:1129). The *Chārucharyāśataka* (Hundred strophes on virtuous conduct) by the tenth-century Sanskrit poet Kshemendra is a good illustration of the genre. A few of these strophes evoke, by their contents, memory of the prescriptions found in the *So kiriā:* morning bath, absention from alcohol, observing purity, etc. (ibid.:1130-1). However, it is not so much the contents (since these are general rules of conduct for high caste people, typical of Brahmanical Hinduism) than the genre itself and the arrangement in hundred principles that inclines me to consider this type of *Śataka* as the direct source of inspiration for the Nizari 'Hundred acts', even if this text is posterior to the *Śikṣāpatri* of the Imamshahis. It is obvious that, in conformity with their favoured methods, the Ismaili Pirs had selected an indigenous model and reworked it according to local requirements and their own ideology. One can therefore surmise that the eighty-four principles of the Ramdev tradition, the eleven or forty-four rules of the Aipanthis, as well as the twenty-nine or thirty-two tenets of the Bishnois, are modelled on the Ismaili compositions which had themselves originally been influenced by a Hindu tradition.[4]

The protection of antelopes (blackbuck) which has become a famous feature of the Bishnoi community and is described as one of their original customs, has itself a more complex and ancient history than is generally assumed. Numerous examples drawn from literature and art show that this sacred animal has become the symbol of 'Aryan Hinduism' (Zimmerman 1982:69), although it also played a role in Buddhism and Shaivism. Much more interesting, because closer to our times, is the present tradition of some Muslim communities concerning the protection of the black buck. The Muslims of Rol (a village connected with Jambha's tradition) avoid harming these animals, and so do the *murīds* (disciples) of a particular *silsila* of Sindhi fakirs established near Jaisalmer. In the absence of research it is impossible to say if this phenomenon is related in any way to the Bishnoi or the Nizari sects. The protection of antelopes does not constitute one of the twenty-nine principles but is mentioned in the thirty-two tenets ascribed to Bilhoji. It is also found among the thirty-six rules of the Jasnathi Panth, a sect which differs very little from the Bishnoi Sampraday and will be described in next chapter.

The most interesting issue, however, concerns the signatures (*chhāps*) of the devotional compositions. Besides a number of authors with Hindu names, such as Bilhoji, Kesoji, Tejoji, etc., many poems are attributed to Muslim Sants: Samas din, Sams paut, Din Suder din, Din Sadar din Samas paut, Tajuddin, Rahimtullah, and Din Muhammad. As we have seen, some of these names are also to be found in the Aipanthi literature, a fact which has been noticed by Maheshwari in his preface to the Ai Mata *bhajans* collected by Choyal (1992:3). However, according to this author (1970, II:485) who is also familar with the Jasnathi tradition, wherever one finds similar *chhāps*, the Jasnathis (and therefore the Aipanthis) have 'taken over' these names from the Bishnois; these authors, he argues, were in reality Muslim disciples of Jambha. Maheshwari states that Samas din (Shamsuddin) was a famous governor and *qāzī* of Nagaur and that one of his descendants Sadr (Suder) who is frequently referred to as his grandson (*pautā*), continued to be a member of the Bishnoi sect (ibid.:483). Needless to say, the explanation does not hold good. The two rulers of Nagaur named Shams Khan, living respectively at the beginning of the fifteenth and sixteenth centuries, have probably nothing to do with Jambha or his sect (Jain 1990:245-6). Instead, the Nizari Pir Sadruddin being generally regarded as the great grand-son of Pir Shams, it will be not be surprising to see him mentioned as '*Samas pautā*' once we have admitted that the Bishnoi sect is connected with Ismailism. Similarly, Maheshwari (ibid.:48) attempts to prove that the author Tajdin (Tajuddin) is the same as Tejoji, a Bishnoi Sant from the Charan caste, without explaining how this poet came to be also given a Muslim name without discarding his original one. It seems more logical to admit that this Tajuddin was the Ismaili Pir who succeeded his brother, Hasan Kabiruddin, and was also known as Prahlad. As has been suggested earlier, Jambha might have been his son or disciple, a reason why the Bishnois would have been originally named Prahladvanshis and Prahladpanthis.

Rahmatullah is presented by Mahesehwari (ibid.:635) as a Muslim poet of Rol, who had become a follower of Jambha. I suggest, in conformity with my basic hypothesis, that he might have been Hasan Kabiruddin's son from whom sprang the line of Kadriwala Sayyids who remained faithful to the Persian Imam. The signature 'Din Muhammad' may refer to Muhammad Shah, the founder of the Pirana sect or to Nuruddin Muhammad 'Satgur Nur', one of the first Nizari *dāīs* of the subcontinent.

Like the Ai Panth literature and to a greater extent the Nizarpanthi composition, the devotional texts of the Bishnoi tradition literally swarm with *ginānic* concepts and terms. All the Nizari motifs with which we are now familiar, *Nikalank avatār, Kāyam rājā,* Kalinga are present in the *vāṇīs* and *sākhīs,* and sometimes directly associated with a type of prophetic song which has already been mentioned, the *āgam vāṇīs.* In one of these texts signed *Lākho sādh,* the tenth *avatār* is even portrayed as riding the horse Duldul (Imam Ali's famous mount); as in the Nizarpanthi *Āgams,* he comes with thirty-three crores of Hindu deities, the Sayyids and Prophets. The figure referred to as Shah Saliṃ (*Sāh Salem*) might well be the fifteenth-century Imam of the time also known as Abud Salam, Salamullah, Islam Shah and Salah Shah (Ivanow, 1953:07). Although the poem has evidently been composed much later, this could be an obcure reminiscence of the time when the sect was still under the authority of the Persian Imam.

The recurrent formula '*Satguru sat panth chalāyā*' (lit. 'the true Guru started the true sect') may also be translated as the Satguru, the Pir as a representative of the divine Imam, established a sect referred to as Sat Panth (one of the cover names of the Nizari religion in the subcontinent). Other *ginānic* themes can be traced, such as the importance of recognizing the Lord (*guru* or *Satguru olakhno*) and the *didār* (divine vision) as the dearest wish of the believers. The thirty-three crore souls are constantly mentioned, and Jambha portrayed as the saviour of the twelve remaining crores. *Daylam deś* appears, generally in the corrupted form of *Dulam deś,* and the *Atharva Ved* is said to be the final revelation. *Das avatār* series also constitute one of the most conspicuous leit-motifs of the Bishnoi literary heritage. Finally, the followers of Jambha are commonly addressed as *momino* (*momin*).

EVOLUTION OF THE BISHNOI COMMUNITY

I propose to conclude this chapter with a few remarks concerning the part played by the process of 'reHinduization'. As for the Nizar Panth, it is not possible, in the present stage of our research, to determine at what time the links with the Persian centre had been severed. However, a glimpse of the progress of reHinduization is offered in the nineteenth-century census reports and gazetteers. Muslim elements, which are at present violently denied, are clearly present: the custom of burying the dead, the wedding ritual, the habit of growing a beard and cutting the *choṭī* (the tuft of hair kept by twice-born Hindus), the uttering of '*bismillāh*' after 'Vishnu', etc. (Erskine 1992:90-1, Munshi and Munshi 1895:76). These are ascribed to the desire of pleasing the local Muslim rulers of this time but one can interpret the facts in a different way. At the end of the last century Islamic customs and rites were still conspicuous enough to attract attention. Therefore, probably under the influence of the Hindu revivalist movements, they were reinterpreted in conformity with the new emerging ideals. Judging by the work of Maheshwari (1970), a further step was made in this century, so that many (if not all) Bishnois prefer to deny the existence of Islamic elements in their sect. Besides, referring to the twenty-nine principles, it is not difficult for Jambha's disciples to appear as high caste Hindus greatly concerned with purity and non-violence, values which seem alien to the majority of Muslims. Whenever it is not possible to erase traces of Islamic influence, attempts are made to reconstruct facts, names and etymologies as in the case of Ramdev. For instance, *Mukām* is said to be a corrupted form of *Muktidām* (sacred place where liberation is granted), *momimo* of *mumukṣa* (he who seeks *mokṣa* or *mukti*, liberation), whereas *jammo, jamo* (*jamā*) referring to the sacred vigil, is believed to derive from the name of its organizer, Guru Jambho.

This trend of evolution can also be observed in the use of an ochre coloured *chādar* over the original green one, the installation of portraits of Jambha in the Bishnoi shrines (although formal idol worship is still prohibited and devotees are requested to cover their head before entering a temple), and the erection of new structures with the appearance of Hindu *mandirs*.

WHO WAS THE FOUNDER OF THE BISHNOI SECT? ALTERNATIVE PERCEPTIONS

As some Muslims believe that Ramdev was in reality one of their coreligionists, a few are of the opinion that Jambha was another Islamic saint. Maheshwari (1970, I:155) reports the curious theory exposed by a British resident, Etkinson (1879) that Jambha might have been the famous Sunni Sufi Shaikh Makdum Jahania 'Jahangasht'. This Pir, however, flourished one century before Jambha and I do not see what could have been his connection with the Bishnoi sect.

The Muslim Qazis of Rol, who claim to be Suhrawardi Sufis, declared that Jambha's actual name was Jam Shah, and that he was a Sufi saint of some unidentified *tarīqa*. For some reason the Hindus he had converted reverted to their original faith, while continuing to rever their Pir and to attend his *dargāh* (*mukām*) near Bikaner. In this way, to repeat the words of one of the qazis, they were 'of neither Ram nor Rahim', i.e. remained without a clear-cut religious identity. As orthodox Muslims, they had once started their prayer with the words '*Bismillāh*' (in the name of Allah) but later on, in order to dissociate themselves from Islam, they took the habit of stopping after the first vowels, so that their invocations sounded as '*Bisem, Bisem*'—as a result of which they came to be referred to as Bishnois, *Bisem* having been confused with *Bisen* (Vishnu).

This amusing and absurd explanation must not divert our attention from other significant facts. The connection between the Bishnoi Panth and the village of Rol has not yet been entirely elucidated, but allusions to a former link can be traced. Firstly, the account of a quarrel between the Silavats of Rol (who are supposed to have built the shrine of Mukam) and Jambha's successors (Maheshwari 1970:438-9), and secondly the claim sustained by the Bishnois regarding some manuscripts of their tradition which the Qazis of Rol held in their possession and refused to restore to them. During my visit to this village, I heard that a few manuscripts, allegedly in Persian, were kept inside the *dargāh* by the Qazis of Rol. Among the titles mentioned was the *Risala ur Rahmatullāh*. Incidentally, one Rahmatullah is believed to have been a poet of this village affiliated to the Bishnoi sect (referred to earlier). Before this manuscript is examined, it is not possible to say if both figures are related and if there is any connection with the Nizari Sayyid of this name. In view of the Bishnoi claims, one can however suggest that a few Muslim communities of Rol, among them most probably the Silavats, may represent former Ismaili groups absorbed into Sunni Islam. Whether they are the authentic descendants of the Suhrawardi saint or ex-Nizaris themselves, it seems logical to deduce that the present Suhrawardi Sufis of the village were instrumental in compelling the Ismailis to embrace Sunni Islam. Therefore, as in the case of the

Nizar Panth, we may be faced with two split sections of the Nizari community: the Bishnois, who have chosen the Hindu identity but have been able to preserve their former heritage, and the Sunni groups of Rol who, logically, have been obliged to discard the major part of it.

The fact that Jambha can be perceived alternatively as a Hindu guru and a Muslim Pir (as he was in this own times, according to the Bishnoi hagiography), in other words, the 'liminality' of his religous identity, appears as a characteristic feature of the Nizari Ismaili tradition of the subcontinent where Pirs could be viewed, according to the context, as Hindu yogis or Sufi dervishes. Whereas I have argued that Ramdev came from a Hindu family which had been converted to Ismailism two generations earlier, in the case of Jambha, the lack of a clear genealogy and many elusive details in his hagiography prevents us from inferring anything concerning his identity. One of my Meghval informants, who was familiar with the Ramdev tradition and the Nizar Panth, connected him with Ugam Si Bhatti, and added that, at all costs, Bishnois and Khojas originally belonged to the same tradition.

Before further evidence can be found, I am personally inclined to think that the Prahladvanshis or Prahladpanthis are in some way connected with Pir Tajuddin and his descendants the Prahaladpautras.

NOTES

1. Maheshwari does not hesitate to speak of 'imaginary beliefs' and denies facts which have been observed directly by many nineteenth and twentieth century witnesses.
2. But for the short a vowel, one of the possible etymologies would have been 'Jambha', referring to a Puranic demon vanquished by Vishnu; Jambha, who is also named Jambheshvar would thus have referred to 'The Lord of Jambha', the God (Vishnu) whom the demon recognized as his master and to whom he submitted. Jambha is sometimes spelled with a short vowel, for example when designating his sayings as *jambhvāṇīs.*
3. The phenomenon has been analysed by Dumont for the Sadhs and the Gosains of Uttar Pradesh (1966:238-9).
4. Whether the principles related to purity and non-violence are Jain or Vaishnava in spirit might be difficult to ascertain; meanwhile Ghurye (1995:205) is of the opinon that the Ramsnehi *sādhus* (who associate themselves with the Ramanandi Sampraday) have been influenced by Jain ascetism: they 'generally are seen walking very warily lest they should happen to crush some vermin under their

feet. Not only do they drink water after straining it through a piece of cloth but also they also commonly avoid drinking water at night.'

5. The parallel ban on tobacco in the Ismaili and Bishnoi 'rules of conduct' might point to the fact that, at least upto the eighteenth century, the Bishnois formed an integral part of the Nizari community submitting to the authority of the Imam. But this detail must be discarded as evidence, since the Khojas would have imitated the Imamshahi *Śikṣāpatri* only in the nineteenth century (thus roughly four hundred years after the Pirana sect had become independent by seceding from the main branch). On the other hand, a legend connected with the trip of Randhir to Amarpuri, where he obtains gold with which the shrine of Jambha was erected, is identical with the Imamshahi account of Imam Shah's ascent to Amarpuri and his bringing back gold later kept at the Pirana shrine, which would testify to some historical link between the Bishnoi and the Pirana Panths.

CHAPTER 8

Jasnath, the Siddhs and the Jasnathi Sampraday

At first sight, the sect connected with Guru Jasnath may appear as a mere offshoot of the Bishnoi Panth with which it presents more than casual similarities. Jasnath (1482-1506) was a younger contemporary of Jambha who lived in the same region and died before him, rituals and literature of both traditions being hardly distinguishable, Maheshwari (1970:II:484) has argued that the Jasnathis took over a number of elements from the Bishnoi Panth, including the signature of its alleged Muslim disciples. Quoting a Bishnoi *bhajan* with the *chhāp* 'Samasdin', he writes: 'several verses of the second *sākhī*, with slight variations, have been, in the name of oral tradition, attributed to Jasnath by the Jasnathi followers and spread as such. Secondly, having spread various other songs composed by Bishnoi poets under the name of Samas Din, these people have tried to prove that he was a disciple of Jasnath which is not correct.' According to the same author, a devotional text of the Jasnathi Sampraday ascribed to the same Samasdin and starting with the words '*movniyā milo milāvo*' (O believer *momin*, 'gather and meet') is in reality the work of a Bishnoi poet named Jodhoji (ibid.: n. 2).

My Bishnoi informants did not claim that Jasnath had borrowed from Jambha, explaining that both had simply drawn their inspiration from the same *bhakti* environment; so argued the Jasnathis with whom I had the opportunity to discuss the question. S. Pareek, author of a few articles on the 'Bishnoi' and Jasnathi movements and *mahant* of a Jasnathi *gaddī*, was of the opinion that Ramdev, Jambha and Jasnath were three religious figures belonging to an originally identical tradition; he termed them 'Siddhs' (ascetics endowed with *siddhīs* or supernatural powers.[1] Kabir, Nanak and Dadu, he added, were to be regarded as Sants, whereas Mira Bai, Tulsi Das, etc., should be referred to as Bhaktas.[2]

Despite the earlier-mentioned similarities with the Prahlad-panthis, the Jasnathis (whom the British occasionally referred to, in gazetteers and census reports, as 'Siddh Jats') have preserved, in their tradition, enough original traits to deserve consideration in a separate chapter.

As usual, a summary of the current 'official' hagiography of the sect will be given first. Hamir and Rupande, a Jat couple residing at Kathriasar (a village near Bikaner) were childless. One night, in a dream, the pious Jat saw a yogi who introduced himself as Guru Gorakhnath (one of the founders of the Nath Sampraday). The yogi ordered him to go to the jungle: there, near a water tank, he would find a miraculous child whom he should adopt without fear. The little boy would be an incarnation of Vishnu-Krishna. On the following morning, Hamir and Rupande directed their steps towards the place indicated by Gorakhnath. On the shore of the lake they saw a beautiful baby who was playing with a snake and a tiger. Remembering the instruction of the Guru, the Jat approached him without fear, as a result of which both animals immediately disappeared.

Tradition has it that the original name of the boy was Jasvant or Jaspal. One day he met Gorakhnath in the jungle and receiving initiation at his hands, adopted the name of Jasnath. He was engaged at the age of ten. However, he decided to 'take *samādhi*' before the nuptial ceremony could be completed. Previously, he had become a *siddh* and performed penance for twelve years in a place now known as Gorakhnalya. Having heard of his decision, Kalal De, the young fiancee who lived with her family in the region of Hissar went to Kathriasar and also took 'living *samādhi*', thus becoming a *satī* of the Jasnathi tradition. Her sister, Pyare Sati, is said to have performed the same sacrifice for which both women are now worshipped by the members of the sect. These buried *satīs,* similar to those of the Ai Panth, do not have *chabūtrās* or *chhatrīs* but graves (*mazārs*) in the Muslim style.

In 1561 Vikram Samvat (AD 1504) Jasnath founded his sect by initiating a Jat, Chaudhari Ramu of Lalandesar village. He gave him the *chulu,* consecrated water similar to the Bishnoi *pāhal,* and tied a black thread around his neck referred to as *selī.* One interesting feature of the Jasnathi tradition is that its founder is regarded simultaneously as an *avatār* of Vishnu (identified with Krishna and with the tenth *avatār* Nikalank) and as an incarnation of Shiva, whereas his *satī*, Kalal De is considered a manifestation of the Goddess Parvati. Another point is worth mentioning: despite the numerous Nath elements traceable in the sect (Jasnath is said to have been a direct disciple of Gorakhnath and the Jasnathi Siddhs, like the Jogis, regularly add the suffix -*nath* to their names), the members generally deny that their *panth* could have been an offshoot of the Nath Sampraday, nor do the Gorakhnathi Jogis regard the Jasnathis as Naths. An attempt at solving this apparent contradiction will be made in the next chapter, when analysing the relation between Nizari Pirs and Nath Jogis.

GADDĪS OF THE SECT

The main seat of the Jasnathi Sampraday is located at Kathriasar, a village included in the district of Bikaner. From Naurangdesar, on the Dungargarh-Jaipur road, Jasnath's birth place is accessible only by camel or jeep. It is a desolate and arid tract where only thorny bushes and trees grow and where millet (*bajrā, jvār*) and *moṭh* (a variety of coarse pulse) constitute the sole crops. Jasnath's *samādhi* or *mandir*, as it is referred to, is located in the middle of this desert among the sand dunes. The entrance to the sacred complex is not marked by any artificial or natural boundaries, but a gate has recently been erected and the construction of a *dharamśālā* (pilgrim's resting place) is planned. Beyond the gate, the devotees and visitors are requested to remove their shoes and sandals, except if they are made of plastic. If one has not been careful enough to carry one pair, there is no other solution than walking bare-foot on the burning sand, a real ordeal for those who are not Siddhs.

The main shrine is a square, white building, reached by a flight of steps covered by a round dome, inside of which the grave of the saint has been installed. The tombstone (once more a typical *mazār*) is covered by an ochre-coloured *chādar* on top of which fly-whisks (*chavrīs*) and a peacock-feather broom (*morpankh*) have been placed. The *mazār* shows the usual north-south orientation and has been erected in front of a recess facing west, like a *mihrāb*. As in the case of Jambha, a colourful picture representing Guru Jasnath has been installed inside the niche, despite the prohibition of idol-worship. In this conventional modern iconography, the founder of the sect appears as a young ascetic, with long, loose hair, his body covered by a tiger skin. He is standing in *abhaya mudrā* (the traditional gesture of protection). As for Ramdev Pir, footprint stones (*pagliyā*) are offered to Jasnath and placed near his grave. Around the main shrine more modest dome-shaped structures are to be found: they contain graves of smaller size but of a similar type. These are regarded as the *samādhis* of Jasnath's disciples.

The Jasnathis recognize four other main *gaddīs*, at Bamblu (near Kathriasar), Likhmadesar and Pundasar, both situated in the vicinity of Bikaner, and Panchla (also referred to as Panchla-siddho-ka or 'Panchla of the Siddhs') near Khimsar, in the district of Nagaur.[3] Each *gaddī* has at its head a *mahant* referred to as Siddh. All Siddhs are householders and add to their names the suffix -*nāth*, as is the custom for the Kānphaṭā Jogis. Their function is hereditary. There are also Jasnathi *sādhus* (celibate renouncers) but, according to S. Pareek, this custom was introduced later into the tradition. All the other lay devotees initiated into the *panth* are known as Sevaks (a common appellation used for other Hindu devotees).

Under the authority of the five *gaddīs* are five *dhāms* (sacred shrines) and twelve *dhāms*. The latter are said to have been established by the twelve disciples of Siddh Rustam, an important figure of the Jasnathi tradition who flourished at the end of the seventeenth century. In the traditional hagiography, he is famous for having demonstrated his supernatural powers in front of the Mughal Emperor Aurangzeb. These twelve sacred places are located in various regions around Bikaner and Nagaur, in modern Haryana, Punjab and Uttar Pradesh. In Rajasthan other Jasnathi strongholds are the regions of Churu, Ganganagar, Barmer and Jodhpur.

After the twelve *dhāms* come the eightly-four *bārīs*: at *bārī* is a sacred place where a Jasnathi *sādhu, sevak* or *satī* have taken their 'living *samādhi*' under a *jāl* (*pilu, salvadora procera*), a tree as sacred to the Jasnathis as the *khejṛā* to the Bishnois. Eighty-four is considered a symbolic figure, since fifty or sixty other *bārīs* are indicated in various regions. Shrines which are not regarded as *gaddīs*; *dhāms* or *bārīs* are referred to as a *sthāpnās* (lit. 'establishments'); a hundred and eight *sthāpnās* are recognized in the tradition. All the remaining places where Jasnath is revered are said to be countless and are known as *bhāvnās* (lit. 'feelings'). According to the Jasnathi saying, 'five *dhāms*, twelve *dhāms*, eighty-four *bārīs*, hundred and eight *sthāpnās* and the rest are *bhāvnās*'. Each *gaddī* or *dhām* has its *mahant*; the *mahants* of a *bārī* have generally two to four villages, that is, fifty to sixty households, under their authority.

Contrary to the Bishnoi Panth, the Jasnathi Sampraday has preserved all the characteristics of a sect without transforming itself into a caste. One finds whole villages where the population consists exclusively of Jasnathis who are clearly identified by their *jāti*, although according to their beliefs, they should not make any discrimination on this basis. In Jodhpur and Barmer a good majority of Jasnathis are Jats, whereas in the region of Sardarshahar and Nagaur many of them are said to belong to the Oswal community (Jain merchants). Otherwise, Brahmans, Darzis, Chhipas, Sunars and Nais are reported as members of the sect which also has a number of Muslim followers. It is said that all the Siddhs (the householder *mahants*) are Jats by caste.

Once or twice a year, the *mahants* of *dhāms* and *bārīs* go to visit their *jajmāns* (here their patrons and disciples) the Jasnathi *sevaks* in their villages. This custom is referred to as *pherī lagānā* (lit. 'set off on one's rounds'). They are escorted by five or ten singers and travel on camel back, in bullock carts and, more recently, in jeeps. They bring with them two sacred *nagāṛās* (drums), a distinctive feature of the Jasnathi Siddhs, testifying to their association with local kingship. On top of these instruments an ochre-coloured banner and a peacock-feather broom are tied. *Mahānts* organize *jāgraṇs* for their *sevaks*, the Jasnathi vigil referred to as as *jammo*. The devotees offer in exchange money, grain, cloth, blankets, and so forth.

Regarding the association of the Jasnathi Siddhs with royal power, two important episodes of the traditional hagiography must be narrated. According to it, Lunkaran Rathore of Bikaner, the son of Bika, was said to have been blessed by Guru Jasnath, as a result of which he was to succeed to the throne after Neroji's death, instead of his elder brother. Similarly, the founder of the Jasnathi Sampraday was said to have taught a lesson to the sultan of Delhi Sikander Lodi. We have seen in the previous chapter that in the Bishnoi hagiography it was Jambha who was associated with Lunkaran and Sikander Lodi.

Rustam, as has already been alluded to, demonstrated the power of his *panth* to the Mughal ruler Aurangzeb who intended to persecute its members. By invoking Guru Jasnath, the famous seventeenth-century Siddh obtained from him a boon which would give birth to the most picturesque custom of the Jasnathi tradition: the power to walk and dance on burning embers without being burnt.

FESTIVALS AND CEREMONIES

The Jasnathis have three main festivals. Each starts with a *jāgraṇ* followed by a *melā* (fair) the following day, a custom which we have already noticed in the Nizarpanthi, Aipanthi and Bishnoi traditions. However, in the case of the Jasnathi Sampraday, these festivals do not fall on the new moon or on the *dūj* following it, but on the seventh day of the bright half of the Hindu month (*saptāmī*). Aśvin Śukl Saptāmī commemorates the *samādhi* of the founder of the sect and is referred to as Asojī. Māgh Śukla Saptāmī is said to be the day when Hansoji, one of Jasnath's disciples, received his *jyot* (the divine light of the guru, a concept reminiscent of the Sikh belief concerning the transmission of Nanak's 'light' to his successors). Finally, Chait Chautā and Saptāmī commemorate other events: the former falls on the day when Kalal De and Pyare De became *satīs* and is a *satī kā melā* which causes hundred of devotees to gather at Kathriasar and Bamblu. On Saptāmī the vigil and the fair consecrated to Jasnath are held.

According to the Jasnathi tradition, the original meaning of the word *jammo* (which, as in the Nizarpanthi and Bishnoi sects, refers to the vigil) is 'gathering, congregation', which correponds to the Arabic *jamāat.* All gatherings of the Jasnathi devotees are called *jammos.* The night session devoted to the singing of hymns in the Jasnathi tradition displays original features which distinguish it from the Bishnoi ritual. The main singer uses two *nagāṛās* and the others sit in a row, in equal numbers, on his right and left. The tempo and melody of the Jasnathi religious hymns are very peculiar and they sound like incantations: they are referred to as '*Jasnāthī rāg*'. The sequence of songs must follow a fixed pattern. For example, it is compulsory to start with a *pad* ascribed to Jasnath himself which must be followed by a composition signed 'Samsoji' (Samas Din, most probably Pir Shams Sabzwari). The other *pads* can be freely chosen from the Jasnathi repertoire of devotional poems and ballads.

During each of the three main festivals, the vigil is supplemented by what is known as the *agni jāgraṇ* (lit. 'fire vigil') among the Jasnathis and as the fire-dance (*āg nṛtya*) with the general public. The session starts like the usual *jāgraṇs*, with the *āratī*, a *pad* by Jasnath, one by Samso and a third one by any Jasnathi saint. When the fourth song, referred to as *nachnya pad* ('dance poem') starts, at the order of the guru who is the *mahant* of the place, the Jasnathi devotees stand up. A round fire-pit has been prepared with fifteen to twenty quintals of wood. When the fire is reduced to glowing embers the ritual dance can begin.

Doning their characteristic ochre coloured turbans, the disciples of Jasnath circumambulate the fire-pit or *dhūṇ*. The *dhūṇ* (*dhūṇā*, *dhūṇī* are synonyms) obviously functions as a sacred hearth and as a *havan kuṇḍ* or sacrificial pit. The Jasnathis jump and dance across the fire, walking on the embers with the ends of their *dhotīs* lifted and held in their hands. Only male devotees practise this ritual. Generally, there is a pause after five or six *bhajans*. After a certain time the fire dancers start to put glowing embers into their mouths, which they soon spit out. This feat is referred to as *matīrā khāna* (lit. 'eating melon'). Later they will scatter the embers and carefully avoid walking on the discarded pieces of burning wood which, having been removed from the *dhūṇ*, having lost their sanctity. After some time, other devotees will reshovel the embers and put them back into the pit. It is believed that the glowing embers cannot harm the Jasnathi devotees as long as they remain inside the fire-pit.

According to the tradition, the *jammo* vigil [including the partaking of *chulu* (*pāhal*) and the *āgni jāgraṇ*], was introduced by Siddh Jasnath to divert the people from their former practices connected with the *vāmmārgī* (left-handed) ceremonies of the type described in Chapter 4 (the *panchmakār* ritual). This detail is of exceptional interest, as it appears to confirm one of my hypotheses, namely that the Nizari Pirs imitated and transformed the Tantric rites prevalent among their converts in order to lead them more easily onto the new path. S. Pareek (personal communication) whom I had asked to explain the meaning of the term *nizārī* in the Jasnathi tradition, replied that it referred to 'a person who keeps chastity' (*brahmācharya*), 'abstains from the sexual practices of the *vāmmārgī* type, even when sitting side by side with his female partner'. Other meanings were suggested by the same informant: *nizārī* (*nejārī*) designated a 'banner bearer' (as in the Ramdev tradition *nejārī* was said to be a corrupt form of *nejādhārī*) and also referred to a 'staunch disciple of the sect'. It has been said earlier that in the Nizarpanthi tradition *nizārī* (*nijārī*) was also interpreted as 'virtuous and chaste'. But here too the non-sectarian observers have generally attributed to this word the reverse meaning and believe that it designates those who engage in Tantric-Shaktic sexual practices. This phenomenon is probably due to the secretive character of the Jasnathi ceremonies in which the non-initiated are not allowed to participate, as well as to the free mixing of devotees of all castes (the main feature of the *jammo*). These ceremonies have earned the Jasnathis a bad reputation with the high caste members of Hindu society who derogatorily call them *trijāts*, an allusion to the fact that they would have changed their caste thrice. At first they belonged to various communities before they were made Jats, and finally, from Jats they were converted into Jasnathis (*sevaks*), as a result of which they started to mix freely with other caste groups, including untouchables. For this reason, no commensality nor intermarriage is tolerated between the Siddhs and the non-Siddh (non-Jasnathi) Jats. It must be mentioned that similar accusations are made against the Bishnois. Ramdev and Mallinath, as we have seen, were believed by the non-Nizarpanthis to be connected with the ill-famed *kuṇḍā panth* where the *panchmakār* ritual would have been allegedly performed. Similarly, the Aipanthis were accused of following secret Tantric-Shaktic practice analogous to the *kuṇḍā panth* where all castes freely mixed, including the unclean groups. Incidentally, I heard that inspite of his alleged status as a Rajput and his high position in politics, the Diwan of Ai Mata, as the *mahant* of the Ai Panth, is styled by high status Hindus as 'the chief of the Gurras' and that his sect is similarly referred to as the 'sect of the Gurras'. The poor esteem in which this religious and political figure of modern India is held, despite his social rank, higher education and financial power, testifies to the fact that purity criterion still dominate Hindu society. As a member of the Ai Panth, according to the teaching of its founder, the Diwan is compelled to mix with devotees of all communities, including Harijans; besides, like the Gaur Brahmans among Hindus and Fakirs among Muslims, he takes 'the gifts of the dead', that is, the belongings of the deceased which are discarded as impure by the family.

THE TEACHING OF SIDDH JASNATH

Jasnath taught people of all castes to revere God in the *nirgūṇ* (non-qualified) form and to give up idol-worship. The *bhū samādhi* ('earth *samādhi*' referring to burial) was adopted instead of cremation and devotees were dissuaded from going on pilgrimages. Jasnath, like Pir Shams in other hagiographical traditions, caused the Ganga to flow in the sands of the desert in order to demonstrate to his followers that it was useless to go so far to 'sink the flowers' (dispose of the ashes) of their dead forefathers; the deceased were buried in the villages, in *kabristāns* (cemeteries similar to the Muslim ones) and, as in the *bhakti* tradition, 'pilgrimage was to be made in one's own heart'.

Jasnath would have required from his disciples a tenth of their income (*dasvand*), a custom which was later replaced by the collection of only a twentieth part (*bīsvand*), in consideration of the poverty of the local population which had to survive in an arid environment.

References to these tithes are found in the Jasnathi literature; for instance: *dasvant kharcho . . . thanai guru farmāyo* ('give a tenth part . . . the Guru has ordered you') and: *guru ko āsā bīsvant bānṭo* ('the Guru expects you to give the twentieth part'). It is not difficult to recognize a typical *ginānic* theme, the significance of which for Nizari Ismailism has already been stressed.

THE LITERARY HERITAGE OF THE JASNATHIS

The sectarian literature is of exceptional richness and comprises devotional compositions of various kinds referred to as *vāṇīs, pads, Simbhu dhārās* (from Sambu, i.e. Shiva) and so on. There are short songs, but also long poems in the form of ballads (*lokgāthās*). We will not be surprised to find that the themes of the longer compositions (as those of the shorter songs) are the usual 'Hindu Ismailized' patterns traced in the *ginans*, and also attested in the Nizarpanthi, Aipanthi and Bishnoi traditions, stories of Harischandra, Prahlad, Raja Bali, or the Pandavas, reconstructed in conformity with Nizari ideals. A large number of these texts have been collected from oral tradition and published. They are now available in libraries.

The Jasnathi literary compositions display the usual Ismaili motifs noticed elsewhere. Reference is made to *Nikalank avatār* with whom, this time, Jasnath is identified; it is believed that the Guru manifested himself in order to save the twelve remaining crores (out of the thirty-three crores of souls which were to be saved from Prahlad's time onwards). The Lord (here Jasnath) is also called *Kāyam rājā* (interpreted as the 'king who is eternal', i.e. God) and Nizar. S. Pareek says that the meaning of the sentence '*Nikalank avatār* will kill Kalang (Kalinga)' was not clear to him, despite his profound knowledge of the tradition. As shown by Gohil (1994:33-42), who is certainly quite familiar with this motif so crucial to the Nizar Panth, these names are related to the same type of prophecy known as *āgam vāṇīs* found in various other sectarian literatures; he has himself reproduced from

S. Pareek the long poem entitled *Nikalank purāṇ* ascribed to the Jasnathi eighteenth-century saint Lalnath (ibid.).

Nikalank avatār is also associated with *das dalam* (most probably *Daylam deś*) glossed by my informant as a synonym of *iśvar* (the Lord, God). As for the other analysed sects, the motif of the *das avatār* is a prominent one. Incidentally, I found one *bhajan* in which Buddha *avatār* (rather unusually) manifested himself together with the five Pandavas to save nine crores of souls. The unconventional association of Buddha with the heroes of the *Mahabharata*, said to have flourished in the previous age of *treta yuga*, is also characteristic of the Khoja tradition (Nanji 1978:113). Among various Islamic references I have noted are the following terms: Pir, *dargāh, didār, bismillāh.*

One interesting theme of the Jasnathi literature is the sharp criticism levelled at both Muslims and Nath jogis. The *bhajan* starting with: '*mahmad mahmad mat kar kāzī* ' ('O Qāzī, do not repeat the name of Muhammad') is similar to a *sabad* ascribed to Jambha. Except when one finds the signature of Jasnath, generally preceded by the name of his guru Goraknath, it is, impossible to distinguish a Jasnathi *bhajan* from a Bishnoi one. The same text, with very few variants, is sometimes given a different *chhāp.*

As other sectarian traditions studied here, the Jasnathis have also a 'manual of conduct' arranged in the form of a poem listing thirty-six principles. Most of them are identical with the tenets attributed to Jambha, including the recommendation to bathe, filter drinking water, abstain from tobacco, and not to kill antelopes or cut green trees. More interesting, insofar as it was not found in the Bishnoi *Untīs niyam* or *Battīs akhāṛī*, are the prescriptions concerning the burial of the dead and the obligatory *bisvant* (twentieth part of the income to be given by each member of the sect).

CONCLUSION

It may be added that, as in the case of the other analysed sects, the process of reHinduization has modifed many features of the Jasnathi tradition. Despite the presence of *kabristāns* and other conspicuous Muslim elements, the Jasnathis are generally regarded as pure Hindus, connected with the Nath Sampraday.

The fact that the Jasnathi tradition is believed to be a distinct sect, although it differs very little from the Bishnoi Panth may once more be explained through the fragmentation process referred to in

Chapter 3; it is not known if Jambha and Jasnath ever met (the Bishnoi and Jasnathi traditions deny such a possibility) but it is probable that the two, operating in the same area, were once closely related, that is, at the time when they were engaged in converting and organizing their communities. However, it can also be surmised that a certain amount of isolation was always kept for fear of attracting the attention of Sunni rulers, which would account for the earlier-mentioned phenomenon. The rest was probably done when the links with the Nizari centre of Persia (and its representatives in the subcontinent) were severed. As a consequence of this event, the two communities became independent and gathered under the banner of their respective Pirs and gurus. It is natural in these circumstances that the Jasnathis, like the Bishnois, while jealously preserving their secret heritage, should start to develop original features which were later viewed as 'popular traditions' and indicated a separate religious movement.

An essential point remains the association of the Jasnathi Sampraday with the tradition of the Nath jogis. The issue, in its broader context, will be discussed in the next chapter.

NOTES

1. The Nath Sampraday mentions the nine Naths and the 'eighty-four Siddhs' among whom figure gurus belonging both to the Hindu and to Buddhist Tantric traditions.
2. I thank Surya Shankar Pareek for having supplied me with this precious information. I quote here from our talks in Bikaner as well as from his letters. Many details are also drawn from an interview conducted by Gulab Kothari (G. Kothari 1990). Pareek is at present preparing a detailed study of the Jasnathi Sampraday for publication.
3. At Bamblu, one can see the *samādhi* (*mazār*) of Hariji, a disciple of Jasnath; next to his shrine is located a small building inside of which a symbol of Jasnath's *samādhi* (again in the form of a Muslim grave) has been erected. This kind of structure, which I have earlier called *chillā mazār* (to use the terms suggested by the Sayyids of Junjala concerning Shams Pir's replicas of graves installed for worship), is also attested to in the Bishnoi tradition: for instance, Jambha's replica of a grave is to be found in the shrine of Sambharatal (R.S. Gupta 1966:50). At Panchla, there is an imposing *maṭh* surrounded by fortified walls. Inside the sacred compound one finds a few halls sheltering rows of *mazārs* said to be the *samādhis* of the previous *mahants* who in this case are celibate renouncers. The *mazārs* are covered with ochre-coloured *chādars,* and *paglyās* are placed in front of them, exactly as in the shrine of Ramdeora. Outside, in the courtyard, a few *chhatrīs* are to be seen. Under the stone canopy small *mazārs* have been installed as in the Nizarpanthi tradition. I have not observed *samādhis* of a more Hinduized type.

CHAPTER 9

The Nizari *Dawa* and the Nath Sampraday

In the *ginānic* tradition a number of elements point to the fact that there has been a strong interaction between Nizari Pirs and yogis of the Nath sect. Here I wish to suggest that in the same way as the interaction with Sufism generated both rivalries and coalescences, encounters with various groups of Nath Jogis in Sind, Punjab, Gujarat, Rajasthan, and elsewhere may have given birth to a similar phenomenon. Unfortunately, whereas a few authors have touched on the process of coalescence between Sufism and Nizari Ismailism in the Persian context (Ivanow 1959:15-16, Corbin 1986:152-4 and passim, Daftary 1990:452-5 and passim), the existence of a similar link between Nathism and Ismailism has never been contemplated to this day.

Coalescence with Sufism has been explained by the sharing of philosophical ideals, the necessity of *taqīyya,* as well as by the usual methods of conversion which gave birth to acculturated forms of Nizari Ismailism. Daftary, following Ivanow, points out that Nizari *dāīs* were sometimes 'disguised as darwishes' and even took formal affiliation into Sufi *tarīqas.* Similarly, they have sometimes been 'appropriated' by orthodox Sunni orders of the Sufis, an issue which was discussed in the first chapter.

I will argue that the coalescence with the Nath Sampraday in the Indian subcontinent operated on exactly the same basis. As stated by Nanji (1978:106) 'the vehicle and the signs employed in conveying the ideas [of Ismailis] depended very much on the milieu in which the *dawa* was operating'. Owing to their importance, it will not be out of place to repeat here the words of the same author (ibid.:68), as they have a direct bearing upon the subject. 'The Pir [the Nizari *dāī*] emerges as a Hindu yogi or a wandering dervish, working totally within the forces current at the time.' It is not surprising, therefore, to find in the *gināns* various yogic references, ranging from the eighty-four *āsans* of hatha-yoga to the *siddhīs* (supernatural powers obtained by ascetism), the technique of *samādhi* and the mystical concept of *śabd.*

In Chapter 5 it was suggested that, at the time when the Nizari preachers started their missionary activities in India the various movements, practices and ideas connected with Nathism had already had a strong influence on the local propulation, in particular on groups like Meghvals and Lohanas. It appears that Sind and Punjab were strongholds of the Jogis. There is evidence that Tantric-Shaktic practices were prevalent among certain groups and it is not illogical to suppose that some untouchables had obtained a high position as gurus and *mahants* in the sect. The missionaries, therefore, could not start their programme of conversion without taking into account the popularity of yogic ideas and practices. In the Khoja tradition, the *dāī* Satgur Nur is portrayed like a yogi when, for example, he is described in a state of *samādhi,* which does not prevent him from showing his superiority over indigenous yogis, by showing a miracle in front of the Nath guru Kanipa. A Meghval legend has it that 'Gusainji', whom I have tentatively identified with Satgur Nur, and who clearly appears as a Shaiva ascetic (for instance in the rock-gallery of Mandore), was 'discovered' by a devotee to be in reality a Muslim fakīr (personal communication Swami Ram Prakash Achyut). We have interpreted the ambiguity of Shams Pir/Samas Rishi as a figure connected with the Ramdev tradition, as ensuing from the fact that Shamsuddin Sabzwari Multani came to Rajasthan and worked among the Meghvals in the guise of a yogi. The Nizari *dāī* Hasan Kabiruddin himself acquired two additional personalities, first as a Suhrawardi Sufi Pir named 'Hasan Darya' and second as a Shaiva ascetic, clad in ochre-coloured clothes, as 'Anant-jo-dhani'.

It is even more intriguing to discover, among the longer *gināns* attributed to Pir Shams, a text entitled *Rājā Govarchand tathā tenī Ben nī Kathā* now available in Gujarati script in the collection of Mukhi Lalji Bhai Devraj (Noorally 1973:85).[1] This is an Ismaili version of the story of the renouncer-king Gopichand, one of the famous yogis of the Nath tradition. A popular ballad on Gopichand is sung in many parts of north India by the so-called 'Bhartrihari Jogis' who are householder Naths (Grodzins-Gold 1994). The singers tell moving stories of Raja Bhartrihari and his nephew Gopichand who, renouncing the throne, received the Nath initiation and became wandering yogis.[2] A part of the story of Gopichand, when he is confronted with his sister, Champa De or Champavati (ibid.:259-64), can be compared with the *ginān* on Govarchand, elsewhere named Gopichand, and his sister Nilavanti. The Nath Jogi Gopichand and the Ismaili Govarchand are the same; both are said to be the disciples of Jalandarnath and the basic theme is identical: the young king becomes an ascetic and his sister tries to dissuade him (Noorally 1973:85). The city of Ujjain is mentioned in the Ismaili text, as well as the name of the yogi's father and mother, all these details being in conformity with the Nath tradition. However, Moir (personal communication) is of the opinion that both texts differ in tone and meaning. The *ginān* is deprived of the rich folk-motifs found in the Nath ballad and has a generally more solemn tone: 'it stresses the importance of immortality and conveys discreetly the syncretic teaching of *Satpanth*'. Besides, the names of the Pirs such as Shams, Sadruddin and Hasan Kabiruddin are briefly mentioned, so as to stress that real salvation lies in the hands of the Satgur (the Pir). In other words, it seems that the appropriation of the yogic ballad by the Nizari preachers testifies to that process analysed by Kassam (1994:233) in which Hindu symbols and allusions provide 'scope for a coherent shift in perspective from Hindu to Isma'ili'. In the specific case studied here, the story of Gopichand might have been chosen and adequately transformed (in the same way as the Tantric rituals were selected and modified according to the Ismaili ideology) to lead smoothly, but inadvertently, into the new path, groups who were initially under the strong influence of the ideals and observances of the Nath Sampraday.

A further stage of interaction is illustrated by *gināns* which, according to Moir (personal communication), are of a later period. They have a more critical attitude towards yogic ideals, such as an emphasis on supernatural powers, ascetism, and penance. In this respect the *ginānic* text '*Guru Hasan Kabīrdīn ne Kāniphā Jogīno Samvad*' ('Discussion between Guru Hasan Kabiruddin and the Jogi Kanipav Nath') is of exceptional interest for our subject. Kanipav, disciple of the famous Kānphaṭā ascetic Jalandarnath, revered as a guru by the untouchable Kalbelya Jogis (snake-charmers) of Rajasthan, goes to see the Nizari Pir Hasan Kabiruddin, son and disciple of Sadruddin because he has not been able to attain salvation through the teaching of his Nath guru. Although Kabiruddin was only a child, he was able to show him the right path and the way towards liberation. Thus, reconstructing the history of the Nath movement, the unknown author of the *ginān* goes so far as to 'appropriate' one of its famous exponents.

If we find a variant of a ballad belonging to the Nath repertoire with the signature of the Nizari *dāī* Pir Shams, the reverse phenomenon is also attested. For example, a version of the Nizarpanthi *āgam vāṇī* (a type of composition which primarily belongs to the Ismaili heritage) is sung by some Kamads of Ramdev with the *chhāp* 'Matsyendranath'. Actually, stating implicitly that Kanipav and Gopichand have become Nizaris or that the Jogi Matsyendranath has adopted the Satpanthi ideas and beliefs is but a way of 'diverting' famous yogis into the Ismaili camp with the aim of enhancing the power and prestige of the *dawa.* This tactic is not fundamentally different from the Ismaili perception of Hindu mythological figures, such as Prahlad, or the Pandavas as Nizari devotees—a belief which is shared by the Nizarpanthis for whom these *bhaktas* of previous *yugas* have been secretly converted to their sect. However, the 'appropriation' of famous yogis, saints and devotees must not only be regarded as a strategy of conversion, or, in Kassam's words (1994:232), a 'technique of transformation'. It has also a more profound, esoteric resonance, as for example in the idea that the Biblical characters Adam, Noah, Moses, Jonas and Seth were in reality Ismailis, whose true identity had been concealed (Marquet 1985:191-3, 197, 231); the principle of *taqīyya* itself thus acquires an esoteric meaning and history can appear as the unveiling of hidden truths, a spiritual revelation. It is not absurd to assume that the Isamili Pirs who operated in the guise of yogis, revealing their real 'identity' only gradually, should have, by their very example, convinced their disciples that the powerful figures of Hindu mythology were not essentially different from their own. 'Shifty' and evasive identities have apparently always characterized the Ismaili preachers for whom the changing of names, garbs, customs and terminologies was simultaneously a necessity of *taqīyya*, a method of conversion, and a way of demonstrating the pervasiveness of their tradition which knew neither geographical nor historical boundaries.

If the Nizaris have absorbed a number of Nath elements, and still more, 'infiltrated' the Nath milieu (very much in the fashion of spies penetrating foreign circles under a forged identity), it is logical that conversely the Naths (when they had been approached by Ismaili missionaries) would have retained certain Nizari influences. We have seen that *mahants* of the Kānphatā tradition were sometimes termed Pirs and that two subdivisions of the yogic Ai Panth (to distinguish it from the homonym sect of Ai Mata) were called *bāṛī dargāh* and *choṭī dargāh*. Much more striking are the Islamic references found in the *Gorakhvāṇīs*, poems ascribed to Guru Gorakhnath. The *sabdī* numbered 118 quoted by Lalram Srivastav (1984:238) is comprised of words such as 'Pir', 'Muhammad' and 'Khudāi'. Schomer (1987:70) quotes famous verses ascribed to the same Nath teacher which say: 'The Hindus call on Ram, the Muslims on Khuda. The yogi calls on the invisible One in whom there is neither Ram nor Khuda.' Schomer rightly connects these ideas with Santism (similar declarations are found in Kabir, Nanak and Dadu), and attributes them, like all other scholars, to the influence of Sufism. The similarities to Ismaili *ginān*s have not been sufficiently emphasized nor explained to this day.

It has already been said that the compositions associated with the Bishnoi and Jasnathi sects were generally classified by Rajasthani authors as 'Sant poetry' and a comparison with Kabir's poems appeared sufficient to account for the presence of numerous Islamic elements. These elements were also given a Sufic origin. In Chapters 7 and 8, I have attempted to demonstrate the connection of these two sects with the Nizari *dawa* by bringing out a series of customs, concepts and terminologies which were typical of Ismailism. In connection with this and the subject of this chapter, attention will now be drawn to the intriguing similarity between another *Gorakhvāṇī* and two devotional compositions ascribed to Jambha and Jasnath.

The verses ascribed to Gorakhnath are (Rizvi 1986, I:339):

Mahmad Mahmad na kari kāzī mahmad kā viṣam bichārā
Mahmad hathi karad je hotī lohai ghaṛī na sārā.

Jambha's *sabad* no. 12 (Gyanprakash 1992:46) reads:

Mahmād Mahmād na kar kāzī Mahmād kā to viṣam vichārū
Mahmād hāth karad jo hotī lohai ghaṛī na sārūn.

As we see, it is identical, word for word, with the *Gorakhvāṇī* but for a few dialectal variations.

It must also be paralleled with a *vāṇī* signed Jasnath (Pareek 24):

Memad Memad mat kar kāzī Memad bikham bichārī
Memad Pir halālī hontā tum kāzī murdārī
Memad hāth karotī hontī loh ghaṛī na sārī.

'Do not repeat the name of Muhammad, o qāzī, Muhammad's ideas are very far from yours,

If Muhammad were a butcher, so you, qazi, are a murderer!
If Muhammad had a saw in his hand it would certainly not be made of iron.'

Far from concluding that Gorakhnath (or any of his followers who used his signature to give authority to his composition) has borrowed from the Ismailis or has been influenced by them, one should rather regard this remarkable phenomenon as the consequence of the 'embeddedness' of some Nizari preachers in the Nath circles. A similar explanation might be given to the curious fact that, at the Nath *maṭh* of Sivaramandap in Kacch, 'the Jogis worship the horse image of Naklank' (*Nikalank avatār*) (Khakhar 1978:53 and Briggs 1989:130). Incidentally, the Nizarpanthis of Gujarat consider Sivaramandap as a sacred place.

A few famous religious figures endowed with a 'dual religious identity' have been regarded by most authors as 'syncretistic' creations of the popular imagination (Husain 1929, Ahmad 1964 and 1969) inspired by the interaction between Hindu beliefs and Sufism. The same process is termed 'yogic syncretism' by Rizvi (1986; I:354) with reference to Muslim yogis. No convincing explanation, however, has been suggested nor has the phenomenon been analysed in all its details and implications. Once more, the term 'syncretism' and the idea of spontaneous exchanges and mutual influences have appeared satisfactory explanations.

A few examples will be provided here, with a view to demonstrating that the issue is more complicated than it seems and that 'spontaneous syncretism' is a cliche that obscures the fact that the phenomenon may have possessed, instead, historical roots. In Sind, Lal Shahbaz Qalandar was known to his Hindu followers as Raja Bhartrihari; Pir Patho became Raja Gopichand and Pir Haji Mango was called Lala Lasraj' (Jasraj) (Ansari 1992:19). The author implicitly seems to admit that these Muslim saints, whom she recognizes as Suhrawardi Sufis, have been 'spontaneously' transformed into Hindu yogis by their Hindu followers so that they could properly worship them. Conversely, Carter (1917:205) argues that the Indus river God, Uderolal, 'has been converted for the benefit of Mussulmans to Sheikh Tahir, so at Sukkur, Zinda Pir, the living God, has become Khwaja Khizr and near Tatta, Shah Jandho, the saviour ferry-man'. The contrary has also been said. Such statements however, are not in conformity with what we know. When after having obtained a boon from some Muslim Pir, say from Muinuddin Chishti of Ajmer, Hindu or Jain women start to visit the shrine regularly and adopt certain practices such as wearing a green sari each Friday, they show their reverence for an Islamic saint without feeling the need to endow him with a Hindu name and personality. Similarly, one does not see the necessity of transforming the religious identity of a Hindu deity so that Mohammedan followers could worship him, as there are numerous examples of Muslims who perform a cult to Hindu goddesses (such as Sitala Mata) without feeling compelled to give them an Islamic 'pedigree'.

The perspective will change if we reconsider the identity of the alleged Suhrawardi saints Lal Shahbaz, Pir Patho and Pir Mango; in the Ismaili tradition the former two saints are clearly regarded as Nizari *dāīs* (Allana 1984:34-5). As far as Pir Mango is concerned (Lalu Jasraj), my Kamad informants have told me an interesting legend which, according to them, accounts for the origin of their *bhekh* and sect, the Kamadiya Panth (a synonym of Nizar Panth). Lalu and Jasraj are regarded as twin brothers born from the dirt of Rama's body while he was taking a bath before performing *pūjā* to the Tantric Goddess, Hinglaj, tutelary deity of the Nath yogis. These 'impure' beings will become great ascetics and they are indeed the model of the untouchable Kamad *sādhus* who recognize in them their ancestors. The story continues with the quarrel of the two brothers, each desiring to take possession of the ochre-coloured robe (*pītāmbar*) the hero of the *Ramayana* has given to them as a token of their religious vocation. Jasraj steals the cloth from his brother and flees. Furious, Lalu goes into the forest and performs penance. Shiva grants him a boon and he receives another ochre-coloured robe. Later, he goes to Thattanagar (in Sind) and pays obeisance to the *mahant* of a *maṭh* who is an Aughar yogi (Aughars were those who did not have their ears split and, thus, were not 'Kānphaṭās'). Lalu requires the ascetic to initiate him into his order. However, the *mahant* notices that, although he has not yet received initiation, the young man is clad in ochre-coloured clothes. He immediately curses him to become a householder and be obliged to earn his livelihood. After Lalu has explained that the robe has been given to him by Shiva as a result of a long penance, the Aughar Nath agrees to initiate him but cannot, of course, withdraw his curse. Lalu leaves the monastery and goes once more into the forest to practice penance. This time Shiva gives him a musical instrument (an allusion to the *tandurā* with which Kamads are associated) and teaches him the *rāgas*. Subsequently, the yogi will be able to earn money and sustain his family by singing devotional songs. We have seen that, according to my hypothesis, the Kamads or Kamadiyas of Rajasthan could be viewed as the counterparts of the Nizari Kamadiyas, though they have evolved in a different way, and that they seemed to be closely connected to Ismailism. For the Sunni Muslims, Maggar Pir or Mango Pir whose shrine is near Karachi, is a Suhrawardi saint connected with the worship of sacred crocodiles (*magar*); for the Kamads he is a Hindu yogi.

The solution would be to assume that, like Lal Shahbaz-Bhartrihari and Pir Patho-Gopichand, Pir Mango-Lalu-Jasraj was neither of the two. This dual personality, typical of so many Nizari *dāīs* in the context of the subcontinent, was aimed at concealing their true identity, so that they could conduct their missionary activities in the inconspicuous Ismaili way. In this case, if my theory is correct, the term 'syncretism' could apply only to the visible consequences or apparent results of this tactic based on *taqīyya*, but not to the phenomenon as perceived in its diachronic dimension.

Consequently, I will argue that 'Bhartrihari', and 'Gopichand' do not refer, in these cases, to the mythical figures of the renouncer kings, but were names purposely assumed by the Nizari missionaries under their yogic guise; in the same way, Sadruddin had called himself Sahadev, and Kabiruddin, Prahlad. This also means that they were to be regarded as reincarnations of these legendary figures.

We can now revert to a brief survey of the Nizarpanthi, Aipanthi, Bishnoi and Jasnathi traditions and consider them in this perspective. In Ramdev's hagiography, the Nath element played a significant role: an Aghori yogi named Balinath (Balaknath) is said to have been his guru, though Ramdev's followers deny any direct connection with the Naths. However, one of my Kamad informants declared that many of them had lived, and still live as Shaiva ascetics, being referred to as Naths, or as Kapri Gosains (according to the legend told above, the legendary Lalu would have been the first Kapri Gosain). Some of them even denied the fact that they were Kamads, though the Kamads themselves identified them clearly with their caste-fellows. My informant's grandfather and great-grandfather had openly used the suffix *-nāth* and were known as Govind Nath and Ram Nath, as testified by an inscription carved on an old *kamandal* (the wandering ascetic's water pot). In Chapter 3 we have seen that certain Nizarpanthis were affiliated to a *gaddī* referred to as Nathani and were initiated by Nath yogis into their own *panth.*

The Bishnoi tradition also contains, though to a lesser extent, a number of Nath terminologies and concepts, but Jogis are the target of sharp criticism, and it does not seem that there has been any attempt at identifying Bishnoi *sādhus* with Naths. In contradistinction to this, the Jasnathi Sampraday, which otherwise appears as a mere variant of Jambha's tradition, tends to identify itself with Gorakhnath's sect. Jasnathis will not claim to be full-fledged Nath jogis, but their hagiography insists that Jasnath's guru was Gorakhnath and a small shrine sheltering a sacred *jāl* tree and a *shiv ling* has been erected near his *samādhi* at Kathriasar. The same apparent paradox can be noticed in the Ai Panth. Although the followers of Ai Mata do not identify themselves with the Naths, the name of their sect is the same as a particular order of the Jogis who worship the Goddess, and their main *gaddī* at Bilara is regarded by Ramdev's traditional worshippers as a centre connected with the Nizar Panth as well as with the Nath Sampraday.

Efforts have been made recently by a few Nizarpanthis to demonstrate that their sect was a section or an offshoot of the Nath Sampraday, or had a similar origin. Despite many common traits shared by both traditions, the main difference (at least, the most conspicuous one), is the emphasis put by Ramdev's followers on the necessity of remaining householders, versus the Nath ideal of renouncement, which even householder Naths admit to be the highest value.

Before concluding, it will be suggested that a few other ambiguous figures of saints endowed with a dual identity may have been connected with Ismailism: Baba Ratan Haji/Ratan Nath-ji, Guga Pir/Goga Dev and Shaikh Tahir/Uderolal (Khaja Khizr/Jhulelal). A few Bishnoi *vāṇīs* mention two of them jointly, associating them, indirectly, with the teaching of the sect. One has therefore the impression that this formula conceals an esoteric meaning known only to the initiated Prahladpanthis:

Bābā Rāwal Hājī Ratan, Khuwāj Khidar Elias . . .

The title 'Rawal' is applied to certain categories of Jogis and Elias the Biblical figure is sometimes identified with the Koranic figure of Khwaja Khidar, who plays an important role for Sufis, as well as for Nizaris.

In a poem (which I found similar to the Ismaili *duā*) the Lalbegis also mention Khwaja Khidar: *Awwal Pīr Asā, Dom Pīr Hazrat Khwāja Kāsā* (Rose 1993,II:201), 'the first Pir is Asa, the second onc Khwaja Khizr'.

Without entering into details,[3] a few points will be suggested concerning the protean figure referred to as Shaikh Tahir, Shah Jhando, Khwaja Khizr, Zinda Pir, Uderolal, Jhulelal or Amarlal. Viewed by many authors as a 'popular deity', a god of the river Indus, patron of sailors and so on, he has seldom been analysed in the role of a spiritual teacher, or founder of a sectarian movement which still exists. According to his traditional followers (the Hindu Sindhi Lohanas), he had established, in the tenth century, a sect known as the Daryashahi Panth (one of his double appellations being also Darya Shah and Darya Nath). He is said to have had disciples among both Hindus and Muslims. The most remarkable feature of his hagiography is the quarrel which followed his death, or rather his *samādhi* (he is said to have disappeared in the water of the Indus, *jal samādhi*, or to have been buried, *bhū samādhi*). As Hindu and Muslim disciples were quarrelling, the Pir's voice was heard: he permitted the former to erect a temple in which a sacred lamp would replace the forbidden idol, whereas the latter were allowed to build a *dargāh*. Both places became sacred to the Daryapanthis, as they were called. The episode is strikingly reminiscent of a famous scene in Kabir's hagiography The weaver saint of Benares is also worshipped by the two communities in two separate, but similar shrines. The Muslim disciples (claiming to be his descendants) perceive him as a Sufi Pir, whereas the Hindu Kabirpanthis view their guru as a Brahman adopted by a Muslim family, who was in reality a divine incarnation. In both cases—the worship of Uderolal and of Kabir—the consequence of the 'split' has been the same: those who continued to revere him with a Hindu identity formed a sect (Kabir Panth, Daryashahi Panth) and preserved a good part of the old religious tradition, which they gradually sought to reHinduize; the Muslim followers, now perceived as 'orthodox' Sunnis, do not have a sect and have lost most of their former heritage, keeping only the reverence for the saint, viewed henceforth as an 'orthodox' Sufi Pir.

Of considerable interest is the fact that the Daryashahi Lohanas do not claim that their sect is a branch of the Nath Sampraday, although they perceive it as a Hindu movement, whereas the Naths themselves consider that what they call the Darya Panth is a section of the Nateshvari order of Jogis or an independent branch, the founder of which was one Darya Nath. Meanwhile, located in Sind, Uderolal's *dargāh* is considered by the local Muslim population as a Sunni Sufi shrine. Confronted with this confused and complicated framework scholars have perceived this ambiguous figure either as an Islamic saint or a Hindu god, each arguing that the 'other community' had adopted him and transformed his personality to suit its own religious ideals.

The Daryashahi tradition, as I could observe it among the Sindhis living in Rajasthan, seems to have a decidedly Ismaili 'flavour'. A. Khan (1980; 312-14) in a monograph on the history of Sind makes a similar suggestion: 'the double nomenclature and a similarity in symbols, and sanctity attached to numerals five and seven suggests that he [Uderolal] might have been an Ismaili *dāī* or was deeply impressed by the Ismaili belief'. Among the elements which might point to a connection with Ismailism, the author mentions the palm of the hand (*panjtan*), the seven objects which are like the 'seven Imams of the Ismailis', five burning lamps and so forth. To this I simply wish to add the description of one of the seven sacred objects, as given by Carter (1978:200): a *timalhī* or *jhāri*, 'a pot containing sacrificial water for distribution in cups'. This detail, the association of a pot full of consecrated water with cups (*piyālās*), is strikingly reminiscent of the Khoja ritual of *ghaṭ-pāṭh* where the water from the holy *ghaṭ* is distributed to the faithful in individual *piyālās* (Nanji 1982:106 and 1988:66, Rajyaguru, n.d.:506). In the Daryashahi tradition, the deified Jhulelal-Zinda Pir is also said to be 'the twenty-fifth *avatār* of the Hindus', a clear reference to the twenty-four incarnations of Vishnu, and is known as *Sachā badshāh* (the 'true emperor'), a Persian designation of the Nizari Imam. Hindu Sindhis frequently declare that 'there is no fundamental difference between Jhulelal-Zinda Pir and Ramdev-Ramshah Pir': both have established similar principles, have had disciples among Hindus and Muslims, and are represented in popular iconography as bearded warriors, mounted on a horse and holding a spear (Jhulelal's other image shows him as a kind of ascetic with a flowing white beard, riding on a fish, in the middle of the Indus river). One of my Sindhi informants had it that 'to have the *darśan* of one is to have the *darśan* of the other'.

According to Briggs (1989:65-6), Ratan Nath was a disciple of Bhartrihari. He is also revered by Muslims. 'Ratannathis are counted as Daryanathis as well'. Although the connection between the two is not explained, the detail is interesting, insofar as the names of both are associated in the verse of the Bishnoi *vāṇī* quoted above. Srivastav (1984) has amply shown the ambiguity of this fascinating character simultaneously viewed as a Nath yogi (Ratan Nath) and as a Muslim saint (Ratan Haji). The exceptional longevity which is attributed to him somehow recalls the alleged immortality of Khwaja Khizr with whom he is linked. A similar ambiguity is reported by Briggs (1989: 66) regarding the nature of his disciple and son Kayanath/ Qaimuddin (created, as legend has it, from the dirt of his body): 'When Kāyanāth died, both Musalmāns and Hindus claimed his body but it disappeared, only the clothes remaining. Hindus built a *samādhi* for him, and Musalmāns a tomb.' The episode, it will be easily noticed, recalls not only the quarrel between Uderolal/Khizr's followers in Sind, but the well-known hagiographical account of Kabir's death, where the rival disciples, lifting the cloth covering the Sant's body, found only flowers which they shared to worship as Kabir's mortal remains, respectively in a *samādhi* and a *dargāh.*

Bouillier (forthcoming) has provided an excellent analysis of Siddha Ratan Nath's Nepali tradition and has attempted to link it to the Punjabi, Hindu and Muslim contexts. She arrives at the conclusion that Ratan Nath was probably a Sufi saint flourishing towards the end of the thirteenth century, whose fame and psycho-physiological methods related to breath control would have attracted the yogis who adopted him and spread his cult in their own circles. This interpretation, interesting as it is, does not satisfy me entirely, except if the epithet 'Sufi' were intended to refer to any Islamic saint of the dervish type, regardless of his affiliation. As has been argued earlier, I do not believe in the necessity of altering a Pir's religious identity before worshipping him except if one assumes that the process occurred only recently, after the revivalist movements had spread their influence. Before the need to affix clear-cut labels had been felt in the subcontinent, there seems to have been no objection, on the part of those who followed the Brahmanical rites, to perform the worship of a Muslim Pir, as is still the case of those who refuse to submit to the pressure of fundamentalists.

I will argue, once more, that Haji Ratan Nath was neither a true Kānphāṭa Jogi nor a Sufi of the Kubrawiya order, as the representatives of this *tarīqā* have attempted to prove. According to Rizvi (1986:320), this Kubrawiya affiliation has been forged with the help of a legend which became a part of the tradition of this Sufi order and was legitimized and recognized as authentic by Mir Sayyid Ali Hamdani. This could be another illustration of the evasive personality of Ismaili missionaries who appeared, depending on the context, as 'yogis or wandering dervishes' (Nanji 1978:26).

The fascinating figure of Goga Dev/Guga Pir, a 'folk deity' of Rajasthan and north India whose fame is no less considerable than that of Ramdev, has been connected by his Muslim *pujārīs* to Baba Haji Ratan Nath. The ubiquitous yogi-cum-Pir has been associated with the Chauhan rulers of Bhatinda in Punjab where his *samādhi-dargāh* is located; Goga himself was, according to tradition, a Chauhan Rajput, as claimed by the Muslim priests in charge of Goga's cult at his main shrine of Gogamedi (district Ganganagar). Legend has it that at his own request he was swallowed by the earth, but had first to be initiated by Gorakhnath, or in other versions by Haji Ratan Nath, sometimes coupled with Uderolal/Zinda Pir (Temple 1993,I:204-6). In popular belief this is supposed to account for the fact that, although he was a Rajput, he was not cremated but buried like a Shaiva ascetic or a Muslim.

A detailed study of the Goga tradition would require at least a separate chapter and involve more extensive field research than has hitherto been done despite the abundant references to the subject in journals, books, and hagiographical publications. Actually, the available material reveals the complexity and richness of the folk tradition connected with Goga, but gives no idea of its original roots. It is generally believed that Goga was a Hindu ruler, although his Muslim priests say that he had been converted to Islam, which was also their case at a later stage. As far as Goga's untouchable *Bhopās* ('popular' priests and healers) are concerned, they claim that their guru and God was 'half-Hindu half-Muslim', like his official *pujārīs* of Gogamedi, the Muslim Chahils.

I will now mention a few details which will show to what extent the 'Goga phenomenon' is reminiscent of what I have observed in the Nizarpanthi and other similar traditions. Goga's *samādhi* at Gogamedi appears outwardly like a *dargāh* in the Sindhi style (similar to the tomb of Mango Pir near Karachi), that is, a square structure topped at each corner by a slender, low minaret. Inside the shrine, Goga's grave was rebuilt in marble by Maharaj Ganga Singh of Bikaner in the twenties. He did however preserve its original Islamic shape. The grave was made to look like a Hindu image by a simple device: a small hero slab representing Goga on his mount was carved out of the marble. According to the Chahils, this was the only detail which prevented the sacred object from being a 'full-fledged' Muslim *mazār*. Goga's shrine looks like a *dargāh* but functions as a temple. The main priests (on duty for eleven months of the year) are Muslims, but Goga's major worshippers are Hindus. In the same way only a minority of Muslims flock to the shrine during the annual *melā*; Brahman priests are appointed by the trust in charge of the shrine only for one month, that is, for the period of the fair. At Gogamedi, at some distance from the main shrine, is a temple-cum-*maṭh* dedicated to one of the founders of the Nath Sampraday. It is named 'Gorakhtila' (Gorakhnath's *dune*) as it is located on the top of sandy hill; incidentally, Goga is also associated with the Jogis and his legend is connected with Gorakhnath through whose blessing he was born. Temples dedicated to Goga may look like traditional platforms with a hero (memorial) stone, or like replicas of the main shrine, sheltering a miniature *mazār* to which *chādars* are offered and whose priests are Hindu; the latter are also referred to as *Gogāmedīs* (Goga's houses).

By assuming that these characters can be connected in some way with Ismailism, and more precisely, might have been missionaries operating in various guises, I am not trying to deny the fact that interactions have also occurred at a deep level between Sufis and Naths. The case of Shaikh Abdul Quddus has been sufficiently studied (Digby 1975, Rizvi 1986:345-6) to prevent our overlooking this phenomenon. In his works, yogic terminologies have been extensively used and Allah compared to (or called) 'Alakh' and 'Niranjan' as in the Nath tradition. Quddus had gone so far as to choose 'Alakh' as his nom-de-plume. There is no doubt that the sixteenth-century Chishti Shaikh was indeed a Sunni Sufi. How can one therefore ascertain whether the saints endowed with a dual yogic-Muslim identity were Ismailis or Sufis?

I suggest that it is ultimately the evasiveness and ambiguity of their personalities and of the traditions connected with them that might tip the scale in favour of Ismailis. Quddus may have gone very far in accepting yogic models and a Hindu name, but his personality does not seem to have appeared ambiguous or elusive. The Shaikh's Chishti affiliation raises no doubt; similarly his partial identification with the Nath Sampraday can be clearly regarded as a conscious choice which could not have led his followers to question his identity.

Hindus may have been attracted by his teaching and become his devotees or disciples, but this factor did not lead to his transformation into an alleged Hindu saint or God. The case of the Nasiruddin Chirag Delhi tradition in Maharasthra, where he appeared with a dual identity, as the Chishti Sufi Nasiruddin and as the Jogi Nagnath (Adinath), has been described by Skyhawk (1993 and 1994). Unfortunately no extensive study of the 'syncretic' sect associated with him has been made to this day.[4]

Let me now conclude with the remark that 'syncretism' may at best be applied to an artificially ossified phenomenon but can by no means account for the extreme diversity of processes which, historically, have led to the analysed situation. In other words, if different causes are able to produce similar results this does not imply that such results have been produced by one single factor whether conveniently labelled 'popular religion', 'syncretism' or 'interaction between Hindu mysticism and Sufism'.

NOTES

1. Once more I have to thank Zawahir Moir for supplying me with a copy of Hasan Kabiruddin's *ginān* and for suggesting her interesting commentaries on this text and on Pir Shams' Govardhan *ginān*. My gratitude also goes to Iqbal Surani who has generously lent me his collection of books on Ismailism, including the *Pīr Shams nā Grantho* where I found Gopichand's story.
2. I must refer to the interesting article written by Catherine Champion (1994) on the Muslim Bhartrihari Jogis of Gorakhpur (Uttar Pradesh).
3. Research on this theme is ongoing.
4. It is unfortunate that Skyhawk's articles give but a confusing idea of the tradition, while revealing a number of fascinating details. A study based on field research would certainly reveal much more. Let us hope that this important task will be completed by the author in the near future.

CHAPTER 10

Ram and Rahim: Nizari Ismailism and the *Sant Paramparā*

The phenomenon of interaction between diverse Muslim traditions, including Sufism and Ismailism in its Indo-Pakistani form and various indigenous movements connected with Nathism and *bhakti,* poses the problem of the origin and development of the *Sant paramparā.* A number of interesting studies have already addressed the question (Vaudeville 1974, Schomer 1987, Matringe 1992, Rizvi 1978). Scholars have generally come to the conclusion that the non-sectarian tradition of the northern Sants and of their Maharashtrian brothers emerged as the result of an encounter between the tradition of Tantric yoga (Nath Sampraday) and the indigenous devotional current which can be dated back to the first centuries of our era. This theory seems to be confirmed by the fact that saints from Maharasthra have traced their lineage from Nath gurus.

As far as Islamic influences are concerned, as observed for example in the poetry of Kabir, Nanak and Dadu (to quote only the most famous Sants), it has been generally agreed that they were the result of interactions with Sunni Sufism (Rizvi 1978, Vaudeville 1974), a current which was also regarded as instrumental in permeating the Nath Sampraday with Muslim elements. While I do not deny these facts, I cannot agree with C. Champion (1976) when she says that 'the historical links between the sect of the Naths and Sufi Islam have been well perceived'. I will argue that on the contrary, the issue has never been properly elucidated to this day. Suprisingly enough, in all these studies, Ismailism has been altogether ignored; the reason is either that this particular tradition is unknown to scholars dealing with Indian religions or that it is considered too minor a phenomenon to have played any significant role.

However, a few authors, such as Nanji (1978), Shackle and Moir (1992) and Mallison (1991a), have given a number of interesting hints on the similarities which exist between the compositions of some Sants and the *ginānic* hymns. As Nanji states (ibid.:14), 'The *ginān* literature was part of a larger, developing tradition on the Subcontinent.' Compositions of medieval Sants and of Nizaris share a good number of traits including the general tone of indigenous *nirgūṇ bhatki* tinged with Nath references and Sufic elements.

Mallison (1991a:97) has pointed out the similarities between a few verses of a *ginān* signed 'Pir Shams', and a *vāṇī* attributed to Kabir:

The Hindu goes to the sixty-eight places of pilgrimage while the Muslim goes to the Mosque. Yet neither the Hindu nor the Muslim knows my Lord, who sits, Pure (Shams).

The Hindu evokes the name of Ram, The Musulman cries; Khuda is One! But the Lord of Kabir pervades all (Kabir).

It is generally inferred that this type of *ginān* evolved later, under the influence of the Sants, which is not impossible if one considers that no Khojki manuscript or other transcriptions have been found which could be dated before the eighteenth century. The idea that Kabir is earlier and his poetry is the model that inspired the Nizaris, seems to be corroborated by the 'existence of works of some of the above poets [the Sants], side by side with the *gināns*, in some of the manuscripts' (Nanji 1978:14). Indeed, in Khojki manuscripts one often finds short *bhajans* of Kabir, Narsingh Mehta, Mira Bai, or Raidas (personal communication, by Z. Moir). Moreover, in a *ginān* ascribed to Shams (but evidently composed later, as most *gināns* in at least their present form) and entitled *Brahma Prakāsh*, the names of Kabir, Ramanand, Dhana, Rohidas (Raidas), Dadu and Nanakshah occur (Shackle and Moir 1992:173) along with those of other famous *bhaktas*. However, I will attempt to show that the integration of these Sants (at an obviously later stage) into the Khoja heritage does not prove that the 'syncretic' teachings of the medieval poets, to use this criticized but convenient adjective, preceeded those of the Nizari Ismailis.

Before resuming the discussion, I will compare two other compositions which display more striking similarities than those chosen by Mallison; the former is ascribed to Pir Shams, the latter to Guru Nanak:

Shams: My mind is my prayer mat, Allah is my Qadi
and my body is my mosque (Nanji 1978:121).

Nanak: Make mercy your mosque, faith your prayer mat
and rightousness your Quran (McLeod 1968:304).

Leaving aside the question of authorship and date of the *ginān,* which cannot be solved for the moment, how do we prove that Nanak's is the earlier version? Let us proceed, then, with the same *ginān;* it further gives the characteristic warning 'listen to me, you Mullas and Qadis' (Nanji ibid.), which is also the tone of Kabir and Nanak's sharp criticism of Muslim theologians and judges, and is exactly the same type of admonition which is found in the Bishnoi and Jasnathi literatures: '*Sunre mullā sunre kāzī*' ('Listen mollahs and Qajis' (Jambha's *sabad* n. 8, Gyanprakash 1992:38) and '*Sambhāl mulla sambhāl qāzī*' ('Take heed mollah, take heed, Qadi', Pareek:25).

If my hypothesis of the Ismaili origin of the Jambha and Jasnath sects has substance, can we admit that these were also later influenced by Kabir and Nanak whose teachings they incorporated into their hymns? Otherwise, can it be that they were simply following the pattern of the *gināns,* either before or after the supposed influence of the Sants? This is an intricate problem for which no easy solution is at hand.

The Meghval worshippers of Ramdev, and other Nizarpanthis were certainly influenced by Kabir when they became Kabirpanthis, probably during the seventeenth-eighteenth centuries, but this may not account for the alleged Kabirian accents of the devotional poetry composed by Ramdev's followers between the fifteenth and twentieth centuries. No such influnce sees to have existed for the Bishnois who rapidly formed a closed group functioning simultaneously as sect and caste. As for the Jasnathis, a connection with the Kabir or Nanak Panth appears still less probable, whereas the Nath Sampraday has evidently played a major role. Maheshwari (1970, I:444) has strangely assumed that Jambha and his movement had influenced the Sikh tradition, a reason why so many similarities could be traced in both sects.

Let us tackle the problem from a different perspective. If we adopt the commonly accepted idea that the original association of Nath, *bhakti* and Islamic elements is a 'creation' of the medieval Sants, one would then come to the conclusion proposed by a few authors such as Dvivedi and Vaudeville that Kabir belonged to a *gṛhastha* Jogi (house-holder Nath) family recently converted to Islam, analogous to the present Muslim Bhartrihari Jogis (Champion 1994:37) who, like him, are mostly weavers by occupation. As far as his Islamic ideals are concerned, they are, of course, said to have been inspired by the Sunni Sufis. Strangely enough, it has never been remarked that the virulent criticism of Sunni judges and theologians could have had a Shia basis instead of having been inspired by the alleged mystical ideals of the Sufis. Kabir's rejection of the *sharīa* (though he was a Muslim by birth and by name), has not, however, its origin in Sufism, as the Shaikhs insisted on associating *sharīat* with *haqīqat* (Muslim law with inner truth) rather than discarding the former, which would have made them heretical to Sunni theologians, as in the famous case of the Sufi Mansur al-Hallaj. Kabir's attitude was thus explained by his Hindu origin and the influence of Hindu Sants, factors which were later instrumental in transforming this Muslim 'heterodox' thinker into a purely Hindu sage. Nothing can be said on the issue of priority in terms of dates of poems and manuscripts, However, in the light of what has been said concerning the spirit of acculturated Nizari Ismailism, it can be suggested that, owing to the particular ideals of this sect adverse to both Sunni and Hindu beliefs and practices, but much more sympathetical to the latter, such 'formulae' which are regarded as creations of the Sants are actually congenial to Ismailism from its very origin. In this respect, Nizari *dāīs* had nothing to learn from the Sants. Therefore the possiblity of influence in the reverse direction cannot be excluded. But it goes without saying that this remains a provisional hypothesis.

First of all, it must be emphasized that, much more than defiance of 'orthodox' Muslims or Brahmanical Hindus, it is the idea of bringing together Hindu and Islamic names, terms and concepts which can be regarded as an important characteristic of the acculturated Nizari tradition. Owing to their particular methods of conversion, the missionaries must have used these 'equivalences' from the very beginning of their mission as reflected in the various legends of the Khoja and Nizarpanthi heritages. It would be surprising if they had had to wait for Kabir's teachings before introducing these ideas into their tradition. According to Z. Moir, this 'strategy', which also corresponds to deeper philosophical ideals, lies in the very nature of the Ismaili *dawa* and cannot be regarded as a model borrowed from the Sant tradition. Instead, later references to Kabir, Nanak, and Mehta play a different role; it seems that owing the extreme popularity of the Sant movement, the authors of the *ginãns* felt compelled to refer to these prestigious figures who appeared so similar to themselves.

THE RISHI MOVEMENT

In the subcontinent Kabir was not the first to convey Hindu-Muslim 'syncretistic' teachings: the Muslim Kashmiri saint Nuruddin 'Rishi' (1377-1438), and the Hindu female ascetic Lal Ded (1317-90) seem to have preceded him. It is unfortunate that those who have dealt with both saints (M. I. Khan 1994, Temple 1990, Kotru 1990 and A. Koul 1929) have not paid more attention to the intriguing fact that their compositions express the same spiritual and religious message, each under a different identity, so that they appear (to repeat Kassam's words concerning the syncretism of Nizari literature) 'as two faces of the same phenomenon' (Kassam 1994:231). Kachru (1981:22), who has noticed that the similarities in the poetry of the two Kashmiri saints has even led, in some cases, to wrong attributions of authorship, does not draw any conclusion on the basis of this statement.

Eager to show that Nuruddin's teachings and his Rishi movement are in strict conformity with the *sharīa,* M.I. Khan follows the later efforts of Sunni Sufis to appropriate his tradition by asserting that the Kashmiri saint's father had been formally affiliated to the Kubrawi *tarīqa* and, therefore, was not fundamentally different from the 'orthodox' Sufis. For this reason he also hushes up a belief reported by A.K. Koul (1929:195) that Nuruddin's father, who was a Hindu, was converted to Islam by a hermit named 'Yasman Rishi'. If this were true, the title 'Rishi', which was to give its name to the movement, had not been introduced by Nuruddin.

M.I. Khan argues that the way the Kashmiri saint uses this title does not prove any direct connection with the indigenous tradition, although reference is made to Hindu figures who symbolize the sages of Kashmir: 'his eulogization of the "legendary" Rishis is not an exact description of a certain band of Rishis but a profound and illuminating portrayal of some living and comprehensible pious men who practised asceticism in their every day life' (ibid.:45). Instead, Rizvi (1986,I:350) does not believe that Nuruddin was a Sufi in the strict sense of the term and, referring to Pirs affiliated to particular Sunni *tarīqas,* stresses that 'these Kashmiri saints [the followers of Nuruddin] preferred to be called Rishis than Sufis'.

Noticing that the Kashmiri saint 'traces the family tree of the Rishis back to Muhammad and not to any local saint of pre Islamic times' and that he gives them Muslim names, M.I. Khan (ibid.:45-6) sees in this very fact the confirmation of his theory concerning the purely symbolic value of this geneaology. For him, the earthly existence of Zulka, Miran and Pilas Rishi defy historical analysis, and he prefers to 'situate them in the world of analogies' to arrive at an approximation of the truth.

I will start with the reverse hypothesis, referring to the mysterious figure of Yasman Rishi mentioned by Koul as having been the Pir who converted Nuruddin's father to Islam. Assuming that these Muslim Rishis are historical, although unidentified, figures, I will, for the sake of comparison, juxtapose two fragments of poems. The former is ascribed to Nuruddin Rishi and quoted by M.I. Khan (ibid.:45) to support his view:

> The first Rishi was the Prophet Muhammad;
> The second in order was Hazrat Uways;
> The third Rishi was Zulka Rishi;
> The fourth in order was Hazrat Pilas.

The latter example is selected from a passage in a devotional song of Lalbegi tradition preserved among the Bhangi-Chuhra community of Punjab (Rose 1990:187). It reads like a semi-imaginary genealogy:

> *Bālā Shāh Santokh Rikh dā* . . .
> Bālā Shāh (Bālmīk Rishi *Bālā* Shāh, guru and god of the Lālbegīs) is son of Santokh Rishi
> Santokh Rikh is son is Sharāp Dit Rikh,
> Sharāp Dit Rikh is son of Āīnak,
> Āīnak is son of Rikhī,
> Rikhī is son of Bikhī,
> Bikhī is son of Mahadev (Shiva),
> Mahadev or Shiv is son of Aut Khanda,
> Aut Khanda is son of Alakh Purukh (the Lord)
> Alakh Purukh is son of Śakt (feminine of *Śakti,* Divin power), Śakt is son Agam (unknowable).

We seem to have here both human figures with distorted names and qualifying attributes of God. If we examine carefully the non-versified genealogies of the Lalbegis as given by Rose (ibid.:184-6), it is easy to deduce that the titles 'Pir' and 'Rishi' like the suffixes *-shāh, -dev,* and *-beg* have been used to refer to the gurus of lineages related to Bala Shah/Balmik Rishi. Bearing in mind this equivalence, another versified genealogy of the same tradition will be given (ibid.:201); already cited in Chapter 5, it had been compared with the Ismaili *duā*:

The first Pir is Asa [Isa, Jesus?],
The second Pir is Hazrat Khwaja Khasa [Khwaja Khizr],
The third Pir is Safa [no interpretation suggested],
The fourth Pir is Dada Giljhapra ['grandfather' Bala Shah].

This list will be again compared with the earlier-mentioned poem of Nuruddin, which goes on beyond the fourth Rishi in this way:

The fifth was Rum Rishi,
The sixth in order was Hazrat Miran;
The seventh (me) is miscalled a Rishi;
Do I deserve to be called a Rishi? What is my name?

The Lalbegi sect (see Chapter 5) has been tentatively connected with the Nizari tradition through the identification of Balmik Rishi/ Bala Shah with the fifteenth-century Ismaili missionary of Dera Ghazi Khan, Sayyid Bala Shah. On the other hand, the combination of a Muslim name with the title Rishi cannot but remind us of the fact that Pir Shams (Pir 'Samas' in the vernacular pronunciation) was also called Samas Rishi in the Ramdev tradition. In the *ginānic* literature one finds more than one reference to Kashmir as a centre of Nizari missionary activities and, although this can by no means be considered as historical evidence, there is nothing absurd in assuming that, as in Rajasthan where its traces have been lost, there existed an Ismaili *dawa* in Kashmir. Pir Shams himself is credited with conversions in Kashmir. What I am trying to suggest is that, owing to *taqīyya,* these activities might have been totally inconspicuous, and that 'Rishi', a standard *ginānic* term for the Arabic 'Momin' (believer), might well have referred in Nuruddin's compositions to the Ismaili saints, as was the case in the Khoja literature (and in the songs of the Nizarpanthis, Aipanthis, Bishnois, Jasnathis and Lalbegis). It is obvious that its secret meaning could only be understood by the initiated followers, for whom it could also function as a 'pass-word' or a cover name.[1] Nuruddin's personality (he was also known as Nand Rishi) is itself suggestive of such a connection. However, if my hypothesis is correct, it must be assumed that the great Kashmiri saint himself gradually drifted away from Ismailism and that his Rishi movement became a kind of detached branch which merged into the Sufi current. His originality is in conformity with the local environment from which the Ismaili *dāīs* had always drawn to teach their converts in a way that would not seem alien to them. It will be even suggested that the Nizari Pirs have been inspired by the folklore connected with the mountainous valleys of Kashmir and Punjab, the legendary abode of the Rishis, when they came upon the idea of calling their converts by this name.

NANAK AND THE SIKH RELIGION

Let us now revert to the medieval Sants of the so-called 'syncretic' type. I will choose the tradition of Nanak as the basis and focus of my analysis. It has already been stated in Chapter 7 that both Jambha and Nanak operated in neighbouring areas (Punjab) during the same period. I have also mentioned the strange idea of Maheshwari who believes that the founder of the Bishnoi Panth inspired the first guru of the Sikhs, which would account for the striking similarities between the two traditions. Finally it has been suggested that this could as well be explained by the fact that both drew from another, common heritage, namely Nizari Ismailism. In formulating this hypothesis, I am aware that I will be accused of forming premature theories upon unsufficient data. Owing to the great popularity of the Sikh tradition, to which innumerable studies have been devoted, some of them by scholars of renown, the idea will probably appear too bold. However, considering all the implications it could have, if indeed borne out, the hypothesis deserves at least some consideration.

The debate over the origin or significance of the Muslim elements in Guru Nanak's tradition (McLeod 1968, Bruce 1987, Ahuja n.d.) has not led to any satisfactory conclusion, and such discussion can continue endlessly. Was this influence due to Sufism, to 'popular Islam', or to the imitation of an already existing model of Sant poetry, for instance that of Kabir (the last hypothesis, dear to McLeod, having the effect of pushing back the issue to an earlier period without solving it)?

We will argue that it is impossible to get out of the vicious circle through endless theoretical debates over the meaning and origin of Muslim concepts and terminologies in Nanak's tradition; philosophical notions are too elusive to have any objective value. A solution may however be suggested by field research, that is, the patient collection of ethnographic data and their examination on the basis of anthropological methods.

Let me start with a picturesque anecdote reported by one of my Bishnoi informants.[2] The event took place shortly after Partition, in the fifties, a period when many sects and communities attempted to assert their identity in Indian society by erecting as many shrines as possible. All the Muslim inhabitants of Abubshahar, a small town in Haryana, had gone to Pakistan, leaving behind two empty mosques. Seeing in this a golden chance, Sikhs and Bishnois immediately occupied the place. Very few accretions were necessary to transform the former into a *gurudwārā* (which was rapidly enlarged and renovated) and the latter into a Bishnoi temple. The case may not be an unusual one. It could be viewed as a universal phenomenon with which historians of religion are perfectly familiar (erection of a Christian church on the site of a Celtic temple, or a mosque at a spot where an old Buddhist *stūpa* had been established). But I argue that in this case it was different. Neither mosque was razed to the ground nor regarded as a former place of worship of the Sikhs and Bishnois. Besides, no other community in the town tried to appropriate these places. My informant suggested that it was precisely because of the similarities shared by these traditions that this peaceful, yet curious, transmutation was possible.

Let us now proceed to a comparative analysis of the Sikh and Khoja traditions. To start with, I will temporarily take for granted the 'official' Sikh belief (which is however not accepted by all Nanakpanthis), according to which there has always been a profound continuity in the movement, from the founder's time to the present period. In other words, it will be assumed, for the requirements of this study, that Nanak's message, the Sanatan movement, the Khalsa, and the Singh Sabha represent but different sides of the same picture, at least if one refers to one original idea and encompassing model.

ORGANIZATION OF THE PANTH

Without dealing with the history and development of the sect nor with its literary tradition—for which the reader may refer to several publications—we will limit ourselves to some specific traits which will be compared to similar features in the Nizari tradition of the subcontinent.

DASVANDH-DASSONDH

Nanak's sect, frequently referred to simply as 'the *panth*' (which was also the case of the secret sect spread in Rajasthan by Ugam Si, Mallinath and Ramdev), has probably been organized from the guru's time onwards; unfortunately very little is known of its beginnings. Later on, we learn that Arjun (the fifth Guru) started to collect from the Sikhs tribute instead of voluntary donations. Each Sikh was required to give a tenth of his income in the name of the Guru, and officers specially appointed for this task were directed to come to Amritsar every year on the first day of Baisakh (April-May) to submit the accounts (Banerjee 1983:59). This tithe was called *dasvandh* (as in the Bishnoi and Jasnathi traditions), a variant of the Nizari word *dassondh.* As is known in Sikh history, this system was later suppressed because of numerous misuses.

DHARAMŚĀLĀ-JAMĀT-KHĀNA

Instead of going to temples or mosques, Nanak's followers were requested to gather in *dharamśālās* (later *gurudvārās*) which were places meant for congregational prayers and the singing of devotional hymns. The Momna Kanbis of Gujarat, who became followers of the Imamshahi sect usually referred to their *jamāt-khānas* as *dharamśālās* (Enthoven 1990, II: 156-7). Both communities, therefore, made a similar use of this word which otherwise does not refer to a shrine but to a resting place for pilgrims. Similarly, the Sikh concept of *sangat* (*sat sang* or *sādh sangat,* the gathering of virtuous or saintly persons) has its equivalent in the Ismaili *jamāt,* the congregation of the faithful with a decisively strong emphasis on the community and in an Islamic rather than in a Hindu sense even in the spirit of the Sant *paramparā.*

GURUDWĀRĀS, SAMĀDHS AND *DARGĀHS*

From a certain period onwards, *dharamśālās* tended to evolve into structures which were closer to indigenous temples and came to be referred to as *gurudwārās* (the Guru's door), like the gathering places of Ramsnehis (a branch of the Ramanandis) which were known as *Rāmdwārās* and those of the Dadupanthis called *Dādūdwārās.* However, the word *dharamśālā* was not discarded. *Gurudwārās* with holy relics functioned simultaneously as shrines (in the sense of temples or *samādhis*) and places for congregational prayers and vigils.

Leaving aside the outer appearance of these *gurudwārās* (which can be accounted for by the architectural fashion of the time), we will focus our attention on the inner design. Idol worship being strictly forbidden according to Nanak's teaching, the usual Sikh temple contains in the middle of the hall a raised platform with a canopy under which the holy book (*Guru Granth Sāhib*) is installed and worshipped, very much like a relic or a sacred image. Incidentally, *gurudwārās* sheltering the funeral monument of some guru or a member of his family display exactly the same structure (a raised platform and canopy), but the book is replaced by the *samādh* of the deceased. *Guru Granth* and *samādh* are both covered with ornate drapes (*chādars*) which are regularly offered to them. Thus it is not difficult to see that these structures look like imitations of a Muslim *dargāh*, whether the *mazār* is represented by a *samādh* or by a book. It will also be suggested that the fact that the holy *Guru Granth* and the *samādh* are identified must not be considered mere coincidence: as will be suggested further, both are the embodiment of the everliving Guru (through the symbols of his body and his word).[3]

RITUALS: *PĀHUL, PĀHAL, PĀYAL* AND *PĀVAL*

Before entering a *gurudwārā* it is compulsory to wash one's feet and cover one's head; the Sikhs prostrate before the *Guru Granth* (or the *samādh*) and pray with their palms open and raised to the sky, after the fashion of Muslims. These details which have been noticed (Ahuja:68-9), have been considered evidence of Islamic influence on Sikhism, although the nature of this influence has not been elucidated.

The main ritual of the Sikhs was called *pāhul* from the very beginning. Originally, the charan-*pāhul* was prevalent; it consisted in the partaking of the consecrated water previously touched by the Guru's foot. After Guru Arjun, the baptismal liquid was prepared by five Sikhs who touched the water with their right thumbs and sanctified it with the recitation of the scriptures (Fauja Singh 1990:57). Still later (maybe from the time of the tenth and last Guru onwards), it was replaced by the *khaṇḍe kī pāhul*: the water put in an iron vessel was stirred with a double-edged dagger and fragments of Nanak *Jāpjī* were recited over it (Banerjee 1983:310). According to a Sikh tradition, the weapon originally used for this purpose was none but Ali's sword, Dhul Fiqār, the double-edged sword.

We are now familiar with the Nizari *pāval* ritual, which was later more frequently referred to as *ami, amit, amṛt,* an indigenous word also extensively used by the Sikhs as a synonym of *pāhul.* Nizarpanthi, Aipanthi and Bishnoi variants of the term applied to similar rituals have also been mentioned such as *pāyal* and *pāhal,* the latter being linguistically closer to the Sikh *pāhul.* Another intriguing similarity must be noted, this time between a Sikh and a Nizarpanthi ritual. The custom of drinking the water (flowing in a channel or stored in a small tank) where all Sikh devotees have washed their feet before entering a *gurudwārā* is strikingly reminiscent of the partaking of the 'polluted' liquid of the *kuṇḍā* where Nizarpanthi followers have acted similarly. In both cases the holy water is called *pāhal* or *pāyal* (see Chapter 4 on the *dasā panth* ceremony). At this stage an important suggestion may be made: in the Sikh, as well as in the Nizarpanthi ritual, the emphasis is on the fact that not only the *amṛt* of a guru's or god's feet is sacred, but also the *pāhal/pāyal* of all initiated devotees. Followers become pure by their initiation and are all equal, that is why their *charanamṛt* is holy, and, I might add, they all deserve the title of *ṛṣi,* contrary to the Brahmanical belief that it can be applied only to the ancient seers who are the ancestors of Brahmans or kings.[4] Finally the syllable which, as in the Bishnoi term *pāhal,* replaces the *-va* and the *-ya* used in Khoja and Nizarpanthi variants. In Punjabi *-hu* often stands for the Sanskrit *-va.* For instance, the Hindi name of one of Rama's sons, Lav (Skt. Lava) will become Lahu.

GURMUKHI AND KHOJKI, *GURU GRANTH, PANDIYĀT-I JAVĀNMARDĪ* AND THE COLLECTIONS OF *GINĀNS*

A number of other elements in the Sikh religion are also suggestive of Ismaili influence. There is the parallel use of a sacred (secret) writing for the purpose of transcribing devotional hymns both the Sikh Gurmukhi (now the alphabet of Punjab), said to have been designed by the second Guru Angad, and the Khojki (supposed to be the creation of Pir Sadruddin) have evolved from mercantile shorthands (Shackle and Moir 1992:35). If the dates are correct, Khojki however preceeded the Gurmukhi script by approximately one century. Another analogy must be stressed: the *Guru Granth,* written in Gurmukhi as a collection of hymns constituting the sacred Scripture of the Sikhs, has incorporated a few songs ascribed to famous non-Nanakpanthi saints, such as Mira Bai, Ravidas, Namdev, and the Muslim Baba Farid. Similarly, as already noted, the Khojki manuscripts gathering Ismaili *ginān*s also contain short hymns signed by non-Nizari Sants and *bhaktas*.

Finally, the symbolic role played by the *Guru Granth*, considered to be the eleventh and last Guru, after Govind Singh's decision, can be compared to that of the *Pandiyāt-i javānmardī* which, incidentally, has been included in the list of Ismaili Pirs and is still mentioned as such during the recitation of the genealogical list of Pirs which is a part of the *duā* (Ivanow, 1953:2-3). Pir 'Pandiyāt-i javānmardī' was equally supposed to replace the Pir when the function of the main *dāī* was suppressed by the Imam so that henceforth no missionary would be referred to as Pir and the former Pir's descendants would simply be called Sayyids. Similarly, the Sikh leaders who came after Govind Singh were no more referred to as Gurus.

GURUSHIP, PIRSHIP AND IMAMATE

Ultimately, it is the whole concept of Guruship (so different from the Hindu ideas of the guru, albeit closer to the Nathpanthi ideals) which can be said to match the Nizari institutions and concepts of Pirship and Imamate. In Sikhism the Sikh gurus had an exceptional importance and though Nanak seems to have stressed the difference between himself as the first Guru of the Sikhs and God who is the Satguru (true guru), there is a definite ambiguity between the two, which is illustrated by the fact that the human guru is much more than a single individuality. Nanak will pass on his divine light to his successors who will be Nanak II, Nanak III and so forth until the tenth and last. This transfer of energy and, we would say, of personality, is reminiscent of the Aipanthi belief mentioned in Chapter 6 that Ai Mata, first guru and founder of the sect, transferred her divine light to her disciple, who became the Diwan and Pir-*murshid* of the *panth*, while he was also regarded as a male incarnation of the Devi. As a guru, Ai Mata also holds an ambiguous position as intermediary between the divinity and the human spiritual guide. Although the same can be said with reference to many founders of sects in the subcontinent, I would argue that the particular relationship which exists between the Sikh guru and the Satguru as God is akin to the Nizari perception of the Pir and the Supreme Pir (the Imam) as overlapping figures. Similarly, the hereditary transfer of the Imamate (like the later hereditary transmission of Guruship in Sikhism) was viewed as a transfer of divine light. If it is true that Nanak rejects the

Hindu theory of *avatārs*, Guru Arjun has composed a poem on the *Das avatār* motif and the belief is subsequently reinforced, namely by Govind Singh in his *Dasam Granth* (later incorporated into the Sikh scripture) listing the twenty-four *avatārs* (another popular series of Vishnu's incarnations which are more often grouped in a series of ten). This collection is also characteristically referred to as *Dasmā Pādshāh kā Granth* (the holy book of the tenth emperor). *Dasmā pādshāh*, refers also to Govind Singh and strongly suggests that he compared himself (or has been compared by his followers) to the tenth incarnation of Vishnu: Nanak X is the last Guru of the series, as Kalki is said to be the last incarnation. Finally, the title *Sachā Pādshāh* which refers to the Supreme Guru in the Sikh tradition corresponds to the Ismaili concept of the Lord equally known as *Sachā Pādshāh* (the 'true emperor').

NANAKSHAHIS HAGIOGRAPHY

A few episodes of Nanak's life appear to have strong Ismaili echoes. Nanak's legendary encounter with the evil spirit of our age, the demon 'Kali yuga', is a theme by no means common in the *bhakti* or *sant* heritage, albeit the original idea is drawn from the Hindu *Kalki purāna* and other similar texts (see Chapter 4). It is naturally reminiscent of the confrontation of *Nikalank avatār* with the demoniac king Kalinga in the *gināns.* Moreover, Nanak's hagiography shares a number of traits with Pir Shams Sabzwari's life, as portrayed in the Nizari tradition; for instance, the interesting episode connected with the city of Multan. When Nanak, during one his trips, reaches this town famous for its numerous Muslim saints, the Pirs send him a bowl of milk to indicate that there is no room for him and the Sikh guru puts a flower in it to explain that his presence will make no difference. A similar legend reported by Nanji (1978:54) concerns Pir Shams: the Sufi Bahauddin Zakariya's son presents him, in the same place, with a bowl of milk; Shams puts a flower into the bowl 'trying to tell him that his presence in the city would prove as unburdensome to him as the flowers were to the milk'. Finally, the famous declaration of Nanak emerging from the river after his three days' disappearance: '*na ko Hindu na Musulmān*' (there is no Hindu nor Muslim) might be compared to a similar utterance of Pir Shams, 'who in this world is a Hindu and who is a Musulman?' (quoted from a *ginān*, see Nanji 1978:121).

A NEW PERSPECTIVE ON THE ORIGIN AND DEVELOPMENT OF THE SIKH PANTH

According to the caretakers of Pir Shams' *dargāh* at Multan (who belong to Twelver Shia Islam but claim to be his descendants), whenever Guru Nanak stopped at Multan, he bowed to the grave of the famous Ismaili *dāī* (personal communication by Z. Moir). What is more, in the fifties a Khoja travelling in Punjab for commercial purposes was told by a Sikh that Nanak had been Pir Shams' disciple (personal communication A. Rahmatoullah). Until after the 'Haji Bibi' case which took place in 1908 (Shackle and Moir 1992:9), intermarriages were reported between Khojas and Sikhs (Nanji 1978:25). What are we to make of all these unconnected facts combined with the traces of Ismaili influence mentioned above?

Curiously enough, those who have described the religious atmosphere of fifteenth-century Punjab have dealt at length with orthodox, 'legalistic' Sunni Islam, Sufism, yoga and Hindu *bhakti*, but not a single word has been said of the Nizari presence. Actually, Punjab had always been a stronghold of the Ismaili *dawa*, and Multan and Ucch were the main *gaddīs*. The local community, having been converted by Pir Shams, was referred to as Shamsi.

In Nanak's time Punjab was under Muslim rule. It was logical that, being subjects of the representatives of the sultanate of the Sunni Afghan Lodis the Shamsis practised *taqīyya*. This enabled them to survive until the Aga Khans urged them to come out of concealment. However the result of a long period of 'precautionary dissimulation' was that, even towards the end of the past century, they were often mistaken for Hindus or categorized by the British census officers as 'half-Hindu half-Muslim' groups. As has been explained, they were later compelled to choose a clear-cut identity, some of them following the Imam of the time, others becoming Sunnis and Twelver Shias, or coming back into the fold of Hinduism. Like the Khojas who had practised *taqīyya* and outwardly appeared to be Hindu merchants, these Shamsis came to be referred to as Guptis. We learn from Rose (1990:403) that among them were not only Sunars but other artisan castes, and 'a good many Khatris'. Curiously, the same author states that in Punjab, Muslim Khatris are known as Khojas.

Guru Nanak, it may be recalled, as all the other Gurus, was a Khatri by caste. Even before Guruship became hereditary, it was a tradition to select the leaders of the sect from among them. Incidentally, the Khatris share at least one common trait with the Khojas (ex-Lohanas converted by Sadruddin to Ismailism and renamed 'Khojas'): both are trade communities and both claim a Kshatriya origin. The association between the Khatri caste and Sikh Guruship, mysterious as it is, is certainly not a coincidence. Considering all these elements, and following the data supplied by the specialists on Sikhism, I am now in a position to present my own theory of the origin and evolution of the Sikh Panth.

Nanak, who appeared with a Hindu identity as is amply attested to in the tradition, may have been in reality a Shamsi 'Gupti' from the Khatri caste, that is, not a direct disciple, but a follower of Shams who, like all his coreligionists in Muslim ruled Punjab practised *taqīyya*, appearing outwardly as a Hindu. For this reason he had nothing to fear from the local authorities who themselves were not hostile to these people. It is obvious that if Nanak had divulged his real identity his career and even his life would have been endangered. However, he did not follow faithfully the path of his ancestors who presumably had been converted by Shams to Ismailism. It was not only his strong personality which prompted him to create his own, separate movement, but the general atmosphere of the time which was favourable to such a move. It may be useful to recall that it is during Nanak's time (1469-1539) that the crisis of the Ismaili *dawa* described in Chapters 1 and 5 occurred. The Nizari sect suffered a serious setback with the quarrel for succession which ensued after Kabiruddin death (d. 1470) and probably during the Pirship of his brother Tajuddin who eventually committed suicide. This was followed by Pir Sayyid Imam Shah's independent behaviour when, after having failed to win the Imam's nomination as the main Pir of the *dawa*, he organized his own community in Gujarat. After his death in 1513, his son Muhammad Shah created a dissident branch at Pirana by claiming that his father was the real and legitimate Imam (Shackle and Moir 1992:7-8). The founder of the Imamshahi sect died in 1533, about six years before Nanak. From this account one can infer that the *dawa* was weakened as a result of this secession and rivalries between the Sayyids of Pirana and the Kadiwala Sayyids who, starting with Kabiruddin's son Rahimtullaḥ, worked for the Persian Imam to whom they had remained faithful. Another consequence was that the area of Multan was no more, as it had earlier been, a prestigious centre of the Ismaili *dawa*. This period has also been characterized, as described in Chapter 5, by the emergence of several independent 'dynasties of Pirs' and by the formation of separate sects, as in the case of the Nizarpanthis, Aipanthis, Bishnois and Jasnathis, not to speak, of course, of the Pirana Panth organized by Sayyid Muhammad Shah. The circumstances were, therefore, congenial to the creation of a new sect by a hypothetical Shamsi Nanak. In the Guru's writings, the emphasis was clearly on the inner religion, the congregational prayers and hymns, moral precepts, charity and the new ideal of purity proposed by the Nizaris, whereas the obeisance to the Persian Imam, the paying of tithes, and so on were discarded. No more was there an intermediary between the Guru (or Pir) and God. In other words, Nanak preserved certain basic characteristics of Ismailism while rejecting others. It is highly probable that he made his major converts among the Shamsis themselves, whether they were Khatris or belonged to other castes.

When Nanak reaches Kartapur after his travels, he preaches and converts people who, by accepting his message and reciting his own composition the *Jāpjī*, are said to 'cast off the burden of the *Atharva Ved*' (Banerjee 1983:93). This rather mysterious phrase is to be found in a composition referred to as *Vārā Bhāī Gurdās*. It says, *guramukhi bhāra atharabaṇi tārā* ('The teaching of the Guru freed his disciples from the burden of the *Atharva Veda*', quoted here from Matringe 1991:43-4 whose translation in French I have rendered in English). Matringe interprets this verse as most scholars do: 'the *Atharva Veda* is the Veda of ritual incantations and magical formulas. The verse means that Nanak freed his disciples from ritualism and superstition.'[5]

In conformity with my hypothesis, I will argue that this phrase conceals a different meaning, known only to the initiated members of the sect. First, it will be noticed that the original word is *atharabāṇi* (*atharvāṇī*) and not *atharaba bāṇi* which would be *Atharva Ved.* As Ahmad (1969:25) reminds us, the Shamsis 'still more deeply influenced by Hinduism than the Khojas' (ibid.), call the corpus of their religious books *Atharva Ved.* Actually, as we learn from direct Nizari sources, there is a *ginānic* composition ascribed to Pir Sadruddin referred to as *Athar Ved* (and not *Atharva Ved*). The variant is meaningful, even if the disappearance of one syllable can give the impression that it is due to a vernacular corruption; for the Ismailis it does not exactly refer to the fourth Veda or *Atharva Veda* but to a fifth Veda, corresponding to the new revelation brought by the Nizari Pirs or *Athar Ved,* that is, the 'eternal Ved' (from *athar, a-sthir,* immovable, stable, permanent) (personal communication, Z. Moir).

This fifth book is taught to the converts but will remain secret till the end of the *kali yuga*, as also stated in the Nizarpanthi prophetic *bhajans*.[6] This 'secret book' refers rather to the teaching of the Nizari Pir and the Ismaili revelation as a whole than to the *ginān* ascribed to Sadruddin, as illustrated in the *ginānic* composition signed by this author:

> *eji bhaṇe pir sadar din sat-gur baramā*
> *athar-ved bhane so mere eji*

> 'Pir Sadruddin the Divine True Guide says
> those who recite the scripture are mine' (Shackle and Moir 1992:113)

or, in a more literal translation:

> 'Pir Sadruddin (who is) Brahma the Satguru says:
> those who recite the *Athar-ved* are mine.'

It will not be out place to add that the *ginān Athar Ved* which is regarded as an Ismailized version of the Hindu *Atharva Veda* is chiefly centred around the worship of *Nikalank avatār* (Lakhani 1973:89). My interpretation of the Sikh verse would thus be: Some Shamsis who owed allegiance to the Imam and paid the *dassondh* were 'freed' from this bondage by accepting the new message of Nanak and severing their links with 'official' Nizari Ismailism.

Finally, let us examine the evolution of the Sikh *panth* from a new perspective. I have argued that Nanak's teaching preserved all the inner, spritual aspects of Nizari Ismailism, particularly as they were already stressed in the Persian context during the 'peaceful' period of Nizari history when the *dāīs* and Imams came into close contact with the local Muslim dervishes. It is precisely this aspect of Guru Nanak's religion which, in my opinion, has given birth to the vague impression of a Sufi influence, while, as McLeod stated from a different perspective, it was clear that there was no such direct impact on the Sikh Guru (McLeod 1968). Nanak had probably modified the *pāval* ritual to create his *pāhal* ceremony and continued the congregational prayers with the singing of devotional hymns. Later on, the *dassondh* (*dasbandh*) was reintroduced by one of his successors, Guru Arjun, who was also a Khatri. In my opinion, this event is suggestive of the fact that the fifth guru had not forgotten the origin of Nanak and of many of his disciples and probably had himself originally belonged to a Shamsi family, so that in seeking to introduce a system of taxes, he spontaneously drew from the *dassondh* model. This implies a secret transmission of certain Nizari elements from one guru to the other or suggests that the whole Sikh community continued to function like a 'detached branch' of the Nizari *dawa*. Even the so-called 'Sanatan period' can be interpreted as a partial return to the concepts of incarnations (*avatārs*) and the belief in the power of deified Pirs, in their 'popular' versions (these practices being, characteristically, centred around the worship of Guga Pir and Sakhi Sarwar).

Finally, let us come to the rise of military ideals and the idiom of the Khalsa. McLeod and others (McLeod 1992:24-5; Matringe 1990) have assumed that what looked like a sudden change of emphasis from the peaceful ideals of Nanak to the warlike accents of Guru Govind Singh, and which led to the transformation of a sect of Sants into a military community, could be explained by the massive recruitment of Jats. During the eighteenth century, the members of this agricultural community had indeed expressed their ambitions in a number of guerilla raids. They even succeeded in creating a kingdom in Alwar (modern Rajasthan). I would argue that if the presence of Jats was instrumental in changing the orientation of the sect and the attitude of its members, a similar phenomenon might have been observed in the Bishnoi and Jasnathi Panths during the same period, as Jats represented a majority in these sects. Instead they continued their peaceful evolution towards a gradual reHinduization. My hypothesis is that, pressed by the political, historical and social circumstances of the time, helped by the presence of the troublesome Jats, the Sikh Gurus and their successors reverted to an old Ismaili ideal: the association of military and political power with spiritual rule (*Pīrāī* and *mīrāī*, Muslim terms which, incidentally, have been used with this purport by Govind Singh). This ideal, I believe, had never been totally forgotten nor abandoned by the Ismailis, as reflected in the warlike *ginān*s and even in the prophetic *bhajans* of the Nizarpanthis: for both, Alamut had remained a magical word and a powerful symbol. The fact that as late as 1970 a Sikh *sādhu* claiming to be *Niṣkalank avatār* (*Blitz*, 8 Dec 1973:15, 12 Jan 1974:3), started a messianic movement in Punjab could also confirm my view.

I would suggest that the memory of a former affiliation to Ismailism has never been lost among the Sikhs who have constantly and variously drawn on it according to the changing circumstances. Thus, they have preserved a continuity which some scholars believe to be only a method of legitimating the *panth* and its alleged changes of orientation. I am convinced, therefore, that these transformations are only shifts of emphasis (as Ismailism has experienced in its checkered history) and that the modern Sikhs are right when they stress the fundamental unity of their sect through time and claim that they are not Hindus.[7] Whether their secret has been concealed as a result of a persistent, albeit uncecessary, *taqīyya* or as the token of some esoteric truth transmitted only to the initiated members, is an issue which remains to be clarified.

KABIR, THE KABIR PANTH AND THE JULAHAS

Even though Nanak was probably not influenced by Kabir during his life time, the teaching of the Muslim saint of Benares was later known to the Sikh gurus and some of his poems incorporated into their scripture. Similarly, his name was mentioned in the *ginānic* literature. Most scholars agree that Kabir (1440-1518) was born in a family of Muslim weavers in the region of Benares, yet no one has asked what kind of Muslim he was. The general assumption is that the form of Islam which plays a role in the history of mystical religious movements can be only Sunni Islam, generally in its Sufi form. Scholars do not seem to consider the existence of Shiism, whether of the Imami (Twelver) or Ismaili type. 'Unorthodox' elements traced in the tradition of Muslim saints are explained by the mystical ideals of Sufism or by the influence of Hindu *bhakti* and yoga. Considering certain Nath elements in Kabir's poetry, as well as the mention of the saint's father as '*baṛā gosāīn*' (the 'Great Gosain', generally a Shaiva ascetic),[8] Dvivedi (1965), followed by Vaudeville (1974) and Gold (1987), has suggested that his ancestors had been householder Jogis (*gṛhastha* Naths) recently, and one would be tempted to add, 'superficially' converted to Islam. Besides, whereas most authors suggest that the sect founded after Kabir represented a betrayal of his dearest ideals, the Kabirpanthis hold the reverse opinion. The *Bījak* which is their sacred book is also held in suspicion by the same scholars (Schomer 1987).

The controversy regarding the alleged 'continuity' of the Sikh tradition can be solved, in my opinion, through the same argument: the Kabir Panth may indeed represent a departure from Kabir's original teaching, but it remains profoundly embedded in the tradition in which he would have originated, Nizari Ismailism. A number of elements appear to point to this fact: the system of tithes (the tenth part of one's earnings given to the Guru) (Keay 1995:145), the theory of the four *yugas* during which Kabir takes a particular form of incarnation (ibid.: 135-7) and the number of souls to be saved at each generation, which is reminiscent of the thirty-three crores motif (ibid.:123). A more extensive study might lead to the discovery of other analogies.

Let us come to my own interpretation of Kabir's tradition. The legend of Shams 'Tabrez' converting the Hindu untouchable weavers by causing the Ganges to flow in front of them may not be based on any historical event, but it may well reflect symbolically the conversion to Ismailism of certain low-caste groups; these weavers were known as Bhambis under their Hindu Gupti identity, and Julahas wherever they practised *taqīyya* under a Sunni guise. Our Julaha and Nyariya informants, who both revered Shams as their Pir and called themselves his *murīds,* also believed that their *murshid* had gone to convert the weavers, 'as far as the Ganga'. This could be interpreted as a massive conversion of these caste groups in various areas of north India through methods which were typical of Ismaili *dāīs*: focussing on the influential leader of a local community, who in turn urged his brothers to embrace the new faith, and could help the missionaries to spread it in other areas. This process has been illustrated in the Nizari legends through the conversion of Meghvals/Meghvars from Sind, Gujarat, Rajasthan and Malwa by Satgur Nur, Shams and Ramdev, and in the local Nizarpanthi tradition through the activities of Khivan Balai and Dharu Megh, not to speak of the Gujarati untouchable saints. We will, therefore, assume that Kabir's ancestors had been converted to Ismailism and, like all the Guptis, lived under a particular guise, though with a 'liminal' identity. If the saint's father was indeed a 'great Gosain', it could have meant that he was one of the local dignitaries of his community, appearing like a half-Muslim half-Hindu Jogi, very much in the fashion of the Rajasthani Kamadiyas or 'Kapri Gosains', as some of them were called. A similar explanation has been suggested by Mumtaz Ali (personal communication).

Kabir probably received his initial instruction from his coreligionists. The *bhakti* tradition has connected him with Ramanand, the fourteenth or fifteenth-century Sant, a connection which was also accepted by the Nizaris in later *gināns* such as Brahm Prakash where one finds the verse *Dās Kabīr guru Rāmānand.* In Kabir's writings, however, reference is made to a certain *Pītāmbar Pīr* over whose mysterious identity much ink has been spilled. Was he an unnamed Sufi saint? Does this appellation stand for the god Krishna or is it a only a symbol of the Guru and of the Lord (Vaudeville 1974:93)? Incidentally, this name which incorporates Hindu and Muslim connotations fits quite well into the Nizari pattern: it might indeed be one of those 'Kapri Gosains' wearing the Hindu ascetic '*pītāmbar*', of the legend told by Rajasthani Kamads (Chapter 9), and endowed with the title of Pirs (very much like Ramdev Pir and Jambha Pir) and, why not, an Ismaili Sayyid *dāī* like Pir Hasan Kabiruddin who is said to have died in 1470, when the Sant Kabir was approximately thirty years old. The Ismaili saint clad in saffron clothes (Upanga 1973:91) and also known as 'Anani-jo-dhani' was the head on the central *gaddī* of Ucch-Multan after the death of Sadruddin (1416?), before the weaver's birth. It is not impossible that his parents chose the name as homage to this 'Pitambar Pir' whose real identity was not to be divulged.

However, as was the case for Nanak, Kabir did not follow in his parents' footsteps. His adult life corresponds with the beginning of troubles and dissensions in the Nizari *dawa* and with an intense activity of various *bhatka* groups such as the movement created by Ramanand. Like Nanak, rejecting the authority of the Imam, and therefore the theory of *avatārs* in its indigenous as well as Ismaili versions, he accepts the values of 'inner religion' and what appears to be the 'syncretic' ideals of the Nizari Pirs: a bold criticism of hypocritical Sunni Muslims and 'Brahmanical' Hindus, coupled with an encompassing vision of the Divine including indigenous and Islamic references: Ram and Rahim, Alakh and Allah. Nanak also had preserved such values.

It is difficult to tell whether or not Kabir intended to create a separate sect. One can only observe what seems to be the result of a 'quarrel of succession' among his disciples. This dispute is illustrated in the famous episode reported in previous chapters: was the dead body of the saint to be cremated or buried? Luckily, in conformity with Hindu symbolism, the body was transformed into flowers, a detail which incidentally recalls the legend of Khivan Balai's martyrdom. These flowers having been shared, Kabir's body divided, so will be his tradition and his teaching. In Keay's book this is illustrated by a picture showing twin shrines and a detailed account of the legendary events (1995: 25, 95-7). The episode and the double shrine of Maghar is also strikingly reminiscent of what happened in the Daryashahi tradition in Sind (see Chapter 9). Drawn into the orbit of Sunni Sufism, some of Kabir's followers integrated his heritage into 'orthodox' mystical Islam, whereas the reHinduized disciples preserved, as usual, a certain amount of 'liminality', together with elements of Kabir's teaching and of the Ismaili ideology and structures with which they had been formerly connected. I suggest that, as for Nanak, the major bulk of the saint's disciples came from the Nizari communities.

To conclude, a few words may be said of Dadu, the Muslim cotton-carder of Gujarat who founded the Dadu Panth. Although he certainly knew Kabir whom he quotes in his compositions, and whom he, undoubtedly admired, I would agree that his movement was not so much inspired by his illustrious predecessor as by his own ideas which he may have drawn from the same background. Cotton-carders (Pinharas, Pinjaras, Dhunis) also formed a 'liminal' community living with an outwardly Muslim 'label'. In Rajasthan and Gujarat they are still major worshippers of Ramdev, with whom, however they tend to dissociate themselves under the influence of Islamic fundamentalist bodies. The same hypothesis will be thus formulated: Dadu who may have belonged to a Gupti family of Gujarat went to preach in Rajasthan a 'reformed' version of Ismailism. He had also Hindu and Muslim disciples (Sant Rajjab, one of his famous followers, identified himself with the Muslim community). However, the sect underwent the same kind of evolution as the Kabir Panth, evolving towards a still more 'Brahmanical' form of Hinduism and ultimately resulting in Dadu's personality being ruthlessly manipulated. From a low-caste Muslim cotton-carder he was made to become a Brahman and a divine incarnation. He was once said to be an *avatār* of Brahma, an unusual choice, as *avatārs* of Vishnu and Shiva were generally preferred, and yet perfectly consistent with my hypothesis, if we remember that in the ginanic tradition the Nizari Pirs, when deified, were regularly viewed as incarnations of Brahma. Nanji (1978) who has not discussed Kabir's or Dadu's traditions from this particular angle seems however to suggest regarding the sixteenth century medieval Sant Dadu Dayal some unexplored Ismaili connection. When discussing the important role of Pir Dadu in Gujarat (a Nizari Sayyid sent by the Imam in the sixteenth century to reorganize the *dawa*), Nanji goes so far as to speculate on a possible connection with the contemporary Hindu mystic Dadu, born in Gujarat in 1544. 'The name "Dadu" is most probably a term of endearment of Indian origin and may quite possibly have been attributed to the Pir after his coming to India' (Nanji 1978:88-9). Here again, the suggestion is made that Dadu, the humble cotton-carder, was so named by his parents as homage to the great missionary of his time. But, even if this were true, there is no doubt that the Sant betrayed his namesake and dissociated himself, like Nanak and Kabir, from the central authoritiy of the *dawa*, namely, the Persian Imam.

Is it a coincidence that Dadu settled and died at Naraina where the main *gaddī* of the Dadu Panth is still located? Is it by mere chance that the nearby place of Bichun also shelters, on the top of a rocky hill, his alleged place of meditation? It might be of some interest to remember that Naraina is supposed to be an old *gaddī* founded by Ramdev's grand-father, Pir Shams' disciple, and is still an important centre of the Nizar Panth; so is Bichun, the *gaddī* of 'Samas Rishi' located at the spot where the Nizari Pir performed his *chillā*, probably on the same elevated stone platform where, two or three centuries later, Sant Dadu would practise his austerities.

How could the confrontation between the local Nizari Pirs and the Gujarati saint who proposed a 'reformed' version of Ismailism have appeared? Were the followers of Ransi Tanwar the first to become his disciples? These important questions will lead me, in the conclusion that follows, to discuss the possible implications of my hypotheses with respect to the various socio-religious orientations prevalent in the Indian subcontinent from the medieval period up to our times.

NOTES

1. The appellation 'Rishi movement' itself recalls what the Bishnois say of 'our Rishi tradition' (*hamarī ṛṣi paramparā*) to which both Jambha and Kabir would have belonged (Krishnanand 1992:80).
2. I thank Krishna Lal Bishnoi for having shared with me, in all sincerity, his profound knowledge of the Bishnoi tradition.
3. In usual Sikh practice in *Gurudwārās* enshrining the *Guru Granth*, it is treated exactly like a Hindu idol: washed, dressed, presented with offerings and even put to sleep.
4. *Ṛṣis* also play a role in Sikh tradition: gurus are compared to them; to stress the similarity of Sikhism with Hinduism a Sikh had declared: 'the mission of Guru Nanak was simply to revive the Vedic religion of the ancient Rishis of Arya Varta' (quoted in Jones 1973:459). Actually this can be, and has been, interpreted as the influence of the Arya Samaj which referred to an allegedly old and pure Hinduism of the times of the *ṛṣis*; but it may have also another

hidden meaning: Nanak also belonged originally to the *ṛṣi paramparā,* that is, to a sect whose followers were called *ṛṣis.*

5. *Atharva Ved* might as well refer to Shaktic-Tantrism, as this was one essential text legitimizing their theories and practices: 'many Saivite Tantras trace their authority to it' (Lorenzen 1991:28). In the same poem, it is said that Nanak 'inverted the Ganges's course' (Matringe 1991:43) which I am inclined to interpret as a meaningful metaphor, similar to that which is illustrated in the legends where Pir Shams causes the Ganga to modify its course and flow in front of the people whom he wishes to convert.
6. As expressed in the *Daylāmi arādh* of Devayat Pir (Shrimali 1993:239), 'four Vedas have become manifested, the fifth Veda has remained secret'.
7. The interesting issue of Sikh identity has been considered by McLeod (1992) and Jones (1973). The latter has emphasized the role of the Arya Samaj in the dispute. The Sikh controversy on this point (are we or are we not Hindus ?) is closely related to the issue of emerging clear-cut identities as briefly discussed in Chapter 5.
8. Later, the titles Gosain-Goswamis also came to be applied to Vaishnava gurus (for instance in the traditions related to Chaitanya and Vallabha, the sixteenth-century Krishnaite mystics).
9. I even heard my Muslim Julaha informant defining his religious affiliation (although he was formally a Twelver Shia) vis-a-vis Pir Shams, his sole *murshid,* by declaring 'we are *murīds*' (and not 'his *murīds*'). *Murīd, momin,* without further specification, were typically elusive *ginānic* appellations, vague and general enough to prevent the non-initiated from perceiving their secret meaning. I am tempted to say that 'Sikh' (disciple), designating Nanak's followers, was an indigenous rendering of the equally elusive *murīd.*

5. Jambha's tomb at Mukam

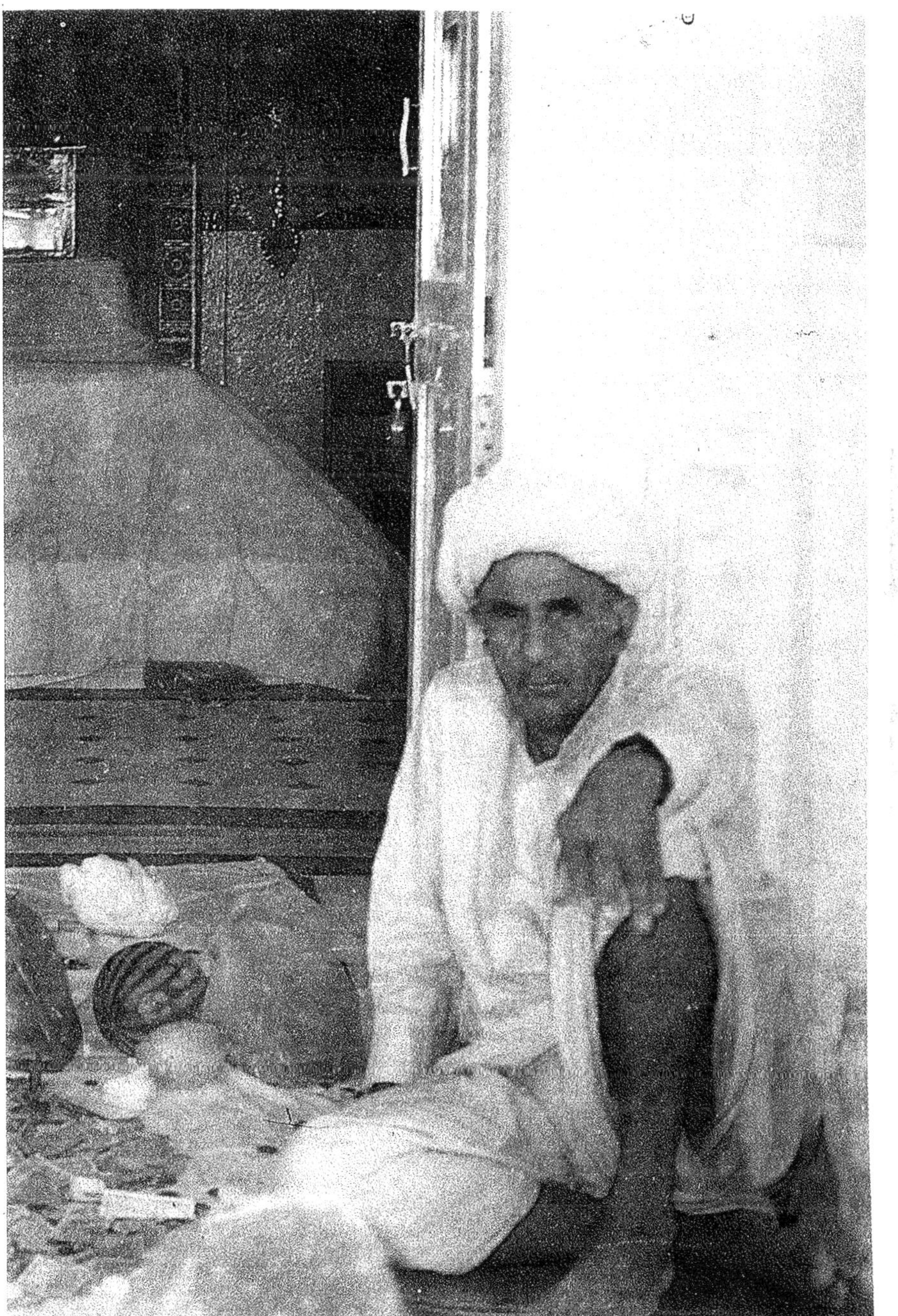

6. The *pāhal* ritual of the Bishnois

7. A shrine or *baḍer* of Ai Mata

8. *Chhatrī*-tombs of Jasnathi gurus

Conclusion

If my hypothesis is correct the present Nizari Ismaili community of South Asia represents but a small part of the former *dawa*. In the areas where Khojas still pay allegeance to the Imam Aga Khan, that is, Sind, Punjab, Gujarat and the region of Bombay, numerous communities have been traced, which may be regarded as having once been affiliated to Ismailism, as in Rajasthan, they are mostly called Nizarpanthis. Rajasthan itself, according to my theories, seems to have been once a stronghold of the Nizari sect, as reflected by the great number of communities which, under various sectarian and religious identities, have preserved a part of the Ismaili heritage and/or reverence of its Pirs. Traces of former Nizari communities have also been spotted in Malwa (Madhya Pradesh) and in the Ganga valley. It is not absurd to suppose that the *dawa* extended even further east, up to Bengal, considering the numerous references to 'Bangaldesh', one of the ancient names of that province, found in the *ginān*s: certain elements, such as the prevalence of a non-Sunni type of law and the 'syncretistic' heritage of the Bauls might point to the same conclusion. Incidentally, the Nizarpanthis consider that what they call the Baul Panth is not fundamentally different from their own sectarian tradition (Gohil 1987:37). Similarly, the teachings of the Sat Panth were not unknown to Akbar at whose *Ibādat khāna* the orthodox Badauni was shocked to see 'even Ismailis', worse for him than Hindus, Jains and Parsis, although it is surprising that the 'heretics' had revealed their identity and publicly exposed a part of their ideas. The curious theory of the Nizarpanthis, however far-fetched it may seem, concerning the influence of their sect upon Akbar's *Dīn-i ilāhī* (Gohil ibid.) might at least mirror the interest which this emperor took in Ismaili ideologies.

If I am of the opinion that the map of the Nizari *dawa* in medieval times must be redrawn to come closer to what has been illustrated in the *ginānic* literature (in terms of the numerous conversions made by various *dāīs* from Kashmir to the Deccan and from Sind to Bengal), I am also aware of the fact that further research must be done and stronger evidence provided. It goes without saying that, even it my suspicions proved correct and were confirmed by others, I will certainly not form the opinion, as I have been at times unfairly accused, that the entire subcontinent had once embraced Ismailim, nor even that all traces of Muslim influence on Hindu communities must be ascribed to the activities of the Nizari Pirs. I am too conscious of the complexities of Hindu-Muslim interactions to be guilty of such gross oversimplification.

However, if we were to admit that so many communities were converted by the Nizari missionaries in such a vast part of the subcontinent, which undoubtedly testifies to the success of the *dawa* and to its effective power, how can we explain its decline and downfall as a result of which Nizari communities now constitute but a minority with limited influence in the few areas where they remain? The issue has been discussed in the previous chapters, but a résumé will not be out of place.

We have seen that, despite a strong organization, the *dawa* suffered many setbacks in history, namely with the formation of 'dissident' branches by various ambitious leaders, from the Fatimid to the Nizari pariod and from Egypt, Syria, and so forth, to Iran and to the Indian subcontinent. The secretive nature of the Nizari mission, dictated by *taqīyya* which was vital for its survival, could have been an instrument of its might (as is the case for all secret societies and organizations), but it could also be a weakness under certain circumstances. This was well understood by the Aga Khans who, knowing that their followers were no longer endangered, encouraged them to come out of concealment and openly profess their religion.

As has been suggested, the gradual drifting away, and in some cases the secession, of various Nizari communities towards the end of the fifteenth century can be explained by internal rivalries (the most conspicious event being the Imamshahi 'dissidence'), and the influence of other religious movements then at their peak, such as Sunni Sufism, non-sectarian *bhakti* or Santism, and the Nath tradition. This type of event may well have been mirrored in a Khoja legend reported by Nanjiani (1918:171). Pir Sadruddin wished to take thirty-six crore Ismailis to visit the Imam in Persia; only twelve crore accepted, whereas the remaining twenty-four did not. As suggested by Z. Moir, these twenty-four crores might symbolize all those groups which separated from the parent body and were forgotten, forming what I have called the 'lost branches of the Ismailis'. While the local Pirs in charge of various Nizari communities were quarrelling among themselves and attempting to ascertain their authority in a particular region by claiming their independance, Sufis, Jogis and Sants could avail of the ensuing confusion and draw them into their orbit. Those who embraced the Sunni religion were compelled to abandon altogether their former beliefs and practices, whereas those who came under the influence of indigenous movements managed to preserve their heritage with little or no change. This led to an astonishing paradox: among the former Nizari communities it is not those who had chosen a clearcut Muslim identity, but the devotees who at present define themselves as 'Hindus', who have preserved the basic elements of what is, undoubtedly, an Islamic tradition. We have seen that after a long period when these communities had subsisted with a 'dual' religious identity, they were forced to declare themselves Sunnis, Twelver Shias or Hindus, if they did not wish to pay allegiance to the Ismaili Imam. It is also towards the end of the last century that Ismailism, which had appeared equally different from Sunni Islam and from the indigenous traditions (without, it must be added, dissociating itself from the Muslim heritage), openly joined the rank of its former adversaries in the Islamic world. But, at that time, it was clear that a good part of the Nizari heritage had already been lost, more correctly appropriated by others. Many Ismaili shrines were now in the hands of Sunni Sufis, Twelver Shias and Hindus, and their Pirs had started a new, unexpected existence under a different identity (as they had themselves once assumed for *taqīyya* purpose).

The adoption of new religious affiliations actually involved more complex processes than suggested. Thus, the Nizari faithful who, being originally a 'Hindu' (in the broad sense of the term, referring to various indigenous traditions) had embraced Ismailism and then was made to adopt the Sunni religion, can be said to have been twice Islamized. But can we say that his brothers who are now proud to call themselves Hindu, (as for example Ramdev's worshippers) have been 'reHinduized'? This would imply that they simply reverted to their former faith. Meanwhile there is ample evidence of the fact that their beliefs had been different from what they are now, and that they have changed more than once their formal affiliation, while preserving secretly their Ismaili heritage. It is only now that appelations like

'Shaktipanthi', 'Nathpanthi', 'Kabirpanthi' are viewed as specific categories within Hinduism. Shifting from the egalitarian views of the Ismailis to the 'universal' ideology of the Arya Samaj and its successors, these ex-Nizari communities were more 'deIslamized' or 'Sanskritized' than reHinduized.

Another important issue has been raised. How can we assert that the studied communities had been formally converted to Ismailism? Is it possible to assume that the Nizari elements found in their literature and practices are the result of a different type of influence, say free exchanges, or the result of a purely spiritual teaching of the Pirs (without any attempt at conversion) or the first steps to an actual conversion programme which had never been achieved?

As evidence of formal, and not 'incomplete', conversion, which was by no means limited to purely mystical preaching, I have mentioned the organizational structure of the Nizarpanthis, Aipanthis, Bishnois and Jasnathis. I have also dismissed the theory of mutual influences through free exchanges of ideas, by stating that a number of specific elements, which are to be found in these traditions, and constitute the secret part of the Nizari teachings, were not divulged to the non-initiated. This means, of course, that influences worked only one way: Sufic, Nath, Vaishnav, Jain ideas could be integrated into the Sat Panth but Satpanthi esoteric beliefs were not expected to spread out of the tightly closed circles of followers. It is only with the breaking up of the Nizari religion into separate branches and dissident sects that Ismaili ideas began to have a certain influence outside these circles and penetrate to some extent other movements. Many of the ex-Nizaris who either founded new sects or became prominent members of other *panths*, no longer felt bound by secrecy and began to reveal the tenets and practices of their former faith.

It is not a paradox if the major role played by propaganda and proselytization in Ismailism goes hand in hand with the secretive nature of the mission; secret societies and organizations of a revolutionary type have always been characterized by this powerful association, and the Nizari Pirs have resorted to methods similar to those used by Tantric gurus. They have created a secret code which also functions as an 'intentional language' where the 'real' meaning of words is kept secret both for security and for esoteric purposes.

The way in which the 'secret' has been transmitted from generation to generation in communities which no longer identified themselves with the main branch of Ismailism is particularly meaningful. The followers of Ramdev, Mallinath, Ai Mata, Jambha, Jasnath, Lal Beg have replaced the requirement of *taqīyya* by another urgency: the necessity of preserving from the outsiders curiosity their sacred esoteric truths. And it is, therefore, in the form of esoteric sects (*gupt panths*) that they have survived to this day, despite all the changes that have affected their open beliefs and practices. Even if they have severed their links with the Ismaili authorities represented by the Imam, it is doubtful that they are dissident Nizaris, if 'dissidence' is to be understood not as a mere shift of allegiance but as the creation of a new movement. Viewed from this angle the Imamshahi sect itself is a 'detached' but not a 'dissident' branch of the Nizari sect and, this is why I have chosen to refer to the studied communities as 'lost branches' of the Ismailis.

If 'dissidence', in our case, implies a reformist attitude, it is now towards the movements led by Kabir, Nanak and Dadu that attention must be drawn; I have argued that the Islamic influences which are traceable in their traditions may not be due to the direct impact of Sufism, but might be explained by the former Ismaili affiliation of these Sants. As I have suggested, it is not the Muslim mystical ideas and terms as such, but an interplay of Islamic and indigenous elements that they have introduced into their works, an association which was already typical of the *ginānic* tradition. However, what they proposed was clearly a 'reformed' version of Ismailism, as illustrated by the fact that they discarded certain of its tenets. The distinction is not difficult to make between the ex-Nizaris who, like the Nizarpanthis, Aipanthis, Bishnois and so on, have preserved the concept of the ten incarnations along with the key figure of *Nikalank avatār* and the 'reformists' who, like Kabir, rejected them. Other Sants who owed nothing to Ismailism, among them Raidas and the Maharashtrian saints, did not feel any urge to introduce Islamic concepts and terms into their literature, in so far as the indigenous *bhakti*, with its local roots, sufficed in itself. But at a later stage both types of Sants converged to form, in the imagination of devotees, a universal symbol of non-sectarian devotion. On the other hand, the sects which emerged after Kabir and Dadu took a somewhat different direction which resembles more the evolution of the 'detached branches' such as the Nizar Panth. And like them, they ended up with a Hindu identity, whereas the followers who had been attracted into the orbit of Sunni Islam saw their heritage vanish together with the emergence of their Muslim identity. Up to the present only one such community has succeeded in escaping the alternative: the Sikhs, who do not identify themselves with the triumphant model of Sunni Islam while claiming that they are not Hindus at the very time when Ismailis have felt the urge to demonstrate publicly that they are no different from Sunnis and are, after all, Muslims like the others (Boivin 1994).

Ultimately, it is the secret of changing values, definitions and identities which is embedded in the faded pages of history. It tells of the fascinating encounter between two religious currents from different origins which had so much in common. The various indigenous beliefs and practices conveniently labelled 'Hinduism' and the Ismaili branch of Shia Islam shared an astonishing capacity for absorption and integration of foreign elements without loosing their coherence or their congenial qualities. Both were, by nature, encompassing and, for this very reason, flexible and tolerant.

Modern conflicts centred around a new idea of Hinduism and Islam, which having been deprived of their fluidity, tend to oppose themselves as monolithic blocks struggling for hegemony, testify to the danger of categorization; the passionate quest for identity is a path open to violence. But as long as Muslims, even in reduced numbers, continue to go on pilgrimage to Ramdeora and as long as Hindus, albeit occasionally, do not cease to utter with reverence the name of Multan, all hope is not lost.

Bibliography

LIST OF ABBREVIATIONS

BEFFO	:	*Bulletin de l'Ecole Francaise d'Extrême Orient*
EFEO	:	Ecole Francaise d'Extrême Orient
EPHE	:	Ecole Pratique des Hautes Etudes
JAS	:	*Journal of Asian Studies*
JBBRAS	:	*Journal of the Bombay Branch of the Asiatic Society*
JRAS	:	*Journal of the Royal Asiatic Society*
JRASB	:	*Journal of the Royal Asiatic Society of Bombay*

Achyut, Ram Prakash. 1960. *Śrī Rāmdev Brahma Purāṇa.* Ajmer: Arya Brothers.

———1985. *Upāsnā kā anāvaraṇ banās rahasya kī pol.* Jodhpur.

Ahmad, Aziz. 1964. *Studies in Islamic Culture in Indian Environment.* Oxford: Clarendon Press.

———1969. *An Intellectual History of Islam in India.* Edinburgh: University Press.

Ahuja, N.D. undated. *The Great Guru Nanak and the Muslims.* Chandigarh: Kirti Publishing House.

Allana, G. 1984. *Ginans of Ismaili Pirs rendered in English verses.* Karachi: Shia Imami Ismailia Association for Pakistan.

Ansari Sarah, F.D. 1992. *Sufi Saints and State Power, The Pirs of Sind, 1843-1947.* Cambridge: CUP.

Asani, A.S.A. 1991. 'The *ginān* literature of the Ismailis of Indo-Pakistan', in *Devotion divine: bhakti traditions from the regions of India.* Ed. Eck D.L. and Mallison F. Groningen: Egbert Forsten, pp. 1-18.

Assayag, Jackie. 1992. 'La déesse et le saint—Acculturation et communalisme hindou-musulman dans un lieu de culte de sud de l'Inde (Karnataka)', *Annales ESC,* July-October 92, nos. 4-5, pp. 789-813.

Bahadur, K.P. 1981. *The Castes, Tribes and Culture of India: Western Maharashtra and Gujarat.* Delhi: Ess Ess Publications.

Banerjee, A.C. 1993. *The Sikh Gurus and the Sikh Religion.* Delhi: Munshiram Manoharlal.

Benett, Peter. 1993. *The Path of Grace, Social Organisation and Temple Worship in a Vaishnava Sect.* Delhi: Hindustan Publishing Corporation.

Bhanawat, Mahendra. 1963. 'Kāmaḍ aur unkā teratālī nātya', *Shodh Patrika,* no. 3, varsh 15, pp. 182-6.

———1986. 'Kūṇḍā panth evam undriyā panth', in *Ajuba Rajasthan.* Udaipur: M. Bhanawat, pp. 32-37.

———'mṛtak sanskār śankāḍāl', pp. 121-7.

Bhatt, M. And Remy, J. 1982. *Le Kalki-Purana,* translated from Sanskrit, followed by a study by Preau A., Preface by Varenne J. Milano: Arche.

Bhattacharyya N.N. 1977. *The Indian Mother Goddess.* Delhi: Manohar.

———1987. *History of the Tantric Religion.* Delhi: Manohar.

Binford, Mira. 1976. 'Mixing in the color of Ram of Ranuja', in Ed. Smith, B.L. *Hinduism, New Essays in the History of Religion.* Leiden: E.J. Brill, pp. 120-42.

Bishnoi, K.L. 1993. *Biśnoī dharm sanskār.* Gangashahar: Dhok Dhora Prakashan.

Bishnoi, Sonaram. 1989. *Bābā Rāmdev: itihās evam sāhitya.* Jodhpur: Scientific Publishers.

Boivin, Michel. 1994. 'The Reform of Islam in Ismaili Shi'ism from 1885 to 1957', in Ed. Delvoye F. 'Nalini' *Confluences of Cultures, French Contributions to Indo-Persian Studies.* Delhi: Manohar, pp. 197-216.

Bose, M. 1984. *The Aga Khans.* Kingswood: Worlds' Work.

Bouillier, Veronique. 1986. 'La caste sectaire des Kānphaṭā Jogī dans le royaume du Nepal: l'example de Gorkha', *BEFEO,* lxxv, pp. 125-75.

———2001. 'Un bricolage hagiographique: Siddha Ratannāth du monastere de Caugherā (Nepal)', *EPHE,* pp. 123-38.

Briggs, G.W. 1920, reprinted 1990. *The Chamārs.* Delhi: Low Price Publications.

———1938, reprinted 1990. *Gorakhnāth and the Kānphaṭā Yogis.* Delhi: Motilal Banarsidass.

Callewaert, W.M. 1988. *The Hindi Biography of Dādū Dayāl.* Delhi: Motilal Banarsidass.

Campbell, J.M. ed. 1899, reprinted 1990. *Gazetteer of the Bombay Presidency, Gujarat Population: Musulmans and Parsis,* vol. IX. Part II. Gurgaon: Vintage Books.

———1901, reprinted 1988. *Gujarat Population: Hindus.* vol. IX. Part I. ibid.

Carter, G.E.L. 1917. 'Religion in Sind', *Indian Antiquary,* vol. XLVI, September 1917, pp. 205-8.

———1918. August 1918, pp. 197-208.

Carstairs, G.M. undated. 'Patterns of Religious Observance in three villages of Rajasthan' in Ed. Vidyarthi L.P. *Aspects of Religion in Indian Society.* Meerut: Kedar Nath Ram Nath, pp. 59-113.

Champion, Catherine. 1994. 'Entre la caste et la secte: un Kissā du repertoire des Bhartrhari Jogī musulmans de la region de Gorakhpur (Uttar Pradesh)' in *Puruśartha* 17, pp. 27-41.

Choyal, Shiv Singh M.Ed. 1992. *Āī panth kī vāṇīā.* Bhavi: S.S.M. Choyal.

Clementin-Ojha, Catherine. 1994. '*La śuddhī* de l'Ārya Samāj ou l'invention d'un rituel de (re) conversion a l'hindouisme', *Archives de Sciences, Sociales des Religions,* 1994, 87 (July-September), pp. 99-114.

Coccari, Diane M. 1990. 'The Bīr Bābās of Banaras and the Deified Dead', in Ed. Hiltebeitel, Alf. *Criminal Gods and Demon Devotees.* Delhi: Manohar, pp. 251-70.

Corbin, Henry. 1986. *Histoire de la philosophie islamique.* Paris: Gallimard.

Crooke, William. 1896, reprinted 1978. *The Popular Religion and Folklore of Northern India.* 2 vol. Delhi: Munshiram Manoharlal.

Currie, P.M. 1989. *The Shrine and Cult of Mu'in al-din Chishti of Ajmer.* Delhi: OUP.

Daftary, Farhad. 1990. *The Isma'ilis, their History and Doctrines.* Cambridge: CUP, Delhi: Munshiram Manoharlal.

Digby, Simon. 1975. 'Abd al-Quddus Gangoh. The Personality and Attitudes of a Medieval Indian Sufi', in *Medieval India. A Miscellany,* vol. 3, pp. 1-66.

———1984. 'Qalandar and Related Groups, Elements of Social Deviance in the Religious Life of the Delhi Sultanate of the Thirteenth and Forteenth Centuries', in Ed. Friedmann Y. *Islam in Asia,* vol. I South Asia. Jerusalem: The Magnesspress, The Hebrew University, pp. 60-108.

District and State Gazetteers of the Undivided Punjab 1893-1935. Reprinted 1993. Delhi: Low Price Publications, 4 vols.

Dowson, John. 1879, reprinted 1982. *A Classical Dictionary of Hindu Mythology and Religion, Geography, History and Literature.* Delhi: Rupa & Co.

Dumont, Louis. 1966. *Homo Hierarchicus-Le système des castes et ses implications*, Paris: Gallimard.

Dutta, S. 1960, reprinted 1990. 'Independant States during the Sultanate of Delhi. A. Rajput States', in Ed. Majumdar, R.C. *The History and Culture of the Indian People. The Delhi Sultanate.* Bombay: Bharatiya Vidya Bhavan, pp. 326-60.

Dvivedi, Hariprasad. 1981. *Nāth-Sampradāy.* Ilahabad: Lokbharati Prakashan.

———1965, reprinted 1994, *Kabīr.* Delhi: Rajkamal Prakashan.

Eliade, Mircea. 1954, reprinted 1972. *Yoga, immortalité et liberté.* Paris: Payot.

Elliot, H.M. and Dowson, J. 1867-1877. *The History of India.* 8 vols. London: Trubner and Co.

Encyclopaedia of Islam, 1978, reprinted 1986. Leiden: E.J. Brill.

Engineer, A.A. 1989. *The Muslim Communities of Gujarat, an Exploratory Study of Bohrās, Khojās and Memons.* Delhi: Ajanta Publications.

Enthoven R.E. 1914, reprinted 1989. *Folklore of Gujarat,* vol. I, Folkore Notes compiled from Materials Collected by A.M.T. Jackson. Delhi: Asian Educational Services.

———1920, reprinted 1990. *The Tribes and Castes of Bombay.* Delhi: Asian Educational Service. 3 vols.

Erskine, K.D. reprinted 1992. *Rajputana Gazetteers.* Gurgaon: Vintage Books. 3 vols.

Frykenberg, R.E. 1989, reprinted 1991. 'The emergence of modern "Hinduism" as a concept and as an institution: A reappraisal with special reference to South India', in Ed. Sontheimer G.D. and Kulke H. *Hinduism Reconsidered.* Delhi: Manohar.

Fuchs, Stephen. 1992. *Godmen on the Warpath, A study of Messianic Movements in India.* Delhi: Munshiram Manoharlal.

Gaborieau, Marc. 1975. 'Legende et culte du saint musulman Ghazi Miya au Nepal occidental et en Inde', in *Objects et Mondes,* Paris, Musee de l'Homme, XV, 3, pp. 289-318.

Gaborieau, M. and Clementin-Ojha C. 1994. 'La montée du prośelytisme dans le sous-continent indien-Introduction', in *Arch. de sc. soc. des Rel.* 1994, 87 (July-September), pp. 13-33.

Gahlot, S.S. and Banshi Dhar. 1989. *Castes and Tribes of Rajasthan.* Jodhpur: Jain Brothers.

Ghay, R.K. 1985. 'Hindu-Muslim Relations during the 1920s with special reference to shuddhī and tablīgh' in *Indian History Congress,* Proceedings of the 46th Session; Amritsar: Guru Nanak Dev University.

Ghurye, G.S. 1953, reprinted 1995. *Indian Sadhus.* Bombay: Popular Prakashan.

Gohil, Nathabhai. 1987. *Saurāṣtranā Harijan Bhakta-Kavio.* Keshod: N. Gohil.

———1994. *Āgamvāṇī.* Ahmedabad: Navbharat Sahitya Mandir.

Gokuldas, 1950. *Maghvanś jāti ke rasm rivāz.* Dumara: Seva Das Rishi.

———1982. *Meghvanś itihas.*

Gold, Daniel. 1987. *The Lord as Guru, Hindi Sants in North Indian Tradition.* New York: OUP.

Grodzins-Gold, Ann. 1989. *Fruitful Journeys, The Ways of Rajasthani Pilgrims.* Delhi: OUP.

———1992. A Carnival of Parting, *The Tales of King Bhartari and King Gopi Chand as Sung and told by Madhu Natisar Nath of Ghatiyali, Rajasthan.* Delhi: Munshiram Manoharlal.

Gunarthi, R.C. 1987. *Rajasthānī jātiyā kī khoj.* Ajmer: Arya Brothers.

Gupta, C.S. 1966. *Census of India 1961—vol. XIV: Rajasthan. Part VII-B: Fairs and Festivals.*

Gupta, R.P. 1993. 'The Politics of Heterodoxy and the Kina Rami Ascetics of Banaras'. Unpublished Ph.D. dissertation. Syracuse: Syracuse University.

Gyanprakash. 1992. *Sri Guru Jāmbheśvar jī dvārā uchharit śabdvāṇī kī Jambhsāgar.* Dehradun: Gyanprakash.

Hamdani, A. al-.1965. *The beginnings of the Isma'ili da'wat in northern India.* Cairo: Sirovie.

Hawley, J.S. 1988. 'Author and Authority in the Bhakti Poetry of North India', *JAS,* no. 2, May 1988, pp. 269-90.

Hedayetullah, M. 1977. *Kabīr: The Apostle of Hindu-Muslim Unity.* Delhi: Motilal Banarsidass.

Herklots and Jafar Sharif. 1921, reprinted 1972. *Islam in India.* Delhi: Oriental Book Reprint Corporation.

Hiltebeitel, Alf. 1988-1991. *The Cult of Draupadi.* 2 vol. Chicago: The University of Chicago Press.

Hollister, J.N. 1953, reprinted 1979. *The Shi'a of India.* Delhi: Oriental Book Reprint Corporation.

Horstmann, Monika, 1994. 'Govinddevji of Vrindaban and Jaipur and its Kachvaha Patrons from the Mid-Seventeenth to the Mid-Eighteenth Century', in Ed. Entwistle, A.W. and Mallison, F. *Studies in South Asian Devotional Literature.* Paris: EFEO, pp. 82-93.

Husain, Yusuf. 1929. *L'Inde mystique au Moyen-age: hindous et musulmans.* Paris: Adrien Maisonneuve.

Ivanow, Wladimir. 1936. 'The Sect of Imam Shah in Gujarat'. *JBBRAS,* 12, pp. 19-70.

———1939. 'The Organization of the Fatimid Propaganda', *JBBRAS,* NS, 15 (1939), pp. 1-35.

———1948. 'Satpanth' in The Ismaili Society (Series A, no. 2) *Collectanea,* vol.I. including 'Some specimens of Satpanth literature' translated by Hooda, V.N. Leiden: E.J. Brill.

———1953. *Pandiyāt-i javānmardī.* Bombay: Ismaili Society.

———1955. 'Shums Tabrez of Multan', in *Professor Muhammad Shafi's presentation volume,* Ed. S.M. Abdullah. Lahore: Majlis-e Armughan-e Ilmi, pp. 109-18.

———1959. 'Sufism and Ismailism: Chiragh-nama', *Revue Iranienne d' Anthropologie,* III (1959), 13-17.

Jaffrelot, Christophe. 1994. 'Les (re)conversions àl'hindouisme (1885-1990): Politisation et diffusion d'une "invention de la tradition"', *Arch. de Sc. soc. des Rel.* 1994, 87 (July-September), pp. 73-98.

Jain, K.C. 1972, reprinted 1990. *Ancient Cities and Towns of Rajasthan.* Delhi: Motilal Banarsidass.

Jamous, Raymond. 1955. ' "Faire", "defaire" et "refaire" les saints: Les Pirs chez les Meo (Inde du Nord)', *Terrain,* 1955, 24, pp. 43-56.

Jasol, Nahar Singh and D.V. Kshirsagar. 1998. *Rāṇī Rūpande aur Mallīnāth.* Jasol: Rani Bhatiyani Trust.

Jones, Kenneth W. 1973. '"Ham Hindu Nahin": Arya-Sikh Relations, 1877-1905', *JAS,* May 1973, vol. XXXII, no. 3, pp. 43-56.

Joshi, S. and Josh B. *Struggle for Hegemony in India 1920-1947-Culture Community and Power.* Vol. III:1941-47. Delhi: Sage Publications.

Joshi, Vinod. 1991. 'Kālbeliyā ek anchālik dharm paramparā—Anthropological Study of Kalbelia (Snake Charmer) Traditional', in *Rajasthan History Shodhak.* Jaipur: Ram Pande.

Kachru, B.B. 1981. *Kashmiri Literature.* Wiesbaden: Otto Harrassowitz.

Kassam, T.R. 1994. 'Syncretism on the model of the figure-ground: A Study of Pir Shams' Brahma Prakāśa', in Ed. Young K.K. *Hermeneutical Paths to the Sacred Worlds of India—Essays in Honour of Robert W. Stevenson.* Atlanta: Scholars Press, pp. 231-41.

——— 1995. *Songs of Wisdom and Circles of Dance—An Anthology of Hymns by the Satpanth Isma'ili Muslim Saint, Pir Shams.* New York: State University of New York Press.

Keay, F.E. 1931, reprinted 1995. *Kabir and his Followers.* Delhi: Mittal Publications.

Khakhar, D.P. 1878. 'History of the Kānphaṭās of Kachh', *The Indian Antiquary,* February 1878, pp. 47-53.

Khan, A.N. 1983. *Multan-History And Architecture.* Islamabad: Institute of Islamic History, Culture and Civilisation, Islamic University.

Khan, A.Z. 1975. 'Isma'ilism in Multan and Sind', *Journal of the Pakistan Historical Society,* 1975, vol. I, pp. 36-57.

———1980. *History and Culture of Sind.* Karachi: Royal Book Company.

Khan, D.S. 1993. 'L'origine ismaelienne du culte hindou de Ramdeo Pir', *Revue de l'histoire des religions,* CCX-1/1993, pp. 27-47.

———1994. 'Deux rites tantriques dans une communaute d'intouchables au Rajasthan', *Revue de l'histoire des religions,* CCXI-4/1994, pp.443-62.

———1995. 'Ramdeo Pir and the Kamadiya Panth', in Ed. Singhi N.K. and Joshi R. *Folk, Faith & Feudalism.* Jaipur: Rawat Publications.

———1996. 'The Kamad of Rajasthan—Priests of a Forgotten Tradition', *JRAS,* vol. 6, Part I, April 1996.

———1997. 'La tradition de Ramdeo Pir au Rajasthan: acculturation et syncretisme?' in Ed. Assayag, J. and Tarabout, G. *Islam et Christinanisme en Inde - Alterité et identité.* Paris: *Puruśartha,* pp. 121-40.

———2001. 'Jambha, fondateur de la secte des Biśnoī au Rajasthan', in Ed. Mallison, F. *Constructions hagiographiques en Inde: entre mythe et histoire.* Paris, EPHE, pp. 337-64.

———1999. 'Sacrifice, Martyrdom and Samadhi in the tradition of the Meghvals of Rajasthan'. Jaipur, pp. 140-52.

Khan, M.I. 1994. *Kashmir's Transition to Islam—The Role of Muslims Rishis (Fifteenth to Eighteenth Century).* Delhi: Manohar.

Kinsley, David. 1986. *Hindu Goddesses—Visions of the Divine Feminine in the Hindu Religious Tradition.* Delhi: Motilal Banarsidass.

Kolff, Dirk H.A. 1990. *Naukar, Rajput and Sepoy—The ethnohistory of the military labour market in Hindustan, 1450-1850.* Cambridge: CUP.

Kothari, Gulab. 1990 'Āgni jāgraṇ ke sādhak Jasnāthī', *Rajasthan Patrika,* 15 April 1990, pp. 13, 16.

Kotru, N. K. 1990. *Lāl Ded: Her Life and Sayings.* Motiyar: Utpal Publications.

Koul, Anand. 1929-30. 'A Life of Nand Rishi', *The Indian Antiquary,* October 1929, December 1929, February 1930, pp. 194-8, 221-4, 228-32.

Krishnanand. 1991. *Vishnu Charitr.* Rishikesh: Gyanprakash.

Lahani, J.H. 1973. 'Pir Sadar Din', in *The Great Ismaili Heroes.* Karachi: Religious Night School, pp. 87-90.

Lalas, Sitaram. 1939. *Śrī Āīmātājī kā sankṣipt-itihās.* Bilara: Lalas.

———1988. *Rajasthani Sabad Kos.* Jodhpur: Chaupasni Siksa Samiti. 9 vols.

Lawrence, Bruce. 1987. 'The Sant Movement and North Indian Sufis', in Ed. Schomer, K. and McLeod, W.H. *The Sants—Studies in a devotional tradition of India.* Delhi: Motilal Banarsidass. pp 359-74.

Lercha, Narayanram. 1990. *Śīr Āī Mātājī kā itihās.* Bilara: Diwan Madho Singh and Moti Babaji.

———1990. *Śrī Āī Mātājī kī bīj vrat kathā.* ibid.

Lewis, Bernard. 1967, reprinted 1985. *The Assassins, a radical sect in Islam.* London: Al saqi Books.

———1982, reprinted 1984. *Les Assassins—terrorisme et politique dans l'Islam medieval.* French translation. Preface by Maxime Rodinson. Paris: Editions Complex.

Lodrick, D.O. 1994. 'Rajasthan As a Region: Myth or Reality?', in Ed. Schomer, K., Erdman, J.L., Lodrick, D.O., Rudolph L.I. *The Idea of Rajasthan: Explorations in Region Identity.* vol. I. Constructions. Delhi: Manohar-American Institute of Indian Studies, pp. 1-44.

Lorenzen, David. 1972, reprinted 1991. *The Kapalikas and Kalamukhas—Two Lost Saivite Sects.* Delhi: Motilal Banarsidass.

Maclean, D.N. *Religion and Society in Arab Sind.* Leiden: E.J. Brill.

Mcleod, W.H. 1968. 'The influence of Islam upon the thought of Guru Nanak', *History of Religions,* vol. VII, 4, pp. 302-16.

———1968, reprinted 1976. *Guru Nanak and the Sikh Religion,* Delhi: OUP.

———1989, reprinted 1992. *Who is a Sikh? The Problem of Sikh Identity,* Oxford: Clarendon Press.

Maheswari, Hiralal. 1970. *Jāmbhojī, Viśnoī Sampradāy aur sāhitya.* 2 vols. Calcutta: B.R. Publications.

———1980. *History of Rajasthani Literature.* Delhi: Sahitya Akademi.

Majumdar, R.C. Ed. 1960, reprinted 1990. *The History and Culture of the Indian People,* vol. VI: *The Delhi Sultanate.* Bombay: Bharatiya Vidya Bhavan.

Makrand Dev. 1970, reprinted 1991. *Sat Kerī Vāṇī.* Ahmedabad: Navbharat Sahitya Mandir.

Mallison, Francoise. 1989, reprinted 1991a. 'Hinduism as seen by the

Nizari Isma'ili missionaries of Western India: the evidence of the *ginān*', in Ed. Sontheimer, G.D. and Kulke, H. *Hinduism Reconsidered.* Delhi: Manohar. pp. 93-113.

———1991b. 'Les chants garabī de Pīr Shams', in Ed. Mallison, F *Litteratures medievales de l'Inde du Nord.* Paris: *EFEO*, pp. 115-38.

———1992a. 'Muslim devotional literature in Gujarati: Islam and Bhakti', in Ed. Mcgregor, R.S. *Devotional Literature in South Asia. Current Research, 1985-1988.* Cambridge: CUP, pp. 89-100.

———1992b. 'La secte ismailienne des Nizārī ou Satpanthī en Inde: Heterodoxie hindoue ou musulmane?', in Ed. Bouez, S. *Ascèse et renoncement en Inde ou la solitude bien ordonnée.* Paris: L'Harmattan, pp. 105-13.

———1997. 'Rencontrer l'Absolu (Maha Pad Kerī Vāt)', in Ed. Assayag and Tarabout op. cit., pp. 265-74.

Marquet, Yves. 1973. *La philosophie des Ihwān al-Ṣafā.* Ph.D. dissertation. Alger: Etudes et Documents.

———1985. *Poesie ésoterique ismailienne: La Tā'iyya de Amir b 'Āmir al-Baṣrī.* Paris: Adrien Maisonneuve & Larose.

Masselos, J.C. 1978. 'The Khojas of Bombay: The Defining of Formal Membership Criteria During the Nineteenth Century', in Ed. Imtiaz Ahmad, *Caste and Social Stratification among Muslims in India.* Delhi: Manohar, pp. 97-116.

Matringe, Denis. 1991. 'Images de la premiere communaute sikhe', in Ed. Mallison, F. 1991b, pp. 39-54.

———1993. '"The Future has come near, the past is far behind": A Study of Saix Farid's verses and their Sikh commentaries in the Adi Granth', in Ed. Dallapiccola, A.L. and Zingel-Ave Lallemant, S. *Islam and Indian Religions.* Stuttgart: Franz Steiner Verlag, pp. 417-43.

———1995. 'Pakistan', in Ed. Chambert-Loir, H. and Guillot C. *Le culte des saints dans le monde musulman.* Paris: GEFEO, pp. 167-96.

Mathur, U.B. 1969. *Ethnographic Atlas of Rajasthan (with Reference to Scheduled Castes and Scheduled Tribes).* Census Publications, Gandhi Centenary Year.

Mayaram, Shail. 1996. *Resisting Regimes: Myth and Memory among the Meos.* Delhi: OUP.

Mishra, R.L. 1994. *Kāyamkhānī vanś kā itihās.* Mandawa: Mishra.

Misra, S.C. 1964, reprinted 1985. *Muslim Communities in Gujarat—Preliminary Studies in their History and Social Organization.* Delhi: Munshiram Manoharlal.

Moir, Zawahir. 1980. *Tarikhe Āīmae-Ismailiya*, vol. 3. Karachi.

———1985. 'A Catalogue of the Khojkī MSS in the library of the Ismaili Institute' London. Unpublished typescript.

———2001. 'The Life and Legends of Pir Shams as Reflected in the Ismaili

Ginans: A Critical Review', in Mallison Ed. op. cit., pp. 365-84.
Mujtaba Ali, S. 1936. *The Origins of the Khojāhs and their Religious Life Today.* Bonn: Ludwig Rohrscheid Verlag.
Mukta, Parita. 1994. *Upholding the Common Life—The Community of Mirabai,* Delhi: OUP.
Mumtaz Ali. 1994. 'Ramdeo Pir: A Forgotten Ismaili Saint', *Sind Review,* vol. 32, April 1995, pp. 24-9.
Munshi, H. and Munshi, D.P. 1895. *Report Mardum Śumārī,* Census Report of Marwar 1891, vol. III. Jodhpur.
Nainsi, Munhat, *Marwār rā pargānā rī vigat,* Ed. Bhatti, N.S. 1968, Jodhpur: Rajasthan Prachya Vidya Pratishtan. 3 vols.
Nanji, Azim. 1978. *The Nizārī Smaiili Tradition in the Indo-Pakistan Subcontinent.* Delmar-New York: Caravan Books.
———1982. 'Ritual and symbolic aspects of Islam in African contexts', in Ed. Martin, R.C. *Islam in local contexts.* (Contributions to Asian Studies, 17). Leiden: E.J. Brill, pp. 102-9.
———1988. '*Shari' at and Haqiqat:* Continuity and Synthesis in the Nizārī Isma (Ismaili Muslim Tradition' in Ed. Ewing, K.P. *Shari' at and Ambiguity in South Asian Islam.* Delhi: OUP, pp. 65-75.
Nanjiani, Sachedina. 1892, reprinted 1918. *Khojā vṛttant.* Ahmedabad: Samasher Bahadur Press.
Noorally, Zawahir (Moir, Z.). 1964. 'The first Aga Khan and the British 1838-1868'. Unpublished M.A. thesis. University of London.
———1973. 'Hazrat Pir Shamsuddin Sabzwari Multani', in *The Great Ismaili Heroes,* op. cit. pp. 83-6.
Norman, H.C. 1908. 'The Kalki avatāra of Viṣṇu' in *Transactions of the third International Congress for the History of Religions.* Vol. II. Oxford: Clarendon Press, pp. 85-8.
Oberoi, Harjot. 1994. *The Construction of Religious Boundaries.* Delhi: OUP.
Pareek, S.S. undated. 'Srīdev Siddh Jasnāthjī: sabad-vāṇī', Bikaner, *Jagti Jot.*
Parry, Jonathan. 1982. 'Sacrificial Death and the Necrophagous Ascetic', in Ed. Bloch, M. and Parry, J. *Death and the Regeneration of Life.* Cambridge: CUP.
Piovano, Irma. 1988. 'Il Cārucāryaśataka di Kśemendra (Kśemendra e le sue opere)', in ed. Gnoli, G. and Lanciotti, L. *Enenda Curaverunt* Rome: Istituto Italiano per il media estremo oriento. LVI, 3, pp. 1129-32.
Orr, W.G. 1947. *A Sixteenth-Century Indian Mystic: Dadu and His Followers.* London: Butterworth Press.
Pemaram 1977. *Madhyakālin Rajasthān me dharmik āndolan.* Vanasthali Vidyapith: Pemaram.
Rajyaguru, Niranjan. 1986. 'Mahapanthane navum parimāṇa āpanārā Khojā Santo' *Urmi Navarachana* (Rajkot), 679, Oct. 86, no. 7, pp. 301-3.

———undated. 'Pirānā panthnī ghaṭpāṭh upasnā', *Urmi Navarachana*, pp. 505-8.

———1995. *Bijamarg gupt path upāsnā.*

Ramanujan, A.K. Ed. 1981, reprinted 1993. *Hymns for the Drowing—Poems for Vishnu by Nammalvar.* Translated from Tamil by Ramanujan. Delhi: Penguin Books India.

Rao, T.V.S. 1980. 'Telugu Folk Additions to Maha Bharata', *Asian Folklore Studies.* 39, 2 (1980), pp. 137-44.

Rehatsek, E. 1880. 'The Doctrines of Metempsychosis and Incarnation among nine heretic Muhammadaṇ Sects', *JRASB*, vol. XIV 1878-80, pp. 418-38.

Rizvi, S.A.A. 1978, reprinted 1986. *A History of Sufism in India.* 2 vol. Delhi: Munshiram Manoharlal.

Rose, H.A. 1919, reprinted 1990. *A Glossary of the Tribes and Castes of the Punjab and North-West Frontier Province.* 3 vols. Delhi: Asian Educational Services.

Roy, Asim. 1983. *The Islamic Syncretistic Tradition in Bengal.* Princeton: University Press.

Ruhela, S.P. 1994. *Sri Shirdi Sai Baba—The Universal Master.* Delhi: Sterling Publishers.

Russell, R.V. and Hiralal. 1916, reprinted 1993. *The Tribes and Castes of the Central Provinces of India.* 4 vol. Delhi: Asian Educational Services.

Sarantal, K. 1979. reprinted 1980. *History of the Khalji. A.D. 1290-1320.* Delhi: Munshiram Manoharlal.

Schomer, Karine and Mcleod, W.H. 1987. *The Sants—Studies in a Devotional Traditional of India.* op. cit.

Shackle, Christopher and Moir, Zawahir. 1992. *Ismaili Hymns from South Asia—An Introduction to the Ginans.* London: School of Oriental and African Studies, University of London.

Sharma, Dasharath. 1983. *Kyam Khan Raso.* Jodhpur: Rajasthan Oriental Research Institute.

Sharma, G.N. 1985. *Rajasthani Studies.* Agra: Lakshmi Narain Agarwal.

Sharma, Manohar. 1977. 'Rāmdevjī Tanvar rī bāt', *Shodh Patrika,* varsh 28, nos. 3-4, pp. 49-53.

Sharma, Mahavir Prasad. 1980-81. *Torawāṭī kā itihās.* Kotputli: Prakashan Samiti.

Sharma, P. 1972. *Maharaja Man Singh of Jodhpur and his times (1803-1943).* Agra: Shiva Lal Agarwal and Co.

Shekhawat, S.S. 1993. *Maālāṇī ke gaurav gīt.* Jasol: Rani Bhatiyani Trust.

Shrimali, Dalpatbhai. 1989, reprinted 1993. *Harijan Sant ane Loksāhitya.* Ahmedabad: Gurdar Granthratna Karyalay.

Siegel, Lee. 1991. *Net of Magic—Wonders and Deceptions in India.* Chicago: University Press.

Singh, Fauja. 1990. *The City of Amritsar—An Introduction.* Patiala: Publication Bureau, Punjabi University of Patiala.

Singh, Jasmer, Singh, Dalbir, Singh, Rajinder Ed. 1993. *Biblography of Sikh Studies*. Delhi: National Book Shop.

Singh, Raghuvir, and Ranawat, M.S. Ed. 1988. *Jodhpur rajya kī khyāt*. Delhi: Bharatiya Itihas Anusandhan Parishad and Jaipur: Panchsheel Prakashan.

Sinha, S. 1962. 'State Formation and Rajput Myth in Tribal Central India', in *Man in India*, XLII, 1 (1962), pp. 35-80.

Solanki, Jituram, undated. *Mālī Likhmī Dās jī kā śāstra*. Ajmer: Arya Brothers.

Somani, R.V. 1976. *History of Mewar (From earliest times to 1751)*. Jaipur: C.I. Ranka and Co.

Srinivas, M.N. 1952. *Religion and Society among the Coorgs of South India*. Oxford: Clarendon Press.

Srivastav, Ramlal. 1984. Ed. 'Hajī Ratannāth', *Yogvāṇī* (Gorakhpur), year 9, no. 1, pp. 228-38.

Stutley, James and Margaret. 1977, reprinted 1985. *A Dictionary of Hinduism—Its Mythology, Folklore and Development 1500 B.C.-A.D. 1500*. London: Routledge and Kegan Paul.

Temple, Richard. 1884, reprinted 1993. *Legends of the Punjab*. 3 vol. Gurgaon: Deepak Reprints.

Thapar, Romila. 1966, reprinted 1986. *A History of India*, vol. 1. London: Penguin Books.

Thomas, R.H. 1855, reprinted 1993. *Memoirs on Sind*. 2 vol. Delhi: Low Price Publications.

Thomas, P.T. 1973. *Sabārīmalai and its Sastha*. Bangalore: The Christian Institute for the Study of Religion & Society.

Tod, James. 1829-32, reprinted 1983. *Annals and Antiquities of Rajasthan* Delhi: M.N. Publishers.

Troll, Christian W. Ed. 1989. *Muslim Shrines in India —Their Character, History and Significance*. Delhi: OUP.

Upanga, A.A.A. 1973. 'Pir Hasan Kabiruddin', in *The Great Ismaili Heroes*, pp. 91-3.

Vaishanav, Bhanvarlal, undated. *Śrī Ramdev Jīvan Līlā kathā*. Ramdeora: Gahlot, M. and Vaishnava, B.

Vaudeville, Charlotte, 1962. *Les Duhā de Ḍholā-Māru*. Pondichery: Institut Francais d'Indologie.

———1974. *Kabīr*. Oxford: Clarendon Press.

Vettam Mani. 1964, reprinted 1989. *Puranic Encyclopaedia*. Delhi: Motilal Banarsidass.

Zimmermann, Francis. 1982. *La Jungle et le fumet des viandes*. Paris: Gallimard-Le Seuil.

———1989. *Le discours des remèdes au pays des épices*. Paris: Payot.

Index of Names

Subject Index